The Dead Sea Scrolls

The Dead Sea Scrolls

and
the Personages of Earliest Christianity

Arthur E. Palumbo. Jr.

Algora Publishing
New York

© 2004 by Algora Publishing.
All Rights Reserved
www.algora.com

No portion of this book (beyond what is permitted by
Sections 107 or 108 of the United States Copyright Act of 1976)
may be reproduced by any process, stored in a retrieval system,
or transmitted in any form, or by any means, without the
express written permission of the publisher.
ISBN: 0-87586-296-9 (softcover)
ISBN: 0-87586-297-7 (hardcover)
ISBN: 0-87586-298-5 (ebook)

Library of Congress Cataloging-in-Publication Data

Palumbo, Arthur E.
 The Dead Sea scrolls : and the personages of earliest Christian / Arthur E.
Palumbo, Jr.
   p. cm.
 Includes bibliographical references and index.
  ISBN 0-87586-296-9 (pbk. : alk. paper)— ISBN 0-87586-297-7 (alk. paper) —
ISBN 0-87586-298-5 (e)
 1. Dead Sea scrolls—Relation to the New Testament. 2. Bible. N.T.—History
of Biblical events. 3. Qumran community. 4. Jesus Christ—Family—Miscel-
lanea. 5. Jesus Christ—Crucifixion—Miscellanea. 6. Christianity—Origin. I.
Title.

BM487.P32 2004
296.1'55—dc22

2004009921

Front Cover: The Scroll of the Rule

© West Semitic Research/Dead Sea Scrolls Foundation/CORBIS
Photographer: Bruce E. Zuckerman

Printed in the United States

To my mother and father

Table of Contents

Introduction	1
Part I The Dead Sea Scrolls	7
Chapter 1. Who Wrote the Dead Sea Scrolls?	9
Chapter 2. The Baptism of John	25
Chapter 3. John's Food and Dress	41
Chapter 4. The First Ones	49
Chapter 5. Zadok	63
Chapter 6. John the Baptist	73
Chapter 7. Dositheus	83
Chapter 8. James the Righteous	91
Leaders of the Dead Sea Scroll Sect	113
Leaders before the New Covenant	113
Leaders of the New Covenant	113
Future Leader of the New Covenant	113
Chapter 9. The Hymn Scroll	115
Chapter 10. The Kittim	121
Chapter 11. The Lion of Wrath	131
Chapter 12. Herod, Agrippa I, and Agrippa II	137
Chapter 13. The Coming Visitation	145
Chapter 14. Khirbet Qumran and the Scrolls	159

PART II. CHRISTIANITY	165
CHAPTER 15. THE FAMILY OF JESUS	167
CHAPTER 16. MICROLETTERS	175
CHAPTER 17. THE TRIAL AND CRUCIFIXION OF JESUS	179
CHAPTER 18. THE HYPOTHESIS	193
CHAPTER 19. THE SLAVONIC JOSEPHUS	225
CHAPTER 20. THE FATE OF THE SON OF JOSEPH	237
CHAPTER 21. SIMON MAGUS	245
CHAPTER 22. SAUL, PAUL, THE PILLARS, AND THE TWELVE	255
CHAPTER 23. THE CREATION OF CHRISTIANITY	275
SUMMARY	283
BIBLIOGRAPHY	295
BOOKS	295
ARTICLES	299
INDEX	301

Introduction

I have always been fascinated with the beginnings of Christianity for as long as I can remember. What *really* happened in the Holy Land in the first century AD? Can we ever know for certain? Or must it remain an unanswerable question that can only come alive by religious faith? When some of the Dead Sea Scrolls were first discovered in cave 1 in 1947, the air was rife with excitement that they might reveal the answer to us at last. Now, more than fifty years after their initial discovery, the scholarly consensus is rather disappointing. Although the Dead Sea Scrolls reveal more fully the religious ideas and beliefs that paved the way for Christianity, they do not tell us anything about the men who created the Christian faith. So we are told, but is this view correct?

Part I of this study is an attempt to deal more realistically with the evidence of the Dead Sea Scrolls. Such a work is desperately needed, because research on the scrolls has been for the most part a continuing process of evasion and distortion in order to lessen their importance and to distance them from the personages of earliest Christianity. This has been accomplished by placing undue reliance in the purported accuracy of paleography and radiocarbon dating and by locating the historical setting from one to two hundred years earlier than the evidence requires.

Paleography is the study of the evolution of a language's script over time in order to determine the relative dates of documents. It can be useful as an additional verification of dates obtained initially from the internal literary evidence of the scrolls, but it can never be the main determinant for arriving at dates. *A carefully worked out theory of the scrolls cannot be discarded solely because it disagrees with the paleographical dating.* Radiocarbon dating is a test for determining the approximate age of fossils and artifacts based on the radioactive decay of the carbon-14 isotope in organic matter. As a result of this technique, we can be very confident that the scrolls belong somewhere within the period from 200 BC to AD 100 and that they are not for example medieval forgeries or documents from the time of the Divided Monarchy. Using radiocarbon dating to fix a time — let us say 75 BC as opposed to AD 50 — is to place too much confidence in the accuracy of this test. The same can be said for paleography, if it is used as the primary dating criterion instead of the information found in the scrolls themselves.[1]

In most theories that have been advanced, the primary element that connects the scroll evidence to the traditional historical sources is the identity of someone known in the scrolls as the "Wicked Priest." This personage is usually identified with some show of evidence as one of the Hasmonaean priest-kings of the second or first centuries BC. Unfortunately, these theories lose credibility mainly because the other personage in the scrolls who is known as the "Teacher of Righteousness" is never found. He was the leader of the Dead Sea Scroll sect and the Wicked Priest's main adversary. The explanation usually given is that the Teacher of Righteousness was not considered important enough to be mentioned in our traditional historical sources. Can we really accept this explanation? Many other personages of far less importance are mentioned often in these sources.

Very few scholars have ever examined the period from 37 BC to AD 71 as the possible setting for the scrolls. Nevertheless, everyone would admit the existence of scroll allusions that only have real relevance in this time period. For example, the scroll writers were opposed to the practices of divorce, polygamy, and marrying nieces. According to our traditional historical sources, the only time when these practices were prevalent was in the period from 37 BC to AD 71. Herod the Great and his descendants indulged in them routinely. As another example, the scroll writers were concerned about the building of a new Temple that would be correctly constructed and would allow the offering of sacrifices in

---

1. The alleged precision of these methods of dating the Dead Sea Scrolls has been questioned by a number of scholars. G. R. Driver's 1965 discussion of paleography still has relevance today: G. R. Driver, *The Judaean Scrolls-The Problem and a Solution*, (New York: Schocken Book, 1965), 410-6. See also "Carbon-14 Tests Substantiate Scroll Dates," *Biblical Archaeology Review* 17 (1991): 72; "New Carbon-14 Results Leave Room for Debate," *Biblical Archaeology Review* 21 (1995): 61; "Maccabees, Zadokites, Christians and Qumran: A New Hypothesis of Qumran Origins" in Robert Eisenman, *The Dead Sea Scrolls and the First Christians* (Rockport: Element, 1996), 80-97; and Norman Golb, *Who Wrote the Dead Sea Scrolls?* (New York: Scribner, 1995), 241, 249-56.

a proper manner. In the entire period from 200 BC to AD 70, there was only one person who actually undertook to rebuild the Temple. Herod the Great began building operations in 23/22 BC and completed the structure in AD 62-4.

In the following pages, I have attempted to connect the scroll allusions to historical events and personages found primarily in the period from 37 BC to AD 71. However, there are indeed *some* allusions to events before this time and I have dealt with these as well.

Dr. Robert Eisler (1882-1949), a brilliant Austrian scholar, created an ingenious theory of Christian beginnings early in the last century. Although everyone has acknowledged his amazing erudition in this area, many have nevertheless disparaged his writings for his controversial theory and his utilization of the Slavonic version of Josephus in it. Nevertheless, it is important to recognize that *no alternative theory yet exists which adequately explains the Slavonic Josephus*. His view was that this source was derived from Josephus himself. I have not hesitated to utilize his writings extensively in this work, as well as the Slavonic version of Josephus as restored by him.

In his theory, he also endeavored to solve the historical problems regarding the death of James the Righteous (usually referred to with the sobriquet "the Just"), who was a brother of Jesus. I am convinced that the Dead Sea Scrolls and specifically the Habakkuk Commentary passage (11:2-8), if rightly interpreted, prove the correctness of his theory and reveal the Teacher of Righteousness as James. Only a few alterations are required in the theory as a result of the new scroll evidence. Should this identification turn out to be wrong as a result of future discoveries, then the only solution is that the Teacher of Righteousness was indeed an unknown figure in the historical record. If Dr. Eisler had only lived long enough to have studied all the Dead Sea Scrolls instead of the few meager fragments that he was able to see before his death in 1949, scroll research would have yielded far different and fascinating results indeed!

After dealing with the Dead Sea Scrolls in Part I, I next take up Jesus and the beginnings of Christianity in Part II.

Admittedly, the explanation put forward in this work as to how and why the Romans crucified Jesus is a surprising one and I will not divulge it in this introduction. However, the way I see it, if something like that explanation did *not* take place, then it is simply inexplicable why the Romans would have crucified Jesus — a peaceful teacher and healer — as a rebel. The only alternative would then have to be that the historical Jesus was really a political revolutionary who attempted in some way to free Israel from the Romans and become its King. This theory has been offered in various forms beginning in the

18th century with H. S. Reimarus, who was the first scholar to study the gospels in a modern critical manner. In fact, Dr. Eisler's theory is usually included in this category also, even though he believed Jesus *unwillingly* became embroiled in an insurrection started by his followers in Jerusalem. Unfortunately, this idea is precisely what makes his theory unlikely at least on this point: Jesus is not portrayed as a dynamic personality in the manner the gospels depict him, but as one who was pushed along on his fateful course by the actions of his followers. In any case, if he was indeed a rebel, then the later Christians, who strenuously strove to live at peace with Rome, must have been the actual creators of the pacifistic Jesus of the New Testament. However, the notion that these unique and time-honored teachings of peace, non-violence, and love were fabrications seems less credible than the explanation being proposed in this work. Notwithstanding, I only offer it as a hypothesis.

There is an official classification system utilized to identify the Dead Sea Scrolls. Take 4Q507 as an example. 4Q is the cave it was discovered in (cave 4 in this instance) and 507 is the scroll or manuscript number. The title of it is Festival Prayers[a] and only three small fragments survive. Take 1QpHab as another example. 1Q is the cave it was discovered in (cave 1 in this instance), p signifies it is a pesher (i.e., a commentary), and Hab identifies that it is a commentary on the biblical book of the prophet Habakkuk. Only one copy was found in cave 1. A complete index of the scrolls utilizing the official classification system can be found in Florentino Garcia Martinez & Eibert J. C. Tigchelaar, eds., 2 vols., *The Dead Sea Scrolls Study Edition* (Leiden: Brill, 1997), Vol. II, 1313-60.

Quotations from the principal Dead Sea Scrolls were taken from the following sources:

1. For the Temple Scroll (11QT), I have quoted verbatim from Michael Wise, Martin Abegg, Jr., and Edward Cook, *The Dead Sea Scrolls: A New Translation* (San Francisco: Harper, 1996), unless otherwise noted.
2. For the Hymns Scroll (1QH), I have quoted verbatim from A. Dupont-Sommer, *The Essene Writings from Qumran*, trans. by G. Vermes (Gloucester: Peter Smith, 1973), unless otherwise noted.
3. For the Damascus Document (CD), the Rule of the Community (1QS), the Rule of the Congregation (1QSa), I have followed for the most part the translations of A. Dupont-Sommer (see the reference above), but have made certain changes in words or phrases that were considered necessary as a result of studying the original Hebrew.
4. For the Nahum Commentary (4QpNah) and the Psalms Commentary (4QpPs[a]), I have followed for the most part the translations of Maurya P. Horgan, *Pesharim: Qumran Interpretations of Biblical Books* (Washington:

Catholic Biblical Assoc. of America, 1979), but have made certain changes in words or phrases that were considered necessary as a result of studying the original Hebrew.
5. For the Habakkuk Commentary (1QpHab), I have followed for the most part the translation of William H. Brownlee, *The Midrash Pesher of Habakkuk* (Missoula: Scholars Press, 1979) or A. Dupont-Sommer (see the reference above), but have made certain changes in words or phrases that were considered necessary as a result of studying the original Hebrew.

Quotations of the Old and New Testaments are from Herbert G. May and Bruce M. Metzger, eds, *The New Oxford Annotated Bible* (New York: Oxford University Press, 1973), unless otherwise noted; and all quotations of Flavius Josephus are from Flavius Josephus, *Jewish Antiquities, Jewish War, The Life, Against Apion*, trans. by H. St. J. Thackeray, R. Marcus, and L. H. Feldman, 10 vols., Loeb Classical Library (Cambridge: Harvard University Press, 1925-65).

This work does not pretend to be the final answer to the mysteries of the Dead Sea Scrolls or to Christian origins. I can only say that I have tried to be as diligent and objective as possible in interpreting the evidence and then placing it into a comprehensive theory. If it accomplishes nothing else, perhaps it will motivate others to begin looking seriously at the period from 37 BC to AD 71 as the proper setting for the scrolls. Or perhaps others will be inspired to study microletters, the Slavonic Josephus, or Marcion in more detail — just to name a few topics.

The reader should not overlook the notes. They are an integral part of the text and should be read along with it.

In closing, thank you for wanting to read this work and may the synapses of your brain be amply stimulated by it.

Arthur E. Palumbo, Jr.

Part I The Dead Sea Scrolls

CHAPTER 1. WHO WROTE THE DEAD SEA SCROLLS?

The Jewish historian Flavius Josephus (ca. AD 37-ca. 100) describes three Jewish sects (i.e., the Pharisees, the Sadducees, and the Essenes) that he states all came into existence ca. 146 BC.[2] By the first century AD, the Pharisees and Sadducees had become members of the establishment supporting the Herodian family and making concessions with the Romans. The Essenes were not interested in politics, but simply accepted the authority of the ruling establishment without argument. Only the newly formed "fourth school of philosophy" in AD 6 was an anti-establishment sect.[3]

The Pharisees were mainly laymen who endeavored to practice the written words of Scripture as accurately as possible. In doing this, they had created a large body of oral tradition that they felt was just as binding as the written Word. However, they were not in agreement about the interpretation of Scripture. Each Pharisaic school offered its own exposition in this area.

The Sadducees comprised the priestly class (most importantly the high priestly families) and the lay nobility. They were the aristocracy of the country. In Jerusalem, they controlled the Temple and the Sanhedrin, which was the ruling body (with certain restrictions) under the Roman occupation. Not accepting the oral tradition of the Pharisees, they followed only the written words of Scripture.

The Essenes were an ascetic, communist, pacifist and celibate sect with many similarities to the Greek Pythagoreans.[4] Living together in small groups

---

2. Ant. XIII, 171-3; XVIII, 11-22; War II, 119-66.
3. Ant. XVIII, 4-10; 23-5; War II, 118.
4. Ant. XV, 371.

throughout the land, they practiced their own private rituals and kept to themselves. Each Essene was to "for ever keep faith with all men, especially with the powers that be, since no ruler attains his office save by the will of God."[5] Not only does Josephus describe them,[6] but also Philo of Alexandria (ca. 20 BC — ca. AD 50) in *Quod omnis probus liber sit* and *Apologia pro Judaeis* and Pliny the Elder (died AD 79) in *Natural History*.[7]

Most scholars have concluded that because of some correspondences with certain traits in the Dead Sea Scrolls,[8] the Essenes wrote the scrolls. However, there are significant differences as well, which makes the identification unlikely.[9] For example, the Dead Sea Scroll sect was not pacifist[10] or celibate[11] and did not reject slavery,[12] as did the Essenes. Furthermore, when one studies the scrolls, one cannot help becoming aware of the pivotal role of priests and the importance of the 364-day solar calendar to the sect yet Josephus, Philo, and Pliny say nothing about these things.

The founder of the "fourth school of philosophy" was Judas the Galilaean. He "threw himself into the cause of rebellion" in opposition to the assessment of property that Quirinius, the governor of Syria, was ordered to take for the purpose of determining the tax that would be levied on the people.[13] In the *Antiquities*, Josephus states that Judas received help from someone called Saddok, who was a Pharisee.[14] As a result of his opposition to the tax assessment, he "perished, and all who followed him were scattered."[15] This all occurred in AD 6.

---

5. Ant. II, 140
6. Ant. XVIII, 18-22; War II, 119-61.
7. All the relevant passages from these classical writers are quoted and commented on in A. Dupont-Sommer, *The Essene Writings from Qumran*, trans. by G. Vermes (Gloucester, MA: Peter Smith, 1973), 21-38.
8. The primary scroll in which correspondences are found is 1QS.
9. Michael Wise, Martin Abegg, Jr., & Edward Cook, *The Dead Sea Scrolls: A New Translation* (San Francisco: Harper, 1996), 13-26.
10. E.g., see 1QM, 1QSa 1:21, 26.
11. E.g., 1QSa 1:4, 9-10; CD 7:6-7. Josephus does mention another order of Essenes that did practice marriage (War II, 160-1), but neither Philo nor Pliny mention it.
12. Rules for the treatment of slaves are found in the scrolls. See CD 11:12, 12:10-1; 4Q159, frags. 2-4, lines 1-2.
13. Ant. XVIII, 1-10, 23-5, War II, 117-8.
14. Ant. XVIII, 3-4, 9, 10, cf. 23-4. Josephus tells us nothing else about this person other than his name (Saddok) and his party affiliation (a Pharisee). As to his party affiliation, we will learn later in this chapter that he was an *anti*-establishment Pharisee. I take the view that he was the opponent of the high priest Simon, the son of Boethus, or perhaps his father in ca. 24 BC. Josephus was probably incorrect in placing him with Judas the Galilean in AD 6.
15. Acts 5:37.

The sect that came into being at that time continued to exist and was led by Judas' descendants.[16]

Josephus identifies the "fourth school of philosophy" as the Sicarii, who were the first group to use violence against the Romans and the Jews who made concessions or even collaborated with them. In the end, some of them committed suicide on the fortress of Masada rather than surrendering to the Romans in AD 73.[17] Others escaped to Egypt during the war, but were captured and tortured.[18] They were called the "Sicarii," because they used a small curved dagger called a "sicae" to kill their enemies.[19] From the "fourth school of philosophy" sprung up even more terrible revolutionary groups like the Zealots during the war period.[20]

Of crucial importance in endeavoring to answer the question "Who Wrote the Dead Sea Scrolls?" is the evidence that from 37 BC to AD 71 there appear to have been other groups claiming to be Pharisees, Sadducees, and Essenes. The best explanation of their existence is that they were factions of the original sects that did not approve of how their erstwhile colleagues were behaving towards the ruling establishment. Either collaboration of some kind or silent assent were the methods being used to deal with the family of Herod and their Roman masters. Rejection of their authority should have been the appropriate response. Let me discuss the evidence below.

During the reign of Herod the Great (37-4 BC), Josephus mentions Pharisees numbering six thousand[21] who refused to take the oath of loyalty to him.[22] Many of them were only fined for their disobedience,[23] but some were executed.[24] However, although the pharisaic leaders Pollion and Samaias and

---

16. James and Simon, who were sons of Judas the Galilaean, were crucified by governor Tiberius Alexander (Ant. XX, 102). Menahem, who was a son or grandson of Judas, was a leader for a time before he was killed by Eleazar, the son of Ananius (War II, 433-48). Eleazar, the son of Jairus, who was a descendant of Judas, was the leader of the Sicarii on Masada (War VII, 253-4, 275, 297).

17. War VII, 253-8; 262; 325. It appears that in some places Josephus used the name "Sicarii" to refer to the descendants and followers of Judas the Galilaean (War IV, 400; 516; VII, 253; 254; 262; 275; 297; 311). In other places, he used the name generically for various groups (War II, 254; 425; VII, 410; 412; 415; 437; 444; Ant. XX, 186; 204; 208; 210). James and Simon, the sons of Judas the Galilaean, and Menaham, a son or grandson of Judas, were certainly Sicarii, but Josephus does not call them by this designation (Ant. XX, 102; War VII, 433-48). Acts 21:38 uses it generically.

18. War VII, 409-19.

19. Ant. XX, 185-8; War II, 254-7.

20. Ant. XVIII, 6-10, 24-5, War VII, 262, 325.

21. Ant. XVII, 42.

22. Ant. XV, 368-72; XVII, 41-5. Ant. XVII, 42 states that the oath was to Caesar as well as to Herod.

23. Ant. XVII, 42-3. The fine was actually paid by Pheroras' wife. Pheroras was Herod's younger brother (War I, 181, 308).

24. Ant. XVII, 44.

their disciples refused to take the oath, they were not fined or executed. Josephus states that they escaped punishment because of Herod's high opinion of Pollion[25] and Samaias.[26] This refusal of Pharisees to take the oath was probably the origin of the anti-establishment faction of the sect.

Josephus also states that the Essenes were excused from taking the oath, because Herod had such a high regard for them.[27] The reason he gives is that when Herod was a boy Menaham the Essene predicted that he would be king.[28] However, this statement about the Essenes not having to take the oath may be incorrect, because Josephus only mentions them in one of the relevant passages[29] and seems to have confused the Pharisees and the Essenes in the other.[30]

The Hasmonaeans were the high priestly and kingly dynasty that ruled over the Jews in the second and first centuries BC. The supporters of the last Hasmonaean priest-king, Antigonus (40-37 BC), were most likely the same as those of his father, Aristobulus II (67-63 BC, died 49BC), and they were the same for his grandfather, Alexander Jannaeus (103-76 BC). They were the Sadducees. Herod the Great endeavored to wipe out all of the Hasmonaeans and their Saducean supporters when he came to power,[31] as well as during his reign.[32] It is unlikely that he got them all. Those who survived would not have approved of the pro-Herodian establishment. They would have become an anti-establishment faction of Sadducees.

In the *Aboth de-Rabbi Nathan*, it is stated that Antigonus of Sokho, who was a disciple of the late third century BC high priest, Simon the Just (ca. 215-ca. 185 BC), had two disciples named Zadok and Boethus. It goes on to say "they taught [Antigonus' words] to their disciples, and their disciples to their disciples. ... [who then] arose and broke away from the Torah and split into two sects, the Sadducees and the Boethusians: the Sadducees after the name of Zadok, the Boethusians after the name of Boethus."[33] The Qara'ite author alQirqîsânî in his

---

25. Ant. XV, 3, 370.
26. Ant. XIV, 172-6.
27. Ant. XV, 371-2.
28. Ant. XV, 373-9.
29. Ant. XV, 371-2.
30. Ant. XVII, 41-2. In other places, Josephus ascribes the gift of prophecy to the Essenes not the Pharisees (War II, 159, Ant. XIII, 311, XV, 373-9, XVII, 345-8).
31. Ant. XIV, 175; XV, 5-10; War I, 358.
32. Ant. XV, 259-66. See also the passage in the Slavonic version of the *War* (Josephus, Bk. III, Appendix, pp. 636-8), about some priests, who meet in secret in order to discuss the wickedness of Herod's rule, and who are executed by him after being denounced by one priest who had attended the meeting. A portion of this passage is quoted later in this chapter.

Kitµb al-Anwµr wal-Marµqib mentions "the Sadducaeans, whose leaders were Zadok and Boethus, appeared after the Rabbanites [i.e., the Pharisees] ... Zadok was the first to expose the Rabbanites and to disagree with them, writing books ... and ... attacking them."[34]

There is a difficulty with the end of the third century BC as the time period when Zadok and Boethus lived. Only the *Aboth de-Rabbi Nathan* provides us with this information and there is no corroborating evidence to support it. However, Herod the Great did make an Alexandrian Jew named Simon, the son of *Boethus*, high priest in ca. 24 BC and he held this office until 5 BC. When his daughter (the second Mariamme) married Herod,[35] he became his father-in-law. Simon, the high priest,[36] or perhaps his father would then be identified with the Boethus of these sources and the founder of the Boethusian family of high priests.[37] In these sources, the Boethusians represent a subgroup of establishment Sadducees based on bloodline, while those founded by Zadok represent an anti-establishment faction of the original sect.

This view would be in agreement with alQirqîsânî who stated that the Sadducees of Zadok and Boethus "appeared *after* the Rabbanites [i.e., the Pharisees]...." As we have seen, the conventional Pharisees and Sadducees (excepting the Boethusian subgroup), originated much earlier than ca. 24 BC.

The *Recognitions of Clement* (Rec.1:54) contains the following important passage. At this point, I am only concerned with the portions in italics:

> For when the rising of Christ was at hand for the abolition of sacrifices, and for the bestowal of the grace of baptism, the enemy, understanding from the predictions that the time was at hand, wrought various schisms among the people, that, if haply it might be possible to abolish the former sin, the latter

---

33. Emil Schurer, *The History of the Jewish People in the Age of Jesus Christ*, vols. I, II, III.1, III.2, rev. and ed. by Geza Vermes, et al. (Edinburgh: T. & T. Clark, 1973/87), Vol. II, 406 note 16.

34. G. R. Driver, *The Judaean Scrolls-The Problem and the Solution* (New York: Schocken Books, 1965), 229, 260-1, 264.

35. Ant. XV, 320-2; XVII, 78; XVIII, 109-10.

36. In one place (Ant. XIX, 297-8), Josephus takes Simon, the son of Boethus, who was appointed high priest by Herod the Great in ca. 24 BC, and Simon Cantheras, the son of Boethus, who was appointed high priest by Herod Agrippa I in AD 41, to be the same person. Howver, this identification is doubtful, because of the length of time between them. Perhaps the latter was actually the *son* of the former. If so, then he was the *grandson* of Boethus not his son. Josephus would have taken the two Simons to be identical by confusing the grandfather with the father in one of his sources.

37. There were four high priests that were descendants of Boethus. They were Simon (ca. 24-5 BC), Joazar (4 BC and again before Ananus, the son of Seth, became the high priest in AD 6), Eleazar (4 BC-?), and Simon Cantheras (AD 41-?). Schurer, *The History of the Jewish People in the Age of Jesus Christ*, vol. II, 229-232.

fault might be incorrigible. *The first schism, therefore, was that of those who were called Sadducees, which took their rise almost in the time of John [the Baptist]. These, as more righteous than others, began to separate themselves from the assembly of the people, and to deny the resurrection of the dead, and to assert that by an argument of infidelity, saying that it was unworthy that God should be worshipped, as it were, under the promise of a reward. The first author of this opinion was Dositheus; the second was Simon.* ANOTHER SCHISM IS THAT OF THE SAMARITANS; FOR THEY DENY THE RESURRECTION OF THE DEAD, AND ASSERT THAT GOD IS NOT TO BE WORSHIPPED IN JERUSALEM, BUT ON MOUNT GERIZIM. THEY INDEED RIGHTLY, FROM THE PREDICTIONS OF MOSES, EXPECT THE ONE TRUE PROPHET; BUT BY THE WICKEDNESS OF DOSITHEUS THEY WERE HINDERED FROM BELIEVING THAT JESUS IS HE WHOM THEY WERE EXPECTING. *The Scribes also, and Pharisees, are led away into another schism; but being baptized by John [the Baptist], and holding the word of truth received from the traditions of Moses as the key of the kingdom of heaven, have hid it from the hearing of the people.* Yea, some even of the disciples of John, who seemed to be great ones, have separated themselves from the people, and proclaimed their own master as the Christ. But all these schisms have been prepared, that by means of them the faith of Christ and baptism might be hindered.[38]

The "Sadducees" who arose "almost in the time of John [the Baptist]" and "began to separate themselves from the assembly of the people" for being "more righteous than others" could not have been the establishment Sadducees. The latter originated in ca. 146 BC. However, they were confused with the establishment Sadducees, because it was actually the latter who did not believe in the resurrection of the dead not the former.[39] Nor could the "Pharisees" who were "baptized by John [the Baptist]" have been the establishment Pharisees, because they along with the establishment Sadducees were opposed to John the Baptist. They would not have accepted baptism from him. These Sadducees and Pharisees are the same ones mentioned in the gospels who go to John to be baptized.[40] They were anti-establishment factions of Sadducees and Pharisees. The "scribes" who were "baptized by John [the Baptist]" could have been in these same factions, because the Sadducees and Pharisees had their own scribes (i.e., Torah scholars).[41]

The very idea of "separating from the people" has been discovered in a text discovered in cave 4 (4QMMT). I quote the relevant portion: "... *we have separated from the majority of the peo[ple ... and from all their uncleanness] [and] from being*

---

38. Alexander Roberts and James Donaldson, *The Ante-Nicene Fathers*, vol. VIII (Grand Rapids: Eerdmans Publishing Co., 1951), 91 (italics and "small caps" mine).
39. War II, 165, Ant. XVIII, 16.
40. Mt. 3:7: "many of the Pharisees and Sadducees ," cf. Lk. 3:7: "the multitudes."
41. Schurer, *The History of the Jewish People in the Age of Jesus Christ*, Vol. II, 323, 329.

party to or going along wi[th them] in these matters."[42] Here is an important point of contact between 4QMMT and the *Recognitions of Clement*. The *Recognitions of Clement* will be touched upon again in this chapter and in more detail in a later chapter. Dositheus and Simon will be discussed in later chapters as well.

In ca. AD 230 Hippolytus of Rome in his *Refutation of all heresies* stated that the original Essenes had divided into four classes, three of which he describes as Zealots and Sicarii ! I quote the passage below:

> They are divided according to their age and do not follow the observances in the same manner, divided as they are into four classes. Indeed, some of them carry the observances to an extreme, going so far as to refuse to hold a piece of money in the hand, declaring it forbidden to carry, look at and fabricate effigies. Also, none of these dare enter a city for fear of passing through a gate surmounted by statues, esteeming it sacrilege to pass beneath an image. Certain others among them, when they hear an individual discoursing on God and his laws, make sure, if he is uncircumcised, that this individual is alone in a place, then threaten him with assassination unless he allows himself to be circumcised. If he does not wish to comply, far from sparing him, they cut his throat. It is on account of this that they have received the name of Zealots; or as some call them, Sicarii. Still others among them refuse to call any man master but God, even though they be maltreated or put to death. And those who have come later are so inferior with respect to the observances, that those who hold to the ancient customs do not even touch them. Should they do so, they wash themselves immediately, as though they have touched a stranger.[43]

These Essenes who resemble Zealots and Sicarii are not the conventional, peaceful Essenes, but an anti-establishment faction that probably would have resembled the Zealots and Sicarii in some ways.

Josephus describes the Essene view of an afterlife as similar to that of the Greeks in that "the body is corruptible ... but ... the soul is immortal." The "virtuous souls" go to a pleasant "abode beyond the ocean," while "base souls" go to "a murky and tempestuous dungeon." [44] However, Hippolytus states that, although the Essenes believe in an immortal soul, they also believe in the resurrection of the body, a final judgement, and a universal conflagration at the end of time.[45] It is Hippolytus' description that is in agreement with the Dead

---

42. Wise, Abegg, Jr., and Cook, *The Dead Sea Scrolls: A New Translation*, 363 (Section C, 7) (italics mine). However, I disagree with the other possible translation that is suggested for "majority of the people," which is "council of the congregation." See also Florentino Garcia Martinez & Eibert J. C. Tigchelaar, eds., *The Dead Sea Scrolls Study Edition*, 2 vols. (Leiden: Brill, 1997), Vol. 2, 800-1.
43. Dupont-Sommer, *The Essene Writings from Qumran*, 32-3.
44. War II, 154-8.
45. Dupont-Sommer, *The Essene Writings from Qumran*, 34.

Sea Scrolls.[46] Josephus is probably describing the original Essenes and Hippolytus an anti-establishment faction.

Whereas Josephus states that the Essenes "will forever hate the unjust and fight the battle of the just," Hippolytus states that the Essene was "to hate no man, neither the wicked nor the enemy, but to pray for them and to fight together with the good."[47] In this instance, Josephus' description agrees with the description in the Dead Sea Scrolls.[48] Hippolytus is probably describing the original Essenes and Josephus an anti-establishment faction.

Philo of Alexandria says of the Essenes that "in vain would one look among them for ... makers of arms, or military machines, or instruments of war, or even of peaceful objects which might be turned to evil purpose."[49] Although Josephus significantly softens Philo's statement by saying that " they carry nothing whatever with them on their journeys, except arms as a protection against brigands,"[50] he nevertheless mentions in another place "John the Essene." He was one of the Jewish *generals* in the revolt and was killed in battle.[51] One must wonder where John the Essene obtained sufficient qualifications to be appointed a general! Doubtless, the answer is that he obtained them from an anti-establishment faction of Essenes, certainly not from the conventional, peaceful Essenes.[52]

Josephus describes the terrible torture that the Romans inflicted on the supposedly conventional Essenes during the war in AD 66-70:

> They make light of danger, and triumph over pain by their resolute will; death, if it come with honour, they consider better than immortality. The war with the Romans tried their souls through and through by every variety of test. Racked and twisted, burnt and broken, and made to pass through every instrument of torture, in order to induce them to blaspheme their lawgiver or to eat some forbidden thing, they refused to yield to either demand, nor ever once did they cringe to their persecutors or shed a tear. Smiling in their agonies and mildly deriding their tormentors, they cheerfully resigned their souls, confident that they would receive them back again.[53]

---

46. See pp. 98-108.
47. Dupont-Sommer, *The Essene Writings from Qumran*, 30.
48. War II, 139-40. Cf. 1QS 1:3-5, 1:9-10, 4:23-5, 9:14-6, 9:21-2.
49. In *Quod omnis probus liber sit* from Dupont-Sommer, *The Essene Writings from Qumran*, 22.
50. War II, 125-6. Is Josephus confusing the conventional Essenes with the anti-establishment Essenes here?
51. War II, 566-8; III, 9-12.
52. One must also wonder if Josephus is confusing the conventional Essenes with the anti-establishment Essenes, when he mentions the marrying order of the sect (War II, 160-1).
53. War II, 151-3.

This description of torture is very similar to that of the persecutions of the Sicarii, who had escaped to Egypt at that time as well:

> Six hundred of them [the Sicarii] were caught on the spot ... were ere long arrested and brought back. Nor was there a person who was not amazed at the endurance and—call it which you will—desperation or strength of purpose, displayed by these victims. For under every form of torture and laceration of body, devised for the sole object of making them acknowledge Caesar as lord, not one submitted nor was brought to the verge of utterance; but all kept their resolve, triumphant over constraint, meeting the tortures and the fire with bodies that seemed insensible of pain and souls that wellnigh exulted in it. But most of all were spectators struck by the children of tender age, not one of whom could be prevailed upon to call Caesar lord. So far did the strength of courage rise superior to the weakness of their frames.[54]

Again, Essenes that are being tortured like Sicarii are not the conventional, peaceful Essenes, but an anti-establishment faction.

Herod the Great (37-4 BC) was hated by his subjects, because of his friendship with the Romans, his un-Jewish (i.e., Hellenistic) ways, his cruelty, and his non-Jewish ancestry.[55] According to the Torah, the king must be Jewish.[56] The Slavonic version of the *War* describes a secret discussion between some priests in Jerusalem as early as 32 BC in which they deny that Herod could be the Messiah expected in the Scriptures because of his cruelty. One of the participants denounced the other priests to Herod and the latter had them all executed.[57] In ca. 25 BC, ten "citizens" conspired together to kill the king, but they were caught and put to death. Josephus notes that their motivation was that they believed Herod was destroying the "customs" of their nation.[58] Before Herod's death from a serious illness in 4 BC the golden eagle attached to the Temple was pulled down, because the Torah forbids the setting up of images of

---

54. War VII, 417-9; cf. XVIII, 23-4.
55. In 39 BC, when Herod surrounded Jerusalem and offered the inhabitants amnesty, Antigonus, the last Hasmonean king, called Herod a "half-Jew" in his response to him (Ant. XIV, 403). The determination of Jewish ancestry was based on the descent of the mother. Herod was called a "half-Jew," because, even though his father, Antipater I, was probably forcibly converted to Judaism by John Hyrcanus I, his mother was Cypros of a noble Nabataean (i.e., Arabian) family. There is no evidence that she converted to the faith. See Lawrence H. Schiffman, *Who Was a Jew?* (Hoboken: KTAV Publishing House, 1985), 12-3.
56. Dt. 17:14-5.
57. Josephus, Bk. III, Appendix, pp.636-8. A portion of this passage is quoted later in this chapter.
58. Ant. XV, 280-91.

any living creature.[59] Two rabbis named Judas, the son of Sepphoraeus, and Matthias, the son of Margalus, instigated the whole affair. Josephus states that they had "a reputation as profound experts in the laws of their country, who consequently enjoyed the highest esteem of the whole nation."[60] Herod executed the rabbis and their followers.[61] It goes without saying that none of the priests in 32 BC, the ten conspirators in ca. 25 BC, nor the two rabbis and their devotees in 4 BC, could be considered pro-establishment Pharisees, Sadducees, or Essenes and the "fourth school of philosophy" was not yet in existence.

After Herod the Great's death in 4 BC, the people whom he had oppressed for so long revolted against his son Archelaus. They demanded (among other things) a reduction in taxes, amnesty to political prisoners, the removal of the high priest chosen by Herod (i.e., Joazar, the son of Boethus)[62] in order to select a "high priest more in accordance with the law and ritual purity."[63] Archelaus was able to put down the rebellion, but only after much bloodshed. Then he went to Rome where emperor Augustus was in the process of deciding whether or not to confirm Herod's will. While the sons of Herod (Archelaus and Herod Antipas) were scheming against each other in Rome for the throne, trouble broke out again in Judea. Varus, the governor of Syria, was able to suppress it for the time being and he left a legion there to keep the peace. However, as soon as he left trouble broke out again, but on a much wider scale. Eventually, three persons came forward as the leaders of the revolt. They were Judas, the son of Ezekias;[64] Simon of Perea, a former slave of Herod; and Athronges, a former shepherd. Varus returned and eventually put down the revolt, which had spread throughout the country (i.e., in Judea, Galilee, Idumea, and Perea). He crucified two thousand individuals who were the most responsible for the revolt before he returned to Syria. Simon was beheaded;[65] Athronges was probably killed along with his four brothers;[66] and Judas, the son of Ezekias, who was probably the

---

59. Ex. 20:4; Lev. 19:4; 26:1; Dt. 4:15-8; 5:8; 27:15.
60. War I, 648.
61. Ant. XVII, 149-67; War I, 647-55.
62. Joazar, the son of Boethus, was the high priest twice — once in 4 BC, and again before Ananus, the son of Seth, became high priest in AD 6 (Ant. XVII, 164-7; XVIII, 2-4; 26).
63. Ant. XVII, 204-10.
64. Ezekias was a "bandit leader," whom Herod the Great captured and killed, along with many of his followers in 47 BC (Ant. XIV, 159; War I, 204-5).
65. Ant. XVII, 273-7; War II, 57-9.
66. Ant. XVII, 278-84; War II, 60-5. In the *War*, the fate of the four brothers is mentioned; whereas in the *Antiquities*, the fate of only three of the brothers is mentioned. The texts are clearly defective. Perhaps there were only four brothers *including* Athronges, and they were all crucified by Varus.

same person as Judas the Galilaean in AD 6,[67] survived the revolt and probably went into hiding.

Within ten years after Emperor Augustus had confirmed Herod's will by giving the territory of Judea, Samaria, and Idumaea to Archelaus (though not with the title of king, but ethnarch instead),[68] it was taken away from him in AD 6 as a result of his corrupt rule. He was banished to Vienna.[69] A Roman governor named Coponius was sent to rule the territory taken away from Archelaus.[70] From AD 6 until the beginning of the Jewish revolt against Rome in AD 66, several governors ruled the territory. For a brief period from AD 41-4, Herod Agrippa I ruled as king also. He was Herod the Great's grandson.

According to Robert Eisler's restored Slavonic version of Josephus' *War*, John the Baptist made his first public appearance in 4 BC during the reign of Archelaus, the son of Herod the Great (4 BC-AD 6). This source records the following information:

> [John] came to the Jews and allured them to freedom, saying: "God hath sent me to show you the way of the law, by which ye shall be freed from many tyrants. And no mortal shall rule over you, but only the Highest who hath sent me." And when the people heard that, they were excited.
>
> But he did nothing else to them, save that he dipped them into the stream of the Jordan and let them go, warning them that they should renounce evil deeds. So would they be given a king who would free them and subject all who are insubordinate, but he himself would be subjected to none. At his words some mocked, but others put faith in him.[71]

The passage in the *Antiquities* about John is significant here as well. It records that John "incited the Jews to liberty and bade them cultivate valour, practice justice toward each other and piety toward God, and to band together through baptism."[72] Robert Eisler has shown that in 4 BC the Galilaean followers of Judas, the Perean followers of Simon, and the followers of Athronges

---

67. Hengel states that Judas, the son of Ezekias, and Judas the Galilaean "can probably be identified." However, the scholarly opinion is roughly divided. See Martin Hengel, *The Zealots*, trans. by David Smith (Edinburgh: T. & T. Clark, 1989), 331-3.
68. War II, 94-7; Ant. XVII, 318-20.
69. War II, 111-2; Ant. XVII, 342-4.
70. War II, 117-8; Ant. XVIII, 1-2.
71. Robert Eisler, *The Messiah Jesus and John the Baptist*, ed. by A. H. Krappe (London: Methuen & Co., 1931), 224-5. For the unrestored version, see Josephus, Bk. III, Appendix, p. 644-5. See also the chapter titled *John the Baptist*.
72. This is Robert Eisler's restoration of this verse (see the chapter titled *John the Baptist*).

were baptized by John the Baptist and accepted him as the true high priest in opposition to the establishment high priest Joazar, the son of Boethus.[73]

A good case can be made that around the turn of the first century AD, John the Baptist established a new sect that united all of the various anti-establishment factions and groups. The anti-establishment factions of Pharisees, Sadducees, and Essenes and the Galilaean followers of Judas, the son of Ezekias, joined it. Some Samaritans must have joined it, since there are several traits in the Dead Sea Scrolls that resemble Samaritan beliefs.[74] Also, in the *Recognitions of Clement* (the lines quoted in "small caps" above) a faction of Samaritans appear as another schism along with the anti-establishment factions of Sadducees and Pharisees. Others probably joined it as well. *This new sect was the Dead Sea Scroll sect.*

According to a passage in the Slavonic version of the *War* (mentioned above), some priests meeting in secret in 32 BC were trying to determine when the last messianic high priest was expected to come.[75] The priests, Ananus and Jonathan, made the following statements:

> But Ananus the priest answered and spake to them: "I know all the books [i.e., the Scriptures]. When Herod fought beneath the city wall,[76] I had never a thought that God would permit him to rule over us. But now I understand that our desolation is nigh. And bethink you of the prophecy of Daniel; for he writes[77] that after the return [of the exiles from Babylon] the city of Jerusalem shall stand for seventy weeks of years [70x7], which are 490 years, and after these years shall it be desolate." And when they had counted the years, they were thirty years and four [remaining]. But Jonathan answered and spake: "The number of the years are even as we have said. But the Holy of Holies, where is he? For this Herod [we] cannot call the Holy One — (him) the bloodthirsty and impure."[78]

According to Ananus' calculation, there were 34 more years to run from 32 BC. This takes us to AD 3.[79] It was probably in this year the new sect, which called itself the "New Covenant,"[80] was established by John the Baptist. He was thought to be the last messianic high priest (i.e., the Holy of Holies, the Holy

---

73. Ant. XVIII, 2-3. Eisler, *The Messiah Jesus and John the Baptist*, 252-67.
74. J. Massingberd Ford, *Revue de Qumran*, "Can we exclude Samaritan influence in Qumran?" Vol. 6, #21, 1967, pp. 109-29.
75. To these priests, the "Holy of Holies" and the "Holy One" was the last messianic high priest (see Dan. 9:24, I Chron. 23:13, Ps. 106:16). See Robert Eisler, "The Sadoqite Book of the New Covenant — Its Date and Origin," *Occident and Orient* (Gaster Anniversary Volume), ed. B. Schindler (London: Taylor's Foreign Press, 1936), 119-20.
76. War I, 342-57.
77. Dan. 9:24
78. Josephus, Bk. III, Appendix, pp. 636-8.

One) who would appear before the Visitation (i.e., the destruction of Jerusalem and the Temple).[81]

In AD 6, Judas the Galilaean left the sect and founded the "fourth school of philosophy" (i.e., the Sicarii), because of some differences over policy. One of these differences was that the Sicarii approved of immediate resistance against abuses. Guerrilla warfare, political assassinations, and outright terrorism were their primary methods of achieving their goal perhaps as a prelude to a final conflict. On the other hand, the New Covenant chose to prepare and wait patiently (if need be) for the one final war ordained by God and led by the Messiah of Israel. There was no doubt in their minds that in due time they would be the certain victors against all the wicked on the earth.

As we have seen, Judas and the Sicarii revolted against the Roman tax assessment, but it would appear that the New Covenant did not. The revolt was a complete failure. Josephus does not mention the Sicarii again until AD 44-8 when Governor Tiberius Alexander crucified James and Simon, two sons of Judas the Galilaean, doubtless for rebellion.[82]

The above hypothesis will explain why both the New Covenant and the Sicarii used some of the same writings. This is proved by the fact that fragments of scrolls left by the Sicarii on Masada were also found in the caves at Qumran and were discovered by archeologists when Masada was excavated in 1963-5.[83] It would also explain why both sects had similar beliefs. Their members had been affiliated with each other before AD 6 and later in the first century some of them probably changed their loyalties on occasion.

The Pharisees, the Sadducees, and the Essenes have some of the same beliefs as those found in the Dead Sea Scrolls also. The reason is that the anti-establishment factions of the three sects brought their beliefs into the New Covenant when it was established.

It is now understandable why theories have been advanced identifying the Dead Sea Scroll sect with the Pharisees (Ginzberg[84] and Rabin[85]), the Sadducees

---

79. Since there are 34 years *remaining* from 32 BC and since there is no "0" year between BC and AD, the calculation would be as follows: 34 — 31 (not 32, since the priests are in 32 BC) - AD 3. See Eisler, "The Sadoqite Book of the New Covenant — Its Date and Origin," 119-20.

80. CD 6:19, 8:21, 19:33-4, 20:12, 1QpHab 2:3. The CD passages mention those who "entered" (CD 6:19, 8:21, 19:33-4) or "made" (CD 20:12) the New Covenant (and the Pact, CD 20:12) in the land of Damascus. These words do not mean that the New Covenant first came into existence in the land of Damascus. They probably mean that the members reaffirmed their original oaths there.

81. This early view that the Visitation to come would be the destruction of Jerusalem and the Temple agrees with the scheme of CD.

82. Ant. XX, 102.

83. Norman Golb, *Who Wrote the Dead Sea Scrolls?* (New York: Scribner, 1995), 131-3.

(North[86] and Schiffman[87]), the Essenes (Dupont-Sommer[88] and Vermes[89]), and the "fourth school of philosophy" (Driver[90] and Roth).[91]

The members of New Covenant did not have to write all the scrolls in their possession. Some of them were probably brought into the sect when it was set up. Some examples are as follows:

1. The pro-Hasmonaean text discovered in cave 4 (4Q448) that praises "Jonathan the king" (i.e., Alexander Jannaeus, 103-76 BC).[92]
2. A very fragmentary text (4Q322-324c) that mentions three persons who lived in the period from 76-63 BC — Queen Salome Alexandra (76-67 BC), the wife of Alexander Jannaeus; Hyrcanus II (63-40 BC), a son of Jannaeus and Salome; and the Roman general M. Aemilius Scaurus.[93] The pro-Hasmonaean faction of Sadducees mentioned above probably brought these two texts into the new sect.
3. 4Q540-1 (a portion of an Aramaic or Hebrew *Testament of Levi*) and 4Q534-6 that prophesy the coming of a great priest who is described as an exceptional teacher and a revealer of many mysteries.[94] It is likely that John the Baptist was believed to be this very personage!
4. The books of Enoch and Jubilees. They are Jewish apocalyptic books that are not included in the Hebrew canon or the Apocrypha but in the Pseudepigrapha. Fragments of both books were found among the Dead Sea Scrolls.[95]

On first reflection, it would appear that Josephus does not explicitly mention the New Covenant. However, there is one interesting possibility that

---

84. Louis Ginzberg, *An Unknown Jewish Sect* (New York: Jewish Theological Seminary, 1976). This book is a revised and updated translation of the author's 1922 German edition. Ginzberg only had the Cairo geniza copies of the Damascus Document (CD) available to him to do his research.

85. C. Rabin, *Qumran Studies* (New York: Schocken Books, 1957).

86. Robert North, "The Qumran 'Sadducees,'" *Catholic Biblical Quarterly* 17 (1955): 164-88.

87. Lawrence Schiffman, "The Significance of the Scrolls," Bible Review 6, no. 5 (October 1990): 18-27, 52.

88. A. Dupont-Sommer, *The Essene Writings from Qumran*, trans. by G. Vermes (Gloucester, MA: Peter Smith, 1973).

89. Geza Vermes, *The Dead Sea Scrolls in English*, 3rd ed. (New York: Penguin Books, 1987).

90. G. R. Driver, *The Judaean Scrolls-The Problem and a Solution* (New York: Schocken Books, 1965).

91. Cecil Roth, *The Dead Sea Scrolls: A New Historical Approach* (New York: W. W. Norton & Co., 1965).

92. Martinez & Tigchelaar, eds., *The Dead Sea Scrolls Study Edition*, Vol. 2, 928-9.

93. Martinez & Tigchelaar, eds., *The Dead Sea Scrolls Study Edition*, Vol. 2, 692-9. If 4Q322, frag. 2, line 6 is completed correctly as "Hyrcanus rebelled [against Aristobulus]," then Hyrcanus' brother Aristobulus II (67-63 BC) is mentioned in the text also.

94. Wise, Abegg, Jr., & Cook, *The Dead Sea Scrolls: A New Translation*, 259-60, 427-9.

95. Schurer, *The History of the Jewish People in the Age of Jesus Christ*, Vol. III.1, 250-68, 308-18.

needs to be considered. A well-known tendency of Josephus was to lay the blame on the "fourth school of philosophy" for inciting the people to revolt against Rome in AD 66 and, as a consequence of this, for the destruction of Jerusalem, the Temple, and the Jewish homeland in AD 70.[96] Furthermore, as has been stated above, he identified the "fourth school of philosophy" with the Sicarii[97] and he described them as "the first" of the revolutionary groups to use violence against the Romans and the Jews who made concessions with them.[98]

What Josephus may have done in order to convincingly lay the blame on the "fourth school of philosophy" for the catastrophe of AD 70 was to portray it in the worst possible light that could be imagined. He could have done this successfully by describing it *solely* as the Sicarii — the prime instigators of the disaster of AD 70, although he was well aware that there were other factions of the opposition who did not use the violent methods of the Sicarii.[99] Thus, the possibility does exist that Josephus' "fourth school of philosophy" was actually more inclusive and referred to *all* opposition factions and groups including the New Covenant. However, Josephus had diplomatic reasons for identifying it solely with the fanatical Sicarii.

---

96. Ant. XVIII, 6, 9, 10, 25.
97. War VII, 252-8, 262.
98. War VII, 262, 325.
99. E.g., see the non-violent protest of the Jews under Governor Pilate regarding the Roman standards and the aqueduct (Ant. XVIII, 55-62, War II, 169-77, see pp. 126-7), as well as the shields (Philo, *The Embassy to Gaius*, 299-305, see pp. 127-8). Also, although Tacitus states that the Jews "chose ... to resort to arms" (*Histories* V.9) when Emperor Gaius (Caligula) tried to have a statue of himself set up in the Temple of Jerusalem in AD 39-41, there were doubtless non-violent protests as well (War II, 196-7, Ant. XVIII, 264).

CHAPTER 2. THE BAPTISM OF JOHN

The many connections between John the Baptist's movement and the Dead Sea Scroll sect have been noticed by many. Some of these are the proximity of time and place,[100] the utilization of Isaiah 40:3,[101] the belief in the destruction of the wicked by fire,[102] the indictment of the Jewish nation,[103] the priestly ties,[104] and the expectation of a messianic personage (i.e., a King).[105] However, because of certain alleged differences (especially the difference between John's baptism and the sectarian ritual ablutions), the conclusion usually reached is one similar to that of Miller Burrows:

> ...John the Baptist probably had some knowledge of the Qumran covenanters and some sympathy with their ideas, though he also differed from them at important points; in some of his ideas and attitudes he may have been influenced by them; he may have visited their settlement, or even possibly have been a member of the sect for a while, though there is no good reason to think so; in any case, in his public ministry ... he was entirely independent of them and was sharply opposed to some of their most characteristic tenets.[106]

---

100. According to Miller Burrows, "the place where John baptized penitents in the Jordan River was not much more than ten miles from the Qumran settlement ...." Miller Burrows, *More Light on the Dead Sea Scrolls* (London: Secker & Warburg, 1958), 57.

101. Mk. 1.2-4, Mt. 3:1-3, Lk. 3:4-6, Jn. 1:23; 1QS 8:14, 9:19. Is 40:3: "A voice cries: 'In the wilderness prepare the way of the LORD, make straight in the desert a highway for our God.'"

102. 1QH 3:28-36, 17:3-4, 1QS 4:11-3, Mt. 3:10=Lk. 3:9, Mt. 3:12=Lk. 3:17.

103. 1QS 9:16-7, 21-3, 10:19-20, CD 8:16, 19:29 (general indictment), 4QMMT (indictment of priesthood), 4QTest (indictment of Herodian family), Mt. 3:7-9=Lk. 3:7-8.

104. 1QS 2:19-23, 1QSa 1:1-3, CD 14:3-6, 11QT, Lk. 1:5-13.

105. 4Q174 (Florilegium), 3:11; 4QpIs^a, frags. 7-10, 3:22; 4Q252 (Pesher on Genesis), 5:1-7, 1QS 9:11, Mt. 3:11, Mk. 1:7-8, Lk. 3:15-6, Jn. 1:26-7.

Significant differences are usually noted between the baptism of John the Baptist and the ritual ablutions referred to in 1QS and CD.[107] John's baptism was given to everyone who came to him and was administered by him, presumably only once. The ritual ablutions of 1QS and CD were restricted to the community itself, were self-administered, and were performed daily. However, have scholars been looking in the right place for evidence of John's baptism, as opposed to the ritual ablutions? I think not. Although the ritual ablutions in 1QS and CD took place *within* the sect, John's baptism *outside* the sect is nevertheless alluded to in the scrolls!

The Council of the Community, which was the lay-levitical sector, and the priestly sector were the main parts of the sect's organization structure.[108] The former was probably synonymous with the group of members called the "Many."[109] Both sectors came together as separate small groups or as one large group at various times:

1. At evening meetings where there were ten men present.[110] A priest always had to be present at these meetings,[111] as well as "a man interpreting the Torah day and night."[112] The latter was probably a levite.[113] At these meetings, which took place every night, they would first share in a special Meal, then recite prayers, and finally discuss various topics.

2. As one body on certain occasions:

    And when the order is given to (gather) the whole Assembly (together) for dispensing justice, or for the Council of the Community,[114] or for a convocation

---

106. Burrows, *More Light on the Dead Sea Scrolls*, 63.
107. Ritual ablutions are mentioned in 1QS 3:4-9, 4:18-22, 5:13; CD 10:10-3. For John's baptism see Mt. 3:1-17, Mk. 1:2-11; Lk. 3:1-20; Jn. 1:19-34, 3:22-4; Acts 10:37, 13:24; Ant. XVIII, 117; Josephus, Bk. III, Appendix, pp. 644-5.
108. B. Thiering, *Redating the Teacher of Righteousness* (Sydney: Theological Explorations, 1979), 131-3, 139-40.
109. A. Dupont-Sommer, *The Essene Writings from Qumran*, trans. G. Vermes (Gloucester: Peter Smith, 1973), 85, note 1.
110. 1QS 6:1-13.
111. 1QS 6:4, 5.
112. 1QS 6:6.
113. B. Thiering, *Redating the Teacher of Righteousness*, 134-5. In the version of the evening meeting found in CD 13:2-4, which was written in AD 65-6, a priest had to be present where there were ten men. However, if there was no priest knowledgeable in the "Book of Meditation" (called simply the "Book" in 1QS 6:7), a knowledgeable Levite could take the place of the priest. A priest *and* a Levite (literally "a man interpreting the Torah day and night," 1QS 6:6) were not required, as in 1QS.

of war, they shall sanctify them for three days so that every member may be rea[dy].[115]

Members could become ritually unclean on occasion. Under no circumstances were they allowed to attend these meetings.[116]

3. At the annual census:[117]

> This is what they shall do, year by year, during all the time of the dominion of Belial. The priests shall pass first, in order, according to (the degree of the excellence of) their spirits, one after another, and the Levites shall pass after them; and thirdly, all the people shall pass, in order, one after another, by Thousands and Hundreds and Fifties and Tens, that every man of Israel may know the place he must occupy in the Community of God according to the eternal plan.[118]

The initiation process utilized by the conventional Essenes was accepted by the New Covenant as well. A comparison of 1QS 6:13-23 with Josephus' description of the conventional Essenes in the *War*,[119] shows this to be the case. The anti-establishment Essenes brought this practice into the New Covenant when they joined it. Let me quote 1QS 6:13-23 below:

> [1st level — Postulant] And every man from Israel who freely volunteers to join the Council of the Community, he shall be examined on his intelligence and his deeds by the man who is the overseer at the head of the Many; and if he is suited to the discipline, he will bring him into the Covenant that he may be converted to the truth and turn away from all perversity: he shall instruct him in all the ordinances of the Community.
> [2nd level — First Year Novice] And when he later comes to present himself to the Many, they shall all consider his case, and according to whatever fate decrees, following the decision of the Many he shall either approach or depart. And when he approaches the Council of the Community, he shall not touch the pure food of the Many until he has been examined concerning his spirit and

---

114. We must differentiate between the nominal and verbal usage of the term "Council of the Community." Here it refers to the actual gathering (verbal usage) as opposed to the organization structure (nominal usage). This explains why the *"whole Assembly"* is mentioned in the passage. Although the Council of the Community was only the lay-levitical sector, at the actual gathering the priests were also present (1QSa 2:3, 2:12-4).
115. 1QSa1:25-7.
116. 1QSa 2:3-4.
117. 1QS 2:19-23, 1QSa 1:8-9, CD 14:3-6, 15:5-6.
118. 1QS 2:19-23, cf. CD 14:3-6. CD has the "sons of Israel" instead of "all the people," and adds the "proselytes," as a fourth group. Also, the "Thousands and Hundreds and Fifties and Tens" are not mentioned.
119. War II, 137-42, 150.

deeds, and until he has completed one full year. Also, let him not mingle his property with that of the Many.

[3rd level — 2nd Year Novice] Then when he has completed one year in the midst of the Community, the Many shall consider his case concerning his intelligence and deeds with regard to the Law, and if fate decrees that he approach the Company of the Community, following the decision of the priests and the majority of the members of their Covenant, his property and also his wages shall be handed over to the overseer of the revenues of the Many; but it shall be inscribed to his credit, and shall not be spent to the profit of the Many.

[4th level — Professed Member] He shall not touch the drink of the Many until he has completed a second year in the midst of the members of the Community. When he has completed the second year, they shall examine him. According to the decision of the Many, and if fate decrees that he approach the Community, he shall be regularly inscribed in his rank in the midst of his brethren in whatever concerns the Law and justice and purity and the mingling of his property; and he may giv e his opinion to the Community together with his judgment.

The usual interpretation of the above passage is that there were four levels of initiation into the Council of the Community. First, "every man from Israel"[120] or "every man born in Israel,"[121] who wanted to begin the initiation process, was examined by the "overseer at the head of the Many" in order to determine if he was capable of being instructed. If he was found to be capable, the overseer brought him into the Covenant, which included the taking of an oath.[122] He was then instructed "in all the ordinances of the Community." At this level, he was still not a member of the Council of the Community. Then, one year later,[123] the postulant went before the Many. If he was found to be qualified, he became a first-year novice and was enrolled into the Council of the Community by having his name inscribed in a register that was updated yearly.[124] He still could not "touch the pure food of the Many" nor "mingle his property with that of the Many." A year later, he was examined by the Many a second time; and if he was qualified, he became a second-year novice. At this level, his property and wages were "handed over to the overseer of the revenues of the Many," but they could not yet be utilized for the benefit of the sect. Also, he could "not touch the drink

---

120. 1QS 6:13.
121. 1QSa 1:6.
122. 1QS 5:7-9. See 1QS 1:16-2:18 for the ceremony of entry into the Covenant.
123. When Josephus is describing the conventional Essene initiation process that was identical to this one, he states that "a candidate anxious to join their sect is not immediately admitted. *For one year ... he remains outside the fraternity ...* (War II, 137, italics mine).
124. 1QS 5:23-4, 6:22, 1QSa 1:8-9.

of the Many." Finally, one year later, he was examined by the Many a third time; and if he was qualified, he was made a professed member of the sect. He could now do all the things that a fully initiated member of the sect could do. The entire process of initiation from the level of a postulant to a professed member took three years.

Of great significance for us here, is the precise meaning of the phrases "every man from Israel" and "every man born in Israel," which are designations given to those individuals who were allowed to begin the initiation process into the Council of the Community. It has been assumed that these phrases refer to those individuals who were Jews by birth. However, is this the correct meaning of these phrases? Who was an Israelite (i.e., a Jew) in the view of the New Covenant anyway?

According to the gospels,[125] John the Baptist is recorded to have made the following statement to those who came to him for baptism:

> You brood of vipers! Who warned you to flee from the wrath to come? Bear fruit that befits repentance, and do not presume to say to yourselves, "We have Abraham as our father"; for I tell you, God is able from these stones to raise up children of Abraham. Even now the ax is laid to the root of the trees; every tree therefore that does not bear good fruit is cut down and thrown into the fire.[126]

Robert Eisler made the following interesting point regarding John's statement:

> ...the most remarkable feature in this sermon to 'the multitudes' is the fact that the preacher refuses to recognize the crowds who stream to him for baptism and purification as children of Abraham, i.e. as Israelites or Jews, but vilifies them as 'sons of vipers' and requires them to undergo a bath of purification like *heathen* proselytes.[127]

There were four requirements for a Gentile to convert to Judaism. The convert must accept the Torah, be circumcised if a male, be immersed in a ritual bath, and offer a sacrifice in the temple (not required after the temple was destroyed). With regard to immersion, which would correspond to John's

---

125. Mt. 3:7-10=Lk. 3:7-9. According to Mt. 3:7, those who came to be baptized by John were "many of the Pharisees and Sadducees," but according to Lk. 3:7, it was the "multitudes."

126. The last line is an allusion to the universal conflagration, which will occur on the Day of Judgment. Cf. Mt. 3:12=Lk. 3:17. See pp. 98-100.

127. Robert Eisler, *The Messiah Jesus and John the Baptist*, ed. by A. H. Krappe (London: Methuen & Co., 1931), 268.

baptism, it has been stated that "the immersion should be seen as an initiatory rite in which the convert is cleansed of his transgressions and impurities and emerges from the bath *as a new person*, starting a new life."[128] Through immersion, a former Gentile was reborn a Jew. G. R. S. Mead further describes proselyte baptism as follows:

> A proselyte or a 'new-comer' ... who would join the church or ecclesia of Israel, had to submit to a baptismal rite, the pre-Christian origin of which is no longer disputed. It was a bath not only of purification but also of regeneration in the presence of legal witnesses. The candidate stood in the water and listened to a short discourse consisting of commandments from the Law. Thereon the gentile convert dipped completely under the water, signifying the drowning of his previous impious and idolatrous self. Thereafter he arose reborn a true Israelite. And this birth was taken in a very literal sense, for after the rite the neophyte, or 'new-born babe,' could no longer inherit from his former gentile relatives; not only so, but according to Rabbinic casuistry he could not even commit incest with one of them.[129]

John understood the purpose of his baptism in the following manner:

> ...the Jews were no more a privileged people; they had forfeited their birthright; Israel itself was now no better than the heathen. Physical kinship with Abraham could no longer be considered a guarantee against the Wrath to come. To escape the trials and terrors of that Day the only way for them was to repent, and so become members of the new spiritual Israel by submitting to a rite similar to that which they arrogantly imposed on the gentiles. What greater humiliation than this could there be to the racial pride of the Jew? But things were so desperate, that it required even this act of humiliation as an earnest of truly sincere repentance and contrition. Unrepentant they were no better than heathen idolaters.[130]

By not properly observing the Torah in all its aspects according to John's strict interpretation (i.e., the only true interpretation in his view), the people coming to him for baptism and taking pride in their supposed Jewish ancestry had actually lost their identity as descendants of Abraham. A true son or daughter of Abraham must "bear fruit that befits repentance," i.e., observe the

---

128. Lawrence H. Schiffman, *Who Was a Jew?*, 26 (italics mine).
129. G. R. S. Mead, *The Gnostic John the Baptizer* (London: John M. Watkins, 1924), 11-2.
130. Mead, *The Gnostic John the Baptizer*, 12-3.

Torah in all its details. Therefore, John required "them to undergo a bath of purification like *heathen* proselytes" in order to be included in the new Israel.

One major precept of the Torah that was being violated was the "royalty law":

> When you come to the land which the LORD your God gives you, and you possess it and dwell in it, and then say, 'I will set a king over me, like all the nations that are round about me'; you may indeed set as king over you him whom the LORD your God will choose. *One from among your brethren you shall set as king over you; you may not put a foreigner over you, who is not your brother.*[131]

By accepting the corrupt rule of the non-Jewish king Herod and his sons, as well as their Roman masters, the people were violating this law. Since Jewish tradition declares that the determination of whether the offspring of a married couple is Jewish follows the mother's ancestry,[132] Herod the Great (37-4 BC) could not be considered Jewish, because his mother Cypros was of a noble Nabatean (i.e., Arabian) family.[133] After Herod's death in 4 BC, his kingdom was divided into three territories ruled by his sons, Archelaus, Herod Antipas, and Philip. Malthace, the Samaritan, was the mother of Archelaus (4 BC-AD 6) and Herod Antipas (4 BC-AD 39).[134] Only Philip (4 BC-AD 33/4) may have been Jewish, since his mother, Cleopatra, was "a native of Jerusalem."[135]

By accepting John's baptism, the people were as a consequence denying the legitimacy of the Romans and Herod and his descendants to rule the nation. As a result of proving their faithfulness to the Torah, God would send them a Messiah of Israel (i.e., a rightful King). He would take back their country from the corrupt ruling establishment and in due time would become the ruler of the world.

John's baptism did not merely consist of John dipping the people one by one into the Jordan River. First, they must have publicly confessed their sins before God.[136] As a consequence of the whole experience (i.e., penitence followed by baptism), their past sins were forgiven. G. R. S. Mead aptly describes this solemn gathering as follows:

---

131. Dt. 17:14-5 (italics mine); cf. 11QT 56:14-5.
132. Lawrence H. Schiffman, *Who Was a Jew?* (Hoboken: KTAV Publishing House, 1985), 9-14.
133. Ant. XIV, 121; XV, 184; War I, 181.
134. Ant. XVII, 20, 250; War I, 562; II, 39.
135. Ant. XVII, 21; War I, 562.
136. Mk. 1:5, Mt. 3:6. Dan 9:4-19 and Neh. 9:6-37 may represent two examples of what this confessing of sins consisted of. See Eisler, *The Messiah Jesus and John the Baptist*, 267-70.

> Deeply stirred by the strenuous exhortations of the teacher and the extraordinary power of a proclaimer so utterly convinced of the near coming of the terrible Day, little wonder that the people, just as in evangelical revivals of our own day, were filled with an agony of penitence which would find relief only in a public confession of their sins. Thereafter they were plunged in the Jordan, signifying no external washing, but a very drowning as it were of the old body of sin....[137]

We can see then that John's baptism outside the sect agrees with Josephus' description below:

> For baptism would only appear acceptable to God if practiced, not for the purification of the body, but for the expiation of sins, after the soul had been thoroughly cleansed by righteousness.[138]

The daily ritual ablutions inside the sect were of a different caliber altogether. They only removed ritual impurity, which could arise from infringements of the purity laws or from inner sin.[139]

On the basis of the above evidence, the phrases "every man from Israel" and "every man born in Israel," take on new meanings. These individuals were men who were certainly circumcised, *but also baptized by John or one of his successors.* Although most of them had traditional Jewish ancestry, this fact no longer counted for anything. All those "from Israel" or "born in Israel" consisted "wholly of newly reclaimed converts, dying to heathenism through the baptism of proselytes and rising regenerated from the water."[140] Once John baptized a man (i.e., once he entered the Covenant of Abraham and became an Israelite), he could then take the next step,[141] which was to go to the "overseer at the head of the Many." If he was found to be capable of instruction, the overseer brought

---

137. Mead, *The Gnostic John the Baptizer*, 10-1.

138. This sentence is part of Robert Eisler's restoration of the *Antiquities* passage about John (Ant. XVIII, 116-9). See the chapter titled *John the Baptist*. Thiering is of the opinion that the sentence in its actual form is in agreement with the sect's understanding of its ritual ablutions (Thiering, *Redating the Teacher of Righteousness*, 65-6). Indeed, the actual reading does appear to agree with the ritual ablutions *inside* the sect (see 1QS 2:25-3:12). However, I have tried to show that John's baptism *outside* the sect is a different rite than the ritual ablutions inside it.

139. "The washing ... remains an ablution for the removal of ritual impurity. What is new [in the scrolls] is that the inward sin is held to defile the flesh, that is, make it ritually impure" (Thiering, *Redating the Teacher of Righteousness*, 66).

140. Eisler, *The Messiah Jesus and John the Baptist*, 269.

141. This next step and the subsequent ones were for laymen only. The priests and Levites had there own process of initiation, which unfortunately is not described in the scrolls.

him into the Covenant (i.e., the Covenant of Moses) by administering an oath to him and by giving him instruction in the Community laws. At the end of one year, he then went before the Many; and if they accepted him, they enrolled him into the Council of the Community and he became a first-year novice. He could *now* participate in the daily ritual ablutions.[142] The first ritual washing was probably celebrated as a special rite to commemorate the individual's entrance into the Council of the Community.[143] At the end of another year and an evaluation, he became a second-year novice, and finally at the end of one more year and another evaluation, he became a professed member. It turns out that there were actually *five* levels of initiation into the Community not four.[144]

It should be noted here that the designation "Judah"[145] (i.e., Jews) has the same meaning as "from Israel," "born in Israel," or simply "Israel," except when it refers to the tribe of Judah,[146] the land of Judah,[147] or the first ones of the Dead Sea Scroll sect.[148]

1QS[149] mentions "those who join them for community, lawsuit and judgment" in addition to those in Aaron and Israel. This phrase is probably referring to proselytes. In CD,[150] proselytes are the fourth group in the sect, preceded by the priests, levites, and the sons of Israel. On the basis of the evidence above, these proselytes were probably uncircumcised Gentiles, who were nevertheless baptized by John. Until they were circumcised, they were outside Israel.

---

142. According to Josephus, the ritual ablutions that the three highest levels of the conventional Essenes participated in were considered to be the "purer kind of holy water" (War II, 138), implying that the postulant level had its ritual washings as well.

143. Thiering understands the first ritual washing of a first-year novice as "a special water-washing ... giving [it] the character of an initiation rite" (Thiering, *Redating the Teacher of Righteousness*, 95).

144. James the Righteous was the leader and high priest of the New Covenant after John (see p. 55). The statement by Hegessippus that James "did not go to the baths" (Eusebius, *The Ecclesiastical History*, 2 Vols., trans. by Kirsopp Lake (Cambridge: Harvard University Press, 1975, Vol. I, 171 (II, 23.4-6) might at first reflection present a problem, since John's baptism and the self-administered ritual ablutions were an important part of the sect's practices. However, Robert Eisenman has offered the interesting suggestion that Hegesippus meant hot water Roman style baths and *not* the cold water ritual ablutions of the sect. These Roman style baths could include anointing oneself with oil and according to Hegesippus, James "did not anoint himself with oil" (Eusebius, *Ecclesiastical History*, Vol. I, 171 (II, 23.4-6).

145. 1QpHab 8:1,12:4; 4QpPs^a 2:14; CD 4:11, 8:3, 19:15.
146. E.g., 4Q252, 5:1; 4QpNah 3:4.
147. E.g., 1QpHab 12:9; CD 4:3, 6:5, 20:26; 4QTest, line 27.
148. CD 7:12, 13.
149. 1QS 5:6.
150. CD 14:4, 6.

Rabbinical discussions of the late first and second centuries AD endeavored to determine at what point in the conversion process a proselyte became a Jew. Was a Gentile who went through immersion, but was not circumcised, a Jew; or was a circumcised Gentile a Jew, even through he did not go through immersion?[151] In the view of the New Covenant, the proselyte had to go through both immersion (i.e., baptism) *and* circumcision before he was considered a Jew. Nevertheless, they were considered to be righteous Gentiles, they could associate with the Congregation of Israel, and they would be included in the New World to come. However, their number was probably not very large and their eventual circumcision was encouraged.

The group called the "simple"[152] were all those individuals who had been baptized by John, but could not or did not want to be initiated into the Council of the Community. This group included women; children at least ten years old; physically and/or mentally handicapped persons; circumcised and baptized men, who, for whatever reason, did not take the oath of the Covenant (this standing was probably discouraged); and baptized, but uncircumcised Gentiles (i.e., proselytes). Only the proselytes were not considered to be in the Congregation of Israel.

Children received appropriate instruction in the "Book of Meditation,"[153] the "precepts of the Covenant" and the "ordinances" from the age of ten, which was the age of baptism.[154] Circumcised and baptized men could take the oath of entry into the Covenant at the age of nineteen and then enroll into the Council of the Community at the age of twenty.[155] Also, men could marry at the age of twenty.[156]

There is an interesting passage in CD. I quote it below:

> Now those who heed Him [God] are the poor of the flock; they will escape at the period of the Visitation. But those who are left will be delivered up to the

---

151. Schiffman, *Who Was a Jew?*, 32-9.

152. 1QpHab. 12:3-5; 1QSa 1:4-6, 19-22, 2:4-10; CD 15:10-11, 15-7. Thiering also understands the designation "Simple" as including others besides only mentally and physically handicapped persons (Thiering, *Redating the Teacher of Righteousness*, 97-100). However, my view of who should be concluded in the Simple defers from Thiering's view.

153. This book was probably for men only. See 1QSa 1:4-5, which shows that instruction in the "Book of Meditation" was not part of the overall instruction when women and children are included along with men.

154. 1QSa 1:6-8. However, from this verse, only *male* children seem to be mentioned, but I believe it is reasonable to conclude that female children were baptized at age ten as well.

155. 1QSa 1:8-9.

156. 1QSa 1:9-11.

sword ... as came to pass at the period of the first Visitation; as He [God] said by the hand of Ezekiel, *A mark shall be put on the forehead of those who sigh and groan;*[157] but those who were left were delivered up to the avenging sword, the avenger of the Covenant.[158]

The Ezekiel verse that is quoted in the CD passage above reads more fully as follows:

And the LORD said to him, "Go through the city, through Jerusalem, and put a mark upon the foreheads of the men who sigh and groan over all the abominations that are committed in it." And to the others he said in my hearing, "Pass through the city after him, and smite; your eye shall not spare, and you shall show no pity; slay old men outright, young men and maidens, little children and women, *but touch no one upon whom is the mark.* And begin at my sanctuary."[159]

The "poor of the flock" are all those who were baptized (i.e., Israel and the Gentile proselytes) and were loyal to the New Covenant. After John baptized them, the passage seems to say that they were allowed to wear the mark X on their foreheads[160] and, as a consequence of wearing it, they would be rewarded "at the period of the Visitation," i.e., the time of God's punishment for all the wicked. In all likelihood, the schismatics would have removed the mark, making their doom a certainty.

The New Covenant hesitated to actually call the unbaptized "Jews" heathen, but this was not the case for the Sicarii. It was another difference of opinion between them. Josephus states the following:

---

157. Ezek. 9:4.
158. CD 19:9-13 (italics mine).
159. Ezek. 9:4-6 (italics mine).
160. "The mark was the Hebrew letter 'tau,' made like an X...." *The New Oxford Annotated Bible*, eds. Herbert G. May and Bruce M. Metzger (New York: Oxford University Press, 1973), 1008, note 4 for 9:1-11. Depending on how it is written, the letter could resemble a Christian cross. See Eisler, *The Messiah Jesus and John the Baptist*, 234-5, 255. CD 19:9-13 implies by the phrase "as came to pass at the period of the first Visitation" that the first ones who withdrew to the land of Damascus before the attack by Antiochus IV Epiphanes and later supported Mattathias and Judas Maccabeus also wore the X on their foreheads. It is interesting that Judas' surname "Maccabeus" probably means "Hammer." See Emil Schurer, *The History of the Jewish People in the Age of Jesus Christ*, vols. I, II, III.1, III.2, rev. and ed. by Geza Vermes, et al. (Edinburgh: T. & T. Clark, 1973/87), Vol. I, 158, note 49. Since the X could also resemble a hammer, is it possible that Judas' wearing of this mark was the true origin of his surname?

> For in those days [the days of Judas the Galilean] the Sicarii clubbed together against those who consented to submit to Rome and in every way treated them as enemies, plundering their property, rounding up their cattle, and setting fire to their habitations; *protesting that such persons were no other than aliens*, who so ignobly sacrificed the hard-won liberty of the Jews and admitted their preferences for the Roman yoke.[161]

The New Covenant preferred to call them "Ephraim and/or Manasseh,"[162] i.e., Samaritans![163] The Jews despised the Samaritans in the first century AD. Jeremias describes the reason for this attitude as follows:

> The Samaritans ... attached great importance to the fact that they were descended from the Jewish patriarchs. This claim was contested: they were 'Cutheans', descendants of the Median and Persian colonists, foreigners [planted in Samaria by the Assyrians in the eighth century BC]. Such was the Jewish view current in the first century AD... , in order to refute any Samaritan claim to blood affinity with Judaism.... Even their recognition of the Mosaic Law [that only the Pentateuch was accepted as binding] and their meticulous observation of its prescriptions did nothing to alter their exclusion from the community of Israel, because they were suspected of an idolatrous cult from their veneration of Mount Gerizim as a holy mountain. The fundamental reason for their exclusion, however, was their origin and not the cult of Gerizim....[164]

In the view of the New Covenant, the unbaptized "Jews," who were referred to as "Ephraim and/or Manasseh," were only making pretenses to be Jews and were excluded from the Congregation of the true Israel. It should be noted here that authentic Samaritans, who were baptized by John, were no longer Samaritans, but Israelites!

Another derogatory designation used by the New Covenant was the "Seekers-After-Smooth-Things."[165] This designation included "Ephraim and/or Manasseh" *and* schismatics from the New Covenant. They thought of schismatics as still Israelites, because they had been baptized by John; but they

---

161. War VII, 254-6 (italics mine).

162. Ephraim: 4QpHos^b 2:3; 4QpNah, frags. 3-4, 1:12, 2:2, 8, 3:5, 4:5; 4QpPs^a 1:24. CD 7:13 refers to the priestly establishment at the time of the founders (see pp. 31-5). Manasseh: 4QpNah, frags. 3-4, 3:9, 4:1, 3, 6. Ephraim and Manasseh: 4QpPs^a 2:18. Ephraim in 4QTest, line 27 refers to the land areas in the north, representing the northern kingdom during the divided monarchy in the Old Testament.

163. Theodor H. Gaster, *The Dead Sea Scriptures*, 3rd ed. (Garden City, NY: Anchor Books, 1976), 341, note 23.

164. Joachim Jeremias, *Jerusalem in the Time of Jesus* (Philadelphia: Fortress Press, 1969), 355-6.

165. 4QpNah, frag. 3-4, 1:2, 7, 2:2, 4, 3:3, 6-7; 4QIsa^c, frag. 23, 2:10.

were presently sinners, who chose not to associate with the New Covenant (i.e., the true Israel). They could return to the sect, but if they did, they would be punished according to the sect's penal code. However, a member who had been in the Council of the Community for more then ten years, but who departed from it, could never return under any circumstances.[166]

After AD 62,[167] there was another means of entry into the sect. There were no longer five levels of initiation, but only two. When baptized and circumcised men reached twenty years of age, they simply went to the "overseer of the Many," and were enrolled into the Covenant by taking the oath and having their names inscribed in a register.[168] Also, the oath was no longer voluntary, as it had been;[169] but mandatory.[170] Let me quote CD 15:7-17:[171]

> On the day on which he speaks with the overseer of the Many, he shall enroll him with the oath of the Covenant which Moses concluded with Israel, the Covenant to rev[ert to] the law of Moses with the whole heart and [with] the who[le] soul to whatever of it is to be done during al[l the per]iod [of wickedness]. And let not the ordinances be made known to him until he has presented himself before the overseer, in case he should be judged simple by the overseer when he examines him. But when he has imposed upon him the oath to return to the law of Moses with all his heart and all his soul, they will [exact re]venge from him if he should become unfaithful. Everything that is revealed from the Law for the multitude of the camp, and which he is capable, the overseer should tell him and command him to study for one full year; and then according to his knowledge he may draw near. The stupid, the mad, the foolish, the demented, the blind, the lame, the crippled, [the deaf], minors: none [of] these [shall enter] in the midst of the Congregation, for the ho[ly] angels [are in the midst of it].

Below is a diagram illustrating how the composition of Israel changed under John the Baptist:

---

166. 1QS 7:22-5.
167. This was the period when Symeon, the son of Clopas, was the leader of the New Covenant and when CD was written (AD 65-6).
168. CD 15:5-6, 7-9. According to CD 14:3-6, after AD 62 the proselytes were also enrolled by having their name inscribed in a register. They took part in the annual census also. However, they did not take the oath because they were outside Israel.
169. 1QS 6:13-4.
170. CD 15:5-6.
171. Also see the cave 4 fragment of CD, 4Q266, frag. 8, col. 1, which fills in some of the lacunas in this passage. Florentino Garcia Martinez and Eibert J. C. Tigchelaar, eds., 2 vols., *The Dead Sea Scrolls Study Edition* (Leiden: Brill, 1997), Vol. 1, 591-3.

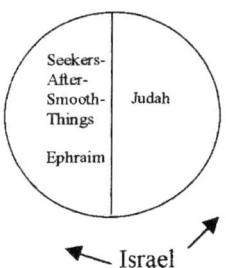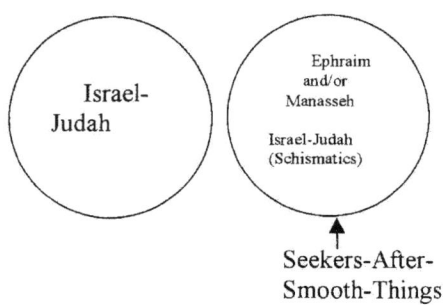

Chapter 2. The Baptism of John

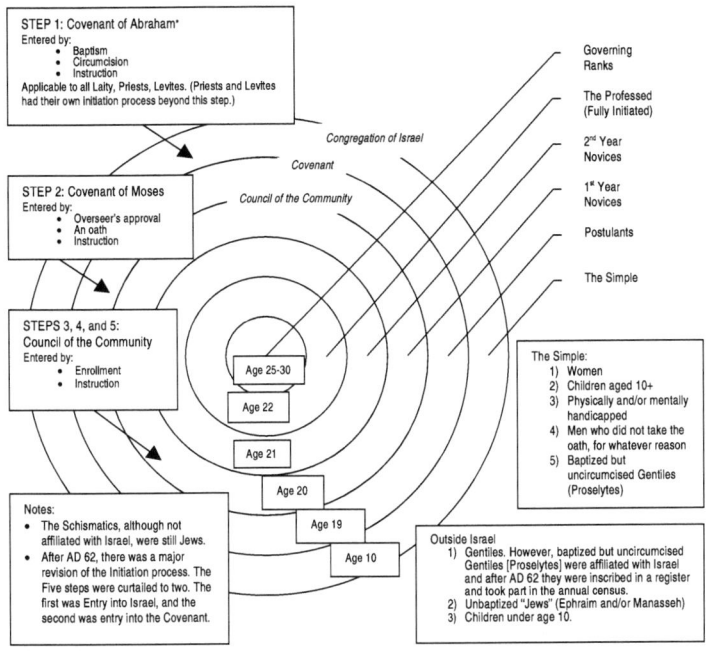

The Five Steps of Initiation

Chapter 3. John's Food and Dress

Something should now be said about John the Baptist's food and clothing. In the gospels,[172] John is said to have worn "a garment of camel's hair, and a leather girdle around his waist; and his food was locusts and wild honey." In the Slavonic version of the *War*, Robert Eisler took the following passages as being authentic statements about John:

> Now at that time there walked among the Jews a man in wondrous garb, for he had stuck on to his body animals' hair wherever it was not covered by his own. But in countenance he was like a savage.[173]

> And when he was brought to Archelaus [4 BC] and the learned doctors of the law had assembled, they asked him who he was and where he had been until then. And he answered and said, "I am a man [Enosh]; as such has the spirit of God called me, and I live on bulrushes [cane] and roots and *tree-fruits*."[174]

> Now his nature was strange and his ways were not human. For even as a fleshless spirit, so lived this man. His mouth knew no bread, *nor even at the passover feast did he taste of unleavened bread, saying: "in remembrance of God, who redeemed the people from bondage is this given to eat, and for the flight only, since the journey was in haste."*[175] But wine and strong drink he would not so much as allow to be brought nigh him. And he loathed (to eat of) any animal. And every act of injustice he exposed. And *tree-fruits*[176] served his needs.[177]

---

172. Mt. 3:4, Mk. 1:6.
173. Robert Eisler, *The Messiah Jesus and John the Baptist*, ed. by A. H. Krappe (London: Methuen & Co., 1931), 224. See also Josephus, Bk. III, Appendix, p. 644.
174. Eisler, *The Messiah Jesus and John the Baptist*, 225. See also Josephus, Bk. III, Appendix, p. 645.

What the Baptist really wore and ate can be determined by his reply to his captors during Archelaus' rule: "I am a man [Enosh]."[178] According to Robert Eisler,[179] the Baptist "regards himself as the reborn antediluvian Enosh"[180] and he practices "the original diet ordained by God for men *before* the fall." The antediluvian diet was a vegetarian diet.[181]

Josephus mentions an individual named "Bannus, who dwelt in the wilderness, wearing only such clothing as trees provided, *feeding on such things as grew of themselves*, and using frequent ablutions of cold water, by day and night, for purity's sake."[182] He says he became "his devoted disciple" and "lived with him for three years." Could John's diet have corresponded to Bannus' diet in which he ate "things as grew of themselves," i.e., fruit, figs, nuts, roots, certain raw plants, etc.? This type of diet would correspond to a raw food vegetarian diet in that cooking or processing is not used in its preparation. The statement in the Slavonic version of the *War* that John did not eat "bread" or drink "wine and strong drink" can be explained by raw food vegetarianism, since they were not food and drink that "grew of themselves." However, the eating of locusts mentioned in the gospels could contradict this dietary practice, if it were not for the fact that locusts can be explained as the "'points' or shoots of some plants."[183]

Unfortunately, a raw food vegetarian diet does not agree with certain statements found in the Dead Sea Scrolls. CD allows for the eating of locusts, as

---

175. Cf. Ex. 11:11. This section in italics is probably Josephus' own idea that was inserted as further evidence for his portrayal of John as a "strange" even "not human" personage. Not eating regular bread is one thing, but not eating even unleavened bread at the Passover feast is something else again! Certainly, people would not, no matter how much they disagreed with the Jewish establishment, have traveled to the Jordan River to be baptized by John during the Passover feast! Nor would John, who had not a good word to say about the ecclesiastical or lay leaders of the country, have traveled to Jerusalem in order to participate in the festivities there! This section of the passage is suggesting that one of these unlikely alternatives actually took place.

176. The phrase "tree-fruits" in italics here and in the passage above actually means "wood-shavings" in Slavonic, but this cannot be correct. The former meaning was probably in mind, but intentionally or not was corrupted to the latter. Robert Eisler believed that the change of "tree-fruits" to "wood-shavings" was done deliberately by Josephus himself to further portray John in a disparaging manner. This was "on par with the malicious statement that he 'stuck over his body' the hair of beasts wherever it was not covered by his own" (Eisler, *The Messiah Jesus and John the Baptist*, 225, 231, 237).

177. Eisler, *The Messiah Jesus and John the Baptist*, 230-1. See also Josephus, Bk. III, Appendix, p. 648.

178. Jn. 1:6: "There was a man [Enosh] sent from god, whose name was John." See Robert Eisler, "The Paraclete Claimant — Simon Magus," *The Quest* 21 (April 1930): 243 note 1.

179. Eisler, *The Messiah Jesus and John the Baptist*, 225, 231, 235-40, 614-5. According to Robert Eisler, John advocates a "*complete* 'return' to the original diet ..." (pg. 236, italics mine) apparently meaning that everyone should be practicing it, but I do not think this idea can be sustained.

180. Gen. 4:26.

181. Gen. 1:29, cf. 9:3.

182. The Life, 11-2 (italics mine).

183. Eisler, *The Messiah Jesus and John the Baptist*, 236.

long as they are cooked alive or drowned first.[184] According to the same scroll, the "wild honey" of the gospels would have to have been filtered.[185] Even fish that had been split with the blood poured out could be eaten.[186] It also conflicts with 1QS and 1QSa that mention the eating of bread and wine in the special Meal of the sect.[187] It is interesting to note that the "wine" used by the sect may have only been unfermented grape-juice,[188] but even the latter had to be prepared before it could be consumed. How can a raw food vegetarian diet be reconciled with these statements of the scrolls?

One possible explanation presents itself. While John was baptizing in the Jordan River, he would not have been able to enter the sect's inner organization for he would have contracted the ritual uncleanness of the people he was associating with! The very existence of the steps in the initiation process gives ample evidence of the sect's extreme views regarding ritual purity. Before he could return to his duties inside the sect, he would have had to undergo a special purification to return himself to ritual cleanliness. This would be the reason why, while John was baptizing in the Jordan River *alone and apart from the sect*, he restricted himself to foods that "grew of themselves" (i.e., a raw food vegetarian diet). When he was *inside the sect*, performing his duties as the sect's high priest, there would be no reason why he could not consume bread, wine, unfermented grape-juice, filtered honey[189] or even some other cooked or processed vegetarian food (i.e., a less strict vegetarian diet). An outsider like Josephus would not have been aware of this distinction.

However, if people who came to John for baptism brought him bread and wine as a gift, what would have been his reason for refusing to accept them if the above explanation is correct? He *must* have refused them, if the statements in the Slavonic Josephus are correct. Of course, one could offer the explanation that these occasions of gift giving were rare and hidden from the view of the large crowd, but this would hang the above explanation on a slender thread indeed. There must have been another reason for John's abstinence from bread and wine.

There is no evidence that the high priest was required to participate in the special Meal of the sect that took place every night wherever ten men were present.[190] At this special Meal, bread and wine were consumed.[191] However,

---

184. CD 12:14-5.
185. CD 12:11-3.
186. CD 12:13-4.
187. 1QS 6:1-8, 1QSa 2:17-22.
188. G. Vermes, *The Dead Sea Scrolls: Qumran in Perspective*, rev. ed., (Philadelphia: Fortress Press, 1981), 94, 111.
189. Even while he was baptizing at the Jordan River, John would not have violated the sect's law (see CD 12:11-3) by consuming *wild* honey as the Gospels state (Mk. 1:6, Mt. 3:4).

"when [Adonai] will have begotten the Messiah among them,"[192] the high priest was certainly required to preside over it with the Messiah of Israel. At this time, the entire Council of the Community would participate in it together.[193] Could it be that John chose to avoid wine until the Messiah of Israel was anointed and he could preside over the special Meal with the latter and the entire assembly together?

One of the requirements of the Nazirite vow was that the person undertaking it consumed nothing that came from the grapevine and this certainly included wine.[194] Also, "no razor shall come upon [the participant's] head" and "he shall let the locks of hair of his head grow long."[195] These requirements of the vow would not be incompatible with the descriptions of John given in our sources. I think John probably undertook a Nazirite vow for the reason given above and this is the most likely explanation why he did not drink wine.

Since bread was also a component of the special Meal, could John have made the decision not to consume bread for the same reason as he did for the wine? I think this was indeed the case.[196] He chose not to consume bread and wine until the Messiah of Israel was anointed and they both could preside over the special Meal together.

While John was baptizing at the Jordan River, he probably did consume a raw food vegetarian diet almost all of the time. But through the charity of some of those who came to him for baptism, he may have been able to consume cooked or processed vegetarian foods from time to time. When he was with the sect, he

---

190. 1QS 6:1-13, 1QSa 2:21-2.

191. 1QS 6:4-5.

192. 1QSa 2:11-2. In a later chapter, I put forward the idea that God's "begetting" of the Messiah of Israel occurred via a ritual of enthronement — the main part being his anointing with oil by the high priest.

193. 1QSa 2:11-22.

194. Num. 6:3-4. The Nazirite vow is described in Num. 6:1-21. See also Jg. 13:4-5, 7, Am. 2:11-2.

195. Num. 6:5.

196. Hegesippus states that James the Righteous, the leader and high priest of the New Covenant after John, "drank no wine or strong drink" and "no razor went upon his head" (Eusebius, *The Ecclesiastical History*, 2 Vols., trans. by Kirsopp Lake (Cambridge: Harvard University Press, 1975), Vol. I, 171 (II, 23.4-6). Both of these characteristics can be explained if James like John undertook a Nazirite vow until the Messiah of Israel was anointed. Nothing is said by Hegesippus about James' abstinence from bread. However, a passage from the Gospel according to the Hebrews, in which we only have quotations from other writers, gives us an important piece of information. It states that "James had sworn not to eat bread from the time that he drank from the Lord's cup until he would see him [Jesus] raised from among those who sleep [i.e., the dead]." After the resurrection, the passage concludes by stating that Jesus "took bread, blessed it, broke it, and gave it to James ... and said to him, 'My brother, eat your bread, for the Son of Adam has been raised from among those who sleep.'" See Robert J. Miller, ed., *The Complete Gospels* (San Francisco: Harper, 1994), 434. The sole value of this passage lies in the fact that it may allude to a tradition that James abstained from eating bread.

certainly would have been able to consume the full spectrum of vegetarian foods available. However, bread and wine would have always been excluded from his diet for the reason given above.

John as the reborn Enosh, the son of Seth and grandson of Adam, also wore the garb of Adam's descendants. After their fall from Paradise, God had made "garments of skins" for Adam and Eve.[197] The word "skins" is a problem here. Would God, who had just commanded Adam and Eve to eat a vegetarian diet[198] and who changed it only after the flood,[199] have killed animals in order to make clothing for them? A vegetarian diet would naturally necessitate that their clothing be from a *living* animal (e.g., animal hair) not a dead one (e.g., animal skin). Early Jewish and Christian interpreters found the idea that God killed animals difficult to accept and explained "garments of skins" as actually meaning garments made from camel's hair, the bark of trees, or something else that did not require the killing of animals.[200] It would appear that John agreed with them.

The description of John's dress in the Slavonic version of the *War* may be correct. It states that "he had stuck on to his body animals' hair wherever it was not covered by his own." However, this description did not set out to praise John. He was portrayed as a "savage," his "ways" were "not human," and he lived as "a fleshless spirit." In another authentic section of the Slavonic version that was not quoted above, he is said to have appeared out of the wilderness "like a wild beast."[201] Wearing the hair of animals where there was none of his own would certainly be consistent with this portrayal. Perhaps John's actual dress was similar to that of Bannus in that he wore "only clothing as trees provided" (i.e., bark or leaves). If John did wear the hair of animals, it was probably camel's hair. It fell off in the spring and was used to make "carpets, saddle-bags, ropes, girdles, and cloaks."[202] The leather girdle around his waist, which is mentioned in the gospels, was inserted in order to identify John the Baptist as the reborn Elijah.[203] The latter was to be the forerunner of the Messiah in Jewish tradition[204] just as John the Baptist was the forerunner of Jesus in Christian tradition.[205]

---

197. Gen. 3:21.
198. Gen. 1:29.
199. Gen. 9:3.
200. Eisler, *The Messiah Jesus and John the Baptist*, 238.
201. Eisler, *The Messiah Jesus and John the Baptist*, 225. See also Josephus, Bk. III, Appendix, p. 645.
202. Eisler, *The Messiah Jesus and John the Baptist*, 239, note 1.
203. 2 Kgs. 1:8. Elijah wore "a garment of haircloth, with a girdle of leather about his loins."
204. Emil Schurer, *The History of the Jewish People in the Age of Jesus Christ*, vols. I, II, III.1, III.2,, rev. and ed. by Geza Vermes, et al. (Edinburgh: T. & T. Clark, 1973/87), Vol.II, 515-6.
205. Mt. 17:9-13, Mk. 9:9-13.

John probably did not require other members of the sect to eat a vegetarian diet. This would explain why cooked or drowned locusts and fish that had been split with the blood poured out[206] were acceptable foods. These foods would not be great departures from a vegetarian diet, but members of the sect could probably eat meat also. Nowhere is there a prohibition against meat eating and, after all, the scrolls were written on parchment, which is actually specially prepared animal skin. However, the blood of the animal could not be eaten, but had to be poured out on the ground.[207] John's garb was probably his own particular choice as well.

The next question we need to ask is why did John practice vegetarianism? I think the answer is that while the temple in Jerusalem was polluted and controlled by a corrupt priesthood sacrifices pleasing to God could not be offered there. Therefore, John refused to eat meat *until* the temple was purified and a righteous priesthood could again sacrifice in it. This practice of his was even stricter than that prescribed in the Bible[208] or even in the Temple Scroll,[209] since the slaughter of animals for food was allowed outside the Temple. Nevertheless, it did correspond to his stern character.

An interesting episode from Old Testament times is worth bringing up here. After the waters of the flood had dried up, Noah offered animal sacrifices to God that had a "pleasing odor" to Him (i.e., the sacrifices were offered in an acceptable manner). It was only as a consequence of this action that God then gave permission to mankind to eat animal flesh![210] As mentioned earlier in this chapter, before the fall God only gave mankind permission to eat a vegetarian diet.[211] It could very well be the case that based on this Old Testament story John chose to forgo eating meat until such time as a proper sacrifice was again offered in a purified Temple by a righteous priesthood.[212]

Why did John wear his peculiar garb? It symbolized the sinfulness of his own day just as it had symbolized the sinfulness of the descendants of Adam after the fall from Paradise. After all, God only clothed Adam and Eve *after* the fall (i.e., sin) had occurred.[213]

---

206. CD 12:13-4.
207. Gen. 9:3-6, Dt. 12:16, 23-4, Lev. 17:10-4, 11QT 53:5-7.
208. Dt. 12:15-28. However, according to Lev. 17:1-7, which is perhaps earlier legislation, animals slaughtered for food had to be brought to the sanctuary and sacrificed as a peace offering.
209. 11QT 53:1-8.
210. Gen. 8:13-22, 9:3.
211. Gen. 1:29.
212. James the Righteous, the leader and high priest of the New Covenant after John, appears to have agreed with John's views in this area, since Hegesippus states that he "did [not] eat flesh" (Eusebius, *Ecclesiastical History*, Vol. I, 171 (II, 23. 4-6).
213. Gen. 3:21.

Chapter 3. John's Food and Dress

To summarize, I think it is likely that John, the great preacher of repentance, believed himself to be the antediluvian Enosh reborn in whose time "men began to call upon the name of the Lord."[214] He intended to practice the antediluvian diet and wear the antediluvian garb until such time as the New Covenant finally gained control of the temple and could again offer sacrifices there that pleased God.

The following Key Terms in the CD Exhortation are discussed in Chapter 4.

Term	CD Reference	Date	Meaning
The First Ones	1:4, 3:10-1, 4:10, 6:2, 8:17, 19:29	187-167 BC	They were Jews who realized their error and returned to the true practice of their faith.
The "Priests"	3:21, 4:2	187-167 BC	The First Ones
Judah (1)	7:12, 13, cf. 14:1	187-167 BC	The First Ones
The Returnees of Israel (1)	4:2	187 BC-167 BC	The First Ones
Ephraim	7:12, 13, cf. 14:1	187-167 BC	The corrupt priestly establishment and its supporters at the time of the First Ones.
The First Visitation	7:21, 19:11, cf. 1:7, 3:10-1, 7:13	169 BC	Antiochus IV Epiphanes' attack on Jerusalem.
20 years grouping	1:9-10	187-167 BC	The period from the appearance of the First Ones to the appearance of Mattathias.
The Remnant (1)	3:13	ca. 167 BC	The First Ones who returned from the land of Damascus to join Mattathias.
The Root of Planting	1:7	167-166 BC	Mattathias, founder of the Hasmoneans.
Sure House in Israel	3:19	164 BC	The rededication of the Temple by Judas Maccabaeus.
The "Levites"	3:21, 4:3	160-159 BC	Some of Judas' followers who returned to the land of Damascus after his death (161 BC).
The Remnant (2)	1:4	ca. 63 BC	Those who preserved the traditions of the First Ones and escaped to the land of Damascus before Pompey attacked Jerusalem in 63 BC.
Zadok	5:5	ca. 24-20 BC	The opponent of the establishment high priest Simon, the son of Boethus, or perhaps Boethus himself. He wrote the Temple Scroll.
Teacher of Righteousness, the Unique Teacher, the Unique One	1:11 20:1, 14 20:32	4 BC-AD 35	John the Baptist
The "Princes"	6:3, 6	ca. AD 37	Those who joined Dositheus in the land of Damascus.
The Period of Wrath, 390 years	1:5 1:6	ca. 315 BC-ca. AD 75	The primary time period in which the CD exhortation is concerned.
The Last Generation	1:12	AD 35-ca. AD 75	The generation prior to the Visitation.
The End of Days	4:4, 6:11	Ended ca. AD 75	A length of time that included the Last Generation but was of uncertain length.
The Visitation	19:10	ca. AD 75	The coming destruction of Jerusalem and the Temple.
"Nebuchadnezzar," Chief of the Kings of Yawan	1:6 8:11, 19:23-4	ca. AD 75	The Roman emperor, probably Nero, who would bring on the coming visitation.

---

214. Gen. 4:26.

The Kings of the Peoples, the Kings of Yawan	8:10, 19:23 8:11, 19:24	ca. AD 75	Rulers of various kingdoms in the Middle East, who would aid the Roman emperor at the coming visitation.
The Man of Mockery, The Man of Lies, the Man who Preaches Lies, Zaw	1:14 20:15 8:13, 19:26 4:19	AD 35-AD 67 or 68	Ananus, the son of Ananus
The Congregation of Traitors, the Princes of Judah, the Builders of the Wall, the House of Peleg	1:14 8:3, 19:15 4:19, 8:18, 19:31 20:22	AD 35- ca. AD 75	Ananus' supporters
The Righteous One, the Teacher, the Teacher of Righteousness	1:20 20:28 20:32	AD 35-AD 62	James the Righteous
The "Nobles"	6:4, 8	AD 65-6	Those led by Symeon, the son of Clopas, to the land of Damascus.
The Interpreter of the Torah, the Star, the Rod, the Voice of the Teacher	6:7, 7:18 7:18, 19 6:4, 7 20:28, 32	AD 62- ca. AD 101	Symeon, the son of Clopas
The Prince of All the Congregation, the Sceptre, he who arises to teach righteousness in the end of days, the Messiah of Aaron and Israel	7:20 7:19, 20 6:11 20:1, 19:10-1, cf. 14:19	ca. AD 75- ca. AD 115	A new leader who was to come at the period of the coming visitation.
The "Sons of Zadok ... who shall stand in the end of days"	3:21-4:1, 4:3-4	ca. AD 75	All members of the sect at the period of the coming visitation.
The Fathers	8:18, 19:31	19th cent. BC	The Patriarchs: Abraham, Isaac, and Jacob
The Period of the Desolation of the Land	5:20, cf. 3:10	586 BC	The fall of Jerusalem under the real Nebuchadezzar
His [God's] Messiah, the Holy One	6:1	Old Testament times	Aaron, the high priest under Moses.
His [God's] Messiah	2:12	No specific date	A uniquely gifted holy priest that appeared in every era of history.
Judah (2)	4:11, 8:3, 19:15, 20:26	4 BC-ca. AD 75	All "Jews" baptized by John the Baptist or one of his successors.
The Returnees of Israel (2)	6:5, 8:16, 19:29	4 BC-ca. AD 75	All "Jews" baptized by John the Baptist or one of his successors (i.e., they became Jews again).
The Well	3:16, 4:3, 4, 9	No specific date	The Torah

Note: Terms with more than one usage are numbered to differentiate each usage. For example: Judah (1), Judah (2).

Chapter 4. The First Ones

The document titled the Damascus Document (CD) was actually discovered by Solomon Schechter in the genizah[215] of a synagogue in Old Cairo in 1896-7. He published it in 1910 with an English translation, introduction, and notes.[216] It was not until the discovery of the Dead Sea Scrolls in the period 1947-52, when fragments of this document were discovered in the caves, that it was realized it actually originated with the Dead Sea Scroll sect. Some previously unknown verses of the document were discovered in the caves as well.

The document is composed of two major sections — the exhortation[217] and the ordinance[218] sections. Although the New Covenant actually came into existence at the turn of the first century AD, it claimed to have originated as far back as the second century BC. The exhortation section alludes to significant periods of their professed history from the beginning right up to the time when the scribe is composing the document. It also predicts events that were to come in the near future. The ordinance section is a compendium of the sect's rules for the present time and for the future. Our main focus in this chapter will be on the exhortation section.

CD was composed in AD 65-6, when a mass exodus of the sect was taking place from Judea to the land of Damascus. The "land of Damascus"[219] was probably the large land area extending northeastwards starting from

---

215. This word is a transliteration of the Hebrew word for "storage room."
216. Solomon Schechter, *Documents of Jewish Sectaries, Vol. 1. Fragments of a Zadokite Work, edited from Hebrew Manuscripts in the Cairo Geniza Collection now in possession of the University Library, Cambridge, and provided with an English translation, introduction, and notes* (Cambridge, 1910).
217. CD 1:1-8:21, 19:1-35, 20:1-34.
218. CD 15:1-16:20, 9:1-14:22 and several cave 4 fragments.

northeastern Galilee to just below the city of Damascus in Syria and southwards on the eastern side of the Sea of Galilee and the Jordan River to just above the city of Pella in the Decapolis. It would have included northeastern Galilee, Gaulanitis, Syria (the region southwest of the city of Damascus), Trachonitis, Batanaea, Auranitis, and the Decapolis (the region northeast of the city of Pella).[220] Josephus mentions this exodus. He states that, because of the unbearable conditions during the governorship of Gessius Florus (AD 64-6), many Jews "were one and all forced to abandon their own country and flee, for they thought that it would be better to settle among gentiles, no matter where."[221]

The writer expected this exodus to be completed before a terrible "visitation" of God took place. This one would be as disastrous (if not more so) as the visitation of Nebuchadnezzar in 586 BC. Those remaining in Judea would be "delivered up to the sword." Some of those in the land of Damascus would return and be destroyed justifying the scribe's quoting of Malachi 3:18: "And they shall distinguish again between the just and the wicked, between whoever serves God and whoever does not serve him."[222] Everyone outside the sect had up to the last moment to make his decision: Be baptized (i.e., enter the "House of Judah") and join the sect in the land of Damascus or face destruction by remaining in Judea. Once the terrible visitation had arrived his fate was sealed. This is explained in the following passage:

> And at the completion of the period [i.e., the end of the "period of wrath"],[223]
> according to the number of those years,
> there will no longer be any joining with the House of Judah,
> but each man shall stand on his fortification:
> the wall is built, the boundary carried far.[224]

---

219. CD 6:5, 19, 7:15 ("to Damascus" in the biblical quotation of Amos 5:26-7), 19 ("to Damascus"), 8:21, 19:34, 20:12, cf. 7:14, the "land of the north."

220. This idea comes from Schonfield, but I have extended the area to include Trachonitis. Also, in his map he has incorrectly reversed the locations of Batanaea and Auranitis. See Hugh J. Schonfield, *The Jesus Party* (New York: Macmillan Pub. Co., 1974), 8 (map of the area), 276-93. The land of Damascus is also called the "desert of the peoples" (1QM 1:3). According to Dupont-Sommer, "the expression 'desert of the peoples' appears in Ezek. xx. 35, where it seems to apply to the Syrian desert between Babylonia and Palestine; here [commenting on 1QM 1:3], it may refer to a desert region in the vicinity of Damascus, since we know that it was in the 'land of Damascus' that the sect sought refuge." See A. Dupont-Sommer, *The Essene Writings from Qumran*, trans. G. Vermes (Gloucester: Peter Smith, 1973), 169, note 2.

221. Ant. XX, 256-6; War II, 277-9.

222. CD 20:20-1.

223. CD 1:5.

224. CD 4:10-2, near quote of Mic. 7:11 ("The wall is built, the boundary carried far").

The only two places in the entire document that allude to the original visitation of Nebuchadnezzar are CD 3:10 and CD 5:20-6:2.[225] In the latter lines, Moses and "His [God's] Messiah, the Holy One" (i.e., Aaron) are referred to as the revealers of God's commandments. Unfortunately, Israel strayed away from them necessitating the visitation of Nebuchadnezzar. CD 5:15-9 also mentions Moses and Aaron during the exodus (i.e., the "first deliverance of Israel").

The evil person who would bring on this new visitation would be the Roman emperor who was reigning at that time. He was probably thought to be Emperor Nero, who was emperor from AD 54-68. The Roman emperor is actually symbolically called "Nebuchadnezzar king of Babylon" in CD 1:6.[226] He is also called the "Chief of the kings of Yawan" (i.e., Greece).

> And in the period of wrath,
> three hundred and ninety years to His delivering them
> into the hand of Nebuchadnezzar king of Babylon,
> He [God] visited them,
> and caused a root of planting to spring from Israel and Aaron
> to possess His land
> and to grow fat on the good things of His earth.
> And they recognized their sin,
> and became conscious of having been guilty.
> And (that) they had been like the blind,
> groping for the way for twenty years.[227]

A "period of wrath" lasting "390 years *to*[228] His delivering them into the hand of Nebuchadnezzar" (i.e., the Roman emperor) is mentioned[229] and this is the primary period of time that the CD exhortation is concerned with. Based on this statement alone, the beginning and ending dates of this period of wrath cannot be determined. Fortunately, CD 20:13-5, which will be discussed in a later chapter, will allow us to determine these dates.

---

225. Note the phrase "the period of the desolation of the land" (CD 5:20).
226. B. Thiering, *Redating the Teacher of Righteousness* (Sydney: Theological Explorations, 1979), 55.
227. CD 1:5-10.
228. Not *after*, as it is usually translated. See I. Rabinowitz, "A Reconsideration of 'Damascus' and '390 Years' in the 'Damascus' ('Zadokite') Fragments," *JBL* 73 (1954), 11-35, note 8b, p. 14.
229. CD 1:5-6.

The "root of planting"[230] alludes to Mattathias,[231] the founder of the high-priestly and kingly dynasty of the Hasmonaeans, who appeared in 167 BC. The "20 years" of "groping"[232] will then take us back to 187 BC.[233] In 187 BC, the "first ones" came into being.[234] They were Jews who realized their error and returned to the true practice of their faith. The phrase "He [God] visited them" alludes to the attack by the Syrian (Greek) king, Antiochus IV Epiphanes, in 169 BC.

> But when God visits the earth,
> all those who despise (the commandments)
> shall draw down on themselves the reward of the wicked;
> when the word shall come that is written in the words of the prophet Isaiah
>   son of Amoz, who said, *There shall come upon thee and thy people,*
> *and upon thy father's house,*
> *days such as have (not) come*
> *since the day when Ephraim departed from Judah.*[235]
> WHEN THE TWO HOUSES OF ISRAEL WERE SEPARATED,
> EPHRAIM RULED OVER JUDAH,
> AND ALL THOSE WHO FELL BACK WERE DELIVERED UP TO THE SWORD,
> WHEREAS THOSE WHO HELD FIRM ESCAPED TO THE LAND OF THE NORTH [the
>   land of Damascus];
> AS HE SAID, *I WILL DEPORT THE SIKKUT OF YOUR KING*
> *AND THE KIYYUN OF YOUR IMAGES*
> *AWAY FROM MY TENT TO DAMASCUS.*[236]
> THE BOOKS OF THE TORAH ARE THE "HUT [sukkat][237] OF THE KING;"
> AS HE SAID, *I WILL LIFT UP THE FALLEN HUT OF DAVID.*[238]
> THE "KING" IS THE ASSEMBLY;[239]
> AND THE "KIYYUN OF THE IMAGES" IS THE BOOKS OF THE PROPHETS
>   WHOSE WORDS ISRAEL DESPISED. ...

---

230. CD 1:7.

231. Robert Eisler, "The Sadoqite Book of the New Covenant: Its Date and Origin," *Occident and Orient* (Gaster Anniversary Volume), ed. B. Schindler (London: Taylor's Foreign Press, 1936), 122.

232. CD 1:9-10.

233. Eisler, "The Sadoqite Book of the New Covenant: Its Date and Origin," 122-3: "The twenty years of the apostate Hellenised high-priests, from the accession of Seleucos IV in 187 BC to the Maccabean revolution in 167 BC."

234. CD 1:4, 4:10, 6:2, 8:17, 19:29.

235. Is. 7:17, quoted in CD 14:1 also.

236. Amos 5:26-7. The quotation does not agree to the Masoretic Text.

237. "Sukkat" means "hut." "Sikkut" in Amos 5:26 is an Akkadian name for the planet Saturn ("Kiyyun" is as well). Because of the similiarity of sukkat and sikkut, the scribe is able to make a play on words.

238. Amos 9:11.

239. Based on the statement "the 'king' is the assembly," the first ones seem to have had no single leader in the period before the first visitation. Robert Eisler notes that it is "a remarkably 'democratic' interpretation given by these New Covenanters, the very reverse of Louis XIV '*l'état c'est moi*'!" (Eisler, "The Sadoqite Book of the New Covenant: Its Date and Origin," 133, note 153).

THEY ESCAPED AT THE PERIOD OF THE FIRST VISITATION [ANTIOCHUS],
BUT THOSE WHO FELL BACK WERE DELIVERED UP TO THE SWORD.
And such shall be the lot of all who enter His Covenant
but do not hold firm to these (precepts)
when He visits them for destruction by the hand of Belial.[240]

The first italicized section of the passage is a quotation of Is.7:17[241] except that the very end of the actual biblical text adds "the king of Assyria." The prophet Isaiah made this prediction to Ahaz, the king of the southern kingdom of Judah. In 734-733 BC, Ahaz made an alliance with Tiglath-pileser, the king of Assyria, against the alliance of Rezin, the king of Syria, and Pekah, the king of the northern kingdom of Israel. Rezin and Pekah were waging war against Judah.[242] The prophet was saying that there were terrible times coming for the kingdom of Judah, because of Ahaz' alliance with the king of Assyria. These times would be as terrible as "when Ephraim (i.e., the northern kingdom of Israel) departed from Judah." This occurred when the northern kingdom seceded from Judah after the death of King Solomon in 922 BC.[243]

The "small caps" section in the passage above[244] refers to the withdrawal of "Judah" (i.e., the first ones) to the land of Damascus, which occurred in the period from after 187 BC to the "first visitation."[245] The sect understood this as the attack by Antiochus IV Epiphanes in 169 BC. "Ephraim" was the priestly establishment of the time and its supporters, who apostatized from Judaism and began practicing the Greek way of life. At some point before this first visitation, "when the two houses of Israel[246] were separated," Judah "escaped to the land of the north" (i.e., the land of Damascus). The statement that "Ephraim ruled over Judah" means that the former were the political leaders of the country at the time of Judah's escape. Along with Ephraim, "those who fell back" from the land of Damascus were "delivered up to the sword"[247] in the visitation of Antiochus.

The statement in the biblical passage (Is 7:17) that "Ephraim departed from Judah" was reinterpreted as referring to *Ephraim's abandonment of the true faith*

---

240. CD 7:9-18, 21-8:2.
241. CD 7:10-2.
242. 2 Kgs. 16:1-20.
243. 1 Kgs. 12:1-33.
244. CD 7:12-18, 7:21-8:1.
245. CD 7:21, 19:11.
246. The designation "two houses of Israel" refers to Ephraim and Judah. They were both considered to be a part of Israel before the time of John the Baptist.
247. CD 7:13, 3:10-1.

preserved by Judah. Unlike the secession of 922 BC, it was Judah that was withdrawing in the physical sense not Ephraim.

In CD 3:21-4:4, the "priests," the "levites," and the "sons of Zadok" are symbolic designations for certain groups that appeared at different periods during the sect's professed history.[248] I quote the passage below:

> *The priests and the levites and the sons of Zadok*
> *who kept the charge of my sanctuary*
> *while the children of Israel went astray from me;*
> *they shall offer me the fat and the blood.*[249]
> The priests are the returnees of Israel[250]
> who went out from the land of Judah;
> and (the levites are) those who joined them.
> And the sons of Zadok are the chosen of Israel,
> The (men) named with a name who shall stand in the end of days.

The first ones who escaped to the land of Damascus were "the priests ...who went out from the land of Judah." For an explanation of the "levites," see below. The "sons of Zadok ... in the end of days" will be all the members of the sect at the time of the coming visitation.

In 169 BC, Antiochus IV Epiphanes (175-164 BC) marched into Jerusalem, massacred many people, and looted the Temple. However, this was not to be the end of his evil for his goal was to destroy the Jewish religion. In 167 BC, he sent Apollonius to Judea as the chief tax collector. He began a campaign of massacre, pillage, and destruction in Jerusalem itself. Then, orders arrived from Antiochus that the practice of the Jewish faith was to be prohibited on pain of death and pagan cults were to be substituted in its place. Apollonius used all means available to him to carry out the orders. Finally, he erected a heathen altar in the Temple (this is the "abomination of desolation" mentioned in Dan. 11:31, 12:11), which was the worst outrage imaginable. It was because of the heroism of Jewish rebels under the leadership of Mattathias and then Judas Maccabeus that the Temple was rededicated in 164 BC. From this event, the Feast of the Dedication of the Temple (Hannukkah) originated.[251]

---

248. Hugh J. Schonfield, *Secrets of the Dead Sea Scrolls* (London: Jewish Chronicle Publications, 1956), 29, 55-7. It should be noted that my identifications of the "priests" and "levites" differ from Schonfield's.
249. Ezek. 44:15 (significantly different from the Masoretic Text).
250. I.e., they returned to the true practice of the faith.
251. 1 Macc. 1:20-4:61; 2 Macc. 5:11-10:9; Ant. XII, 233-360; War I, 27-43.

Chapter 4. The First Ones

> But because of those who clung to the commandments of God
> (and) survived them as a remnant,
> God established His Covenant with Israel forever,
> revealing to them the hidden things
> in which all Israel had strayed ...
> But they defiled themselves by the sin of man
> and by the ways of defilement,
> and they said, "This is ours!"
> And God in His marvelous mysteries
> forgave their iniquity
> and blotted out their sin;
> and He built for them a sure House in Israel
> such as did not exist from former times until now.[252]

The "remnant" of the above passage were the first ones from the land of Damascus who returned to join Mattathias (i.e., the "root of planting") in 167 BC. The "sure House in Israel" is an allusion to the Temple rededicated by Judas Maccabeus in 164 BC.

The passage contains an interesting line: "He (i.e., God) built for them a sure House in Israel such as did not exist from former times until now." "Now" refers to the sect in the land of Damascus in AD 65-6. At that time, it would appear that the sect had its own Sanctuary, i.e., a portable Tabernacle and an altar on which sacrifices were offered. This idea is the best explanation for certain passages found in CD.[253] Doubtless, it would have been constructed in accordance with the description found in Ex. 26 and 27 and, in order to keep its location a secret, it would probably have been moved on a regular basis. This line is implying that a proper Sanctuary only existed two times in history! One time was the rededicated Temple in 164 BC (i.e., the sure House in Israel), although it eventually became polluted too. The other was the Tabernacle in the land of Damascus.

The sect's escape in AD 65-6 from coming disaster in Judea was seen as being a repetition of the Exodus from oppression in Egypt during Old Testament times. Thus, it was perfectly legitimate that, as ancient Israel had a Tabernacle in the Sinai desert where its God could dwell, the new Israel had one in the "*desert of the peoples*"[254] (i.e., the land of Damascus) as well. Seeing that the polluted

---

252. CD 3:12-14, 17-9.
253. CD 4:18, 5:6, 6:16, 16:13-4, 11:17-23. CD 1:3 refers to the capture of Jerusalem by the Roman general Pompey in 63 BC (see below). CD 12:1-2 is in the "rule of the settlement of the cities of Israel," not in the "camps" rule. CD 6:11-4 is not saying that the sect did not offer sacrifices, but that sacrifices were useless if they were not offered properly.
254. 1QM 1:3 (italics mine).

Temple in Jerusalem was due to be destroyed by a new Nebuchadnezzar and its rededication would not happen as was the case with the Temple in 164 BC, a new dwelling place for Israel's God was certainly needed. For the time being, this was a portable Tabernacle as described above.

There were precedents for the building of a Sanctuary outside of Jerusalem. When Egypt was under Persian rule (525-401 BC), a Temple was built by a Jewish community on the island of Elephantine in the Nile in Egypt. It was destroyed by the Egyptians in 410 BC. Later it was rebuilt, but sacrifices were not permitted.[255] When the Jews, who returned from the Babylonian Exile, would not allow the Samaritans to participate in the rebuilding of the Temple, they built their own Temple on Mt. Gerizim in ca. 330 BC. It was destroyed by John Hyrcanus I in ca. 130 BC.[256] Finally, when Alexander IV Epiphanes became king in 175 BC, the high priest Onias III fled to Egypt and had a Temple built at Leontopolis in the Nile Delta.[257]

In 161 BC, the pro-Greek party with the high priest Alcimus at its head corresponded with the Syrian king, Demetrius I Soter (162-150 BC) asking him for help against Judas Maccabeus and his party. Demetrius I sent his general, Bacchides, to force the people to accept Alcimus as the high priest. When he believed his mission was a success, Bacchides returned to Syria.[258] However, Alcimus again asked for help from Demetrius I. The king sent another general named Nicanor with a large army to Judea. After an unsuccessful battle with Judas at Capharsalama, Nicanor marched to Jerusalem and threatened to burn down the Temple if Judas and his army were not surrendered to him. However, Judas was eventually able to defeat Nicanor in a decisive battle northwest of Jerusalem. Nicanor was killed in the conflict. Thereafter, the battle was celebrated annually as Nicanor's Day on 13th Adar (i.e., March.).[259] Shortly after Nicanor's defeat, Demetrius I sent Bacchides again with another army that did defeat and kill Judas Maccabeus (161 BC).[260]

---

255. John J. Rousseau and Rami Arav, *Jesus and His World* (Minneapolis: Fortress Press, 1995), 281.
256. Rousseau and Arav, *Jesus and His World*, 206, 281; Ant. XIII, 254-6; War I, 63.
257. Ant. XIII, 62-73; War VII, 427-32.
258. 1Macc. 7:5-25, 2 Macc. 14:3-10, Ant. XII, 391-7.
259. 1 Macc. 7:26-50; 2 Macc. 14:12-15:36; Ant. XII, 402-12.
260. 1 Macc. 9:6-21, Ant. XII, 422-34.

Chapter 4. The First Ones

When Judas died in 161 BC, the Greek party again got the upper hand.[261] The "levites"[262] who joined the "priests" in the land of Damascus were some of the followers of Judas who went there in 160-159 BC.[263]

When Jonathan (161-143/2 BC), the brother of Judas, became the leader of Judas' party, Bacchides again came to Judea at two different times for the purpose of destroying Jonathan and his followers in order to aid the pro-Greek party.[264] The first time he had some success in his endeavor and fortified many cities of Judea including the citadel in Jerusalem.[265] The second time (two years later) he realized that trying to destroy Jonathan's army would be too difficult if not impossible. Therefore, he made peace with Jonathan and swore never to make war on him again.[266] By the time Jonathan became the high priest in 152 BC, the pro-Greek party had lost all its political power.[267]

In the first year of John Hyrcanus I's reign (135/4-104 BC), the Syrian king, Antiochus VII Sidetes (138-129 BC), devastated the country and surrounded Jerusalem with Hyrcanus I shut inside. A settlement was eventually reached between them, although the terms were severe for Hyrcanus I. As part of the deal, Jerusalem was saved from complete destruction, but the walls were pulled down.[268] With the death of Antiochus VII in 129 BC, the country was completely free of the Syrians.[269]

In 88 BC, the Pharisees initiated a treasonable correspondence with Demetrius III Eucerus (ca. 95-88/7 BC) against the Jewish king Alexander Jannaeus (103-76 BC). Demetrius III came with an army, the Jewish rebels joined him, and together they defeated Alexander Jannaeus at Shechem. But then, preferring to be ruled by a Jewish rather than a Syrian king, a large number of Jews returned to Jannaeus and Demetrius III was forced to return to Syria. When Jannaeus had captured the remaining rebel Pharisees, he had eight hundred of them crucified in full view of the city while he was feasting with his concubines. The throats of their wives and children were cut in front of them while they were still alive![270] There is no evidence that Demetrius III had ever tried to enter Jerusalem. However, it is possible that, when he had beaten

---

261. Ant. XIII, 1.
262. CD 4:2-3.
263. Schonfield, *Secrets of the Dead Sea Scrolls*, 20-1.
264. 1 Macc. 9:32-72; Ant. XIII, 12-7, 22-34.
265. Ant. XIII, 14-6.
266. Ant. XIII, 32-4.
267. 1 Macc. 10:15-45; Ant. XIII, 43-57.
268. Ant. XIII, 236-48.
269. Ant. XIII, 250-3, 273.
270. Ant. XII, 376-84; War I, 89-100.

Janneaus at Shechem, he decided to march to Jerusalem. This could be the real reason why a large number of Jews (six thousand according to Josephus) went over to Jannaeus forcing Demetrius III to leave the country.[271]

There is an interesting passage in 4QpNah that has relevance for this time period. I will quote it below:

> [Where is the lion's den, the cave of the young lions? (Nah. 2:12a) The interpretation of it concerns Jerusalem, which has become] a dwelling for the wicked ones of the Gentiles. Where the (1) lion went to enter, the (2) lion's cub [and no one to disturb (Nah. 2:12b). The interpretation of it concerns (2) Deme]trius, King of Greece, who sought to enter Jerusalem on the advice of the Seekers-After-Smooth-Things, [but God did not give Jerusalem] into the power of the kings of Greece from (1) Antiochus until the rise of the commanders of the Kittim; but afterwards [the city] will be trampled [...]. The (3) lion tears enough for his cubs and strangles prey for his lionesses (Nah. 2:13a). [The interpretation] concerns the (3) Lion of Wrath, who smites by his great ones and his partisans.[272] [And fills with prey] the cave and his den with torn flesh (Nah. 2:13b). The interpretation of it concerns the Lion of Wrath....[273]

The scribe interprets the "lion's den" of Nah. 2:12a and 2:13b as referring to Jerusalem that he states has become "a dwelling for the wicked ones of the Gentiles."[274] Three lions are referred to in this section of 4QpNah and they are noted in the above quotation (both the commentary portion and the corresponding biblical verse) with the same number. The statement that "God did not give Jerusalem into the power of the kings of Greece from Antiochus until the rise of the commanders of the Kittim" will only agree with the known historical record in one way. Antiochus VII Sidetes had to be the first lion[275] and Demetrius III Eucerus had to be the "lion's cub"[276] (i.e., the second lion). The third lion (i.e., the "Lion of Wrath"),[277] who lived in the first century AD, will be discussed in a later chapter. The "Seekers-After-Smooth-Things" were the Pharisees who asked Demetrius III for help against Alexander Jannaeus.

---

271. John M. Allegro, *The Dead Sea Scrolls: A Reappraisal* (New York: Penguin Books, 1975), 107-8.
272. The Hebrew words translated here, as "his partisans" is literally the "men of his counsel (or Council)." The designation is also found at 1QpHab 9:10 and 4QpPs^a, frags. 1-10, 2:19. "Their partisans," which is literally the "men of their counsel (or Council)," can be found at 1QpHab 5:10 and 4QpNah, frags. 1-2, 2:8.
273. 4QpNah, frags. 3 and 4, 1:1-6.
274. 4QpNah, frags. 3 and 4, 1:1.
275. 4QpNah , frags. 3 and 4, 1:1 (Nah. 2:12b).
276. 4QpNah, frags. 3 and 4, 1:1 (Nah. 2:12b).
277. 4QpNah, frags. 3 and 4, 1:4 (Nah. 2:13a).

The individual referred to by the name "Antiochus" could *not* have been Antiochus IV Epiphanes as the passage is usually interpreted. The reason for this is that from his reign "until the rise of the commanders of the Kittim" (i.e., the Romans under Pompey in 63 BC) Demetrius I Soter sent his generals Bacchides and Nicanor to Judea and they *did* have Jerusalem in their power at various times. On the other hand, although Antiochus VII did surround Jerusalem and have the city in his power, Demetrius III only "sought to enter" the city being forced to leave the country instead. Therefore, only from Antiochus VII to the coming of the Romans Jerusalem was not in "the power of the kings of Greece."

One common characteristic of the Seekers-After-Smooth-Things at all times was that they tended to make concessions in some way with Gentiles. An example of this attitude can be seen in the description of the pro-Greek party in the days of Antiochus IV Epiphanes. The First Book of Maccabees states that "in those days lawless men came forth from Israel, and misled many, saying, 'Let us go and make a covenant with the Gentiles round about us, for since we separated from them many evils have come upon us.'"[278] Further on, the same source states that "they joined with the Gentiles and sold themselves to do evil."[279] This attitude agrees with the pro-Greek party headed by Alcimus who asked Demetrius I for help against Judas Maccabeus' party. It also agrees with the Pharisees who asked Demetrius III for help against Alexander Jannaeus. A first century AD example of this type of individual was Tiberius Iulius Alexander who was the sole governor of Judea from AD 46-8. Josephus states that he was an Alexandrian of Jewish ancestry who nevertheless "did not stand by the practices of his people."[280]

No history is alluded to again until the capture of Jerusalem by the Roman general Pompey in 63 BC:

> For because of the unfaithfulness of those who abandoned Him [God]
> He hid His face from Israel and its Sanctuary
> and delivered them up to the sword.
> But remembering the Covenant of the first ones,
> He left a remnant to Israel
> And did not deliver them to destruction.[281]

---

278. 1 Macc. 1:11.
279. 1 Macc. 1:15.
280. Ant. XX, 100-1.
281. CD 1:3-5.

The reason why these verses must refer to a later visitation than the one of Antiochus IV Epiphanes in 169 BC is because God *"remembering the Covenant of the first, ... left a remnant to Israel."*[282] When this new visitation occurred, the events concerning the first ones had been in the past. The only significant one after Antiochus, but before the destruction of Jerusalem and the temple in AD 70, was the visitation of Pompey in 63 BC.

"Those who abandoned Him" were Queen Alexandra (76-67 BC); her son, the high priest Hyrcanus II (76-67 BC and 63-40 BC); and the Pharisaic establishment who supported them.[283] The brother of Hyrcanus II, Aristobulus II, was the high priest and king from 67-63 BC and he supported the Sadducees like his father Alexander Jannaeus (103-76 BC).[284] The sect probably approved of Aristobulus II like they did Jannaeus,[285] but the high priesthood of the former lasted only four years. Pompey made Hyrcanus II the high priest again from 63 to 40 BC, but he was not given a royal title.[286] Aristobulus II and his family were sent to Rome in chains.[287] A large number of other Jewish prisoners were sent to Rome as well.[288]

While Pompey had Aristobulus II under arrest and was considering the best way to take Jerusalem in 63 BC, "the partisans of Aristobulus [Sadducees] [were] insisting on a battle and the rescue of the king, *while those of Hyrancus [Pharisees] were for opening the gates to Pompey.*"[289] Josephus continues on as follows:

> The party of Aristobulus, finding themselves beaten [by the partisans of Hyrcanus], retired into the temple, cut the bridge which connected it with the city, and prepared to hold out to the last. *The others admitted the Romans to the city and delivered up the palace.* Pompey sent a body of troops to occupy it under the command of Piso, one of his lieutenant-generals. That officer distributed sentries about the town and, failing to induce any of the refugees in the temple to listen to terms, prepared the surrounding ground for an assault. *In this work the friends of Hyrancus keenly assisted him with their advice and services.*[290]

---

282. CD 1:4-5 (italics mine).
283. Ant. XIII, 408-11, War I, 110-4.
284. Ant. XIII, 293-7, 408-9. Hyrcanus I (135/4-104 BC) deserted the Pharisees and went over to the Sadducees. The Pharissees did not regain their power until the reign of Queen Alexandra (76-67 BC). Therefore, under Aristobulus I (104-103 BC) and Alexander Jannaeus (103-76 BC) the Sadducees were in power.
285. 4Q448 praises Alexander Jannaeus.
286. Ant. XIV, 4-7, 73-6, XX, 244, War I, 120-2, 153-4.
287. Ant. XIV, 79; War I, 157-8.
288. Emil Schurer, *The History of the Jewish People in the Age of Jesus Christ*, vols. I, II, III.1, III.2, rev. and ed. by Geza Vermes, et al. (Edinburgh: T. & T. Clark, 1973/87), Vol. I, 241.
289. War I, 142 (italics mine); cf. Ant. XIV, 58-9.
290. War I, 143-4 (italics mine); cf. Ant. XIV, 59-63.

Although Pompey was able to gain control of the city without a battle, as a result of the aid he received from Hyrcanus' supporters, a siege was still required to take the Temple where Aristobulus' supporters entrenched themselves.

When the Romans finally breached the Temple wall after a siege of three months, Josephus describes the scene as follows:

> Then it was that many of the priests, seeing the enemy advancing sword in hand, calmly continued their sacred ministrations, and were butchered in the act of pouring libations and burning incense; putting the worship of the Deity above their own preservation. *Most of the slain perished by the hands of their countrymen of the opposite faction*; countless numbers flung themselves over the precipices; some, driven mad by their hopeless plight, set fire to the buildings around the wall and were consumed in the flames. Of the Jews twelve thousand perished; the losses of the Romans in dead were trifling, in wounded considerable.[291]

If the passages from Josephus quoted above are examined, especially the phrases in italics that refer to the partisans of Hyrcanus (Pharisees), one will quickly realize that it is *they* who would be considered the "Seekers-After-Smooth-Things" by the sectarians *not* the partisans of Aristobulus (Sadducees). They opened the gates of Jerusalem to Pompey and aided him in every way, even killing their fellow countrymen in the assault on the Temple. On the other hand, the partisans of Aristobulus (i.e., the Sadducees) "retired into the temple ... and prepared to hold out to the last" and, while they were being slain by the Romans, "calmly continued their sacred ministrations ... putting the worship of the Deity above their own preservation."

The "remnant" mentioned in the previously quoted passage from CD,[292] which survived the visitation of Pompey in 63 BC, were Sadducees who preserved the traditions of the first ones by escaping to the land of Damascus. Other Sadducees chose to remain in Judaea with Aristobulus II. Although it does not explicitly state that this remnant had escaped to the land of Damascus, there is some evidence that it did. The archeological evidence for this flight of a group of Sadducees to the land of Damascus will be provided in a later chapter.[293]

---

291. War I, 150-1 (italics mine); cf. Ant. XIV, 64-71.
292. CD 1:3-5.
293. See the chapter titled *Khirbet Qumran and the Scrolls*.

Chapter 5. Zadok

And concerning the prince [i.e., the king] it is written, *He shall not multiply wives for himself*.[294] As for David, he did not read the sealed book of the Torah, which was in the Ark (of the Covenant). For it was not opened in Israel from the day (that) Eleazar and Joshua and the Elders died, (nor) when (the children of Israel) served (the goddess) Ashtoreth;[295] and it remained hidden (and) was (not) revealed until Zadok arose. And David's deeds were praised, except for Uriah's blood,[296] and God forgave him for that.[297]

According to the above passage, Zadok brought to light the "sealed book of the Law, which was in the Ark." It had been kept secret from Israel until his coming. I take the view that Zadok (or Saddok) was the opponent of the high priest Simon, the son of Boethus, or perhaps his father in ca. 24 BC. Josephus was probably incorrect in placing him with Judas the Galilean in AD 6.[298] Zadok surely did not find the Temple Scroll (11QT) in the Ark. God must have revealed it to him, as the new Moses.[299] He wrote it in 22-21 BC and it was probably known as the "book of the *Second* Torah."[300] The sect probably believed that

---

294. Dt. 17:17, cf. 11QT 56:18-9.
295. Jos. 24:29-31, 33; Jg. 2:7-10, 11-4. According to these biblical verses, it was only *after* the death of the Elders that the people of Israel began worshipping Baal and Ashtoreth. I have tried to translate this passage with this idea in mind.
296. 2 Sam. 11:1-27.
297. CD 5:1-6.
298. Ant. XVIII, 3-4, 9, 10.
299. Dt. 18:15: "The LORD your God will raise up for you a prophet like me [Moses] from among you, from your brethren — him you shall heed."
300. Florentino Garcia Martinez & Eibert J. C. Tigchelaar, eds., *The Dead Sea Scrolls Study Edition*, 2 vols. (Leiden: Brill, 1997), Vol. 1, 367 (4Q177, 3:13-4) (italics mine).

Hilkiah, the high priest during King Josiah's reign (i.e., 628-609 BC) found the book of the *First* Torah in the Temple.[301] The "book of the law" discovered by Hilkiah "was" or at least "contained" the book of Deuteronomy.[302]

King David was excused for having many wives, because he did not know the Deuteronomy passage (i.e., the king "shall not multiply wives for himself").[303] The true meaning of it was disclosed by the following prohibition in 11QT: "He [i.e., the king] is not to take another wife in addition to her; no, she alone shall be with him as long as she lives."[304] The Deuteronomy passage did not just restrict the king to taking only a "reasonable" number of wives, but it actually restricted him to taking only *one* wife. In the view of the sect, since 11QT was not brought to light until the time of Zadok, King David could not have known that he was prohibited from taking more than one wife.[305]

CD 4:7-8 states that "all those who entered (the Covenant) after them (i.e., the first ones) are "to act according to the exact tenor of the Torah in which the first had been instructed." How could the first ones and those who came "after them" have practiced the *same* Torah, if the former did not have the book of the Second Torah (i.e., 11QT)? The writer of CD must have believed that, although the first ones did not have a *written* book of the Second Torah (Zadok wrote it many years later), they were practicing it nonetheless, because of their great wisdom and piety.

A priest or at least someone extremely knowledgeable of the Temple ritual must have composed 11QT. Although our sources do not state that Zadok was a priest, what makes this identification likely is that in the scrolls it is the priests, the sons of Aaron, who are called the "sons of Zadok."[306] This designation also reveals the special standing accorded to Zadok by the sect.

---

301. 2 Kgs. 22:1-23:30, 2 Chr. 34-5. 2 Kgs. 22:8: "And Hilkiah the high priest said to Shaphan the secretary, 'I have found the book of the law in the house of the LORD.' And Hilkiah gave the book to Shaphan, and he read it."

302. *The New Oxford Annotated Bible*, eds. Herbert G. May and Bruce M. Metzger (New York: Oxford University Press, 1973), 214 (Introduction to Deuteronomy), 487-8, note 8-10 for 22.1-20.

303. King David reigned from 1000 to 965 or 961 BC. The book of Deuteronomy only came to light when the high priest, Hilkiah, found it during the reign of King Josiah (i.e., 628-609 BC).

304. 11QT 57:17-8, cf. CD 4:20-5:1. All quotations of 11QT in this chapter are taken from Michael Wise, Martin Abegg, Jr., and Edward Cook, *The Dead Sea Scrolls: A New Tanslation* (San Francisco: Harper, 1996), 457-92.

305. Yigael Yadin, *The Temple Scroll: The Hidden Law of the Dead Sea Sect* (New York: Random House, 1985), 227-8. However, I do not agree with him that Zadok was the Teacher of Righteousness and the founder of the Dead Sea Scroll sect.

306. 1QS 5:2, 9; 1QSa 1:2, 24, 2:3; 1QSb 2:22; 4Q174 1:17. The only exception is CD 3:21-4:4 where, commenting on a unique version of Ezek. 44:15, a symbolic meaning is given to the term.

The Pentateuch[307] and other sources were probably used in its composition. It has been suggested that the scroll is made up of four separate units, which are the following: 1) a festival calendar, 2) a collection of purity laws, 3) a law for the king, and 4) a description of the Temple and its courts.[308]

Some evidence that old sources were utilized in its composition is as follows:

1. 11QT 47:7-18 states that only the skins of clean animals that had been sacrificed in the Temple could be brought into Jerusalem. According to Josephus,[309] the Syrian king, Antiochus III (223-187 BC), because of the help he received from the Jews, granted them certain concessions. In a proclamation, he stated (among other things) that the skins of unclean animals were not to be brought into Jerusalem. However, 11QT expands on this ruling by excluding from the city even the skins of *clean* animals that were not sacrificed in the Temple.[310]
2. 11QT 34:6 mentions "rings" in the slaughterhouse of the Temple. Various Talmudic sources state that John Hyrcanus I (135/4-104 BC) introduced rings into the slaughterhouse.[311]
3. 11QT 64:7-13 has a ruling that traitors should be hung alive on a tree (i.e., crucified). The source of this ruling is probably derived from Alexander Jannaeus' crucifixion of the Pharisees, who initiated a treasonable correspondence with the Syrian king Demetrius III in 88 BC.[312] I quote the passage below:

> If a man is a traitor against his people and gives them up to a foreign nation, so doing evil to his people, you are to hang him on a tree until dead. On the testimony of two or three witnesses he will be put to death, and they themselves shall hang him on the tree.
>
> If a man is convicted of a capital crime and flees to the nations, cursing his people and the children of Israel, you are to hang him, also, upon a tree until dead.
>
> But you must not let their bodies remain on the tree overnight; you shall most certainly bury them that very day. Indeed, anyone hung on a tree is accursed of God and men, but you are not to defile the land that I [God] am about to give you as an inheritance.[313]

---

307. The Pentateuch is the first 5 books of the Old Testament, which are Genesis, Exodus, Leviticus, Numbers, and Deuteronomy. It is synonymous with the Hebrew Torah.
308. A. M. Wilson and L. Wills, "Literary Sources of the Temple Scroll," *Harvard Theological Review* 75 (1982): 275-88.
309. Ant. XII, 146.
310. Yadin, *The Temple Scroll: The Hidden Law of the Dead Sea Sect*, 186-8.
311. Yadin, *The Temple Scroll: The Hidden Law of the Dead Sea Sect*, 136-40.
312. Ant. XIII, 379-83; War I, 96-8.
313. Cf. Dt. 21:22-3.

4. In referring to the king's bodyguard, 11QT states, "twelve thousand warriors ... shall never leave him alone, lest he be captured by the nations."[314] Also, they "shall stay with him always, day and night, in order to protect him from any sort of sin and from a foreign nation, lest he be captured."[315] These rulings may very well be alluding to Alexander Jannaeus (103-76 BC). When he was fighting Obedas, king of the Arabs, he was ambushed and almost did not escape with his life.[316] However, it may be alluding to other Hasmonaean rulers as well: Jonathan (161-143/2 BC) was captured and put to death by Tryphon,[317] Simon (143/2-135/4 BC) and his two sons were slain by his son-in-law, Ptolemy[318] and Antigonus (40-37 BC) was executed by the order of Antony.[319]

Sifting through the research that has been done on 11QT, I believe the following passage is correct:

> The Jewish king seems to be a reality, not just a rather abstract speculation. Our document presents through biblical notions of kingship an antithesis to some *real* Jewish king, and its author is willing to correct the defects of kingship which he has observed.[320]

Thiering has placed the composition of the scroll in ca. 20 BC during Herod the Great's reign (37-4 BC). However, she curiously reasons that the scroll was composed by the Essenes in the "hope of persuading Herod to re-establish the Zadokite high priesthood in power." Because he intended to rebuild the temple, "they produced their own plan, in the form of a 'lost' biblical book, to ensure that it would be built in an acceptable way."[321]

I believe that Thiering is on the right track in placing the composition of the scroll during Herod's reign, but a careful study of it will show that it is clearly *anti-Herodian*. It is not in any way supportive of Herod or even hopeful that he could be persuaded to accept its tenets. *The evidence shows that the writer had*

---

314. 11QT 57:7.
315. 11QT 57:11.
316. Ant. XIII, 375-6; War I, 90-1.
317. I Macc. 12:41-13:23; Ant. XIII, 187-96.
318. I Macc. 16:11-7; Ant. XIII, 228-9.
319. Ant. XIV, 487-91, War I, 357.
320. M. Hengel, et al., "The Polemical Character of 'On Kingship' in the Temple Scroll: An Attempt at Dating 11Q Temple," *Journal of Jewish Studies* 37 (1986): 31.
321. B. E. Thiering, *Redating the Teacher of Righteousness* (Sydney: Theological Explorations, 1979), 205-6.

to have been a contemporary, who disapproved of Herod the Great's reign. Let us review some of the evidence below.

11QT, following Deut. 17:15, states the following: "From among your brethren you shall appoint a king. You must not put a foreigner over you, he who is not one of your brethren."[322] This rule has perfect relevance regarding Herod. Jewish tradition declares that the determination of whether the offspring of a married couple is Jewish follows the mother's ancestry.[323] Herod's father, Antipater II, was an Idumaean. Antipater I, the father of the latter, was probably forcibly converted to Judaism by John Hyrcanus I in his conquest of Idumea in 129 BC.[324] Dt. 23:8 states that Idumaeans of the third generation "may enter the assembly of the Lord."[325] Based on this biblical passage, Herod would have been an Idumaean of the third generation. However, Herod's mother, Cypros, was of a noble Nabatean (i.e., an Arabian) family[326] and there is no evidence that she converted to Judaism. On this basis, Herod was *not* Jewish and could *not* be king according to 11QT! Regardless of the facts, Herod's friends spread the belief that he was a Jew descended from the first families who returned from the Babylonian exile. His enemies spread the belief that he was a Philistine (i.e., a pagan) whose ancesters were natives of Ascalon.[327] Correctly following his mother's ancestry, the Slavonic Josephus calls Herod "an Arabian, uncircumcised."[328]

The scroll states that the king "may not take a wife from any of the nations. Rather, he must take himself a wife from his father's house — that is, from his father's family. He is not to take another wife in addition to her; no, she alone shall be with him as long as she lives. If she dies, then he may take himself another wife from his father's house, that is, his family."[329] This passage is first a prohibition against the king marrying a non-Jew (she must also be from his father's house and family)[330] and secondly it is a prohibition against polygamy

---

322. 11QT 56:14-5.
323. L. H. Schiffman, *Who Was a Jew?* (Hoboken: KTAV Publishing, 1983), 9-14.
324. Ant. XIII, 257-8; XIV, 8-9.
325. Dt. 23:7-8: "You shall not abhor an Edomite [i.e., an Idumaean], for he is your brother ... The children of the third generation that are born to them may enter the assembly of the Lord."
326. Ant. XIV, 121; XV, 184; War I, 181.
327. Emil Schurer, *The History of the Jewish People in the Age of Jesus Christ*, vols. I, II, III.1, III.2, rev. and ed. by Geza Vermes, et al. (Edinburgh: T. & T. Clark, 1973/87), Vol. I, 234, note 3.
328. Josephus, Bk. III, Appendix, p. 636. Need I remind the reader that this discussion of genealogy only has relevance *before* the time of John the Baptist?
329. 11QT 57:15-9.
330. It is interesting that after the death of her husband, Aristobulus I, Salome Alexandra married his brother, Alexander Jannaeus. Since she was in Jannaeus' house and family, their marriage would have been in conformity with this ruling (Ant. XIII, 320-3, 405-8, War I, 85, 107-9).

and divorce. The relevance of these prohibitions with regard to Herod is clear. He had ten wives, nine of whom were living at the same time, and probably an unknown number of concubines.[331] It appears that only Mariamme (the Hasmonean princess) was given the title of queen.[332] It is known that Herod had a wife (Malthace) who was a Samaritan.[333] There is no evidence that she converted to Judaism.[334] Furthermore, Herod divorced his first wife Doris in order to marry Mariamme, whom he later executed in 29 BC.[335] He also divorced the other Mariamme, the daughter of the high priest, Simon, the son of Boethus.[336]

11QT 66:15-7 states that "no man is to marry his brother's daughter or his sister's daughter; that is abhorrent." It is known that one of Herod's wives was the daughter of his brother.[337]

A large portion of 11QT is concerned with a detailed description of the ideal temple that should be built in Jerusalem.[338] Herod started the rebuilding of the temple in either 23-22 BC (the fifteenth year of his reign)[339] or 20-19 BC (the eighteenth year of his reign).[340] The actual temple building itself was completed in one and a half years, but the entire structure was not completed until AD 62-4.[341] It was Herod's greatest building achievement, but it was not anything like the temple described in 11QT. Our writer is again revealing his opposition to Herod. At no other time from 200 BC to AD 70, *but only during Herod's reign*, was there an actual effort made to rebuild the temple. For the building of such a massive and elaborate structure, a period of time was unquestionably required for planning the whole operation. I think Schurer is correct in understanding the 23-22 BC date (i.e., the fifteenth year) as "the start of building preparations."[342] The date 20-19 BC (i.e., the eighteenth year) was the date that the building actually began.

---

331. Ant. XVII, 19-20; War I, 511-2, 562-3.
332. War I, 485.
333. Ant. XVII, 19-29; War I, 511-2.
334. Samaritans were despised by the Jews and were considered to be on par with Gentiles. In the fourth century AD, conversions of Samaritans to Judaism were actually prohibited. See Joachim Jeremias, *Jerusalem in the Time of Jesus* (Philadelphia: Fortress Press, 1969), 352-8.
335. Ant. XIV, 300; XV, 232-9; War I, 431-3, 443-4, 590-1.
336. Ant. XVII, 78.
337. Ant. XVII, 19; War I, 563. cf. CD 5:7-11.
338. 11QT 2-13, 30-45:7.
339. War I, 401.
340. Ant. XV, 380.
341. Ant. XV, 421-3; XX, 219-23.
342. Schurer, *The History of the Jewish People in the Age of Jesus Christ*, Vol. I, 292, note 12.

The high priest is envisioned as superior to the king: "He [the king] must not go to battle prior to coming to the high priest to inquire of him about the judgment of the Urim and Thummim."[343] Also, there was to be a council of twelve laymen (called "princes"), twelve priests, and twelve levites, who "are to deliberate with him [the king] on matters of justice and Law, and he [the king] must not become too proud for them or do anything on counsel other than theirs."[344] This reduction of the king's authority is completely relevant to Herod, who had complete authority over the state as the emperor's nominee and who appointed or deposed high priests as he saw fit.[345]

According to the scroll, the army was to be made up of only Jewish men[346] and they "must guard themselves against all manner of impurity, indecency, iniquity, and shame."[347] Furthermore, twelve thousand men selected from the army were to be the king's bodyguard at all times[348] and they "must be truthful men, God-fearing, despising unjust gain, mighty warriors."[349] However, if the enemy was completely destroyed in a war ordained by God, which was prognosticated by the high priest,[350] booty could be taken and divided among the king, priests, Levites, and the army at a stated amount.[351] A condemnation of mercenaries is certainly implied here. Herod's army included mercenaries composed of Thacians, Germans, and Gauls.[352]

11QT 57:20-1 states the following: "Nor is he [the king] to desire any field, vineyard, wealth, or house, or any precious thing in Israel, so as to steal [it] [...]." It is certain that Herod had the Hasmonean nobility and their supporters killed, confiscating all their wealth.[353]

11QT 58:3-15 seems to envision a peaceful state with little concern for offensive warfare, but a great deal of concern for the defensive kind. There seems

---

343. 11QT 58:18-9. The Urim and Thummim were precious stones connected to the breastplate of the high priest, which were used to determine God's will.
344. 11QT 57:11-5.
345. Schurer, *The History of the Jewish People in the Age of Jesus Christ*, Vol. I, 316-7; Ant. XV, 161-82, War I, 433-4 (Hyrcanus II, the Hasmonaean high priest, is executed); Ant. XV, 322 (Jesus, the son of Phiabi, is removed from the high priesthood); Ant. XVII, 78 (Simon, the son of Boethus, is removed from the high priesthood); Ant. XVII, 164-7 (Matthias, the son of Theophilus, is removed from the high priesthood).
346. 11QT 57:1-5.
347. 11QT 58:17.
348. 11QT 57:5-11.
349. 11QT 57:8-9.
350. 11QT 58:18-21.
351. 11QT 58:11-5.
352. Ant. XVII, 198; War I, 672.
353. Ant. XIV, 174-5; XV, 5-10; 260-6; War I, 357-8.

to be a real need for protecting the interior of the country from a possible invasion from outside. It always stresses that a portion of the army must remain in the cities to protect them, while the other portion is to go to battle.

Although the possible revolt of his own subjects was certainly a major cause of anxiety for Herod,[354] there was some reason to be concerned with invasion from outside as well. The Romans under Marcus Licinius Crassus experienced a disastrous defeat against the Parthians at the battle of Carrhae in 53 BC and the latter invaded Syria and Judea in 40 BC[355] and again in 38 BC.[356] Until 20 BC, when the Parthians finally returned to Emperor Augustus the prisoners of war and the standards captured at Carrhae,[357] there must have been anxiety at least among the common people that the Parthians would invade Syria and Judea again. Anthony's retreat following his invasion of Parthia in 36-34 BC[358] would certainly not have lessened their anxieties. Furthermore, the Arabs (Nabateans), since the time Herod made war with them as a result of Cleopatra's instigation in 32-31 BC, were hostile to him.[359] In 10-9 BC, another war actually broke out between Herod and the Arabs.[360] In the light of all these concerns, it is understandable why Herod built or strengthened many fortresses throughout the land (especially two called Herodium,[361] Alexandrium,[362] Hyrcania,[363] Macherus,[364] and Masada[365]) and established the military colonies of Gaba in Galilee and Esebonitis (Heshbon) in Perea.[366]

Among the variations to Dt. 17:16 in 11QT 56:15-7, there is one noteworthy addition. The latter passage states the following: "The king is not to multiply horses for himself, nor shall he return the people to Egypt *to wage war* and thereby increase for himself horses,[367] silver, and gold. I [God] have said to you, 'You shall never again return that way.'" The meaning of the words in italics is not

---

354. Ant. XV, 291.
355. Cook, et al., eds., *The Cambridge Ancient History*, Vol. X (Cambridge: Cambridge University Press, 1952), 47-50; Schurer, *The History of the Jewish People in the Age of Jesus Christ*, Vol. I, 278-280, 282.
356. Cook, et al., eds., *The Cambridge Ancient History*, Vol. X, 50; Schurer, *The History of the Jewish People in the Age of Jesus Christ*, Vol. I, 251-2, 282-3.
357. Cook, et al., eds., *The Cambridge Ancient History*, Vol. X, 254-64.
358. Cook, et al., eds., *The Cambridge Ancient History*, Vol. X, 71-4.
359. Ant. XV, 108-20, 123-60; War I, 334-85.
360. Ant. XVI, 271-85.
361. War I, 419.
362. Ant. XVI, 13.
363. Ant. XVI, 13.
364. War VII, 163-77.
365. War VII, 285-94.
366. Ant. XV, 294, War III, 36.
367. It is interesting that according to Josephus Herod "distinguished himself above all by his skill in horsemanship ... " (War I, 429).

clear. It could mean that the king could not start a war with Egypt, but the more likely meaning is that the king could not send troops to help Egypt against her enemies.

Herod was closely involved in Egyptian affairs in the early years of his reign because of his support for Antony, the Roman general, and the marriage of the latter to Cleopatra, the queen of Egypt, in 37 BC. Civil war broke out between Antony and Octavian in 32 BC, but Octavian was finally victorious at the naval battle of Actium in September 31 BC. Realizing the predicament he was in for supporting Antony, Herod quickly took measures to transfer his support for Octavian. In August 30 BC, Antony and Cleopatra committed suicide.[368] Thus, whether it was to support Antony or Octavian later on, there was at least a concern that Herod would send troops to Egypt.

Even after Octavian became Emperor (Augustus) and Egypt was made into a Roman province, there was still anxiety that Herod would send troops to Egypt for various reasons until peace was made between Rome and Ethiopia in 22-21 BC.[369] C. Cornelius Gallus (the first Roman governor of Egypt) could have been given aid in order to crush revolts there and to protect the borders.[370] In 25-24 BC, Herod actually did send five hundred soldiers to Egypt to help Aelius Gallus (the successor to C. Cornelius Gallus) in his campaign against Arabia.[371] Then, C. Petronius (the successor to Aelius Gallus) could have been given aid in his conflict against the Ethiopians.[372] Thus, possible military excursions to Egypt until 22-21 BC were indeed a cause for concern and the writer alluded to this fact by adding the words in italics when he composed 11QT. This was especially true for him, since God was supposed to have said, "You shall never again return that way."[373]

11QT 59:13-8 states the following: "But the king whose heart and eyes whorishly depart from My [God's] commandments shall never have a descendant sitting on the throne of his fathers. Indeed, I shall forever cut off his seed from ruling Israel. If, however, he walks in My precepts, observing My commandments, and does what I regard as upright and good, then he shall never fail to have one of his sons sitting on the throne of the kingdom of Israel, forever." Further, 11QT 57:19-20 states, "he [the king] must not pervert judgment or take a

---

368. Cook, et al., eds., *The Cambridge Ancient History*, Vol. X, 66-115, 318-21; Schurer, *The History of the Jewish People in the Age of Jesus Christ*, Vol. I, 296-302.
369. Cook, et al., eds., *The Cambridge Ancient History*, Vol. X, 242.
370. Cook, et al., eds., *The Cambridge Ancient History*, Vol. X, 239-41.
371. Cook, et al., eds., *The Cambridge Ancient History*, Vol. X, 241, 247-54; Ant. XV, 317-8.
372. Cook, et al., eds., *The Cambridge Ancient History*, Vol. X, 241-2.
373. Dt. 17:16, 11QT 56:17-8.

bribe to pervert righteous judgment." After Herod's death in 4 BC, a Jewish delegation in Rome asked Augustus to put an end to the Herodian line. In recounting Herod's reign, they accused him of many things including savagery of the worst kind, executions and confiscation of property, corruption, and perversion.[374] In defense of the king, his friend, Nicolas of Damascus, could only say that the accusations should have been brought up when he was alive and could have been tried for them, not when he was dead.[375] Surely, this characterization of Herod is in complete opposition to the king envisioned in the passages of 11QT. Zadok (or Saddok), who composed the document in 22-21 BC, was again revealing his opposition to the king.

The leadership structure that is envisioned in 11QT is as follows (the higher up the table, the greater the authority):[376]

Ranking	The Community Leadership Structure	
1	High Priest	Priests
2	King / Second Priest	Laity / Priests
	The King's Council of 36, consisting of:	
3	*12 Head Priests*	Priests
4	Priests	
5	*12 Head Levites*	Levites
6	Levites	
7	*12 Tribal Heads (Princes)*	
8	Chiefs of Thousands, Chiefs of Hundreds, Chiefs of Fifties, and Chiefs of Tens	Laity

---

374. Ant. XVII, 304-11.
375. Ant. XVII, 315-6.
376. 11QT 31:4-5, 42:12-7, 57-8.

Chapter 6. John the Baptist

> And God considered their works,
> for they had sought Him with a perfect heart;
> and He raised up for them a Teacher of Righteousness
> to lead them in the way of His heart
> and to make known to the last generations
> what He would do to the last generation,
> the congregation of traitors.[377]

John the Baptist is mentioned in CD as the "Unique Teacher,"[378] the "Unique One,"[379] and above as "a Teacher of Righteousness," who "made known to the last generations what He would do to the last generation...."[380] According to the Slavonic version of the *War*, Josephus has John first appear in the reign of Archelaus (4 BC-AD 6). In fact, John the Baptist first appears in 4 BC after the death of King Herod. I quote Robert Eisler's restored version of the Slavonic passage about John below:

---

377. CD 1:10-2.
378. CD 20:1, 14.
379. CD 20:32.
380. CD 1:10-2. Robert Eisler identified John the Baptist with the Unique Teacher/One and the Teacher of Righteousness in CD. See Robert Eisler, "The Sadoqite Book of the New Covenant: Its Date and Origin," *Occident and Orient* (Gaster Anniversary Volume) B. Schindler, ed. (London: Taylor's Foreign Press, 1936), 125, 137. However, I do not take the view that *all* the references to the Teacher of Righteousness in CD refer to John the Baptist (see p. 60). In *Redating the Teacher of Righteousness*, Thiering tentatively identified John the Baptist as the Teacher of Righteousness of the scrolls and Jesus as the Wicked Priest/Man of Lies [B. Thiering, *Redating the Teacher of Righteousness* (Sidney: Theological Explorations, 1979), 207-14]. In her later writings, she claimed to have discovered a code in the gospels and the Acts that further supported her initial hypothesis. For a review of her theory, see N. T. Wright, *Who Was Jesus?* (Grand Rapids: Eerdmans, 1993), 19-36.

Now at that time [4 BC] there walked among the Jews a man in wondrous garb, for he had stuck on to his body animals' hair wherever it was not covered by his own. But in countenance he was like a savage. This man came to the Jews and allured them to freedom, saying: "God hath sent me to show you the way of the law, by which ye shall be freed from many tyrants. And no mortal shall rule over you, but only the Highest who hath sent me." And when the people heard that, they were [excited].[381] *And there went to him all Judaea and the region around Jerusalem.*[382]

But he did nothing else to them, save that he dipped them into the stream of the Jordan and let them go, warning them that they should renounce evil deeds. So would they be given a king who would free them and subject all who are insubordinate, but he himself would be subjected to none. At his words some mocked, but others put faith in him.

And when he was brought to Archelaus [ruled from 4 BC to AD 6] and the learned doctors of the Law had assembled, they asked him who he was and where he had been until then. And he answered and said, "I am a man; as such has the spirit of God called me, and I live on bulrushes [cane] and roots and *tree-fruits.*"[383] But when they threatened to torture him if he did not desist from these words and deeds, he said: "It is meet rather for *you* to desist from your shameful works and to submit to the Lord your God."

And Simon, a scribe, arose in wrath and said: "We read the divine books every day. But thou, only now come forth like a wild beast from the wood, durst thou teach us and lead the multitudes astray with thy accursed speeches?"

And he flung himself forward to rend his body. But he said in reproach to them: "I will not reveal to you the secret that is among you,[384] because you desired it not. For this cause has unspeakable misfortune befallen you and for your own doing." And when he had thus spoken, he went away to the other side of the Jordan. And since no man durst hinder him, he did as he had done before.[385]

---

381. The Slavonic passage actually has "glad" here, but Robert Eisler has given good reasons why it was originally probably "excited." Robert Eisler, *The Messiah Jesus and John the Baptist*, ed. by A. H. Krappe (London: Methuen & Co., 1931), 224, note 7, 246-7.

382. Robert Eisler takes the words in italics to be a Christian interpolation (Eisler, *The Messiah Jesus and John the Baptist*, 224, note 8).

383. The phrase "tree-fruits" in italics here actually means "wood-shavings" in Slavonic. However, the former meaning must have been intended by the latter. See the chapter titled *John's Food and Dress* for an explanation of this problem.

384. The "secret that is among you" was that the identity of the Messiah of Israel was known, although he had not been formally anointed into his office as yet. Since, as will be seen below, Judas the Galilean was the only messianic claimant to have survived the revolt of 4 BC, John must have expected him to be this personage.

385. Eisler, *The Messiah Jesus and John the Baptist*, 224-6. For the unrestored version, see Josephus, Bk. III, Appendix, p. 644-5.

The War Scroll (1QM) describes the military tactics, weapons, and ritual for the final war of the righteous against the wicked. Two major sections seem to be contained in the scroll. They are cols. 2-9, the earlier section, and cols. 1, 15-9, the later one.[386]

The former section describes a forty years war in which the first six years would be to liberate the land and regain control of the temple. Then the first "year of release" would come when the righteous would rest from war and set up the new Temple organization. Finally, there would come a thirty-three year period in which war would be waged against all the other nations of the world. In this period, there would be twenty-nine years of actual warfare and four more years of release.[387]

The latter section is mainly concerned with the final battle against the "Kittim" (i.e., the Romans) and their allies. The "sons of light" (i.e. the righteous) would be successful for the first three engagements, then the "sons of darkness" (i.e., the wicked) would be successful for the next three engagements, and finally God himself would intervene to insure a decisive victory for the sons of light.[388] According to Davies, "col. I is a summary of the entire Final War, and brings together the visions of cols. II-IX as well as of XV-XIX, visions which otherwise remain juxtaposed in blatant contradiction."[389]

1QM 1, 15-9 comes from a later period (i.e., AD 65-6) when Symeon, the son of Clopas, was the leader of the sect. He is the "Chief Priest" mentioned in this section of the War Scroll.[390] There is a mass exodus of the sect to the land of Damascus taking place at this time, but it is stated that the sect would return to Judea when the time came to execute the final war against its enemies:

> The Deportation of the desert shall fight against them [the sect's enemies]; fo[r war] (shall be declared) on all their bands when the Deportation of the sons of light returns from the desert of the peoples [the land of Damascus] to camp in the desert of Jerusalem.[391]

---

386. Philip R. Davies, *1QM, The War Scroll from Qumran: Its Structure and History* (Rome: Biblical Institute Press, 1977), 24-5, 68-9; Thiering, *Redating the Teacher of Righteousness*, 105-9, 172, 201 note 51.
387. 1QM 2:1-7.
388. 1QM 1:12-5.
389. Davies, *1QM, The War Scroll from Qumran*, 113.
390. 1QM 15:4, 16:13, 18:5.
391. 1QM 1:2-3 in A. Dupont-Sommer, *The Essene Writings from Qumran*, trans. by G. Vermes (Gloucester, MA: Peter Smith, 1973), 169.

At the time of their return to Judea the second Nebuchadnezzar (i.e., probably Nero) would have destroyed Jerusalem. That is the reason for the use of the designation "desert" of Jerusalem. The city would then be in ruins.

It was during the events of 4 BC that 1QM 2-9 was written.[392] As will be remembered, the Jews revolted against the Romans and the Jewish establishment at this time. Varus, the legate of Syria, had to come to Judea to put down the revolt, which he did after crucifying two thousand rebels. Three messianic claimants had come forward to lead the people in their efforts. They were Judas, the son of Ezekias (probably the same person as Judas the Galilean); Simon of Perea; and the former shepherd, Athronges. Only Judas survived.

The hierarchical organization in 1QM 2-9 is similar to that which is described in 11QT except that the "Prince of all the Congregation"[393] (i.e., the King) is given more authority than the "Chief Priest."[394] This would make sense, since the lay leader would be better equipped to conduct war. According to Thiering, when compared to 11QT, "both have been reduced in status, so that neither is superior according to title. But the lay leader now has an overall rule which is not given to the Chief Priest. ... There is an equality of status, with much greater power given to the lay ruler."[395] The Chief Priest was John the Baptist. The "Prince of all the congregation" would be the messianic claimant (i.e., Judas, Simon or Athronges) who was successful against his enemies. This would mean that God condoned his leadership. Since Judas was the only one who survived the revolt, he must have been awarded this office.

Although Judas was able to escape from the Romans and go into hiding, John the Baptist was arrested according to the above quoted Slavonic passage. Fortunately, he was let go. The release of John at this time can be explained as follows:

> Only the desire of Archelaus, owing to his uncertain position as unconfirmed heir to the throne, not to exasperate unnecessarily his subjects, can account for the release of their leader, the accused Baptist, on this occasion. Had Archelaus got him into his hands 'after he had received the ethnarchy from Augustus' and begun 'to harass the Jews with intolerable oppression,' the Baptist would not have come off so easily.[396]

---

392. It should be noted that Thiering places the composition of 1QM 2-9 to about AD 6, when the Essenes formed an alliance with Judas the Galilaean's movement (Thiering, *Redating the Teacher of Righteousness*, 206-7).
393. 1QM 5:1-2.
394. 1QM 2:1.
395. Thiering, *Redating the Teacher of Righteousness*, 123.
396. Eisler, *The Messiah Jesus and John the Baptist*, 303.

The leadership structure that is envisioned in 1QM 2-9, if we accept a continuity with 11QT, is as follows (the higher up the table, the greater the authority):[397]

Ranking	The Community Leadership Structure	
1	Prince (King)	Laity
2	Chief Priest	Priests
3	Second Priest	
4	12 Head Priests	
5	26 Heads of Divisions	
6	Priests	
7	12 Head Levites	Levites
8	26 Heads of Divisions	
9	Levites	
10	12 Tribal Heads (Princes)	Laity
11	26 Heads of Divisions with Officers	
12	Chiefs of Thousands, Chiefs of Hundreds, Chiefs of Fifties, and Chiefs of Tens	

When the New Covenant came into being probably in AD 3, 1QS 1:1-4:26, 5:20b-7:25, and 1QSa were written to describe the aims, organization, rules, and penal code for the sect. 1QSb was also written, as a collection of blessings for the sect and its leaders.[398]

In these documents, the (High) Priest was again the leader over the entire sect followed by the Messiah of Israel.[399] The latter was also called the "Prince of the Congregation."[400] Control of the property was the responsibility of the twelve head levites or overseers.[401] If we accept a continuity with 1QM 2-9, the leadership structure is as follows (the higher up the table, the greater the authority):[402]

---

397. 1QM 2:1-6, 3:13-7, 5:1.

398. I believe that Thiering correctly shows that there are four separate units in 1QS in which certain changes in the organization of the sect can be discovered. They are: 1) 1:1-4:26, 5:20b-7:25 (with 1QSa and 1QSb); 2) 5:1-20a; 3) 8:1-15a, 9:12-26; and 4) 8:16b-9:11. However, my interpretations of them differ from Thiering's in many ways. See Thiering, *Redating the Teacher of Righteousness*, 107-9, 125-79.

399. 1QSa 2:12-7.

400. 1QSb 5:20.

401. 1QS 6:12, 20, cf. CD 9:16-20, 13:2-14:18, 15:7-17. Thiering makes a good case that the overseers were levites and controlled the property of the sect, but I do not agree with her that the twelve tribal heads were also overseers (Thiering, *Redating the Teacher of Righteousness*, 137-41). After AD 62 when Symeon, the son of Clopas, was the leader of the New Covenant and CD was written (AD 65-6), it appears that the overseers were priests (CD 14:6).

402. 1QS 2:19-21, 6:8-9, 1QSa 1:22-5, 1:27-2:3, 2:11-7, 1QSb 5:20.

Ranking	The Community Leadership Structure	
1	The (High) Priest, (Messiah of Aaron)	PRIESTS
2	Messiah of Israel, Prince (King)	LAITY
3	12 Head Priests[a]	PRIESTS
4	26 Heads of Divisions	
5	Priests	
6	12 Head Levites (Overseers)	LEVITES
7	26 Heads of Divisions	
8	Levites	
9	12 Tribal Heads	LAITY
10	26 Heads of Divisions with Officers	
11	Chiefs of Thousands, etc.	
12	Judges	
13	Officers	
14	Wise Men[b]	

a. Thiering is of the opinion that these twelve head priests were superior to the other priests not solely because of their office, but because of their Zadokite lineage as well (Thiering, Redating the Teacher of Righteousness, 4, 63,126). In my opinion, all the priests in the sect were considered equal as to their descent and the designations "sons of Zadok" and "sons of Aaron" applied to them all.

b. The "wise men" were the members of the Council of the Community who were not in the ranks of government.

The writer of 1QSa believed that he was living in the "end of days."[403] When the Messiah of Israel was anointed into his office the "last period" of history would commence. Then at a Council of the Community meeting he would preside over the sect's special Meal with the (High) Priest (i.e., John the Baptist)[404] who would be the first to bless the first fruits of bread and wine.[405] 1QSa starts off its description of this meeting as follows:

> [This is the sea]ting plan of the men of renown, [those summoned to] the gathering of the Council of the Community, when [God] begets the Messiah with them [i.e., when the Messiah is anointed to his office] .... [406]

This rite was to be repeated from then on when at least ten men were present.[407] In due time, the Messiah of Israel would lead the sect in the final war against its enemies.[408]

---

403. 1QSa 1:1.
404. 1QSa 2:12-22.
405. 1QSa 2:18-20.
406. 1QSa 2:11-2.
407. 1QSa 2:21-2.

Chapter 6. John the Baptist

It was expected that all those men along with their families who had been baptized by John during the revolt of 4 BC and were still alive would now join the sect en masse. 1QSa describes this situation as follows:

> And this is the rule for all the Congregation of Israel in the end of days, when they [i.e., those baptized in 4 BC] gather [in community to wa]lk in obedience to the law of the sons of Zadok the priests and of the members of their Covenant who have refus[ed to walk in] the way of the people ... On their arrival they shall gather them all together, including the children and the women, and they shall read into [their] ea[rs] all the precepts of the Covenant and shall instruct them in all their ordinances lest they stray in [their] st[ray]ing.[409]

Judas the Galilean was probably anointed as the Messiah of Israel in AD 3. For reasons unknown the final war had to be postponed. Then, because of certain disagreements with the leadership, Judas left the sect in AD 6 and founded the "fourth school of philosophy" (i.e., the Sicarii). As a result, a further postponement was required and Judas was labeled a false Messiah. Nevertheless, the real Messiah of Israel was still expected to arise in the near future.

The tax revolt led by Judas in AD 6 was a failure and he "perished, and all who followed him were scattered."[410] John the Baptist, who had been baptizing again in the Jordan River, was implicated in the affair, although he did not really approve of it. After the revolts of 4 BC and AD 6 the Jewish establishment had lost all patience with would be prophets and messiahs. Furthermore, now that a Roman governor was in office the Sanhedrin had to be more vigilant in watching out for possible revolts. John was in serious danger of being arrested a second time and this time it would not go so well for him. The decision was made to take refuge in the land of Damascus and lead the sect while in exile.

In AD 15/16, an individual who was to become the Messiah of Israel (he will be identified in a later chapter) prematurely declared himself to be this personage and caused a schism in the sect. Many laymen and perhaps some levites and priests went over to him.

It was at this time that 1QS 5:1-20a was written in order to deal with these schismatics. It is stated that the members were to "separate themselves from the Congregation of perverse men."[411] Such a man "is not to enter into the waters to

---

408. 1QSa 1:21, 26; 1QSb 5:20-9.
409. 1QSa 1:3-5.
410. Acts 5:37.
411. 1QS 5:1-2.

share in the pure food of the men of holiness, for a man is not pure unless he be converted from his malice."[412] The property was now under the control of "the sons of Zadok the priests who keep the Covenant, and under the authority of the majority of the members of the Community."[413] Perhaps the reason why there was no mention of a "Holy of Holies" (i.e., a high priest) in this section of 1QS[414] was that John the Baptist, who was leading the sect while in exile, was not actually present with it on a daily basis.[415]

Luke 3:1-3 states the following:

> In the fifteenth year of the reign of Tiberius Caesar ... the word of God came to John the son of Zechariah in the wilderness; and he went into all the region about the Jordan, preaching a baptism of repentance for the forgiveness of sins.

Luke 3:21-2 implies that John baptized Jesus "in the fifteenth year of the reign of Tiberius Caesar" as well. Furthermore, soon after Jesus was baptized by John and went to Jerusalem to celebrate the Passover John 2:19-20 records the following dialog that was supposed to have occurred between some people and Jesus:

> Jesus answered them, "Destroy this temple, and in three days I will raise it up." The Jews then said, "It has taken forty-six years to build this temple, and will you raise it in three days?"

AD 28 appears to be the year that both passages are indicating. Starting from the death of Emperor Augustus on August 19, AD 14 the fifteenth year of Tiberius would take us to AD 28.[416] Starting from the date that the building of the Temple began in 19 BC forty-six years would take us to AD 28 as well.[417] What is the significance of AD 28? It has nothing to do with the date of John's first appearance, which we have seen was 4 BC, or the date of Jesus' baptism,

---

412. 1QS 5:13-4.
413. 1QS 5:2-3.
414. It does mention "all who are volunteers for the holiness of Aaron and for the house of truth in Israel" (1QS 5:6).
415. In two later sections of 1QS, which were written after the death of John the Baptist (AD 35), the "Holy of Holies" is mentioned. At 1QS 8:5-6 (cf. 8:8-9), it refers to three priests (8:1) and at 1QS 9:6-7, it again refers to the high priest.
416. Jerry Vardaman, Edwin M. Yamauchi, eds. *Chronos, Kairos, Christos* (Winona Lake: Eisenbrauns, 1989), 58-61. It should be noted that Vardaman postulates that Luke 3:1 was corrupted from the "second year" (AD 15), which was the original reading, to the "fifteenth year" (AD 28).
417. Emil Schurer, *The History of the Jewish People in the Age of Jesus Christ*, vols. I, II, III.1, III.2, rev. and ed. by Geza Vermes, et al. (Edinburgh: T. & T. Clark, 1973/87), 292, note 12. If we start from 20 BC, the date would be AD 27.

which we will see was probably AD 3. What it really gives us is the date of John's *return* from exile in the land of Damascus.

Why did John return from the land of Damascus in AD 28? Perhaps he expected the last period of history to begin in AD 36 and he returned to prepare for it.[418] The time from 4 BC (the first appearance of John) to AD 37 was exactly 40 years or one generation according to CD.[419] AD 37 would be the beginning of the next generation. A new Messiah of Israel would be anointed into his office in that year and the final war would soon begin. Doubtless as the critical period approached, John's discourses at the Jordan became more zealous and the people in turn became more excited politically.

In AD 35, Herod Antipas had John put to death at the fortress of Machaerus, because he feared that his teaching might lead to a revolt. The Slavonic Josephus states that John died *after* Philip the tetrarch (Herod Antipas' brother) died in AD 34[420] and the *Antiquities* passage states that Herod Antipas' defeat by the Arabs in AD 36 was God's punishment on him for killing John.[421] According to Robert Eisler, "the statements of both sources indicate with a high degree of probability that the Baptist was arrested and executed in AD 35."[422] John's arrest and death must have postponed the sect's war plans again.

I will end this chapter by quoting the *Antiquities* passage about John[423] as restored by Robert Eisler:[424]

> Some of the Jews, however, regarded the destruction of Herod's army as the work of God, who thus exacted a [very just][425] retribution for John, surnamed the Baptist. *For Herod killed him, a wild man with a shaggy body and clothed in animal's hair, who incited the Jews to liberty and bade them cultivate valour,* practice justice toward each other and piety toward God, and to band together through baptism.[426] For baptism would only appear acceptable to God if practiced, not for the purification of the body, but for the expiation of sins, after the soul had been thoroughly cleansed by righteousness.[427] *And when the masses banded together — for they were roused to the greatest revolt by the words*

---

418. The last period of history was originally thought to have begun in AD 3, but this date would now have been revised to AD 37.
419. CD 1:11-2, 20:13-5, cf. 4QpPs^a 2:7-8.
420. Josephus, Bk. III, Appendix, 646-8; Ant. XVIII, 106.
421. Ant. XVIII, 109-119.
422. Eisler, *The Messiah Jesus and John the Baptist*, 291.
423. Ant. XVIII, 116-9.
424. Eisler, *The Messiah Jesus and John the Baptist*, 245-50. Robert Eisler's restorations are in italics.
425. Robert Eisler takes the words in square brackets to be a Christian interpolation. Josephus did not approve of John (Eisler, *The Messiah Jesus and John the Baptist*, 248).
426. This verse actually reads as follows: "For Herod slew him, a good man, who bade the Jews cultivate virtue, practice justice toward each other and piety towards God, and come together through baptism."

which they heard — [428] Herod feared that the powerful influence which he exercised over men's minds might lead to some act of revolt; for they seemed ready to do anything upon his advice. Herod therefore considered it far better to forestall him by putting him to death, before any revolution arose through him, than to rue his delay when plunged in the turmoil of an insurrection. And so, through Herod's suspicion, John was sent in chains to Machaerus, the fortress already mentioned, and there slain. Now *some*[429] Jews believed that the destruction of Herod's army was the penalty inflicted upon him to avenge John, God being wroth against Herod.

---

427. This verse actually reads as follows: "For thus immersion would appear acceptable to God, if practiced, not as an expiation for certain offenses, but for a purification of the body, after the soul had already been previously cleansed by righteousness."

428. This verse actually reads as follows: "And when the others banded together — for they were highly delighted to listen to his words —...."

429. Robert Eisler takes the original word here to be "some," rather than "the," which is the present reading (Eisler, *The Messiah Jesus and John the Baptist*, 248).

CHAPTER 7. DOSITHEUS

With the death of John the Baptist in AD 35, James the Righteous, the brother of Jesus, became the new leader and high priest of the New Covenant. The sect continued to use 1QS 1:1-4:26, 5:20b-7:25, 5:1-20a, 1QSa, and 1QSb, as it did under John's leadership, but Jerusalem became its place of residence instead of the settlement of Khirbet Qumran.

Unfortunately, very soon after James assumed the leadership, a schism occurred in the sect. Its leader was someone named Dositheus. 1QS 8:1-15a and 9:12-26 were written by the schismatics in order to form a new organization and they decided to make Khirbet Qumran their residence again. 1QS 8:12-4[430] states that they moved back to the desert settlement:

> And when these things come to pass for the Community in Israel at these appointed times, they shall be separated from the midst of the habitation of perverse men to go into the desert to prepare the way of Him: as it is written, *In the wilderness prepare the way of .... Make straight in the desert a highway for our God.*[431]

In their organization document, the individual called the "interpreter,"[432] who was probably a levite,[433] was Dositheus. Ranked below him were three priests (only three became schismatics) and twelve men, who were called the fifteen "elect ones."[434] The shortage of levites (Dositheus was probably the only

---

430. See also 1QS 9:19-20.
431. Is. 40:3.
432. 1QS 8:11-2.
433. B. E. Thiering, *Redating the Teacher of Righteousness* (Sydney: Theological Explorations, 1979), 134-5, 169, 176. Thiering identified the interpreter of 1QS 8:11-2 with the prophet of 1QS 9:11, as I do.

83

one) appears to have been remedied in a unique way. Twelve men, who had reached the highest lay governing ranks, received two more years of specialized training.[435] With the additional training, they were "set apart (as) holy,"[436] i.e., they acted the part of levites, and they became the elect ones along with the three priests. In 1QS 8:20-9:2, which is part of a later organization document, they are called perfectly holy men (1QS 8:20) and rules are recorded for them.[437] The laity were probably the main participants in the schism. In order to fill the offices that were vacated by the twelve men (elect ones) and left empty by other laymen who did not go over to Dositheus, additional promotions had to be made (perhaps prematurely in some cases) to fill the lay ranks of government.

If we accept a continuity with the previous organization, the leadership structure of the schismatics is as follows (the higher up the table, the greater the authority):[438]

	The Community Leadership Structure	
Ranking		
1	The Interpreter	LEVITES:
2	15 *Elect Ones* consisting of:	
3	3 *Priests* plus	Priests
4	12 *Men* (Acting Levites)	
5	12 Tribal Heads	
6	26 Heads of Divisions with Officers	
7	Chiefs of Thousands, Chiefs of Hundreds, Chiefs of Fifties, and Chiefs of Tens	LAITY
8	Judges	
9	Officers	
10	Wise Men	

In ca. AD 37, the schismatics led by Dositheus moved to the land of Damascus. The Mandaean tradition in the *Haran Gawaita* about 60,000 (!) Mandaeans fleeing from Judea to "Hauran" (i.e., Auranitis) may be referring to this movement to the land of Damascus.[439] Also, "King Ardban" of the *Haran Gawaita* may be the Parthian king Artabanus III (ca. AD 12-38).[440]

---

434. 1QS 8:1-2, 6, 9:14, 17-8. Thiering identified the three priests and twelve men as the elect ones, as I do (Thiering, *Redating the Teacher of Righteousness*, 166-9).

435. I agree with Thiering's interpretation of 1QS 8:10-1 (Thiering, *Redating the Teacher of Righteousness*, 167, 173).

436. 1QS 8:11.

437. Thiering, *Redating the Teacher of Righteousness*, 171, 173.

438. 1QS 8:1-12.

439. Hugh J. Schonfield, *The Jesus Party* (New York: Macmillan, 1974), 283.

The schismatics introduced above are the "princes"[441] referred to in the following passage from CD:

> And God remembered the Covenant of the first ones
> and raised out of Aaron men of understanding
> and out of Israel sages,
> and He caused them to hear (His voice) and they dug the well:
> The well which the princes dug,
> which the nobles of the people delved with a rod.[442]
> The well is the Torah,
> and those who dug it are the returnees of Israel
> who went out from the land of Judah
> and were exiled in the land of Damascus;
> all of whom God called princes,
> for they sought him
> and their (glory) is denied by the mouth of no man.
> And the rod is the interpreter of the Torah;
> as Isaiah said, *He has made a tool for His work.*[443]
> And the nobles of the people are they that come to dig the well
> with the precepts that the rod decreed,
> that they may walk in them during all the period of wickedness,
> and without which they shall not succeed
> until the Teacher of Righteousness arises in the end of days.[444]

Because the schism was eventually healed, the princes are referred to with approval in the above passage, but any allusion to Dositheus' leadership is carefully avoided.

The "nobles,"[445] who came after the princes, were all the loyal sectarians who were withdrawing to the land of Damascus when CD was written in AD 65-6 in order to escape the coming visitation. Symeon, the son of Clopas, led this mass exodus. He is called the "interpreter of the Torah,"[446] the "rod,"[447] and in other places in the same document, the "voice" of the Teacher.[448] In a later chapter, it will be shown that Symeon was actually a brother of Jesus.

---

440. Edwin M. Yamauchi, *Pre-Christian Gnosticism*, 2nd ed. (Grand Rapids: Baker, 1983), 132-5.
441. CD 6:3, 6.
442. Num. 21:18.
443. Is. 54:16.
444. CD 6:2-11.
445. CD 6:4, 8.
446. CD 6:7.
447. CD 6:4, 7, 9.
448. CD 20:28, 32.

The beginning of the passage states that "God *remembered* the Covenant of the first ones."[449] This means that the two withdrawals of the princes and the nobles to the land of Damascus had to have occurred *after* the time of the first ones (187-167 BC). Also, the withdrawal that occurred before 63 BC cannot be identified with those of the princes and the nobles either, because at that time, God "hid His face from Israel and its sanctuary and delivered them up to the sword."[450] This line refers to the capture of Jerusalem by the Roman general Pompey. There is no allusion to an attack by a foreign power in the passage quoted above.

CD 7:18-21 belongs in AD 65-6 as well:[451]

> And the star is the interpreter of the Torah
> who came to Damascus; as it is written,
> *A star has journeyed out of Jacob*
> *and a sceptre is risen out of Israel.*[452]
> The sceptre is the prince of all the Congregation,
> and at his coming *he will break down all the sons of Seth.*[453]

The "star" and the "interpreter of the Torah" again refer to Symeon, the son of Clopas. The "scepter" and the "prince of all the Congregation" will be identified in a later chapter.

4Q174 with 4Q177[454] were probably written in this period as well. 4Q177 1:8-9 states that they "will flee [... like a b]ird from its spot and will be exiled from His [God's] land."[455] The "interpreter of the Torah" is also mentioned.[456]

1QS 8:16b-9:11, the final section of 1QS that reveals changes in the organization of the sect, was written in ca. AD 40 after the schism led by Dositheus had been healed.[457] From then on until the mass exodus in AD 65-6, the settlement in the land of Damascus remained a distant outpost of the sect.

---

449. CD 6:2.
450. CD 1:3-4.
451. These lines are inserted in a passage (CD 7:12-18, 7:21-8:1) that refers to the withdrawal of the first ones in the period before the first visitation (187-169 BC). Perhaps through carelessness, the scribe added CD 7:18-21, which refers to the withdrawal that was occurring in his own time (AD 65-6). It was to be followed by a terrible visitation to come.
452. Num. 24:17.
453. Num. 24:17. The designation "sons of Seth" is interpreted as the "sons of pride." See Theodor H. Gaster, *The Dead Sea Scriptures* (Garden City: Anchor Books, 1976), 3rd ed., 110, note 33.
454. Thiering, *Redating the Teacher of Righteousness*, 180.
455. Florentino Garcia Martinez and Eibert J. C. Tigchelaar, eds., 2 vols., *The Dead Sea Scrolls Study Edition* (Leiden: Brill, 1997), Vol. I, 363 (4Q177 1:8-9).
456. Martinez and Tigchelaar, *The Dead Sea Scrolls Study Edition*, Vol. I, 353 (4Q174 1:11), 365 (4Q177 2:5).

Chapter 7. Dositheus

The property is now under the control of the priests only[458] and was not to be mingled with the property of the "men of deceit who have not purified their way to be separated from perversity and walk in perfection of way."[459]

Although the sectarians resided predominantly in Jerusalem, they were not to enter the Temple, which they considered to be polluted. Their prayer and right conduct would take the place of sacrifices.[460] Actually, this rule, which was put into writing in this section of 1QS, had been the unwritten policy since the sect began.

Since the organization was so similar to the one originally created by John the Baptist, the scribe could state that "they shall be governed by the first ordinances in which the members of the Community began their instruction."[461]

The "Messiah of Aaron"[462] was James the Righteous, who became the unrivaled leader and high priest of the sect, and the "Messiah of Israel"[463] was still to come. In some other early sources, Dositheus is identified with the prophet, who was predicted by Moses in Deut. 18:15-8.[464] This confirms that he became the "prophet" referred to in 1QS 9:11 when the schism was healed.

At this time, I think it is likely that the twelve perfectly holy men actually *became* levites, i.e., they were reborn into the tribe of Levi and lost their original tribal genealogy based on their father's descent. This action may have been a part of the agreement that healed the schism. A special rite at some point after the completion of the training was probably required to make this official. Although there is no clear evidence for this metamorphosis in the scrolls, it does seem to be the direction that their training was headed. Starting out as tribal heads or chiefs of laymen, they then became with two additional years of training twelve perfectly holy men (i.e., *acting* levites) Finally, they became after a special rite, if my suggestion is correct, twelve levites. The process probably became a continuous one and did not end with the first twelve.

I also think it is likely that the twelve head levites *became* priests after a period of training. They would now be considered sons of Aaron, as well as sons of Levi. This probably occurred after a special rite also. As with the twelve

---

457. It should be mentioned that Thiering places 4QTest and 1QM 1, 15-9 in the same time period (not specified by her) as 1QS 8:16b-9:11 (Thiering, *Redating the Teacher of Righteousness*, 171-2). I place the former documents later in AD 65-6.
458. 1QS 9:7.
459. 1QS 9:8-9.
460. 1QS 9:3-5.
461. 1QS 9:10.
462. 1QS 9:11.
463. 1QS 9:11.
464. S. J. Isser, *The Dositheans: A Samaritan Sect in Late Antiquity* (Leiden: E. J. Brill, 1976), 127-31.

perfectly holy men becoming levites, the process probably became a continuous one and did not end with the first twelve.

Early in the history of Israel all levites (i.e., sons of Levi) *were* priests-the terms were synonymous. At some point during the period of the monarchy, only levites, who were also sons of Aaron, were allowed to officiate as priests. The other levites became only secondary ministers in the Temple.[465] The result was that, as Schurer states, "the 'priests' stood to them [the levites] in the relation of a privileged family vis-á-vis the tribe in general. For Aaron, the patriarch of the priests, was a great-grandson of Levi."[466]

The trend from ca. 20 BC to AD 64 was to give the levites a higher status. In 11QT (written ca. 20 BC), along with a higher status, they were allowed to perform certain priestly duties.[467] Herod Agrippa II, during the time of Albinus' governorship (AD 62-4), gave permission to the levite hymn singers in the Temple to wear linen robes like the priests. He also gave permission to the levite gate-keepers, whose status was lower than that of the levite hymn singers, to learn the hymns like the latter.[468] If my suggestion is correct, at long last, the levites in the New Covenant received their due.

The hypothetical special rites, which would officially make the perfectly holy men levites and the head levites priests are not without support. We know that an establishment priest of this time, who "had been examined and accepted by the Sanhedrin in regard to his fitness, was sanctified for office by a special act of consecration."[469]

If we accept a continuity with the previous organizations, the leadership structure is as follows (the higher up the table, the greater the authority):[470]

---

465. Emil Schurer, *The History of the Jewish People in the Age of Jesus Christ*, vols. I, II, III.1, III.2, rev. and ed. by Geza Vermes, et al. (Edinburgh: T. & T. Clark, 1973/87), Vol. II, 250-1.
466. Schurer, *The History of the Jewish People in the Age of Jesus Christ*, Vol. II, 253.
467. Jacob Milgrom, "The Temple Scroll," *Biblical Archaeologist* 41 (1978): 105-20.
468. Ant. XX, 216-8.
469. Emil Schurer, *The History of the Jewish People in the Age of Jesus Christ*, Vol. II, 244.
470. 1QS 9:10-1.

Chapter 7. Dositheus

THE COUNCIL OF THE COMMUNITY		PRIESTS
LAITY	LEVITES	
		Messiah of Aaron (High Priest)[a]
Messiah of Israel (Prince or King)		
	Prophet	
		12 Head Priests
		26 Heads of Divisions
		Priests
	12 Head Levites (Overseers)	After a special rite, they became Levites.
	26 Heads of Divisions	
	Levites	
12 Perfectly Holy Men	After a special rite, they became Levites.	
12 Tribal Heads		
26 Heads of Divisions with Officers		
Chiefs of Thousands, etc.		
Judges		
Officers		
Wise Men		

a. Based on 1QM 1, 15-9, which was written in AD 65-6, this title was changed to Chief Priest. After AD 62, this was one of the titles of Symeon, the son of Clopas.

CHAPTER 8. JAMES THE RIGHTEOUS

During the last generation (i.e., AD 35-ca. 75), James the Righteous (usually referred to with the sobriquet "the Just"), a brother of Jesus, became the leader and high priest of the sect. In CD, except when a future Teacher of Righteousness is mentioned[471] and when John the Baptist is referred to as *a* Teacher of Righteousness,[472] James is mentioned as *the* "Teacher"[473] and *the* "Teacher of Righteousness."[474] He is always the Teacher of Righteousness in the Pesharim, which are commentaries on various Biblical books, usually one of the Prophets. Robert Eisenman was the first researcher to identify James with the Teacher, but there are significant differences between his theory and mine.[475]

Ananus, the son of Ananus, is the "Man of Mockery,"[476] the "Man of Lies,"[477] "Zaw,"[478] and the "Wicked Priest"[479] of the Dead Sea Scrolls. We know that the Wicked Priest was actually a member of the New Covenant, because 1QpHab

---

471. CD 6:11.
472. CD 1:11.
473. CD 20:28.
474. CD 20:32.
475. See especially "James the Just in the Habakkuk *Pesher*" in Robert Eisenman, *The Dead Sea Scrolls and the First Christians* (Rockport: Element, 1996), 111-217. One of the differences between his theory and mine is that he believes Ananus is the Wicked Priest and Paul is the Man of Lies. I take both designations to be references to Ananus. Prior to Eisenman, Gaster [Theodor H. Gaster, *The Dead Sea Scriptures*, 3rd ed. (New York: Anchor Books, 1976), 16-7] and Schonfield [Hugh J. Schonfield, *Secrets of the Dead Sea Scrolls* (London: Jewish Chronicle Publications, 1956), 106-11, 151-60] got very close to identifying James with the Teacher, but never went all the way.
476. CD 1:14.
477. CD 20:15, 8:13, 19:26.
478. CD 4:19.
479. 1QpHab 8:8, 11:4, 12:2, 8, cf. ("the priest") 8:16, 11:12.

states that he "was called by the *name of truth* at the beginning of his rise to power"[480] and the sectarians believed that truth resided only within the sect.[481]

At some point after James became the leader of the sect Ananus caused a schism in it. A large number of priests, levites, and laity sided with him against James, left the sect,[482] and joined or rejoined the Jewish establishment as a sort of private association.[483] This was the "congregation of traitors" mentioned in CD 1:12.[484] In order to have successfully accomplished this action, it is likely that Ananus had been a high-ranking and influential priest in the sect. If this was not the case, it would be difficult to explain how he could have persuaded a large number of sectarians to join him.

1QpHab states that the Wicked Priest "ruled over Israel."[485] This statement is always taken to mean that the he was a ruling establishment high priest. However, although Ananus was in fact the official high priest for three months in AD 62,[486] I do not think the statement is referring to this period only. Since according to the sect members of Israel could only be "Jews" who submitted to John's baptism, Israel here refers to the large number of schismatics that the Wicked Priest became the leader of (i.e., "ruled over"). The whole period when Ananus "ruled over" them would *include* the period when he was the official high priest in AD 62, as well as when he was one of the leaders at the beginning of the Jewish revolt in AD 67-8.[487]

Because the "princes of Judah" were the schismatics,[488] they "entered the Covenant of conversion,"[489] i.e., they received John's baptism. They will be

---

480. 1QpHab 8:8-9 (italics mine).
481. 1QS 4:5, 3:17-22, 1QpHab 7:10.
482. See 1QpHab 2:1-2: "those who have betrayed with the Man of Lies [Ananus]."
483. The Pharisees joined "local fellowships or brotherhoods" called "haburot" (sing. "haburah"). See F. F. Bruce, *New Testament History* (Garden City: Anchor Books, 1969), 78. This private association of the schismatics may have been similar to one of these.
484. In CD, others names are given to the congregation of traitors. It is also called the "House of Peleg" (Peleg means "divide," CD 20:22) and its members are called the "builders of the wall" (a reference to Ezek. 13:10-1, CD 4:19, 8:12, 18, 19:24-5, 31) and the "princes of Judah" (a reference to Hos. 5:10, CD 8:13, 19:15).
485. 1QpHab 8:9-10.
486. Ant. XX, 197-203.
487. War IV, 158-61.
488. Could the designation "princes of Judah" have a secondary meaning? Could it also be alluding to the real princes of Judah, i.e., Herod the Great and his descendants, who indulged in all the improper practices that the schismatics are accused of indulging in? Robert Eisler unequivocally identified the princes of Judah, as Herod and his descendants. Eisler, "The Sadoqite Book of the New Covenant: Its Date and Origin," *Occident and Orient* (Gaster Anniversary Volume) B. Schindler, ed. (London: Taylor's Foreign Press, 1936), 124-5. Cf. 4QpPs^a, frags. 1-10, 3:7: "the princes [of wickedn]ess who have oppressed [God's] holy people."
489. CD 19:15.

destroyed in the coming visitation by the "Chief of the kings of Yawan," i.e., the Roman Emperor (probably Nero), as is explained in the following passage:

> This is the day when God will make a visitation; as He said,
> *The princes of Judah were like those who remove the bound,*
> *I shall pour out Anger upon them like water.*[490]
> For they entered the Covenant of conversion
> but did not depart from the way of traitors;
> and they defiled themselves in the ways of lust
> and in the riches of iniquity;
> and they took revenge and bore malice, each towards his brother,
> and each man hated his fellow,
> and they refused their help each man to him who is flesh of his flesh,
> and they had shameful commerce
> and made themselves strong for the sake of riches and gain,
> and each man did what was good in his eyes,
> and each one chose the stubbornness of his heart,
> and kept not themselves from the people and its sin
> but lived in license deliberately,
> walking in the ways of the wicked; of whom God said,
> *Their wine is the poison of serpents*
> *And the head of asps is cruel.*[491]
> The serpents are the kings of the peoples
> and their wine is their ways:
> and the head of asps is the Chief of the kings of Yawan
> who will come among them to wreak vengeance.
> But all this they [the schismatics] have not understood
> who build the wall[492] and cover it with whitewash;
> for he [Ananus] walks after the wind and raises whirlwinds
> and preaches lies to men,
> against all of whose congregation the Anger of God has been kindled.[493]

The designation "kings of the peoples"[494] probably refers to several small kingdoms located in the Middle East that were allies of the Romans and often furnished troops to them, as the situation required. The rulers of these kingdoms

---

490. Hos. 5:10.
491. Dt.32:33.
492. Could the designation "builders of the wall" have a secondary meaning? Could it also be alluding to the wall which Herod Agrippa I started to build in the north of Jerusalem, but which the Romans would not allow him to complete? It would have made the city impregnable to attack. See Ant. XIX, 326-7: War II, 218-22. Robert Eisler put forward the idea that the designation alluded to this wall. See Robert Eisler, "The Sadoqite Book of the New Covenant: Its Date and Origin," 124.
493. CD 19:15-26, cf. CD 8:2-13.
494. CD 8:10, 19:23.

were often called kings, though not always, and Rome placed them in power.[495] They included the kingdoms of Emesa, Commagne, Lesser Armenia, and Pontus in the north. The territories in the north (Trachonitis, Batanea, Gaulanitis, Auranitis, Iturea, Galilee, Samaria, and part of Perea) and in the south (Judaea, Idumaea, and part of Perea) were often split up or joined together to create additional kingdoms at various times. The kingdom of Nabatea (Arabia),[496] which was located east of the Dead Sea, was probably included as well.[497]

As inheritors of Greek culture, all the rulers of the kingdoms mentioned above, except perhaps the kingdom of Nabatea, could be called the "kings of Yawan," i.e., Greece.[498]

Three practices, which the schismatics are accused of and which are included under the general category of "lust,"[499] should be mentioned here. They are divorce,[500] polygamy,[501] and marrying nieces.[502] Herod the Great and his descendants indulged in these practices routinely. In fact, the only time from 200 BC to AD 70 when these practices were commonplace was from 37 BC to AD 70 (i.e., the period of Herod and his descendants). In joining the Jewish establishment, it appears that the schismatics adopted the practices of the former.

What was considered to be the beginning of this schism is alluded to in 1QpHab:

> O traitors, why do you stare and stay silent when the wicked one overwhelms one more righteous than he? [Hab. 1:13b]. The explanation of this concerns the House of Absalom and their partisans, who were reduced to silence[503] by the reprimand[504] of the Teacher of Righteousness [James], and (so) did not help him against the Man of Lies [Ananus], who rejected the Torah in the midst of their entire (congregation).[505]

---

495. Emil Schurer, *The History of the Jewish People in the Age of Jesus Christ*, vols. I, II, III.1, III.2, rev. and ed. by Geza Vermes, et al. (Edinburgh: T. & T. Clark, 1973/87), Vol. I, 316-7, 448-51, 471-83, 561-73; G. R. Driver, *The Judaean Scrolls: The Problem and a Solution* (New York: Schocken Books, 1965), 218-22.

496. Schurer, *The History of the Jewish People in the Age of Jesus Christ*, Vol. I, 575-86.

497. The reference to the "kings of the north" in 1QM 1:4 probably refers to all of these kingdoms that were located in the north only.

498. Driver, *The Judaean Scrolls: The Problem and a Solution*, 218-22.

499. CD 4:20, 8:5, 19:17.

500. CD 4:20-1.

501. CD 4:20-1, 5:2.

502. CD 5:7-8.

503. The Hebrew word for "were reduced to silence" should not have the active sense (i.e., "kept silent"), as it is usually understood. See H. G. M. Williamson, "The Translation of 1QpHab, 5, 10," *Revue de Qumran* 9 (1977), 263-5; Driver, *The Judaean Scrolls: The Problem and a Solution*, 271-2.

Absalom was King David's son, who revolted against his father.[506] Therefore, the designation "House of Absalom" in the above passage refers to traitors to the New Covenant. Since Ananus was a priest himself, the House of Absalom should probably be identified with the disloyal priests and "their partisans" to the disloyal laymen and levites.

It would appear that the split between the two camps had been progressing for some time before the event alluded to in this passage. What seems to have occurred is at a full Assembly meeting, the Teacher of Righteousness (i.e., James) reprimanded the members probably for some infringements of the Torah instigated by the Man of Lies (i.e. Ananus). As the passage states, the Man of Lies "rejected the Torah in the midst of their entire (congregation)."[507] They were "reduced to silence" by the reprimand[508] and it was the final provocation for the "House of Absalom and their partisans." They decided to withdraw their support for the Teacher and to give it all to the Man of Lies. As the passage states, "[they] did not help him against the Man of Lies" and the Teacher was "overwhelmed" according to the term used in the biblical passage. The actual physical split between the two camps was soon to come.

Ananus' family was a very powerful high-priestly family in the Jewish establishment in Jerusalem. In AD 6-15, his father (Ananus) had been the establishment high priest and all of his five sons had been high priests at some time as well.[509] Because of the influence of Ananus' family with the priestly establishment, his efforts to destroy the New Covenant were given tacit, if not outright, approval. 1QpHab states, "he plotted to destroy completely the Poor" (i.e., the New Covenant).[510] The passage continues on as follows:

---

504. The Hebrew word for "reprimand" "always has the idea of 'deserved punishment' or 'justified reprimand.' Consequently ... the reprimand must be addressed *by* the Teacher" (Williamson, "The Translation of 1QpHab, 5, 10," 264).

505. 1QpHab 5:8-12.

506. 2 Sam. 15:1-18, 33.

507. This line of the passage seems to state that the Wicked Priest rejected the *whole* Torah. Perhaps it should be understood as being in agreement with Jas. 2:10: "For whoever keeps the whole law but fails in one point has become guilty of all of it."

508. This is the answer to the question put forward by the biblical passage: "*O traitors, why do you stare and stay silent....*" The reprimand by the Teacher of Righteousness did it.

509. Ant. XX, 198. His sons were Eleazer (high priest, AD 16-7), Jonathan (AD 36-7), Theophilus (AD 37-41), Matthias (sometime during Herod Agrippa I's reign, AD 41-4), and Ananus (3 months in AD 62).

510. 1QpHab, 12:6. 4QpPs[a], frags. 1-10, 2:14-5 mentions "the ruthless ones of the covenant who are in the House of Judah [i.e., the schismatics], who plot to destroy completely those who observe the Torah...."

> And as for that which He [God] said, *Because of the blood of the city and the violence (done to) the land* [Hab. 2:17], the explanation of this is "the city" is Jerusalem, where the Wicked Priest committed abominable deeds and defiled the Sanctuary of God;[511] "and the violence (done to) the land," these are the towns of Judah where he stole the goods of the Poor.[512]

Robert Eisler created an ingenious theory early in the last century, which endeavored, among other things, to solve the historical problems regarding the death of James the Righteous.[513] I think the Dead Sea Scrolls, and specifically 1QpHab 11:2-8, if rightly interpreted, prove the correctness of his theory. The new evidence requires only a few alterations in it.

In AD 62, when Ananus was the establishment high priest for three months, he had James the Righteous killed by having him pushed off the pinnacle of the temple and clubbed to death when he hit the pavement below.[514] This event appears to be alluded to in CD when it states, "they banded together against the life of the Righteous One."[515]

According to Josephus,[516] it was in the interval between the death of Festus (AD 60-2), who died in office, and the arrival of the new Roman governor, Albinus (AD 62-4), that the high priest Ananus saw his opportunity to destroy James and his associates. I will quote the passage below and show by brackets where Robert Eisler believed certain Christian deletions were made in the text. The supposed contents of these deletions will be explained in the accompanying notes:

> Possessed of such a character ("rash in his temper and unusually daring"),[517] Ananus thought that he had a favourable opportunity because

---

511. Since a corrupt priesthood already polluted it, the "Sanctuary of God" could *not* refer to the Temple in Jerusalem. It probably referred to the *Synagogue* of the New Covenant, which the Wicked Priest "defiled" by ordering covert executions right in its midst. Contact with corpses caused defilement (Num. 19:1-22).

512. 1QpHab 12:6-10.

513. Robert Eisler, *The Messiah Jesus and John the Baptist*, ed. by A. H. Krappe (London: Methuen & Co., 1931), 540-46.

514. Arthur Palumbo, "1QpHab 11:2-8 and the Death of James the Just," *The Qumran Chronicle* (Vol. 3, No. 1-3, Dec. 1993).

515. CD 1:20.

516. Ant. XX, 200-3.

517. Ant. XX, 199. However, in another place Josephus gives high praises especially to Ananus, the son of Ananus, but also to Jesus, the son of Gamalas, in a eulogy to them (War IV, 319-25, cf. War IV, 151, where Ananus is called a "man of profound sanity"). They both became the most notable leaders in the first period of the revolt.

Festus was dead and Albinus was still on the way. And so he convened the judges of the Sanhedrin and brought before them a man named James, the brother of Jesus who was called the Christ [ ],[518] and certain others. He accused them of having transgressed the law and delivered them up to be stoned [ ].[519] [*The people, when searching (later on) for the cause of the fall of Jerusalem and the destruction of the temple, believed that this suffering happened to our nation through the wrath of God, because of what those men dared to do*].[520] Those of the inhabitants of the city who were considered the most fair-minded and who were strict in observance of the law were offended at this. They therefore secretly sent to King Agrippa urging him, for this was not the first time that Ananus had acted unjustly, to order him to desist from any further such actions. Certain of them even went to meet Albinus, who was on his way from Alexandria, and informed him that Ananus had no authority to convene the Sanhedrin without his consent. Convinced by these words, Albinus angrily wrote to Ananus threatening to take vengeance upon him. King Agrippa, because of Ananus' action, deposed him from the high priesthood which he had held for three months and replaced him with Jesus the son of Damnaeus.

A major problem that is encountered in any examination of James' death is that the passage of Josephus does not agree with Hegesippus. This latter passage is now extent only in Eusebius' *Ecclesiastical History*.[521]

Epiphanius, who also gives us some very important information about James, records that "so many before us have told of him, both Eusebius and Clement and others."[522] This statement appears to be a reference to Eusebius' *Ecclesiastical History* where the Hegesippus passage is quoted and where it is

---

518. A Christian hand deleted something here, because as Eisler states, "Josephus is accustomed to insert a reference harking back to the first mention of a name reintroducing a person for the second time" (Eisler, *The Messiah Jesus and John the Baptist*, 143). Jesus is first mentioned in Ant. XVIII, 63-4, which has been tampered with by Christians also (Eisler, *The Messiah Jesus and John the Baptist*, 62).

519. According to Eisler, "It is not improbable that Josephus wrote some lines about the occasion which James had given for the proceedings of Ananus, and did not altogether omit to state the grave provocation which led to the trial by the Sanhedrin" (Eisler, *The Messiah Jesus and John the Baptist*, 546). A Christian, who did not approve of them, would have deleted them.

520. According to Origen, who wrote in the third century, Josephus stated that the destruction of Jerusalem was a result of divine punishment for the death of James, but in Origen's estimation Josephus should have ascribed the cause of the disaster to the death of Jesus instead. See Schurer, *The History of the Jewish People in the Age of Jesus Christ*, Vol. I, 430-2; S. G. F. Brandon, *The Fall of Jerusalem and the Christian Church*, 2nd ed. (London: S.P.C.K., 1968), 110-4. A Christian deleted the words in italics so that the passage would not contradict Origen's view that Jesus' (not James') death brought about Jerusalem's desolation (Eisler, *The Messiah Jesus and John the Baptist*, 141-4). Eusebius seems to have read a passage from Josephus with lines almost the same as the italicized words. See Eusebius, *The Ecclesiastical History*, 2 vols., trans. by Kirsopp Lake (Cambridge: Harvard University Press, 1975), Vol. I, 177 (II, 23. 20).

521. Eusebius, *Ecclesiastical History*, Vol. I, 170-5 (II, 23.3-18).

522. Eisler, *The Messiah Jesus and John the Baptist*, 541.

stated that Clement of Alexandria's version of the story was in agreement with that of Hegesippus.[523] Yet the narratives of Epiphanius and Eusebius do *not* agree. For example, James only has access to the Holy Place of the Temple in Eusebius,[524] but in Epiphanius James has access not only to the Holy of Holies, but is even "connected with the priesthood" and wears the diadem of the high priest![525]

For this reason, Robert Eisler put forward the view that Epiphanius had a more complete version of Hegesippus in *his* Eusebius than we have in *our* Eusebius. Christian scribes tampered with both versions, but with *his* more drastically than *ours*. Now only ours exists.[526] The diagram below should help to clarify this idea:

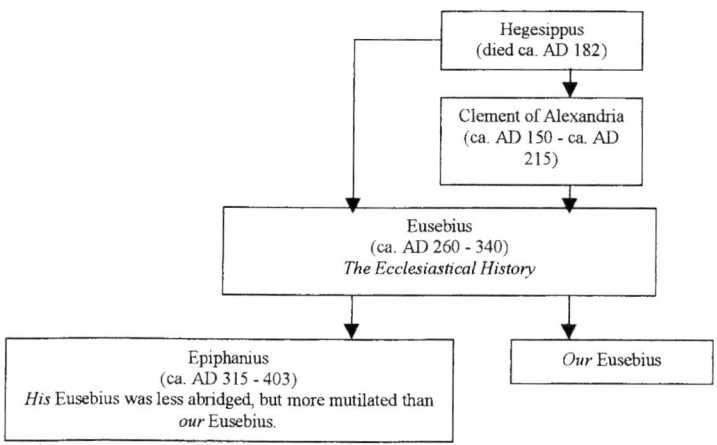

I quote the Hegesippus passage below and, where necessary, comment on it in the notes:

> The charge of the Church passed to James the brother of the Lord, together with the Apostles. He was called the "Just" by all men from the Lord's time to ours, since many are called James, but he was holy from his mother's womb. He drank no wine or strong drink, nor did he eat flesh; no razor went upon his head; he did not anoint himself with oil, and he did not go to the baths. He

---

523. Eusebius, *Ecclesiastical History*, Vol. I, 104-5 (II, 1.3-5), 168-71 (II, 23.3), 176-7 (II, 23.19).
524. Eusebius, *Ecclesiastical History*, Vol. I, 171 (II, 23.6-7).
525. The Syriac and Latin versions of Eusebius, Jerome (ca. AD 342-420), and Andrew of Crete (ca. AD 660-740) also state that James had access to the Holy of Holies and not only to the Holy Place, as Eusebius has it (Eisler, *The Messiah Jesus and John the Baptist*, 541-2).
526. Eisler, *The Messiah Jesus and John the Baptist*, 541, 545.

Chapter 8. James the Righteous

alone was allowed to enter into the sanctuary, [or the Holy Place] for he did not wear wool but linen,[527] and he used to enter alone into the temple and be found kneeling and praying for forgiveness for the people, so that his knees grew hard like a camel's because of his constant worship of God, kneeling and asking forgiveness for the people. So from his excessive righteousness he was called the Just and Oblias, that is in Greek, "Rampart of the people and righteousness," as the prophets declare concerning him.[528] Thus some of the seven sects among the people, who were described before by me (in the Commentaries),[529] inquired of him what was the "gate of Jesus,"[530] and he said that he was the Savior. Owing to this some believed that Jesus was the Christ. The sects mentioned above did not believe either in resurrection or in one who shall come to reward each according to his deeds, but as many as believed did so because of James. Now, since many even of the rulers believed, there was a tumult of the Jews and the Scribes and Pharisees[531] saying that the whole people was in danger of looking for Jesus as the Christ. So they assembled and said to James, "We beseech you to restrain the people since they are straying after Jesus as though he were the Messiah. We beseech you to persuade concerning Jesus all who come for this day of the Passover, for all obey you. For we and the whole people testify to you that you are righteous and do not respect persons. So do you persuade the crowd not to err concerning Jesus, for the whole people and we all obey you. Therefore stand on the battlement [or the pinnacle][532] of the temple that you may be clearly visible on high, and that your words may be audible to all the people, for because of the Passover all the tribes, with the Gentiles also, have come together." So the Scribes and the Pharisees mentioned before made James stand on the battlement of the temple, and they cried out to him and said: "Oh just one, to whom we all owe obedience, since the people are straying after Jesus who was crucified, tell us what is the gate of Jesus?" And he answered with a loud voice: "WHY DO YOU ASK ME CONCERNING THE SON OF MAN? HE IS SITTING IN HEAVEN ON THE RIGHT HAND OF THE GREAT POWER, AND HE WILL COME ON THE CLOUDS OF HEAVEN."[533]

---

527. See below.

528. Eusebius, *The Ecclesiastical History*, Vol. I, 172-3, note 1: "The tradition is obviously confused. Oblias may be an inaccurate transliteration of the Hebrew for 'Rampart of the People,' but the reference to the prophets defies explanation."

529. Eusebius, *The Ecclesiastical History*, Vol. I, 377 (IV, 22.7). According to Hegesippus, the seven sects are the Essenes, Galileans, Hemerobaptists, Masbothei, Samaritans, Sadducees, and Pharisees.

530. Eusebius, *The Ecclesiastical History*, Vol. I, 172-3, note 1: "The 'Gate' of Jesus is ... a puzzle, but it may be connected with the early Christians' name for themselves of 'the Way.'" The "Gate of Jesus" is mentioned again below.

531. Brandon mentions the view of Schwartz that "the Sadducees," which Josephus states that Ananus was a member of (Ant. XX, 199), was replaced in the original account with the "Scribes and Pharisees" to make it agree with the gospels, where the latter are the enemies of Jesus. See S. G. F. Brandon, *Jesus and the Zealots* (New York: Charles Scribner's Sons, 1967), 123 note 1. The "Scribes and Pharisees" are mentioned two more times below.

532. The "battlement" or the "pinnacle" of the Temple (as the word can be translated) was located on the Temple's southeastern corner. This is the side adjacent to the Kidron Valley. See John Marco Allegro, *The Treasure of the Copper Scroll* (New York: Anchor Books, 1964), 103-7, 175, 177.

And many were convinced and confessed at the testimony of James and said, "Hosanna to the Son of David." Then again the same Scribes and Pharisees said to one another, "We did wrong to provide Jesus with such testimony, but let us go up and throw him down that they may be afraid and not believe him." And they cried out saying, "Oh, oh, even the just one erred." And they fulfilled the Scripture written in Isaiah, "Let us take the just man for he is unprofitable to us.[534] Yet they shall eat the fruit of their works."[535] So they went up and threw down the Just, *and they said to one another, "Let us stone James the Just," and they began to stone him since the fall had not killed him,*[536] but he turned and knelt saying, "I beseech thee, O Lord, God and Father, forgive them, for they know not what they do." And *while they were stoning him* one of the priests of the sons of Rechab, the son of Rechabim,[537] to whom Jeremiah the prophet bore witness,[538] cries out saying, "Stop! What are you doing? The Just is praying for you." And a certain man among them, one of the laundrymen,[539] took the club with which he used to beat out the clothes, and hit the Just on the head, and so he suffered martyrdom. And they buried him on the spot by the temple, and his gravestone still remains by the temple. He became a true witness both to Jews and to Greeks that Jesus is the Christ, and at once Vespasian began to besiege them.[540]

Robert Eisler explained his theory regarding the death of James in AD 62 as follows:

---

533. For the explanation why James' answer is in "small caps," see below.

534. This verse is actually from the Wisdom of Solomon 2:12, not from Isaiah.

535. Is. 3:10.

536. According to Robert Eisler, the words in italics here and again immediately below were interpolated in order "to remove the apparent contradiction to Josephus' words 'delivered them up to be stoned,' quite regardless of the improbability thereby imparted into the narrative. For since there were actually no loose stones lying about the marble floor of the temple courts, the Jews ... would have had the difficult task of breaking up the pavement, unless they had brought with them stones concealed in their garments ... But that would of course have defeated their main object, namely, to represent the affair to the Romans as an accident" (Eisler, *The Messiah Jesus and John the Baptist*, 546).

537. Eusebius, *The Ecclesiastical History*, I, 174-5, note 2: "The text of Hegesippus must be corrupt, for Rechabim is only the Hebrew plural and merely repeats the previous phrase."

538. Jer. 35:1-19. Cf. 2 Kgs. 10:15-28, 1 Chr. 2:55. The Rechabites were a religious community founded by Jonadab, the son of Rechab, in the 9th century BC. They followed a nomadic way of life in the desert and resembled the Nazirites (Num. 6:1-21, Jg. 13:4-5, 7, Am. 2:11-2) in that they did not partake of anything that came from the grapevine, which of course included wine. It is interesting that Epiphanius replaced the Rechabite priest of the Hegesippus passage with Symeon, the son of Clopas! See Eusebius, *The Ecclesiastical History*, I, 174-5, note 2.

539. Although the Christians believed rather naively that this individual was a laundryman, who just happened to be there at the time, he was actually one of Ananus' men whose sole purpose was to finish James off, if he survived the fall (Eisler, *The Messiah Jesus and John the Baptist*, 545-6).

540. Eusebius, *Ecclesiastical History*, Vol. I, 170-5 (II, 23.3-18, "small caps" and italics mine). James' death is erroneously placed immediately before the Roman siege of Jerusalem in AD 70. Furthermore, it was actually Vespasian's son Titus, who led the siege. Vespasian was proclaimed emperor in July of AD 69 and stayed in Alexandria until the summer of AD 70. By August/September, AD 70, Jerusalem was in the hands of the Romans. See Schurer, *The History of the Jewish People in the Age of Jesus Christ*, Vol. I, 500-1, 508.

Chapter 8. James the Righteous

On the simple assumption that the longer extract from Hegesippus preserved by Epiphanius has been mutilated even more drastically than in Eusebius, it is possible to make quite good sense of the story of the martyrdom of James. The Sanhedrin condemned him to be stoned ... because he, whom the hierarchy could of course never have recognized as a regular high priest, had actually entered the Holy of Holies and immediately in front of it had pronounced the sacrosanct, secret name of God in the prayer of the Day of Atonement. The sentence of stoning passed upon James and his accomplices (i.e., the priests who officiated with him and conducted him to the sanctuary) at an illicit session of the Sanhedrin convened by the high priest Ananus could not be executed forthwith. The fanatics therefore devised the cunning expedient of inviting the old Saddiq to deliver an address from the roof of the temple to the Jewish and heathen pilgrims streaming in for the feast of the Passover. When he consented AND ONCE MORE AVAILED HIMSELF OF THE OPPORTUNITY TO PROCLAIM JESUS TO THE CROWDS AS 'THE SON OF MAN WHO WAS TO RETURN ON THE CLOUDS OF HEAVEN,'[541] he was pushed over the parapet and dispatched beneath with the wooden club. The object of the whole plot can only have been to enable his enemies to represent to the Romans that the Saddiq had met with an accidental death from a fall through giddiness ... [his enemies maintaining] that the Sanhedrin's solemn death sentences were carried out, so to speak, by the direct avenging intervention of the Deity.[542]

If the identification of James as the Teacher of Righteousness of the Dead Sea Scrolls is correct, then he could not have been a Christian. Nevertheless, the traditional sources tell us that he was the leader of the church after the death of Jesus.[543] This idea probably arose as an accepted belief sometime after the destruction of Jerusalem in AD 70. Among other things, a sect that recorded in 4QpNah[544] that God was *against* "anyone hanged alive upon the tree," i.e., crucified, would certainly not have believed in a *crucified* Messiah. The same thing can be said about the approved use of crucifixion for certain treasonable offenses, which is recorded in the Temple Scroll (11QT).[545] It is highly unlikely that a sect that believed in such a Messiah would have allowed crucifixion to be used as a form of capital punishment.

As will be seen in a later chapter, Jesus left the New Covenant, disobeyed the Torah on many points, and did not keep the Sabbath in a proper manner.

---

541. For the explanation why these words are in "small caps," see below.
542. Eisler, *The Messiah Jesus and John the Baptist*, 545-6 ("small caps" mine).
543. Acts 15:12-21, 21:17-26, Gal. 1:19, 2:9, 12.
544. 4QpNah, frags. 3-4, 1:8-9.
545. 11QT 64:7-13.

James, who adhered to the Torah in as strict a manner as possible, must have thought that his brother was nothing less than a false prophet, who deserved God's curse: "a hanged man is accursed by God."[546] Certainly, John the Baptist, the founder of the New Covenant, would have felt the same way.

The Mandaeans have preserved some interesting traditions in this regard. Even today, they are a small community resident in the Tigris-Euphrates valley. During the first half of the last century, scholars translated and published many of their religious texts, which may have preserved some traditions from the first century AD. When the West discovered them in the 17th century, they were erroneously called the "Christians of St. John," because they venerate to this day John the Baptist as a great prophet. However, they regard Jesus as a liar and a deceiver, i.e., a false Messiah! These beliefs show up most clearly in their book titled the *Sidra d'Yahya* (i.e., *The Book of John*). [547]

In the Hegesippus passage, the establishment leaders make a curious request of James. It is inexplicable as a Christian addition. They ask him "we beseech you to *restrain* the people since they are straying after Jesus as though he were the Messiah"[548] and, further, they urge him to "*persuade the crowd not to err concerning Jesus.*"[549] These are extraordinary demands to make, if we accept the Christian view that James was the leader of the church. Why would they expect James to preach *against* Jesus? Brandon asked the following pertinent question: "How ... could the Scribes and the Pharisees have chosen the leader of the Christian community itself to give such public instruction as would lead the people away from a view of Jesus which they (the Scribes and Pharisees) regarded as dangerous?"[550] Davies reasoned that since the scribes encouraged James to preach against Jesus, "we must infer their assumption that he was free to do so if he had so chosen."[551] The fact is that James was not really a Christian and would have had no desire to endorse a crucified Messiah.

---

546. Dt. 21:23, cf. 11QT 64:12.

547. Edwin M. Yamauchi, *Pre-Christian Gnosticism*, 2nd ed. (Grand Rapids: Baker Book House, 1983, 117-42, 229-33; E. S. Drower, "Mandaean Polemic," *Journal of the School of Oriental and African Studies* 25 (1962): 438-48. The important passages of the *Sidra d'Yahya* have been translated into English by G. R. S. Mead, *The Gnostic John the Baptizer* (London: John M. Watkins, 1924), 29-96; idem, "The Gnostic John the Baptizer," *The Quest* (October 1925): 1-24; idem, "The First Gnostic Community of John the Baptizer," *The Quest* (January 1926): 179-97.

548. Eusebius, *The Ecclesiastical History*, Vol. I, 173 (II, 23.10, italics mine).

549. Eusebius, *The Ecclesiastical History*, Vol. I, 173 (II, 23.10-1, italics mine).

550. Brandon, *The Fall of Jerusalem and the Christian Church*, 98.

551. A. Powell Davies, *The First Christian: A Study of St. Paul and Christian Origins* (New York: Farrar, Straus, ad Cudahy, 1957), 180.

Nevertheless, the passage states that many of the people, who were gathered together at the festival, were "straying after Jesus as though he were the Messiah."[552] This was *as a result* of James' testimony about Jesus.[553] But if James was not really a Christian, they could not have been converted to the faith on account of anything that he said. The view that James converted many to the faith must be a Christian addition to the passage.

The Passover was always a time of increased political agitation. What is likely to have occurred is that among the jubilant "Jewish and heathen pilgrims streaming in for the feast of the Passover"[554] there was a large body of Christians that instigated a "tumult of the Jews."[555] They enthusiastically demonstrated in word and deed that Jesus was the Messiah. As will be seen in a latter chapter, the Christian movement had gained considerable popular support by this time in preaching their crucified Jesus to the masses.

The establishment leaders probably *expected* James to preach *against* Jesus from the pinnacle of the Temple, but they were well aware that nothing he said would really have quieted the crowd down. Their sole purpose was to bring about his death and to make it look like an unfortunate accident to the Romans. However to their surprise, James uttered some sort of revelation about the Messiah to come, which was pleasing to the *whole* crowd, but at the same time, did *not* sanction the crucified Messiah of the Christians.

Because of the evidence of the Dead Sea Scrolls, the part of Robert Eisler's statement quoted in "small caps" above is no longer correct. Although the Christians certainly interpreted the "Son of Man" passage in Daniel[556] as a reference to Jesus,[557] there is no evidence that a Messianic interpretation was ever given to this passage by the Dead Sea Scroll sect.[558] Also, James' revelation, as recorded in the Hegesippus passage above (the part quoted in "small caps" also), must be one of the Christian additions to the text.

As a result of James' words, the already ecstatic Passover celebrants became excited even more and the establishment leaders became enraged beyond measure. Ananus gave the signal and one of his men,[559] who had been hiding on

---

552. Eusebius, *The Ecclesiastical History*, Vol. I, 173 (II, 23.10).
553. Eusebius, *The Ecclesiastical History*, Vol. I, 171 (II, 23.8-10), 173-5 (II, 23.12-4).
554. Eisler, *The Messiah Jesus and John the Baptist*, 545. It is quoted above.
555. Eusebius, *The Ecclesiastical History*, Vol. I, 173 (II, 23.10).
556. Dan. 7:13-4.
557. Mk. 13:24-7, Mt. 24:29-31, Lk. 21:25-8, Mt. 25:31-46.
558. The pseudepigraphal book known as Enoch contains a section titled the Parables (Chapters 37-71), which refers to the "Son of Man." However, this section is the only section of Enoch that was *not* found among the Dead Sea Scrolls (Schurer, *The History of the Jewish People in the Age of Jesus Christ*, Vol.III.1, 252-4, 257-9).

the pinnacle, pushed James down from the height. Since he was not killed when he hit the pavement below, he was finished off with a wooden club by another of Ananus' men. It is interesting to note that a third or fourth century AD Jewish source states that when the Sanhedrin sentenced someone to be stoned, but had lost its power to execute the penalty, the person *"either falls from the roof* or a wild beast tramples him to death."[560]

Although left curiously unmentioned in the Hegesippus passage, the Romans probably had to intervene to put down the disturbance, which would have gotten way out of hand after James uttered his revelation from the pinnacle. Josephus' passage about James, as we now have it, is also silent about any Roman intervention. Perhaps in the original versions of both passages this was not the case.

During the period from ca. AD 59 to AD 62 James and the New Covenant had considerable influence and support, especially among the lower priests. In ca. AD 59, a conflict broke out between the high priests and the regular priests, who were allied with the "leaders of the populace of Jerusalem." Sometimes actual fighting even broke out in the streets. Furthermore, the high priests arrogantly sent slaves to the threshing floors to steal the tithes, which belonged to the regular priests. Josephus states that the result of this was "that the poorer priests starved to death."[561] Brandon had suggested that James "was closely identified with the ordinary priests in their antagonism towards the sacerdotal aristocracy."[562]

This popularity probably gave James the political strength necessary to make his bold move against the priestly establishment. It also allowed him to escape any significant retribution from it at least during the high priesthood of Joseph Cabi (AD 61-2) and the governorship of Porcius Festus (AD 60-2), who died in office.[563] However, this handling of the affair changed when Ananus, whom Josephus states was "rash in his temper and unusually daring,"[564] became the establishment high priest in AD 62. He summoned James to appear for trial before the Sanhedrin. The latter must have appeared before the body voluntarily. Robert Eisler explained the situation as follows:

---

559. For the likely identity of this individual, see the chapter titled *Saul, Paul, the Pillars, and the Twelve*.
560. Eisler, *The Messiah Jesus and John the Baptist*, 544 (italics mine).
561. Ant. X, 179-81; cf. 205-7.
562. Brandon, *Jesus and the Zealots*, 121.
563. Ant. XX, 182-97; War II, 271-2.
564. Ant. XX, 199.

Chapter 8. James the Righteous

> The high priest Ananus ... profited by the interregnum in the Roman governorship after the death of Festus, when the commander was a mere military tribune, more easily accessible to a bribe, to summon a meeting of the Sanhedrin, a thing which he had no right to do without the governor's consent. The tribunal itself then summoned James and his companions, put them on trial, and condemned them to be stoned for impiety. It nowhere appears from Josephus, as has been rashly assumed by those who wished to discover an irreconcilable contradiction between his account and that of Hegesippus, that Ananus and his followers were in a position to execute this sentence forthwith. We can well imagine that the Roman military tribune could be moved to connive at the assembling of seventy worthy elders, without taking cognizance of the fact, since it was evidently a session of a purely academic character. But it is a very far cry from that to the toleration of an arbitrary arrest by the Sadducees of a popular leader with a considerable following even among the loyalists, as appears from the strong protest subsequently made to Albinus, or indeed to the toleration of the lynching of such a man by the excited mob. There is not the least reason to suppose that the deputy-governor would have committed himself so far as that. The execution of the death sentence must accordingly have been brought about by a mischievous ruse, the nature of which the account of Hegesippus permits us clearly to recognize.[565]

According to Josephus, the illegality of Ananus was that he convened the Sanhedrin without the consent of the governor. Now, although in all likelihood the Sanhedrin still had the power to judge infringements of the Mosaic Law under the Roman occupation,[566] it is highly unlikely that it could utilize capital punishment on anyone who was found guilty of a severe infringement of it.[567] Capital punishment was reserved exclusively to the Romans.[568] The first governor, Coponius, came to Judaea with "full powers, including the infliction of capital punishment."[569] None of the later governors lost these powers. The only exception to this appears to have been that the Sanhedrin could use capital punishment on any foreigner who went beyond the stone balustrade into the inner court of the Temple. This court was reserved only for Jews.[570]

Josephus simply meant that the Sanhedrin had to obtain the governor's approval before it could meet for any reason; and in this case, it was for a trial

---

565. Eisler, *The Messiah Jesus and John the Baptist*, 543-4.
566. Richard W. Husband, *The Prosecution of Jesus* (Princeton: Princeton University Press, 1916), 32-3, 150-1.
567. Husband, *The Prosecution of Jesus*, 178-81; William R. Wilson, *The Execution of Jesus* (New York: Charles Scribner's Sons, 1970), 7-14.
568. One of the penalties that the Jews could inflict was the forty lashes — actually thirty-nine lashes less one (Dt. 25:3, II Cor. 11:24). Thirty-nine lashes were administered so that, if there were a miscount, forty lashes would never be exceeded.
569. War II, 117-8; cf. Ant. XVIII, 2.

regarding an infringement of the Mosaic Law. Ananus did not do this, because the new governor (Albinus, AD 62-4) had not yet arrived to take office. As punishment for convening an illegal session of the Sanhedrin, King Agrippa took the high priesthood away from him and gave it to Jesus, the son of Damnaeus (ca. AD 62-3).

Although Robert Eisler did not mention this point, the Day of Atonement episode must have occurred during the high priesthood of Joseph Cabi (AD 61-2)[571] in September-October of AD 61 (the Jewish month of Tishri). James' death must have occurred at the Passover during Ananus' high priesthood in March-April of AD 62 (the Jewish month of Nisan).

The affair concerning James is alluded to in 1QpHab 11:2-8. The Biblical verse being commented on is the following:

> *Woe to the one [the Wicked Priest] who gives his neighbors drink, pouring out his venom/anger, even making (them) drunk, so that God looks (with condemnation) upon their festivals* [Hab. 2:15].[572]

The Biblical verse is interpreted as follows:

> The explanation of this concerns the Wicked Priest [Ananus], who pursued the Teacher of Righteousness [James], making him reel[573] with his venomous anger on the House of his revelation,[574] because[575] at the festive

---

570. Ant. XV, 417; War V, 193-4; VI, 125-6. An inscription in more than one language, which was placed at regular intervals in the stone balustrade, stated the following: "No foreigner is to enter within the balustrade and embankment around the sanctuary. Whoever is caught will have himself to blame for his death which follows" (Josephus, Bk. VIII, pp. 202-3, note d).

571. Ant. XX, 196; cf. War VI, 114.

572. The Biblical Book of Habakkuk actually has "so that (*you*) look upon their *nakedness*," but 1QpHab quotes the verse as "so that *God* looks upon their *festivals*." The early translation of Dupont-Sommer appears to have been correct here. See A. Dupont-Sommer, *The Dead Sea Scrolls-A Preliminary Survey*, trans. By Margaret Rowley (Oxford: Basil Blackwell, 1952), 27.

573. The Hebrew word here can mean a number of things: to swallow up (an idiom for to destroy), to engulf, to overwhelm, to confuse, to confound, and to make reel. For the translation of the Hebrew word as "making ... reel" here and later in the passage, see See William H. Brownlee, *The Midrash Pesher of Habakkuk* (Missoula: Society of Biblical Literature, 1979), 181-2.

574. The Hebrew for "on the House of his revelation" is usually translated as "to or at the house of his exile," but see L. H. Silberman, "Unriddling the Riddle, A Study in the Structure and Language of the Habakkuk Pesher," *Revue de Qumran* III, no. 11, 1961), 357-60; and Brownlee, *The Midrash Pesher of Habakkuk*, 182-5. The word for "revelation" is a Piel infinitive derived from the Hebrew root that means "reveal" or "uncover." In Silberman's view, the pronominal suffix ("his") refers to God.

575. The Hebrew letter translated here as "because" usually means "and" or "but," but less often, it can be translated as a conjunction. See Ps. 60:13 and Gen. 15:2 as examples of this usage. See W. L. Holladay, ed., *A Concise Hebrew and Aramaic Lexicon of the Old Testament* (Grand Rapids: Eerdmans, 1971), 85.

period of rest of the Day of Atonement, he [James] had appeared in splendor unto them,[576] making them reel [577] and causing them to stumble on the Day of Fasting, (which in their error is) the Sabbath of their rest.

How did the scribe who wrote 1QpHab interpret the biblical passage (Hab. 2:15)? He seems to have recognized two main events being revealed that were each connected with a festival. If we take them in the actual order of their occurrence (this is made clear by the word "because" in the commentary portion), the first one is then as follows:

> Woe to the one (the Wicked Priest) who gives his neighbors drink, ... even making (them) drunk, so that God looks (with condemnation) upon their festival.

The commentary portion applicable to it is as follows:

> The explanation of this [is that] ... at the festive period of rest of the Day of Atonement, he (the Teacher of Righteousness) had appeared in splendor unto them, making them reel and causing them to stumble on the Day of Fasting, (which in their error is) the Sabbath of their rest.

The "drink" that the Wicked Priest gave was false teaching. The schismatics became "drunk" in wholeheartedly supporting it instead of the true teaching of the Teacher of Righteousness.

James was killed because several months before he had entered the Temple Holy of Holies on the Day of Atonement to make atonement for Israel, as the rightful high priest. Only the authorized high priest, whose appointment was made by Herod Agrippa II beginning from ca. AD 59,[578] was allowed to enter this inner room and only on this holy day.[579] James had been dressed in the special linen attire when he entered and exited the Holy of Holies. As the passage states, "he had appeared in splendor unto them."

The special vestments of the high priest were usually made up of eight items. They were as follows: the linen coat, the linen breeches, the linen girdle, the linen turban, the breastplate, the ephod (a sort of apron with shoulder-straps), the blue robe, and the gold headband fastened to the turban.[580]

---

576. For the translation of the Hebrew verb as "had appeared in splendor unto them," see Brownlee, *The Midrash Pesher of Habakkuk*, 185-6.
577. Those who believe that the verb translated here and above as "making ... reel" should be translated as "destroy" (literally, "swallow up"), have to explain what use the next verb "causing ... to stumble" would then have.
578. Schurer, *The History of the Jewish People in the Age of Jesus Christ*, Vol. II, 231-2.
579. Schurer, *The History of the Jewish People in the Age of Jesus Christ*, Vol. II, 275-6, 296.

However, when he performed the Day of Atonement ritual,[581] which included entering the Holy of Holies twice,[582] he only wore the linen garments (i.e., the first four items listed above).[583] It is worth mentioning that Hegesippus stated that James "alone was allowed to enter into the sanctuary [i.e., the Holy Place as opposed to the Holy of Holies preserved by Epiphanius], *for he did not wear wool but linen....*"[584]

The Dead Sea Scroll sect utilized a solar calendar of 364 days and the Jewish establishment of the time utilized the traditional Jewish lunar calendar of 354 days.[585] Because of the different calendars, the holy days and even the Sabbaths would not fall on the same days.[586] James' entry into the Holy of Holies most likely occurred according to the solar calendar used by the New Covenant. According to the solar calendar, the Day of Atonement always occurred on the 10th of Tishri and on Friday.[587] What was the day according to the Jewish establishment? If I have interpreted the phrase "(which in their error is) the Sabbath of their rest" correctly,[588] it was the Sabbath for them, which always fell in both calendars on Saturday (i.e., the seventh day). Therefore, for the New Covenant, the day was Friday and the Day of Atonement. For the Jewish establishment, the day was Saturday and the Sabbath.

Because the schismatics were Israelites (i.e., they had been baptized by John the Baptist or one of his successors), they should have wholeheartedly

---

580. Ex. 28-29; Ant. III, 159-87; War V, 231-6.

581. For a description of the Day of Atonement ritual, see Lev. 16:1-34. Num. 29:7-11 specifies the additional sacrifices for the Day of Atonement in addition to the "sin offering of atonement." Cf. 11QT 25:10-16, 26:3-13, 27:1-10.

582. The high priest entered the Holy of Holies first to make atonement for the priests (Lev. 16:11-4) and second for the people (Lev. 16:15-22).

583. Lev. 16:4, 23-4, 32.

584. Eusebius, *Ecclesiastical History*, Vol. I, 171 (II, 23.6, italics mine).

585. Schurer, *The History of the Jewish People in the Age of Jesus Christ*, Vol. I, 587-601.

586. Michael Wise, Martin Abegg, Jr., & Edward Cook, *The Dead Sea Scrolls: A New Translation* (Harper Collins: New York, 1996), 296-301, 318. Regarding the Sabbath, "the Qumran calendars attached the Sabbath, like all the other festivals, to a specific date. Thus even the Sabbaths, which might have offered a moment's peace, instead became battlegrounds for the calendar wars" (pg. 318).

587. Schurer, *The History of the Jewish People in the Age of Jesus Christ*, Vol. I, 600-1.

588. The Hebrew word for "Fasting" could be in the construct *or* absolute state. This allows for the possibility that there are *two* two-word construct chains rather than one long four-word chain. One of the benefits of interpreting the phrase "Sabbath of their rest," as actually referring to the Sabbath, is that it reduces the number of references to the Day of Atonement in the passage. In the usual interpretation, the Day of Atonement is referred to *four* times. They are the "festive period of rest," the "Day of Atonement," the Day of Fasting," and the "Sabbath of ... rest." This is unnecessary repetition. Nevertheless, it is not incorrect to refer to the Day of Atonement, as the "Sabbath of ... rest." In fact, this holy day is called "a sabbath of solemn rest" (Lev. 16:31). Work was not allowed on the Day of Atonement or the Sabbath (Lev. 16:29-31, 23:26-32, Ex. 31:15, 35:2), but only on the Day of Atonement was "self-denial" (i.e., fasting) practiced (Brownlee, *The Midrash Pesher of Habakkuk*, 188).

accepted the day as the Day of Atonement and the Teacher of Righteousness as the legitimate high priest. However, they regarded the day as the Sabbath and the establishment high priest as the legitimate office holder. As a consequence of their position, the action taken by the Teacher of Righteousness caused them to "reel" and "stumble" and "God look[ed] (with condemnation) upon their festival (referring to the Sabbath)."

The second main event the scribe recognized as being revealed in the biblical passage (Hab. 2:15) is as follows:

> Woe to the one (the Wicked Priest) ... pouring out his venom/anger ... so that God looks (with condemnation) upon their festival.

The commentary portion applicable to it is as follows:

> The explanation of this concerns the Wicked Priest, who pursued the Teacher of Righteousness, making him reel with his venomous anger on the House of his revelation....

Because of the Wicked Priest's (Ananus') "venom/anger," he "pursued" the Teacher of Righteousness (James), finally "making him reel" by having him pushed down from the pinnacle of the temple on the day that was accepted by the establishment as the Passover.[589] The "House" is the Temple and "his revelation" is James' utterance about the coming Messiah to the crowd below. It could be said that Ananus "pursued" him from the time he assembled the Sanhedrin trial as the establishment high priest to when he had James pushed off the pinnacle of the Temple.[590] The phrase "making him reel" would be an appropriate allusion to the way he was pushed to his death. It is interesting that according to Robert Eisler James' fall was supposed to appear to the Romans as "an accidental death from a fall through giddiness."[591] As a result of this evil deed, "God look[ed] (with condemnation) upon their festival (referring to the Passover)."

Those arrested with James,[592] who had "officiated with him and conducted him to the Sanctuary,"[593] probably met their ends in some clandestine manner as

---

589. Because of the different calendars, we do not know if the Passover when James met his death was accepted as such by the New Covenant.
590. Although it was not Ananus himself who pushed James down from the pinnacle of the Temple, he *did* give the order, via a signal, to one of his men to do so. The meaning of the phrase "making him reel with his venomous anger" is that the push to death came quickly and suddenly like a snake's lethal bite!
591. Eisler, *The Messiah Jesus and John the Baptist*, 546, the phrase is quoted above.
592. Josephus mentions them as "certain others" (Ant. XX, 200).

well. Their deaths are probably alluded to among the Wicked Priest's other sins in lQpHab 8:13, 9:1, 9:9-10, 12:6, and 12:8-9.

Another important document is the Commentary (Pesher) on Psalm 37 (4QpPs^a). It contains the following passages:

> The interpretation of it [Ps. 37:14-5] concerns the wicked ones of Ephraim and Manasseh who will attempt to lay a hand on the Priest and his partisans in the time of testing that is coming upon them. But God will save them from their hand, and afterwards they [i.e., the wicked of Ephraim and Manasseh] will be given into the hand of the ruthless ones of the Gentiles for judgment.[594]

> *The wicked man observes the righteous man and seeks [to kill him. But the LO]RD [will not abandon him into his hand and will not let him be co]ndemned when he is judged.*[595] The interpretation of it concerns the Wicked [Pri]est who ob[serv]es the [Teach]er of Righteous[ness and seeks] to kill him [because of the legal decisions] and the Torah that he sent to him,[596] but God will not ab[andon him into his hand] and will not [let him be condemned when] he is judged. But as for [him (i.e., the Wicked Priest), God will] pay [him] his due, giving him into the hand of the ruthless ones of the Gentiles to wreak [vengeance] on him.[597]

This Commentary was most likely composed prior to James' trial before the Sanhedrin. Its states that "Ephraim and Manasseh ... *will attempt* to lay a hand on the Priest [i.e., the Teacher of Righteousness] and his partisans [i.e., his priestly accomplices] in the time of testing that is coming upon them" (italics mine). It further states "God *will not abandon him* into [the Wicked Priest's] hand and *will not let him be condemned* when he is judged" (italics mine).

These predictions in 4QpPs^a turned out to be very wrong. The Teacher of Righteousness was *not* saved, but in fact was condemned and killed. It also predicted that the *Gentiles* would punish the Wicked Priest (i.e., Ananus). This turned out to be wrong as well, because it was the Idumaeans who killed Ananus at the end of AD 67 or the beginning of AD 68.[598] The Idumaeans were people

---

593. Eisler, *The Messiah Jesus and John the Baptist*, 545.

594. 4QpPs^a, frags. 1-10, 2:18-20. That Ephraim and Manasseh would "be given into the hand of the ruthless ones of the Gentiles for judgment" could be understood as a prediction of the destruction of Jerusalem and the Temple in AD 70.

595. Ps. 37:32-3.

596. Perhaps the "[legal decisions] and the Torah that [James] sent to [the Wicked Priest, Ananus]" was a copy of 4QMMT, which the former sent to Herod Agrippa I probably in AD 41. See the chapter titled *Herod, Agrippa I, and Agrippa II*. He may very well have sent another copy to Simon Cantheras, the son of Boethus, who was the establishment high priest at the time (AD 41-?) selected by Agrippa I (Ant. XIX, 297, 313).

597. 4QpPs^a, frags. 1-10, 4:7-10.

who lived south of Judea. Hyrancus I (135-104 BC) forced them to be circumcised and accept the Torah.[599] In the first century AD, they considered themselves to be Jews.[600] Unbaptized Idumaeans would have been considered to be Ephraim and/or Manasseh by the New Covenant, not Gentiles. It is not known how the sect would have reinterpreted these passages in order to avert the accusation of false prophecy in the document.

Ananus met his end when the Idumaeans killed him and the high priest Jesus, the son of Gamalas. They both became the most notable leaders in the first period of the revolt.[601] The Idumaeans were allies of the Zealots. After the latter opened the gates of the city for the former, they went on a rampage of looting and killing. Josephus gives us the following information:

> The fury of the Idumaeans being still unsatiated ... they went in search of the high priests; it was for them that the main rush was made, and they were soon captured and slain. Then, standing over their dead bodies, they scoffed at Ananus for his patronage of the people and at Jesus for the address which he delivered from the wall. They actually went so far in their impiety as to cast out the corpses without burial, although the Jews are so careful about funeral rites that even malefactors who have been sentenced to crucifixion are taken down and buried before sunset.[602]

Josephus further states that Ananus and Jesus were "seen cast out naked, to be devoured by dogs and beasts of prey."[603] Ananus' fate is alluded to in 1QpHab 9:8-12:

> The explanation of this [Hab. 2:8b] concerns the Wicked Priest [Ananus] whom, because of the iniquity committed against the Teacher of Righteousness [James] and his partisans, God delivered into the hand of his enemies to humble him with a destroying blow in bitterness of soul because he had done wickedly to His Elect One.

Furthermore, another fragmentary passage from the same scroll mentions "the priest, who rebelled [and trans]gressed the statutes of [God ... (any

---

598. War IV, 314-8.
599. Ant. XIII, 255-8; War I, 63.
600. War IV, 270-84.
601. War II, 563-8, IV, 158-61, 238, 314-25.
602. War IV, 314-8.
603. War IV, 324-5.

supposed translation here is very conjectural) to] punish him on account of wicked judgements. They inflicted on him the horrors of evil diseases and vengeance on his corpse of flesh."[604] It should be noted that Ananus "rebelled" from the sect as the leader of the schismatics.

The writer of 1QpHab gives a brief summarization of Ananus' wicked career in the following passage:

> *Woe to him who builds a town on murder and founds a city on crime! Is it not from the Lord of Hosts? The people labor for fire and the nations exhaust themselves for nothingness* [Hab. 2: 12-3]. The explanation of this word concerns the Preacher of Lies [Ananus] who led many astray to build his town of vanity[605] on murder and to found a congregation on deceit for the sake of his glory, that many people might labor in his service of vanity and conceive in [wo]rks of deceit; that their labor might be for nothingness, that they might come to judgment of fire for having insulted and outraged the Elect Ones of God.[606]

---

604. 1QpHab 8:16-9:2.

605. Ananus did indeed undertake some building operations in the winter of AD 66-7. Josephus states the following: "In Jerusalem Ananus the high-priest and all the leading men who were not pro-Roman *busied themselves with the repair of the walls* and the accumulation of engines of war. In every quarter of the city missiles and suits of armour were being forged; masses of young men were undergoing a desultory training; and the whole was one scene of tumult" (War II, 648-9, italics mine). Nevertheless, I think Schonfield's suggestion is more on the mark: "It is not by any means certain that the commentator is thinking here of Jerusalem, or of an actual city. Rather does he appear to be speaking metaphorically of an edifice of lies built up by the Prophesier of Untruth [i.e., the Preacher of Lies] to serve his own ends, thus leading his wretched dupes to their damnation in assisting him in his fell designs against God's Elect." See Schonfield, *Secrets of the Dead Sea Scrolls*, 101.

606. 1QpHab 10:5-13.

LEADERS OF THE DEAD SEA SCROLL SECT

LEADERS BEFORE THE NEW COVENANT

Leader	Date of Appearance	Title	Comments
Mattathias	167 BC	Root of Planting.	The founder of the Hasmonaeans.
Zadok (Saddok)	ca. 24 BC	Messiah of Aaron.	He wrote the Temple Scroll.

LEADERS OF THE NEW COVENANT

Leader	Date of Appearance	Title	Comments
John the Baptist	4 BC	Teacher of Righteousness, Unique Teacher, Unique One, Messiah of Aaron.	The founder of the New Covenant.
Dositheus	AD 35	Interpreter, Prophet.	The leader of a schism that was eventually healed.
James the Righteous	AD 35	The Teacher of Righteousness, Messiah of Aaron.	He was killed through the machinations of Ananus in AD 62.
Symeon, the son of Clopas	AD 62	Rod, Star, Interpreter of the Torah, Voice of the Teacher, Chief Priest.	The leader of the mass exodus to the land of Damascus in AD 65-6.

FUTURE LEADER OF THE NEW COVENANT

Leader	Date of Appearance	Title	Comments
Identity unknown.	ca. AD 75	Prince of All the Congregation, Sceptre, Branch of David, he who arises to teach righteousness in the end of days, Messiah of Aaron and Israel	As the military leader, he will take back the Holy Land from the second "Nebuchadnezzar." As the high priest, he will officiate in a simple Tabernacle, as the proper Temple would not be completed for 60 years.

Chapter 9. The Hymn Scroll

Dupont-Sommer describes the hymns found in the Hymn Scroll (1QH) as follows:

> With their lofty mysticism these songs are outpourings of the soul in which the author expresses in turn his adoration of God, his total submission to the divine will, his love for the Most High God and his hatred of Belial, his despair and his sudden leaps of infinite hope, his mortal anguish at the thought of the imminent end of the world, and his triumphant joy in the dreams of eternal bliss in the bright company of the angels.[607]

Several of the hymns describe someone who is in exile and someone who is in prison, undergoing severe mental and physical distress. In an earlier chapter, it was determined that John the Baptist went into exile in the land of Damascus from AD 6 to AD 28. On this basis, it would be possible to conclude that John wrote the sections of the hymns that describe an exile. On the other hand, it was also mentioned previously that Herod Antipas had John executed at the fortress of Machaerus in AD 35. Although there is no good reason to question the gospel evidence that John was kept in prison for a period of time before he was finally put to death,[608] there is still a problem in concluding that he could have written the sections of the hymns that describe imprisonment.

First of all, he was never released from prison at any time before his death. Secondly, even if the gospel evidence could be trusted that John was able to

---

607. A. Dupont-Sommer, *The Essene Writings from Qumran*, trans. By G. Vermes (Gloucester: Peter Smith, 1973), 199.
608. Mt. 11:2-6, 14:5, Mk. 6:20.

correspond with someone from prison,[609] it would be a far cry from that to believe that he would have been allowed to dictate the hymns to an associate. Even more unlikely would be the idea that he would have been given parchment and writing implements to do the task himself. Therefore, it must be concluded that John could not have written the sections of the hymns that describe imprisonment.

Given that the hymns are imbued with the doctrines and experiences of John, how can we explain how the hymns were written? Dupont-Sommer was on the right track when he made the following statement:

> It is even possible that the hymns in which the Teacher of Righteousness seems to express himself are, in reality, *not his own work but that of one of his disciples speaking as it were through the teacher's mouth*. With regard to the Gatha of the Avesta, it is in the same way open to question whether, in spite of the 'I,' the author was Zoroaster himself or one of his very early disciples. A similar hypothesis is not to be excluded with respect to the Hymns. But be this as it may, the collection is at least to be considered as an ancient work of the sect, authentically and profoundly stamped with the personality and doctrine of the Teacher.[610]

It is likely that all of the hymns were written not by John the Baptist, but by his successor, James the Righteous, "speaking as it were through [John's] mouth." In a later chapter, the idea is put forward that John the Baptist and James the Righteous, both being Messiahs of Aaron, were considered earthly embodiments of the heavenly being Melchizedek. Therefore, the idea would not be far fetched that the sectarians believed James could have "remembered" the private experiences of John.

I would now like to quote a few sections of the hymns below:

> And they, they [have led] Thy people [astray].
> [Prophets of falsehood] have flattered [them with their wor]ds
> and interpreters of deceit [have caused] them [to stray];
> and they have fallen to their destruction for lack of understanding
> for all their works are in folly.
> For (I was) despised by them,
> and they had no esteem for me when Thou didst show Thy power in me.
> For they drove me out of my land like a bird from its nest
> and all my companions and friends were driven far from me
> and they considered me a broken vessel.

---

609. Mt. 11:2-6.
610. Dupont-Sommer, *The Essene Writings from Qumran*, 200 (italics mine).

Chapter 9. The Hymn Scroll

And they, interpreters of falsehood and seers of deceit,
devised plans of Belial against me,
bartering Thy Law which Thou hast graven in my heart
for the flattering words (which they speak) to Thy people.
And they stopped the thirsty from drinking the liquor of Knowledge,
and when they were thirsty they made them drink vinegar,
so that God saw their error,
so that they were in madness at their feasts,
so that they were taken in their nets.[611]
For Thou, O God, despisest every thought of Belial:
it is Thy counsel that shall remain,
and it is the thought of Thy heart that shall stand fast for ever.[612]

And shaking and trembling seized me
and all my bones cracked,
and my heart melted like wax before fire
and my knees slipped like water descending a slope;
for I remembered my faults
and the unfaithfulness of my fathers
when the wicked arose against Thy Covenant
and the wretched against Thy word.
And I said, It is because of my sins
that I am abandoned far from Thy Covenant.
But when I remembered the might of Thy hand
together with the greatness of Thy mercy
I rose up and stood,
and my spirit stood upright in the face of the blows.
For [I] leaned on Thy favours
and on the greatness of Thy mercy.[613]

And I, I was the butt of the in[sults of] my [en]emies,
an object of quarrelling and dispute to my companions,
an object of jealousy and wrath to those who had entered my Covenant,
an object of murmuring and contention to those I had gathered together.
And [all who a]te my bread
lifted the heel against me.
And all who joined my assembly
spoke evil of me with a perverse tongue.
And the men of my [counc]il rebelled

---

611. I have restored the lines in italics from Dupont-Sommer's original translation. See A. Dupont-Sommer, *The Dead Sea Scrolls-A Preliminary Survey*, trans. by E. Margaret Rowley (Oxford: Basil Blackwell, 1952), 74. Also see Florentino Garcia Martinez and Eibert J. C. Tigchelaar, eds., 2 vols., *The Dead Sea Scrolls Study Edition* (Leiden: Brill, 1997), Vol. 1, 168-9 (12:11-2). See also the translation of 1QpHab 11:2-8 in the chapter titled *James the Righteous*.

612. Dupont-Sommer, *The Essene Writings from Qumran*, 211-2 (Hymn H, 4:9-13).
613. Dupont-Sommer, *The Essene Writings from Qumran*, 213-4 (Hymn H, 4:33-37).

and murmured round about.
And they went among the sons of misfortune
slandering the Mystery which Thou hast sealed within me;
but it is in order that my [wa]y might be exal[ted],
and it is because of their sin
that Thou hast hidden the fount of understanding
and the secret of truth.
And their heart was nought but misfortunes,
they conceived [schemes of Be]lial.
They opened a treacherous tingue
like serpents' venom which causes thorns to grow,
and like creatures which creep in the dust
they hurled [poison] of asps like arr[ow]s [of the Pit]
impossible to charm.
And it became an incurable pain
and a malignant wound in Thy servant's members,
so that [the spirit] staggered
and strength was consumed
and he could not stand.[614]

And to (my) distress they added still more.
They shut me up in the darkness
and I ate the bread of groaning
and my drink was in tears without end.
For my eyes were darkened because of sorrow
and my soul (was plunged) in bitterness every day.
Fea[r] and sadness encompassed me
and shame covered (my) face.
And my br[ead] was changed into quarrelling
and my drink into an enemy that entered my bones
causing the spirit to stagger
and consuming strength.
They changed the works of God by their transgression
according to the Mysteries of sin.
For [I was] bound with unbreakable cords
and with chains impossible to sunder,
and a stou[t] wall [held me shut up]
[and] bars of iron and door[s of bronze].
[And] my [pri]son was like the Abyss without [...]
[and the bonds of Be]lial bound my soul without any [escape ...].[615]

[And confu]sion was on me
as (on) those who go down into Sheol,

---

614. Dupont-Sommer, *The Essene Writings from Qumran*, 216-7 (Hymn J, 5:22-9).
615. Dupont-Sommer, *The Essene Writings from Qumran*, 217-8 (Hymn J, 5:33-9).

and among the dead my spirit searched.
For [my] li[fe] reached to the Pit
[and] my soul fainted [within me]
day and night without rest.
And it grew like a burning fire shut up in [my bones],
and its flame devoured for many days
exhausting (my) strength for (long) times
and destroying my flesh for (long) seasons.
And the billows flew [towards me]
and my soul was oppressed within me unto destruction,
for my strength had vanished from my body.
And my heart ran out like water
and my flesh melted like wax,
and the strength of my loins was prey to terror
and my arm was undone from its ligaments
without any power to move my hand.
[And] my [fo]ot was caught in irons
and my knees slipped like water
and I could make no step;
and walking was forbidden to the nimbleness of my feet
[for my arms were] bound with chains of staggering.
But Thou hast made the tongue in my mouth to grow without going back,
and there was none to [sil]ence (it).
[For the tong]ue of the disciple[s] (was given) to me
to restore the spirit of them with the word.
The lips of [falsehood] were all of them dumb [...].[616]

---

616. Dupont-Sommer, *The Essene Writings from Qumran*, 229-30 (Hymn O, 8:29-36).

Chapter 10. The Kittim

The Chaldean conquerors of the biblical book of Habakkuk are reinterpreted in 1QpHab, as referring to an invading people called the "Kittim." Although this designation was once thought to be referring to the Greek Seleucid kingdom of Syria in the second century BC, there is now no disagreement among scholars that it refers to the Romans.

It is stated that the Kittim "sacrifice[617] to their standards and ... their weapons of war are their objects of veneration."[618] There is simply no evidence that the Greeks worshipped their standards, but there is much evidence that the Romans did so.[619] It is also stated that they "*come*[620] from (remote) shores of the sea, to dev[our a]ll the peoples as an eagle, but without being satisfied."[621] That

---

617. The Hebrew verb here is an active participle. "The period of time indicated by ... a participle active, either as an attribute or predicate, must be inferred from the particular context." Quoted from E. Kautzsch, ed., *Gesenius' Hebrew Grammar*, 2nd Eng. ed. (Oxford: Clarendon Press, 1985), 356.

618. 1QpHab 6:4-5. The Romans actually did sacrifice to their standards in the temple court in August/September of AD 70 (War VI, 316).

619. A. Dupont-Sommer, *The Essene Writings from Qumran*, trans. By G. Vermes (Gloucester: Peter Smith, 1973), 343-4.

620. The Hebrew verb form that is used when referring to the Kittim is almost always in the imperfect tense. This tense can be translated in three major ways. The tense can mean that the actions of the Kittim are repetitive in the past (i.e., they *used to do* such and such), they are continuing into the present (i.e. their actions are *unfinished*), or they are expected in the future (i.e., they are *predictions*). See William H. Brownlee, *The Midrash Pesher of Habakkuk* (Missoula: Scholars Press, 1979), 23; Burrows, *The Dead Sea Scrolls*, 140-2; Kautzsch, ed., *Gesenius' Hebrew Grammar*, 313-9, 335-62. Verbs in italics in this chapter are in the Hebrew imperfect tense and can be translated in one of the three major ways described above.

621. 1QpHab 3:11-2.

they came "from (remote) shores of the sea" is a very appropriate description of the Romans, but a very inappropriate one for the Syrian Greeks.[622]

The major disagreement has to do with whether the Romans were the Republican Romans (from before 27 BC when Caesar Augustus became Emperor) or the Imperial Romans (after 27 BC). It has been generally accepted by most scholars that the Republican Romans are being referred to and that the Kittim specifically refers to the forces of General Pompey, who captured Jerusalem in 63 BC. Some scholars believe that 1QpHab was composed shortly before the Romans captured Jerusalem and others believe it was composed shortly after the capture.[623]

There is no valid reason why the Imperial Romans could not be referred to by the designation "Kittim," especially when an attack was actually expected by them in the near future or when they were in the very process of attacking. This could have been the case in the entire period from before the beginning of the revolt in the summer AD 66 to before Jerusalem was finally in the hands of the Romans in August/September of AD 70.[624] In the summer of AD 66, the priests stopped accepting sacrifices and gifts from all foreigners. Josephus has this to say about the incident. Note particularly the portion in italics:

> Eleazar, son of Ananias the high-priest, a very daring youth, then holding the position of captain,[625] persuaded those who officiated in the Temple services to accept no gift or sacrifice from a foreigner. *This action laid the foundation of the war with the Romans; for the sacrifices offered on behalf of that nation and the emperor were in consequence rejected.* The chief priests and the notables earnestly besought them not to abandon the customary offering for their rulers, but the priests remained obdurate. Their numbers gave them great confidence, supported as they were by the stalwarts of the revolutionary party; but they relied above all on the authority of the captain Eleazar.[626]

The Jews were certainly familiar with the Romans legions and their methods of warfare and these experiences could have been utilized in the writing of 1QpHab. A short list of some of their experiences will suffice to prove this:

---

622. Dupont-Sommer, *The Essene Writings from Qumran*, 344.
623. Miller Burrows, *The Dead Sea Scrolls* (New York: The Viking Press, 1955), 123-42.
624. War II, 409-10; VI, 407, 435.
625. The "captain of the Temple" ranked just below the high priest. See Joachim Jeremias, *Jerusalem in the Time of Jesus* (Philadelphia: Fortress Press, 1969), 147, 160-2.
626. War II, 409-10 (italics mine).

1. In 63 BC, Pompey laid a three month siege on Jerusalem and twelve thousand Jews were massacred when the wall was finally breached.[627]
2. In 37 BC, Herod the Great and the Roman legate of Syria, C. Sosius, laid another siege on Jerusalem and much bloodshed followed after the walls were finally taken.[628]
3. After the death of Herod the Great (4 BC), Varus, the legate of Syria, had to come to Judea with two legions and auxiliaries to put down a revolt of the Jews (called the War of Varus). The city of Sepphoris in Galilee was burnt and its inhabitants were turned into slaves. Emmaus, whose inhabitants fled from the Romans, was also burnt. Before Varus returned to Antioch, he had two thousand rebels crucified.[629]
4. Cestius Gallus, the legate of Syria, commanded the first Romans troops against the Jews in AD 66 for the purpose of crushing the Jewish revolt. He marched his army from Antioch to Ptolemais and captured several rebellious cities and towns on his way to Jerusalem. However, while endeavoring to capture the holy city, for some reason, he unexpectedly ordered a retreat. This soon turned into a tragic defeat for the Romans and a joyous victory for the Jews.[630]

The following additional information about the Kittim can be found in 1QpHab:

- They "[ar]e swift and mighty in war."[631]
- They "*march* ... to smite and plunder the cities of the land (or earth)."[632]
- "Their whole purpose is to do evil, and with cunning and deceit they *conduct* themselves with all peoples."[633]
- They "*thresh* the land with their horses and with their beasts."[634]
- "They *deride* the great and *scorn* the esteemed [and] at kings and commanders they *mock* and *scoff* at great armies."[635]
- They "*gather* their wealth with all their loot as fish of the sea."[636]

---

627. Ant. XIV, 69-73; War I, 138-53.
628. Ant. XIV, 468-86; War I, 342-357.
629. Ant. XVII, 286-98; War II, 66-79.
630. War II, 499-555.
631. 1QpHab 2:12-3.
632. 1QpHab 3:1-2.
633. 1QpHab 3:5-6.
634. 1QpHab 3:10.
635. 1QpHab 4:2-3.
636. 1QpHab 6:1-2.

- "They *distribute* their yoke and their tax burden, their food, upon all the peoples, year by year, in order to lay waste many lands."[637]
- They "*destroy* many with the sword; youths, mature men, and old men, women and (even) children."[638]

Furthermore, the following information about the "commanders of the Kittim"[639] can be found in 1QpHab:

- They "*scorn* the fortresses of the peoples and with derision *laugh* at them."[640]
- "With a great army they *surround* them to take them, and with dread and terror they *are given* into their hand."[641]
- "Through the counsel of [their] house of guil[t]," they "*come*, each one after the other, to devastate the [earth]."[642]

The cryptic designation "house of guilt" probably refers to "the house or family of the Caesars."[643]

In the above passages from 1QpHab, the Kittim are described as being aggressive and ruthless conquerors of the earth. The passages are evidently based on the Jews' past and present experiences with the Romans, as well as their knowledge of how other nations had suffered and were continuing to suffer under the "dominion of the Kittim."[644]

The only allusion to the Kittim that "predicts" a strictly future event is 1QpHab 9:4-7. I quote the passage below:

> And as for that which He [God] said, *Because thou hast plundered many nations all the remnant of the peoples will plunder thee* [Hab. 2:8a], the explanation of this concerns the last priests of Jerusalem who heap up riches and gain by

---

637. 1QpHab 6:7-8.
638. 1QpHab 6:10-2.
639. 1QpHab 4:5, 10. The Hebrew word that is translated "commanders" can also mean "governors" or "generals." See Brownlee, *The Midrash Pesher of Habakkuk*, 78, 81. Another possibility is "rulers." See Maurya P. Horgan, *Pesharim: Qumran Interpretations of Biblical Books* (Washington: Catholic Biblical Assoc. of America, 1979), 14.
640. 1QpHab 4:6-7.
641. 1QpHab 4:7-8.
642. 1QpHab 4:11-3.
643. G. R. Driver, *The Judaean Scrolls-The Problem and a Solution* (New York: Schocken Books, 1965), 200-1.
644. 1QpHab 2:13-4.

plundering the peoples. But in the end of days, their riches, together with their plunder, will be delivered into the hands of the army of the Kittim; for it is they [the Kittim] who are *the remnant of the peoples.*

It states that in the "end of days" the Kittim will obtain the "riches" and the "plunder" belonging to "last priests of Jerusalem."

An event closely corresponding to this "prediction" actually occurred in August/September of AD 70. I quote the passage from Josephus below:

> During those same days, one of the priests named Jesus, son of Thebuthi, after obtaining a sworn pledge of protection from Caesar, on condition of his delivering up some of the sacred treasures, came out and handed over from the wall of the sanctuary two lampstands similar to those deposited in the sanctuary, along with tables, bowls, and platters, all of solid gold and very massive; he further delivered up the veils, the high-priests' vestments, including the precious stones, and many other articles used in public worship. Furthermore, the treasurer of the temple, by name Phineas, being taken prisoner, disclosed the tunics and girdles worn by the priests, an abundance of purple and scarlet kept for necessary repairs to the veil of the temple, along with a mass of cinnamon and cassia and a multitude of other spices, which they mixed and burnt daily as incense to God. Many other treasures also were delivered up by him, with numerous sacred ornaments; those services procuring for him, although a prisoner of war, the pardon accorded to the refugees.[645]

The money and other valuables that had flowed into the Temple before the war by way of the Temple tax,[646] priestly dues, voluntary offerings, gifts, and private funds were enormous.[647] The writer of 1QpHab believed these accumulations were nothing but the "riches and gain" collected by a corrupt priesthood "plundering the peoples" and deposited in a polluted Temple. The "last priests of Jerusalem" gladly took the peoples' wealth under the pretense of being a legitimate priesthood, which in the view of the New covenant they were not.

---

645. War VI, 387-91.
646. Although the priestly establishment required the Temple tax of a half-shekel to be paid on an *annual* basis by every male Jew of twenty years old or more, the Dead Sea Scroll sect had an ordinance that required it to be paid only once in a lifetime. See Emil Schurer, *The History of the Jewish People in the Age of Jesus Christ*, Vols. I, II, III.1, III.2, rev. and ed. by Geza Vermes, et al. (Edinburgh: T. & T. Clark, 1973/87), Vol. II, 270-2 and Florentino Garcia Martinez and Eibert J. C. Tigchelaar, eds., 2 vols., *The Dead Sea Scrolls Study Edition* (Leiden: Brill, 1997), Vol. 1, 308-9 (4Q159, frags. 1 col. II + 9).
647. Emil Schurer, *The History of the Jewish People in the Age of Jesus Christ*, Vol. II, 279-81.

Two occurrences (or perhaps one ongoing occurrence) are described by Josephus and should be mentioned here. The high priests are actually accused of stealing the tithes from the regular priests! I quote the passages below:

> At this time King Agrippa [II] conferred the high priesthood upon Ishmael, the son of Phabi [ca. AD 59-61]. There now was enkindled mutual enmity and class warfare between the high priests, on the one hand, and the priests and the leaders of the populace of Jerusalem, on the other. Each of the factions formed and collected for itself a band of the most reckless revolutionaries and acted as their leader. And when they clashed, they used abusive language and pelted each other with stones. And there was not even one person to rebuke them. No, it was as if there was no one in charge of the city, so that they acted as they did with full license. *Such was the shamelessness and effrontery which possessed the high priests that they actually were so brazen as to send slaves to the threshing floors to receive the tithes that were due to the priests, with the result that the poorer priests starved to death.* Thus did the violence of the contending factions suppress all justice.[648]

> Now the high priest Ananias [ca. AD 47-59, but very influential afterwards] daily advanced greatly in reputation and was splendidly rewarded by the goodwill and esteem of the citizens; for he was able to supply them with money: at any rate he daily paid court with gifts to Albinus [Roman governor, AD 62-4] and the high priest [Jesus, son of Damnaeus, ca., AD 62-3]. *But Ananias had servants who were utter rascals and who, combining operations with the most reckless men, would go to the threshing floors and take the tithes of the priests; nor did they refrain from beating those who refused to give. The high priests were guilty of the same practices as his slaves, and no one could stop them. So it happened at that time that those of the priests who in olden days were maintained by the tithes now starved to death.*[649]

Nearly the same thing that is said of the "last priests of Jerusalem" is said of the Wicked Priest (i.e., Ananus). I quote the passage below:

> The explanation of this [Hab. 2:5-6] concerns the Wicked Priest who was called by the name of truth at the beginning of his rise to power; but when he ruled over Israel, his heart rose up and he abandoned God and betrayed the precepts because of riches, and he stole and heaped up the riches of the men of violence [i.e., the schismatics][650] who rebelled against God. And he took the riches of the peoples to add to himself guilty sin. And he followed the ways of a[bo]mination in every kind of unclean defilement.[651]

---

648. Ant. XX, 179-81 (italics mine).
649. Ant. XX, 205-7 (italics mine).

How did the Wicked Priest steal and amass the riches of the schismatics? The New Covenant required their professed members in the Council of the Community to give all their property and wages over to it to support the sect (1QS 6:18-23). At a later date, it required its members to give a percentage of their wages over to care for those in need (CD 14:12-6). In the same way, the Wicked Priest probably required his followers to provide funds to his organization in order to carry out his nefarious deeds. So under the pretense of being a legitimate leader, he was only stealing the wealth of his supporters in the view of the New Covenant.

Like the other "last priests of Jerusalem," Ananus, when he was the official high priest for three months in AD 62, oversaw the collection of the money and other valuables that streamed in from all over in order to fill the coffers of a polluted Temple. As the passage states,[652] "he took the riches of the peoples to add to himself guilty sin."

All of Ananus' evil activities are referred to under the general statement that "he followed the ways of abomination in every kind of unclean defilement."[653]

The "last priests of Jerusalem" would also include the revolutionary party of the Zealots,[654] who made the Temple their place of residence throughout the war period.[655] Their leaders were priests.[656] Josephus states that one of them (i.e., Eleazer, the son of Simon or Gion[657]) "had in his hands the Roman spoils, the money taken from Cestius [Gallus], and a great part of the public treasure...."[658] In a speech made by Ananus to a general assembly of the people in Jerusalem, the following statement was made about the Zealots:

---

650. The designation "men of violence," which can also be translated as "men of apostasy" (see Brownlee, *The Midrash Pesher of Habakkuk*, 140-2) refers to the schismatics. They "rebelled against God" (1QpHab 8:11-2) just as the Wicked Priest "rebelled [and trans]gressed the statutes of [God ...]" (1QpHab 8:16-7). Cf. "the "company of violence/apostasy" in Martinez and Tigchelaar, *The Dead Sea Scrolls Study Edition*, Vol. 1, 174-5 (1QH 14:5). The "men of war" mentioned in CD 20:14, which is derived from Dt. 2:14, 16 and refers to the rebellious Israelites in the wilderness with Moses for forty years, is a reference to the schismatics as well.
651. 1QpHab 8:9-13.
652. 1QpHab 8:12.
653. 1QpHab 8:12-3.
654. War II, 651, IV 160-1.
655. War IV, 151-2, 204, 216, 228, 577-8; V, 5, 9-10.
656. War IV, 224-6.
657. War IV, 225.
658. War II, 564.

> Is it not enough to bring tears to the eyes to see on the one hand in our Temple courts the very votive offerings of the Romans, *on the other the spoils of our fellow countrymen who have plundered and slain the nobility of the metropolis*, massacring men whom even the Romans, if victorious, would have spared?[659]

In the italicized statement in the above passage, the Zealots (referred to as "our fellow countrymen" by Josephus) are accused of stockpiling "spoils" in the Temple from pillaging and killing the "nobility of the metropolis." This entire hoard seized by the Zealots clearly corresponds to 1QpHab 9:4-7 (quoted above) about the "last priests of Jerusalem" accumulating "*riches and gain by plundering the peoples.*"

Rhoads concluded his discussion of the Zealots with the following statement:

> Of the fate of the Zealots we cannot be certain. Although their numbers were small, they participated in the defense of the city against the Roman siege.... However, since the Zealots included priests among their number, they may have been among those priests who held out in the sanctuary after the temple had been burned ... and who bargained for their lives with the temple treasures ... [see War VI, 387-91 quoted above]. Others apparently fled to the forest of Jardes [near the fortress of Machaerus on the east side of the Dead Sea] which was later overrun by the Romans....[660]

The references to the Kittim in the War Scroll (1QM) can also be easily explained, if it were composed in the first century AD. The scroll refers to the "Kittim of Asshur"[661] and something about the "Kittim in Egypt" (there is a lacuna in the text here).[662] In 65 BC, Syria became a Roman province and was ruled by legates (governors) from then on.[663] After AD 23, four legions were stationed there.[664] Likewise, in 30 BC, Egypt became a Roman province and from then on a prefect (governor) ruled it.[665] After AD 23, two legions were stationed there.[666] The Kittim of Asshur were the Roman legions stationed in

---

659. War IV, 181-2 (italics mine).
660. David M. Rhoads, *Israel in Revolution: 6-74 C. E.* (Philaddelphia: Fortress Press, 1976), 109-10.
661. 1QM 1:2 in Dupont-Sommer, *The Essene Writings from Qumran*, 169.
662. 1QM 1:4 in Dupont-Sommer, *The Essene Writings from Qumran*, 170. See also Martinez and Tigchelaar, *The Dead Sea Scrolls Study Edition*, Vol. 1, 112-3.
663. Schurer, *The History of the Jewish People in the Age of Jesus Christ*, Vol. I, 135-6, 243-66.
664. Schurer, *The History of the Jewish People in the Age of Jesus Christ*, Vol. I, 362 note 42; S. A. Cook, et al., eds. *The Cambridge Ancient History*, Vol. X (Cambridge: Cambridge University Press, 1952), 224.
665. Cook, et al, eds. *The Cambridge Ancient History*, Vol. X, 239-41; Schurer, *The History of the Jewish People in the Age of Jesus Christ*, Vol. I, 358.
666. S. A. Cook, et al, eds. *The Cambridge Ancient History*, Vol. X, 224, 286.

Syria and the Kittim in Egypt (if that is what is mentioned here) were the legions stationed in that country. There is really no need to identify the former group with the Greek Seleucids of Syria (312-129 BC) and the latter with the Greek Ptolemies of Egypt (304-44 BC), as is sometimes done.[667] The Roman Emperor is called the "king of the Kittim" in 1QM,[668] which is an appropriate designation for him, as the overall ruler of the Roman Empire.

---

667. H. H. Rowley, *The Teacher of Righteousness and the Dead Sea Scrolls* (Manchester: Manchester University Press, 1957), 139-40; Idem, *The Zadokite Fragments and the Dead Sea Scrolls* (Oxford: Blackwell, 1952), 64-6.
668. 1QM 15:2 in Dupont-Sommer, *The Essene Writings from Qumran*, 191.

Chapter 11. The Lion of Wrath

The Jewish historian Josephus characterizes Gessius Florus, the last governor of Judea before the revolt (AD 64-6), as the most corrupt and violent of all the previous governors:

> ...Gessius ... ostentatiously paraded his outrages upon the nation, and, as though he had been sent as hangman of condemned criminals, abstained from no form of robbery or violence. Was there a call for compassion, he was the most cruel of men; for shame, none more shameless than he. No man ever poured greater contempt on truth; none invented more crafty methods of crime. To make gain out of individuals seemed beneath him: he stripped whole cities, ruined entire populations, and almost went the length of proclaiming throughout the country that all were at liberty to practice brigandage on the condition that he received his share of the spoils.[669]

In May AD 66, Florus robbed the temple treasury of 17 talents. Because of this and his handling of the riots in Caesarea, the patience of the Jews came to an end. They raised a commotion against his rule, hurled insults at him, and ridiculed his greed by passing a basket around asking for donations, "as for an unfortunate destitute."[670]

The next day, despite the supplications of the chief priests and notable citizens, he delivered the city over to his soldiers for plunder and murder. The troops entered houses and slaughtered everyone found inside, they killed those who were running through the streets, and pillaged everything in sight. Many

---

669. War II, 277-9; cf. Ant. XX, 252-8.
670. War II, 290-9.

were brought before Florus and after first being scourged, they were crucified. Josephus states that about 3600 people (including women and children) were massacred.[671] However, most important for our purpose is the following statement of Josephus:

> The calamity was aggravated by the unprecedented character of the Roman cruelty. For Florus ventured that day to do what none had ever done before, namely, *to scourge before his tribunal and nail to the cross men of equestrian rank, men who, if Jews by birth, were at least invested with the Roman dignity.*[672]

The equestrian order was the second one in Roman society and the emperor controlled admission.[673] The order was open to all Roman citizens, who were eighteen years of age, born free, of good character and possessed a census rating of 400,000 sesterces ($20,000). Entrance into it carried with it the right to wear certain insignia, which included a gold ring and a narrow purple stripe on your tunic. Most importantly, individuals in the order usually filled the civil and military posts of the emperor. Almost all the governors of Judea were of the equestrian order.[674]

This deed of Florus described in the passage from Josephus quoted above is also referred to in 4QpNah, frags. 3-4, 1:6-9. Florus is there called the "Lion of Wrath," (i.e., the third lion)[675] and these Jews of the Roman equestrian order, who were crucified, are called "Seekers-After-Smooth-Things." I quote the passage below:

> The interpretation of it [Nah. 2:13b] concerns the Lion of Wrath, [who brings about a sentence of] death on the Seekers-After-Smooth-Things, when he hangs men up alive [upon the tree, as was the penalty for such as these] in

---

671. War II, 301-11.
672. War II, 308 (italics mine).
673. The order of rank was as follows: the senatorial nobility, the equestrians or knights, the freedmen, and the plebs.
674. S. A. Cook, ed., et al., *The Cambridge Ancient History*, Vol. X (Cambridge: Cambridge University Press, 1952), 185-8, 215-7; H. Mattingly, *Roman Imperial Civilization* (London: Edward Arnold, 1959), 13, 40, 76, 120, 125 ff., 151, 204; W. S. Davis, *A Day in Old Rome* (New York: Biblio and Tannen, 1963), 139-59; Emil Schurer, *The History of the Jewish People in the Age of Jesus Christ*, Vols. I, II, III.1, III.2, rev. and ed. by G. Vermes, et al. (Edinburgh: T. & T. Clark, 1973/87), Vol. I, 357-61.
675. For the specific identity of the first two lions, see the chapter titled *The First Ones*. They are both Gentiles. If 4QpNah is to be consistent, then the Lion of Wrath (i.e., the third and last lion) should be a Gentile also. However, the usual interpretation is that the Lion of Wrath is Alexander Jannaeus — a Jewish king! See Schurer, *The History of the Jewish People in the Age of Jesus Christ*, Vol. III.1, 430-2.

Israel before. For regarding anyone hanged alive upon the tree, [it] reads: *Behold I am against yo[u] say[s the Lord of Hosts].*

The Seekers-After-Smooth-Things crucified by Florus must have been schismatics from the New Covenant (i.e., they had been baptized by John the Baptist or one of his successors). The statement that it was "the penalty for such as these *in Israel* before" implies that it was happening *in Israel* again at the time the document was written. Therefore, 11QT 64:7-13 applied to them.[676] This passage states basically that traitors that went over to the Gentiles were to be hung alive on trees until dead (i.e., crucified). God's curse (i.e., "anyone hung on a tree is accursed of God and men")[677] applied to them as well and this is indirectly alluded to by the biblical statement "behold I am against you says the Lord of Hosts."[678] By becoming Roman knights, they would have been considered traitors of the worst kind.

The passage from 4QpNah also alludes to an event from the past when the same death sentence was used on other Seekers-After-Smooth-Things. As it states, crucifixion was "the penalty for such as these in Israel before." This is an allusion to Alexander Janaeus' crucifixion of 800 Pharisees in 88 BC. As we saw in an earlier chapter, these Pharisees' treasonable correspondence with the Syrian king Demetrius III Eucerus (ca. 95-88/7 BC) was already alluded to in 4QpNah, frags. 3-4, 1:1-3.

The 4QpNah passage continues as follows:

> *I shall burn up yo]ur [abundance in smoke,] and the sword will devour your lions. And [I] shall cut off its [pr]ey [from the earth,] and [the voice of your messengers] will no [longer be heard.*[679] The inter]pretation of it: "your abundance" are the detachments of his army th[at are in Jerusale]m and "his lions" are his great ones [... who perished by the sword] and "his prey" are the riches that the [prie]sts of Jerusalem have amas[sed][680] which they will deliver [... E]phraim, will be given Israel [...] (col. 2). And "his messengers" are his couriers/clerks, whose voice will no longer be heard by the Gentiles.[681]

---

676. 11QT 64:7-13 significantly modifies Dt. 21:22-3, which refers to hanging a man on a tree *after* being put to death.
677. 11QT 64:12, cf. Dt. 21:23. Dt. does not have "and men."
678. Nah. 2:14.
679. Nah. 2:14.
680. 1QpHab 9:4-5 mentions the "last priests of Jerusalem who heap up riches and gain by plundering the peoples."
681. 4QpNah, frags. 3-4, 1:9-2:1.

The Lion of Wrath is still being referred to this portion of the passage and it can be explained as follows:

1. "Your abundance" is interpreted as "the detachments of his army that are in Jerusalem" and "his lions" as "his great ones ... who perished by the sword." These may be allusions to the fate of the Roman cohort left by Florus on his withdrawal to Caesarea. It was massacred by the Jewish rebels in August/September of AD 66.[682]
2. "His prey" is interpreted as "the riches that the priests of Jerusalem have amassed...." As mentioned above, Florus did indeed rob the Temple treasury of seventeen talents and Josephus later states that he desired to get even more.[683]
3. "His messengers" is interpreted as "his couriers/clerks, whose voice will no longer be heard by the Gentiles." These individuals could have been letter carriers in Florus' army or members of his staff handling correspondence.[684] This is probably a "prediction" of the fate of Florus, who was expected to meet up with a terrible end in the near future. It should be noted here that although there is more the one messenger, there is only *one* "voice" and it is Florus.

Another passage from 4QpNah alludes to another event in this period:

> Yet she too w[ent] into exile, [into captivity. Even] her children, too, are dashed to pieces on every street corner, and for her honored ones they will cast lots, and all [her] g[rea]t [ones were bound] in fetters.[685] The interpretation of it concerns Manasseh in the last period, whose reign over Is[rael] will be brought down [...] his wives, his children, and his infants will go into captivity. His warriors and his honored ones [will perish] by the sword.
>
> [You too will be drunk] and you will be hidden.[686] The interpretation of it concerns the wicked ones of E[phraim ...] whose cup will come after Mannasseh [...].[687]

The earlier document, 4QpPs^a, refers to all the unbaptized "Jews" as "Ephraim"[688] or "Ephraim and Manasseh."[689] 4QpNah now understands Manasseh[690] as a separate group from Ephraim.[691] Manasseh receives its

---

682. War II, 329-32, 449-56.
683. War II, 329-32.
684. Schurer, *The History of the Jewish People in the Age of Jesus Christ*, vol. I, 370.
685. Nah. 3:10.
686. Nah. 3:11a.
687. 4QpNah, frags. 3-4, 4:1-6.
688. 4QpPs^a 1:24.
689. 4QpPs^a 2:18.
690. 4QpNah, frags. 3-4, 3:9, 4:1, 3, 6.

punishment first and is followed by Ephraim. A careful examination of Josephus' statements during the early war period can identify the events that are being alluded to in the above quoted passage. The designation "Manasseh" refers to the peace party. It included Herod Agrippa II, his family members, his generals, as well as other establishment people, who left Jerusalem by necessity or otherwise in the period from AD 64-6.[692] As the passage states, their rule over Israel was ended and they went into "captivity" with their "wives," "children," and "infants." Furthermore, their "warriors" and "honored ones" were killed during the fierce fighting between the peace party and the rebels that occurred in that same period.[693] After the defeat of Cestius Gallus in Nov. AD 66, the people assembled in the Temple to appoint new leaders and generals to conduct the war.[694] This new leadership is what goes under the designation "Ephraim whose cup will come after Manasseh." They are also called the "Seekers-After-Smooth-Things in the end of days."[695] In the same way as the past Seekers-After-Smooth-Things had made treasonable communications with the Gentiles, so Ephraim is now accused of secretly desiring to do the same thing with the Romans.[696] This is why the Zealots and the Idumaeans endeavored to execute all the leaders and notable individuals towards the end of AD 67 and early in AD 68.[697] 4QpNah was probably written in early AD 67.

---

691. 4QpNah, frags. 3-4, 1:12, 2:2, 8, 3:5, 4:5.
692. War II, 406-7, 556-8.
693. War II, 417-24, 523-6.
694. War II, 562-8.
695. 4QpNah, frags. 3-4, 2:2.
696. War IV, 244-58.
697. War IV, 305-17, 326-44, 353-65.

Chapter 12. Herod, Agrippa I, and Agrippa II

4Q Testmonia (4QTest) is an important document from the first century AD. The first lines consist of a brief introduction that contains Deut. 5:28-9. This is followed by three biblical quotations and each one refers to a different messianic figure. The first quotation (Dt. 18:18-9) refers to a Prophet like Moses, the second one (Num. 24:15-7) refers to a royal Messiah, and the third one (Dt. 33:8-11) refers to a priestly leader. Finally, the last lines of the document are a quote from the sectarian *Psalms of Joshua*, which quotes Jos. 6:26 and offers an interpretation of it. I quote the last lines of 4QTest below:[698]

> At the time when Joshua finished praising and giving thanks with his praises, he said, *"cursed be the man who builds this city; with his firstborn shall he lay its foundation and with his last-born shall he set up its gates."*[699] And, behold, a man accursed, the one of Belial, shall arise to be a fowl[er's sn]are[700] to his people, and destruction [or terror] to all his neighbors. And he shall arise [...] that the two of them may be instruments of violence.[701] And they shall rebuild[702] [this city and will es]tablish for it a wall and towers, to create a refuge of wickedness [and a great evil] in Israel,[703] and a horrible thing in Ephraim,[704] and in

---

698. This document was first published by John M. Allegro in *Discoveries in the Judean Desert, Qumran Cave IV*, Vol. V (Oxford: Clarendon Press, 1968), 57-60. The quotation follows Allegro's translation unless otherwise noted. Also see Florentino Garcia Martinez & Eibert J. C. Tigchelaar, eds., *The Dead Sea Scrolls Study Edition*, 2 vols. (Leiden: Brill, 1997), Vol. 1, 354-7 (4Q175), cf. Vol. 2, 750-3 (4Q379, frag. 22 col. II).

699. Josh. 6:26 (in italics).

700. Ps. 91:3: "For he will deliver you from the snare of the fowler and from deadly pestilence." Also, see Hos. 9:8 where it says of the false prophet: "A fowler's snare is on all his ways."

701. The phrase "instruments of violence" appears to be taken from Gen. 49:5: "Simon and Levi are brothers; weapons [or instruments] of violence are their swords."

Judah[705] [... and they] shall cause pollution in the land, and great contempt among the sons of [Jacob, and they shall pour out bl]ood like water on the rampart of the daughter of Zion, and in the boundary of Jerusalem.[706]

This last passage seems to refer to three individuals — a father (the "cursed ... man") and his two sons — the oldest and the youngest, if we take Josh. 6:26 literally. Also, in the Masoretic text of Jos. 6:26 after "this city" is added "Jericho." However, since the version of Jos. 6:26 that was utilized in this document omits Jericho, it would appear that the writer was able to identify the city with Jerusalem.

It seems clear that there must be some relationship between the three biblical quotations (i.e., Deut. 18:18-9, Num. 24:15-7, and Deut. 33:8-11) and the last quotation from the *Psalms of Joshua*. The three righteous persons alluded to by the biblical passages are set in opposition to the three despised person alluded to in Jos. 6:26 and its commentary.

That no scholar has identified the three despised persons with members of the Herodian dynasty is difficult to understand. A good case can be made that the "cursed ... man" is Herod the Great, "his firstborn" is Herod Agrippa I, and "his last-born" is Herod Agrippa II. There is evidence that Herod and Agrippa I were considered to be messianic figures by their supporters.[707] As will be seen

---

702. The translation of "they shall rebuild" is literally "they shall return and build," which is Allegro's translation of it, but see Francis Brown, *The New Brown-Driver-Briggs-Gesenius Hebrew and English Lexicon* (Peabody: Hendrickson Publishers, 1979), 998 (shall return and build = shall build again = shall rebuild).

703. "Israel" here refers to all "Jews" baptized by John the Baptist (see pp. 16-7, 20). They are mentioned again a few lines down as the "sons of Jacob [i.e., Israel]."

704. "Ephraim" here refers to the land areas in the north representing the northern kingdom of Ephraim (or Israel) during the divided monarchy in the Old Testament. It does *not* refer to all "Jews" not baptized by John the Baptist, as is usually the case. The reason is that the writer of the document would not have described the rebuilding of Jerusalem by the three accursed men as a "horrible thing" to the unbaptized "Jews." "The basis for the use of 'Ephraim' to designate Israel was provided by the unfortunate outcome of the Syro-Ephraimite War (734-732), in which the N kingdom of Israel saw itself robbed of its peripheral territories, which were turned into the Assyrian provinces of Dor, Megiddo, and Gilead; and Israel was reduced to its central territory, the old settlement area of the tribes of Manasseh and Ephraim. Since Ephraim had long since overshadowed Manasseh in its importance ... , the designation of the rump state as Ephraim suggested itself automatically and endured, too, when this remnant was made into the Assyrian province of Samaria ten years later" ("Ephraim," *The Interpreter's Dictionary of the Bible*, 4 vols. (New York: Abingdon, 1962).

705. "Judah" here refers to the land areas in the south representing the southern kingdom of Judah during the divided monarchy in the Old Testament.

706. Cf. 4QpPs^a, frags. 1-10, 3:7: "the princes [of wickedn]ess who have oppressed His [God's] holy people ... will perish like smoke that is los[t in the w]ind."

707. Robert Eisler, *The Messiah Jesus and John the Baptist*, ed. by A. H. Krappe (London: Methuen & Co., 1931), 136-40, 547-50, 554-61, 578-9.

below, Agrippa II was still alive when this document was written (AD 66) and the development of Messianic ideas connected with him were still premature.

The Prophet, the royal Messiah, and the priestly leader alluded to by the biblical quotations were three messianic leaders of the New Covenant. In AD 66, the Prophet was someone unknown to us,[708] the royal Messiah was probably still to come, and Symeon, the son of Clopas, was the priestly leader.

Herod, Agrippa I, and Agrippa II were all designated kings and had the power to appoint high priests to the temple.[709] Below is a chart that lists the land areas that Herod, Agrippa I, and Agrippa II had jurisdiction over. It should be noted that all three of them had some jurisdiction over land areas in the south (designated as "Judah" in the commentary to Jos. 6:26) and in the north (designated as "Ephraim" in the commentary).[710]

Land Area	Did Herod have jurisdiction?	Did Agrippa I have jurisdiction?	Did Agrippa II have jurisdiction?
Southern lands designated as "Judah" in 4QTest.			
Idumea	Yes	Yes	No
Judea	Yes	Yes	"Curator of the Temple" in Jerusalem only, which included the power to appoint high priests.[a]
Perea (southern half)	Yes	Yes	The cities of Julias and Abila with fourteen neighboring villages only.[b]
Northern lands designated as "Ephraim" in 4Qtest.			
Abila (near Damascus)	No	Yes	Yes
Gaulanitis	Yes	Yes	Yes
Trachonitis	Yes	Yes	Yes
Auranitis	Yes	Yes	Yes
Batanea	Yes	Yes	Yes
Galilee	Yes	Yes	The cities of Tiberias and Tarichea with their surrounding districts only.[c]
Samaria	Yes	Yes	No
Perea (northern half)	Yes	Yes	No

a. Ant. XX, 222.
b. Ant. XX, 159; War II, 252.
c. Ant. XX, 159; War II, 252.

---

708. Dositheus, who was the Prophet, was probably dead.
709. For a complete list of the high priests and whom they were appointed by, see Emil Schurer, *The History of the Jewish People in the Age of Jesus Christ*, Vols. I, II, III.1, III.2, rev. and ed. by G. Vermes, et al. (Edinburgh: T. & T. Clark, 1973/87), vol. II, 29-32.
710. For excellent summaries of the lives of Herod, Agrippa I, and Agrippa II, see Schurer, *The History of the Jewish People in the Age of Jesus Christ*, vol. I, pp. 287-329 (Herod), pp. 442-54 (Agrippa I), and pp. 471-83 (Agrippa II).

Herod the Great, who ruled from 37 BC to 4 BC, initiated several building projects in Jerusalem and the surrounding area,[711] but his most famous and ambitious project was the rebuilding of the temple.[712] Furthermore, he ordered numerous executions during his reign. They included the Hasmonaean nobility and their supporters,[713] Aristobulus III,[714] Joseph (the husband of Herod's sister Salome),[715] Hyrancus II,[716] Mariamme,[717] Alexandra,[718] Costobar (the second husband of Salome) and the sons of Babas,[719] the ten conspirators,[720] Alexander and Aristobulus,[721] some Pharisees,[722] the rabbis Judas and Matthias and their followers,[723] and Antipater.[724]

Agrippa I (AD 41-4) endeavored to build a new northern wall in Jerusalem, but it could not be completed. The emperor ordered the construction to be stopped.[725] This is clearly alluded to in the above quoted passage: "they (i.e., Herod, Agrippa I, and Agrippa II) shall rebuild this city and will establish for it a wall and towers." The towers being referred to here could be the three built by Herod (i.e., Hippicus, Phasael, and Mariamme),[726] although the wall that was being constructed by Agrippa I had or was to have ninety towers as well.[727] Agrippa I also ordered executions by attacking the Christian community and having James *and* John, the sons of Zebedee, beheaded.[728] Peter (Cephas) was arrested, but somehow he was able to escape.[729] Perhaps other Christians were

---

711. (A theatre in Jerusalem and a amphitheatre in the plain near it) Ant. XV, 268; (a hippodrome in Jerusalem probably built by Herod) Ant. XVII, 255, War II, 44, Schurer, *The History of the Jewish People in the Age of Jesus Christ*, Vol. I, 304 note 56; (a royal palace/castle in the upper city) Ant. XV, 318, War I, 402, V, 156-85; (reconstructed the fortress attached to the Temple and named it Antonia) Ant. XV, 292, 409, XVIII, 91, War I, 401, V, 238-47; (a theatre, amphitheatre and hippodrome in Jericho probably built by Herod) Ant. XVII, 161, 178, 194, War I, 659, 666, Schurer, *The History of the Jewish People in the Age of Jesus Christ*, Vol. I, 304 note 56, Vol. II, 55. Herod undertook numerous other building projects throughout the country and even beyond its borders (Schurer, *The History of the Jewish People in the Age of Jesus Christ*, Vol. I, 304-8).

712. Ant. XV, 380-425; War I, 401-2.
713. Ant. XV, 5-10, cf. XIV, 175; War I, 358-60.
714. Ant XV, 50-6; War I, 437.
715. Ant. XV, 80-7.
716. Ant. XV, 161-82; War I, 431-4.
717. Ant. XV, 218-39; War I, 438-44.
718. Ant. XV, 247-52.
719. Ant. XV, 259-66.
720. Ant. XV, 280-91.
721. Ant. XVI, 361-94; War I, 538-51.
722. Ant. XVII, 41-5.
723. Ant. XVII, 149-67; War I, 647-55.
724. Ant. XVII, 182-7; War I, 661-4.
725. Ant. XIX, 326-7; cf. War II, 218-20; for a description of the wall, see War V, 147-58.
726. War IV, 161-75.
727. War IV, 156-8.

executed as well, because Acts also adds that the king "laid violent hands upon *some* who belonged to the church."[730]

Agrippa II (AD 53-92/3) had timber imported from the north to support the temple when its foundation was sinking, but because of the outbreak of the war, the work was not started.[731] When the building of the temple was completed during the governorship of Albinus (AD 62-4), he had the city paved with white stone so the workers who built the temple would not go unemployed.[732] In order to support the peace party against the rebels, Agrippa II sent troops to Jerusalem soon after the war broke out. Josephus stated that "for 7 days there was slaughter on both sides, neither of the combatants surrendering the portion of the town which they occupied."[733] This led to the burning of the house of the high priest Ananias, the palaces of Agrippa II and his sister Berenice, and the public archives. These events occurred ca. August, AD 66.[734]

Because the interpreter of Jos. 6:26 had to utilize whatever was originally contained in the biblical passage (i.e., "his firstborn," "his last-born," "its foundation," and "its gates"), he was forced to give more flexible meanings to these terms than was intended by the text. The biblical text was fixed and could not be changed. Therefore, "his firstborn" was understood to mean *the first descendant of Herod to be king*[735] and "his last-born" was understood to mean *the last descendant to be king*. Furthermore, laying "its foundation" was understood to mean *the first steps in the building of the city* and setting up "its gates" was understood to mean *the final steps*.

The curse of Jos. 6:26 seems to have had disastrous results for the "cursed ... man" and "his firstborn." Herod died in 4 BC of a terrible disease[736] and Agrippa I died suddenly of a disease in AD 44.[737] It was probably expected that Agrippa II would die in this manner also. Their deaths as a result of diseases and their building activities in Jerusalem were probably the main reasons why the scribe was able to use Jos. 6:26 as an allusion to them in the first place. 4QTest was

---

728. Acts 12:2. For the evidence that *both* brothers were executed by Agrippa I, see Robert Eisler, *The Enigma of the Fourth Gospel* (London: Methuen & Co., 1938), 59-77, 95-8.
729. Acts 12:3-19.
730. Acts 12:1 (italics mine).
731. War V, 36; Ant. XV, 391.
732. Ant. XX, 219-22.
733. War II, 424.
734. War II, 426-7.
735. None of Herod's sons were designated kings (Schurer, *The History of the Jewish People in the Age of Jesus Christ*, vol. I, 341, 354).
736. Ant. XVII, 146-8, 168-74, 188-91; War I, 644-7, 656-8, 665-6.
737. Ant. XIX, 343-53; Acts 12:19-23.

probably written after the burning of the high priest's house, the palaces, and the public archives in ca. August, AD 66.

We now need to discuss 4QMMT. One writer describes this document as follows:

> The *Manifesto* [i.e., 4QMMT] is a position paper of some kind and juxtaposes the views of three parties: a "we" group, a "you" individual who is a ruler, and a "they" group who are doing things in the Temple that the "we" group condemns. The "we" group further tries to persuade the "you" ruler to support them in this condemnation. [738]

As a "position paper" it contains a list of more than twenty legal interpretations in which the "we" group differed from the "they" group. Each legal interpretation is stated in this way: "concerning X, we say this about it." The "you" ruler is most likely a king, because Solomon, and especially David, are presented to him as righteous rulers whose lives should be copied.[739]

A good case can be made that the "you" ruler was Herod Agrippa I and the "they" group was the priestly establishment of the time. Josephus characterizes Herod Agrippa I as follows:

> On entering Jerusalem, he offered sacrifices of thanksgiving, omitting none of the ritual enjoined by our law.[740]

> He enjoyed residing in Jerusalem and did so constantly; and he scrupulously observed the traditions of his people. He neglected no rite of purification, and no day passed for him without the prescribed sacrifice.[741]

It would seem only natural that a king like Herod Agrippa I, who endeavored to obey the Torah in every detail, would catch the attention of the sectarians. Could he be persuaded to accept their legal interpretations instead of those of the corrupt priestly establishment? Could this be their chance to regain control of the Temple? It was these hopes that initiated their sending this "position paper" to him. This probably occurred at the beginning of his reign (AD 41).

The tone of the document is very conciliatory, since its purpose was to persuade the king to accept their legal views. Although it is admitted that the

---

738. Michael Wise, Martin Abegg, Jr., & Edward Cook, *The Dead Sea Scrolls: A New Translation* (San Francisco: Harper, 1996), 28.
739. Wise, Abegg, Jr. & Cook, *The Dead Sea Scrolls: A New Translation*, 364 (Section C, 4, 6).
740. Ant. XIX, 293.
741. Ant. XIX, 331.

sect "separated from the majority of the peo[ple],"⁷⁴² the people are still considered to be "holy."⁷⁴³ We know from a previous chapter, that this was not the actual view of the sectarians. However, if they admitted their true view, the king would have considered it an insult. This would hardly have helped them in their purpose. In addition, they endeavored to assure the king of their own honest intentions: "And you k[now that no] unfaithfulness, deception, or evil are found in our hands, for we have given [some thought (?)] to [these issues.]."⁷⁴⁴

Based on the traditional method of determining Jewish ancestry, which is through the descent of the mother,⁷⁴⁵ it is doubtful that Herod Agrippa I could be considered Jewish.⁷⁴⁶ Although his father, Aristobulus, was the son of Herod and Mariamme, the Hasmonean princess,⁷⁴⁷ his mother, Berenice, was the daughter of Costobar, an Idumaean, and Herod's sister, Salome.⁷⁴⁸ Salome's mother was Cypros, who was descended from a noble Nabatean (i.e., Arabian) family.⁷⁴⁹ Therefore, Berenice could not be considered Jewish based on her ancestry, and there is no evidence that she converted to the faith.⁷⁵⁰

However, as was discussed in an earlier chapter, the traditional method of determining Jewish ancestry was not longer used by the New Covenant. If Herod Agrippa I had already been circumcised and was baptized into the new Israel, he would be considered Jewish irrespective of his ancestry. The only modification would be that the king would not have to undergo the long process of initiation into the New Covenant. The relinquishment of this single requirement for him in exchange for securing control of the Temple and the government would not be an unreasonable concession! Nevertheless, he would still have to learn the sect's strict interpretation of the Torah and follow it precisely. The king's family and subjects would have to submit to baptism also

---

742. Wise, Abegg, Jr., and Cook, *The Dead Sea Scrolls: A New Translation*, 363 (Section C, 7). However, I disagree with the other possible translation that is suggested for "majority of the people," which is "council of the congregation." See also Martinez & Tigchelaar, eds., *The Dead Sea Scrolls Study Edition*, Vol. 2, 800-1.

743. Wise, Abegg, Jr. & Cook., *The Dead Sea Scrolls: A New Translation*, 362-3 (Section B, 75-6, 79).
744. Wise, Abegg, Jr. & Cook., *The Dead Sea Scrolls: A New Translation*, 363 (Section C, 8-9).
745. Lawrence H. Schiffman, *Who Was a Jew?* (Hoboken: KTAV Publishing, 1985), 9-14.
746. Schiffman, *Who Was a Jew?*, 13-4.
747. War II, 222.
748. Ant. XVIII, 133.
749. Ant. XIV, 121; War I, 181.
750. Dt. 23:8 states that a third generation Idumaean "may enter the assembly of the Lord." By counting back to his great great grandfather Antipater I, who was forcibly converted to Judaism by John Hyrcanus I in 129 BC, it is discovered that Herod Agrippa I was an Idumaean of the fifth generation. However, under the circumstances this precept would have had no effect because his mother Berenice was not Jewish.

and the establishment priests, levites and laymen would *not* be excused from having to undergo the applicable initiation process.

The attempt of the New Covenant to gain the king's support quickly turned into a failure. The later writing of 4QTest, in which Herod Agrippa I was condemned along with his grandfather Herod the Great and his son Herod Agrippa II, was the unfortunate result.

Chapter 13. The Coming Visitation

Under the leadership of John the Baptist and then James the Righteous, the sect thought of itself as living in the "end of days"[751] or the "last generation."[752] The "last period"[753] of history would commence with the Messiah of Israel formally entering into his office (i.e., being anointed by the high priest). In due course, he would lead the sect in the forty-year war mentioned in the War scroll. In this war, the righteous would regain control of the Temple and the land, and then conquer all the nations of the world. All the wicked on the earth would be destroyed. 4QpPs^a states that "at the end of the forty years ... there will not be found on earth any [wi]cked man."[754] This is probably an allusion to the war. A passage from 1QpHab,[755] which refers to it as a "judgment" or "chastisement" on "all the Gentiles" and "all the wicked ones of His people," is quoted below:

> The explanation of this word [Hab. 1:12] is that God will not destroy His people[756] by the hand of the Gentiles, but into the hand of His Elect One[757] God will give the judgment of all the Gentiles. And at their chastisement,[758] all

---

751. 1QpHab 9:6.
752. 1QpHab 2:7, 7:2.
753. 1QpHab 7:7, 12.
754. 4QpPs^a 2.7-8.
755. 1QpHab 5:3-6.
756. I.e., the true Israel, the sectarians.
757. See also 1QpHab 5:4, 9:12, 4QpPs^a, frags. 1-10, 2:5, 3:5, 4QpIsa^d 1:3. Since 1QpHab was written in AD 68, "His [God's] Elect One" would actually refer to the Messiah of Aaron and Israel who was still to come (see below), but in the time period we are discussing it could still equally well refer to the Messiah of Israel.
758. I.e., all the Gentiles.

the wicked ones of His people[759] will be convicted (by those) who have kept His commandments in their distress.[760]

In another place, 1QpHab states that "on the Day of Judgment, God will eradicate all the idolaters and the wicked from the earth."[761] In 1QS, the "dominion of perversity" will be destroyed "at the appointed time of the Visitation," which is also called "the appointed time of the decisive Judgment":

> But in His Mysteries of understanding and His glorious Wisdom God has permitted a period for the existence of perversity; and at the appointed time of the Visitation He will destroy it forever. Then truth shall arise in the world forever; for (the world) has defiled itself in the ways of wickedness under the dominion of perversity until the appointed time of the decisive Judgment.[762]

The Day of Judgment and the Visitation in these passages refer to the same event. It would be God's Last Judgment and the New Creation of the world. After the forty-year war, God himself will resurrect the dead[763] and judge all of mankind. The wicked, who had been killed by the war, will be raised from a place of punishment in the underworld. Then, all the wicked will be judged and suffer a second death through a universal conflagration,[764] ending in their complete annihilation. 1QS has this to say about what can be expected for the wicked at the Visitation:

> ...it consists of an abundance of blows administered by all the angels of destruction in the everlasting pit by the furious wrath of the God of vengeance, of unending dread and shame without end, and of the disgrace of destruction by the fire of the regions of darkness. And all their times from age to age are in most sorrowful chagrin and bitterest misfortune, in calamities of darkness till they are destroyed with none of them surviving or escaping.[765]

1QpHab mentions the second death of the wicked on the Day of Judgment:

---

759. I.e., the schismatics.
760. I.e., the faithful sectarians.
761. 1QpHab 13:2-3.
762. 1QS 4:18-20.
763. This concept is most clearly expressed in 4Q521, frags. 2 col. II:11-2 of the Dead Sea Scrolls: "And the Lord will perform marvelous acts such as have not existed, just as he sa[id,] [for] he will heal the badly wounded *and will make the dead live*, he will proclaim good news to the poor ... " (italics mine, cf. frags. 7+5 col. II:6). Cf. Lk. 11:22, Mt. 11:5, Is. 29:18-9, 35:5-6, 61:1. Florentino Garcia Martinez & Eibert J. C. Tigchelaar, eds., 2 vols., *The Dead Sea Scrolls Study Edition* (Leiden: Brill, 1997), Vol. II, 1044-5.
764. 1QH 3:28-36, 17:13-4.
765. 1QS 4:12-4.

> The explanation of this [Hab. 2:4a] is that [the wicked] will receive twofold to themselves [and be treated] with[out loving]-kindness at their judgment [...].[766]

On the other hand, all the righteous (i.e., those alive and those resurrected from a place of bliss in the underworld) will be awarded with the earth — purified from all evil through the universal conflagration — to enjoy for all eternity. They will have passed through the conflagration, as though it was only "warm milk."[767] 1QS has this to say about what can be expected for the righteous at the Visitation:

> ... it consists of healing and abundance of bliss, with length of days and fruitfulness, and all blessings without end, and eternal joy in perpetual life, and the glorious crown and garment of honour in everlasting light.[768]

1QpHab 8:1-3 states that the righteous would escape a second death on the Day of Judgment:

> The explanation of this [Hab. 2:4b] concerns all those who observe the Torah in the House of Judah.[769] God will deliver them from the House of Judgment because of their affliction and their faith in the Teacher of Righteoueness.[770]

The above discussion about the Day of Judgment explains why 1QpHab states that "God will sentence [the Wicked Priest] to complete destruction,"[771] even though he was already dead in this scroll.[772] His second death or complete annihilation would occur on the Day of Judgment. This is actually referred to in 1QpHab as well:

---

766. 1QpHab 7:14-7.
767. Thiering mentions the Zoroastrian idea about the destruction of the wicked by liquefied metal at the end of time, which the righteous would experience as only "warm milk." She understands this idea to be the "probable influence" of the universal conflagration belief. See B. E. Thiering, *Redating the Teacher of Righteousness* (Sydney: Theological Explorations, 1979), 69-70.
768. 1QS 4:6-8.
769. "All those who observe the Torah in the House of Judah" refers to all true Israelites (i.e., all "Jews" baptized by John the Baptist) except the schismatics, because they did not practice the Torah according to the interpretation of the New Covenant any longer.
770. I.e., James the Righteous.
771. 1QpHab 12:5-6. See also 1QpHab 11:15: "[G]od will make him (the Wicked Priest) reel by heap[ing] up his [humilia]t[ion upo]n [him], and the pain [...]."
772. 1QpHab 9:8-12, 8:16-9:2.

And as for that which He [God] said, *"the confines of many nations and the bonds of thine own soul"* [Hab. 2:10], the explanation of this (is that) it is the House of Judgment where, in the midst of many peoples, God will put His judgment; and from there He will raise him [the Wicked Priest] up for the Judgment. Then in their midst He will pronounce him guilty and will damn him with the fire of brimstone.[773]

Although 11QMelch is very fragmentary,[774] it describes the heavenly priest-king Melchizedek, who is the leader of the "sons of heaven"[775] or "all the Elim [of the heights]."[776] He will come as a judge to proclaim salvation for the righteous and punishment for the wicked, including Belial (Satan) and "the spirits of his lot."[777] The complete atonement would not occur until the "D[ay of Atone]ment," which was at "[the en]d of the tenth [ju]bilee." Melchizedek would nonetheless "restore them, and proclaim liberty to them,[778] relieving them of the burden of all their iniquities ... in the first week of the jubilee (that occurs) after [the n]ine jubilees."[779] He is also referred to as the "Heral[d who pro]claims peace"[780] and as the "[One An]ointed of the spir[it]."[781] Although there is a significant lacuna in the document at the applicable point, Dan. 9:26 is probably quoted with reference to this personage: "After the sixty-two weeks, an Anointed one shall be cut off." [782]

The sect split up the last era of earth's history into ten jubilees. Since a jubilee is 49 years long, this last era would be 490 years long.[783] It would correspond to the sacred number of "seventy weeks of years" found in Dan. 9:24.[784] 11QMelch seems to be saying that in the first week[785] of the tenth and final jubilee the "Herald" and the "One Anointed with the spirit" will be "cut off," i.e., put to death. The quotation from Daniel states *"after* sixty-two weeks." If we

---

773. 1QpHab. 10:2-5.
774. The translation of 11QMelch utilized here is from Paul J. Kobelski, *Melchizedek and Melchiresa* (Washington, DC: The Catholic Biblical Association of America, 1981), 3-23.
775. 11QMelch 2:5.
776. 11QMelch 2:14. "Elim," which literally means "gods," refers to the heavenly angels.
777. 11QMelch 2:12.
778. Lev. 25:10.
779. 11QMelch 2:6-7.
780. 11QMelch 2:16, 18.
781. 11QMelch 2:18.
782. 11QMelch 2:18. Kobelski inserts Dan. 9:25 ("Until an Anointed One, a Prince, there shall be seven weeks") instead of Dan. 9:26 (Kobelski, *Melchizedek and Melchiresa*, 6, 9, 21). However, see Michael Wise, Martin Abegg, Jr., & Edward Cook, *The Dead Sea Scrolls: A New Translation* (New York: Harper Collins, 1996), 457.
783. $10 \times 49 = 490$.
784. $70 \times 7 = 490$.
785. One week equals seven years.

multiply sixty-three weeks times seven years, we will get four hundred and forty-one years. If we do the same with nine jubilees times forty-nine years, we will get four hundred and forty-one years as well. This will be made clear in the following diagram:

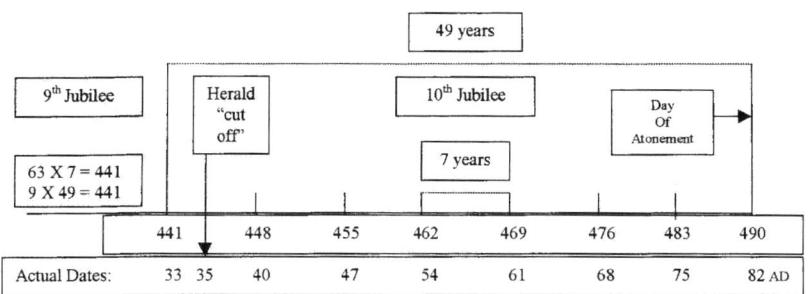

The "Day of Atonement" at the end of the tenth jubilee (i.e., the 490th year of the last era) in this scheme would correspond to God's Day of Judgment, except that *now* Melchizedek would be the judge instead of God. Although not mentioned in 11QMelch, the fighting of the forty-year war would have to commence in 450 (actual date: AD 42) and the Messiah of Israel would probably be anointed in 448 (actual date: AD 40).

The Herald and the One Anointed with the spirit, who was "cut off," was probably John the Baptist, the founder of the New Covenant. Herod Antipas executed him in AD 35. In the diagram above, John's death occurs in "the first week of the jubilee (that occurs) *after* the nine jubilees," i.e., in the first week of the tenth jubilee. The Day of Atonement/Day of Judgment would be expected in AD 82.[786]

A good case can be made that those leaders of the sect with the title of "Messiah of Aaron" were thought to be the successive earthly embodiments of the heavenly being Melchizedek. This series would also include certain priests of special holiness that lived prior to the formation of the New Covenant, as well as the leader titled the "Messiah of Aaron and Israel,"[787] who was still to come when CD was written. The ten[788] earthly embodiments of Melchizedek were probably the following priests:[789] Melchizedek,[790] Aaron,[791] Zadok,[792] Hilkiah,[793]

---

786. Of course, other possible dates could be used in the diagram, as long as the death of the Herald occurs in the first week of the tenth jubilee.
787. CD 12:23-13:1, 14:19, 19:10-1, 20:1.
788. Ten is a sacred number to the sect. See Roger T. Beckwith, "The Significance of the Calendar for Interpreting Essene Chronology and Eschatology," *Revue de Qumran* 10 (1980), 168.

Mattathias,[794] Judas Maccabeus,[795] Zadok,[796] John the Baptist,[797] James the Righteous,[798] and the awaited "Messiah of Aaron and Israel" (see below).

Melchizedek is presented as a very highly exalted heavenly being in 11QMelch. For example, when the author cites Isaiah 61:2 ("to proclaim the year of the LORD'S favor"), he substitutes Melchizedek for God's most holy name, i.e. Yahweh.[799] In ancient times, this name was translated "LORD," because it was considered to sacred to be pronounced. As another example, the name "Elohim," which is almost always used as a name for God,[800] is used to refer to Melchizedek in three places.[801] However, it would be wrong to assume that Melchizedek is identified as God Himself in this document. In another place, it is stated that "Melchizedek will exact the ven[geance] of E[l's] (i.e., God's) judgments"[802] not his own judgments.[803] Also, the heavenly angels are referred to by the name "Elim" (i.e., "gods").[804]

A very interesting hymn has come to light from cave 4, which is known as the Self-Glorification Hymn. We now know that it had been one of the hymns of 1QH, but since so very little of it had been preserved there, its importance was not really noticed until the cave 4 copies became available. The name given to it is very appropriate, since the writer exalts himself to a very lofty level. It is likely that James the Righteous, who was an earthly embodiment of the heavenly being Melchizedek, composed it. I quote a portion of the hymn below:

> [...] my glory is incomparable and besides me no-one is exalted, nor comes to me, for I reside in [...], in the heavens, and there is no [...] I am counted among the gods[805] and my dwelling is in the holy congregation; [my] des[ire] is

---

789. According to CD 2:12, a uniquely gifted holy priest appeared in every era of history.
790. Gn. 14:17-24, Ps. 110:4.
791. Lev. 8-9. The sect called Aaron "His [God's] Messiah, the Holy One" (CD 6:1). See also Dan. 9:24, I Chron. 23:13, and Ps. 106:16.
792. 2 Sam. 8:17, 1 Chr. 12:23-38, 15:11-3.
793. 2 Kgs. 22:1-23:30, 2 Chr. 34-5.
794. 1 Macc. 2:1-69; Ant. XII, 265-84.
795. 1 Macc. 3:1-9:22; Ant. XII, 285-434.
796. See the chapter titled *Zadok*.
797. See the chapter titled *John the Baptist*.
798. See the chapter titled *James the Righteous*.
799. 11QMelch 2:9.
800. Kobelski lists three instances in the Old Testament, when "Elohim" is used for other beings other than God (Moses, Ex. 4:16, 7:1; the ghost of Samuel, 1 Sam. 28:13; Baal, 1 Kg. 18:24). See Kobelski, *Melchizedek and Melchiresa*, 60, note 35.
801. 11QMelch 2:10, 16, 23.
802. 11QMelch 2:13. This is another allusion to Is. 61:2, as is 11QMelch 2:9.
803. Kobelski, *Melchizedek and Melchiresa*, 73-4.
804. 11QMelch 2:14.

Chapter 13. The Coming Visitation

not according to the flesh, [but] all that is precious to me is in (the) glory (of) [...] the holy [dwel]ling. [W]ho has been considered despicable on my account? And who is comparable to me in my glory? Who, like the sailors, will come back and tell? [...] Who bea[rs all] sorrows like me? And who [suffe]rs evil like me? There is no-one. I have been instructed, and there is no teaching comparable [to my teaching ...] And who will attack me when [I] op[en my mouth]? And who can endure the flow of my lips? And who will confront me and retain comparison with my judgment? [... friend of the king, companion of the holy ones ... incomparable, f]or among the gods[806] is [my] posi[tion, and] my glory is with the sons of the king. To me (belongs) [pure] gold, and to me, the gold of Ophir [...].[807]

Under the leadership of Symeon, the son of Clopas, the scheme of the end of days, the Visitation, and God's Last Judgment and New Creation underwent a major change. This can be noticed clearly in CD. It makes the following statement:

"Now from the day when the Unique Teacher [John] was taken, until the end of all the men of war who turned back with the Man of Lies [Ananus], (there shall pass) about 40 years."[808]

CD was written in AD 65-6, which is about thirty years after the Baptist had died. Now the start of the end of days[809] begins with the year of his *death*, as the passage above states ("from the day when the Unique Teacher was taken"). The period from 4 BC (the first appearance of John the Baptist) to AD 35 (the date of John's death) is about 40 years or one generation. The last generation[810] would then be from AD 35 to ca. AD 75.[811] The Visitation is now understood by the sect not as God's Day of Judgment after the forty-year war and a universal conflagration, but as the destruction of Jerusalem and the Temple by a new "Nebuchadnezzar" (i.e., the Roman emperor, probably Nero) in ca. AD 75. At this time, all the schismatics, to whom "God's anger was kindled,"[812] would be destroyed, since it would be the "end of all the men of war who turned back with

---

805. The word here for "gods" is "Elim." They are the heavenly angels.
806. Again, the word here for "gods" is "Elim." They are the heavenly angels.
807. 4Q491c (4QSelf-Glorification Hymn^b), frag. 1, 6-12 in Martinez & Tigchelaar, eds., *The Dead Sea Scrolls Study Edition*, Vol. II, 979-81, cf. 1QH^a, 26 top (Vol. I, 201); 4Q427, frags. 7, col. 1+9 (Vol. II, 897); 4Q471b, frags. 1-3 (Vol. II, 953).
808. CD 20:13-5.
809. CD 4:4, 6:11.
810. CD 1:12.
811. It is *ca.* AD 75, because CD 20:15 has "*about* 40 years."
812. CD 2:1, 8:13, 18, 19:26, 31, 20:16.

the Man of Lies [Ananus]."[813] Perhaps alluding to the death of their leader, the schismatics would have to live through a period with "no king and no prince, no judge, nor anyone to rebuke with justice."[814] The attack on the city and Temple would conclude the 390-year "period of wrath,"[815] which would then have begun in ca. 315 BC.[816]

Therefore, the statement of CD is accurate.[817] John the Baptist did indeed make known to the "last generations" (i.e., 6 BC-AD 35 and AD 35-75) what God would do to the "last generation" (i.e., AD 35-75).

In the land of Damascus at the "period of the Visitation,"[818] a new leader will be anointed into his office. He is called the "Messiah of Aaron and Israel,"[819] "he who arises to teach righteousness in the last days,"[820] the "Prince of all the Congregation," and the "scepter."[821] In 4Q174, he is also called the "branch of David, who will arise with the Interpreter of the Torah ... [in] the [e]nd of days."[822] The latter, who is Symeon, the son of Clopas, will anoint the former into his office and then accept a demotion in rank. This new leader is also called the "Last Priest who will stretch out his hand to smite Ephraim."[823] "Ephraim" here is probably those in the Jewish establishment that go over to the second Nebuchadnezzar at the time of the Visitation in order to save their skins. As can be seen, this individual would unite the offices of high priest and king into one great office.[824]

---

813. Cf. CD 1:17, 2:1.
814. CD 20:16-7. This is an allusion to Hos. 3:4.
815. CD 1:5-6.
816. 390 — 75 = 315.
817. CD 1:10-2.
818. CD 19:10-1 states the following: "Now those who heed Him [God] are the poor of the flock; they will escape at the period of the Visitation. But those who are left [in Judea] will be delivered up to the sword when the Messiah of Aaron and Israel comes (into his office) [in the land of Damascus]...." In other words, the Messiah of Aaron and Israel will be anointed and the Visitation will take place at the same time.
819. CD 12:23-13:1, 14:19, 19:10-1, 20:1.
820. CD 6:11.
821. CD 7:20-1.
822. Martinez & Tigchelaar, eds., *The Dead Sea Scrolls Study Edition*, Vol. I, 353 (4Q174 1:11-2).
823. 4QpHos^b 2:3 in Maurya P. Horgan, *Pesharim: Qumran Interpretations of Biblical Books* (Washington: Catholic Biblical Assoc. of America, 1979), 149.
824. Perhaps 4Q521, frag. 2 col. II:1-2 refers to this personage. It reads as follows: "[for the heav]ens and the earth will listen to His Messiah, [and all] that is in them will not turn away from the precepts of the holy ones." See Martinez & Tigchelaar, eds., *The Dead Sea Scrolls Study Edition*, Vol. II, 1044-5. However, Edward F. Cook translates the phrase "His Messiah," as actually plural (i.e., "his Messiahs). It must be admitted that the plural form would better agree with the second line, which mentions the "holy ones"(plural). See Edward E. Cook, *Solving the Mysteries of the Dead Sea Scrolls* (Grand Rapids: Zondervan Publishing House, 1994), 166-7.

Chapter 13. The Coming Visitation

The sectarians at this time would be called the "sons of Zadok" and the "chosen of Israel ... who shall stand in the end of days."[825]

The new leader's first order of business would be to purify Israel:

> And all among those who have entered the Covenant
> who have breached the bound of the Torah,
> when the Glory of God appears in splendor to Israel[826]
> they will be cut off from the midst of the camp,
> and with them all who did evil in Judah[827]
> in the days of its trials.[828]

After the second Nebuchadnezzar destroyed Judea, the sect in the land of Damascus would begin efforts to take back the land. In his role as the Prince of all the Congregation, the new leader would direct these efforts.[829] Just as the Israelites of Old Testament times crossed the Jordan River under the leadership of Joshua, the son of Nun, in order to begin the conquest of the Holy Land,[830] so would the sectarians do the same under the leadership of the Prince of All the Congregation. After taking back the land, they would then initiate a terrible war against all the nations of the world in which they would eventually be victorious.

It would take six years to conquer the Holy Land followed by a "year of release," when there would be rest from war. Normally, this year of release would also include setting up a new Temple organization, but in this case, a new Temple had to be built first. Nevertheless, with the Holy Land in proper hands again, the new leader in his role as the Messiah of Aaron and Israel, would offer the first sacrifices in the redeemed land (i.e., he would "expiate their iniquity").[831] The simple Sanctuary that the sect had originally built in the land of Damascus would be utilized for this purpose. After this, twenty-nine more years of actual war and four years of release would be required to conquer the world. All of this warfare would comprise the forty-year war.

The first sacrifices offered in the land will fall on the same year as the Day of Atonement had fallen in the 11QMelch diagram above, i.e., AD 82.[832] It would

---

825. CD 4:3-4.
826. I.e., when the Messiah of Aaron and Israel is formally anointed into his office.
827. I.e., the schismatics in Judea.
828. CD 20:25-7.
829. Although very fragmentary, 4Q285, frag. 5 may actually describe an incident in which the "Branch of David" orders the captured "king of the Kittim" (i.e., the Roman Emperor) to be put to death. See Wise, Abegg, Jr., & Cook, *The Dead Sea Scrolls: A New Translation*, 293.
830. Jos. 1-6.
831. CD 14:19.
832. Ca. AD 75 + 7 years = ca. AD 82, which would be the first year of release.

appear that under the leadership of Symeon, the son of Clopas, the Day of Atonement of 11QMelch was not understood as the Day of Judgment any longer, but as the first actual Day of Atonement to be held in the redeemed land.

If 60 years were allowed for the building of the new city and Temple,[833] 490 years would be completed from the beginning of the period of wrath.[834] If this chronology is correct, a new city of Jerusalem and a new Temple would be built by ca. AD 175.[835] It is likely that in this scheme Last Judgment and the New Creation were expected in the far distant future.[836]

Below is a diagram of the 490-year period under Symeon, the son of Clopas:

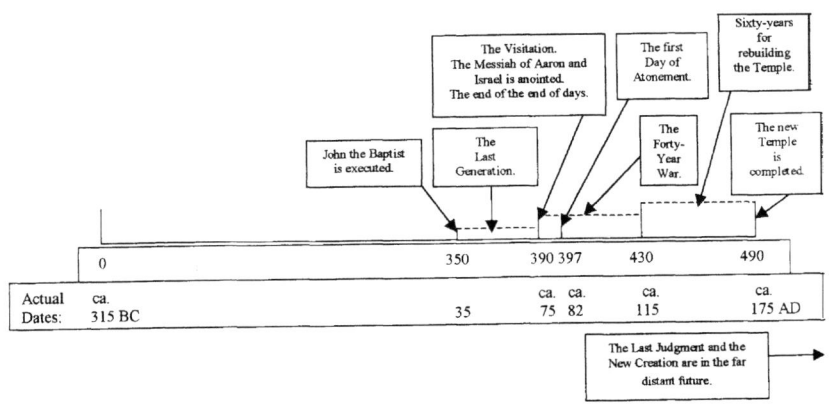

Cestius Gallus, the legate of Syria, commanded the first Romans troops against the Jews in AD 66 for the purpose of crushing the revolt. He marched his army from Antioch to Ptolemais and captured several rebellious cities and towns on his way to Jerusalem. However, while endeavoring to capture the holy city, he unexpectedly ordered a retreat for some reason. It soon turned into a tragic defeat for the Romans and a joyous victory for the Jews.[837] This was a momentous event to the people in Jerusalem, including the writer of 1QpHab,

---

833. It is interesting to note that Josephus states that it took approximately 80 years (ca. 20 BC-ca. AD 60) to totally complete the building of Herod's temple, although it took only 17 or 18 months to build its inner Sanctuary (Ant. XV, 380-2; 421-3; XX, 219-23; War I, 401-2).

834. 390 + 40 + 60 = 490.

835. ca. AD 75 + 40 + 60 = ca. AD 175.

836. According to the Book of Enoch and other texts, the Last Judgment and the New Creation would occur 980 years (i.e., two 490-year periods) after the building of a new Temple. See Beckwith, "The Significance of the Calendar for Interpreting Essene Chronology and Eschatology," 188, 190, 195-7.

837. War II, 499-555.

who was still residing in the city and observing the events taking place there. Nevertheless, the people were realistic enough to know that the Romans would make another attempt to capture the city. The question was when.[838]

After subduing all of Galilee[839] and most of the country surrounding Jerusalem by May/June of AD 68, Vespasian, who had been made the new Roman general after Gallus' defeat, returned to Caesarea to begin preparations for the siege of Jerusalem.[840] Since Scripture stated that Nebuchadnezzar's siege of Jerusalem in 586 BC took eighteen months and in the nineteenth month the city and the Temple were destroyed,[841] the writer of 1QpHab came to the conclusion that the Roman siege and destruction would take approximately the same length of time. Therefore, if he assumed that the siege would begin in June/July of AD 68, he must have expected that the Romans would destroy Jerusalem and the Temple early in AD 70. This date was significantly different from the scheme of CD, which placed the destruction in ca. AD 75. However, it was based on the reality of the situation at the time.

The unexpected death of Emperor Nero on June 9th of AD 68 changed Vespasian's plans.[842] He postponed his military actions against Jerusalem for a full year and he entrusted his son, Titus, with the continuance of the war.[843] In July of AD 69, Vespasian became Emperor.[844] The death of Nero and the delay of Vespasian's attack were certainly Godsends to the defenders of Jerusalem.

Three passages in 1QpHab allude to these events. I quote them below:

> And God told Habakkuk to write down the things which will come to pass in the last generation, but the completion of the period He made not known to him.[845]

---

838. The writer of 1QpHab "predicts" that in the end of days the "riches" and "plunder" of the "last priests of Jerusalem" will be "delivered into the hands of the army of the Kittim" (1QpHab 9:4-7). This is certainly an allusion to the capture of Jerusalem and the Temple, if not to the destruction as well.
839. War IV, 120.
840. War IV, 366-77, 410-50, 486-91.
841. 2 Kg. 25:1-12, Jer. 39:1-14, 52:4-16. According to Scripture, the siege lasted from the 10th month of King Zedekiah's 9th year to the 4th month of his 11th year, which equals 18 months. In the 5th month of his 11th year, the Temple, the King's house, and all the houses of any significance in Jerusalem were burnt down and the walls around the city were razed.
842. War IV, 491.
843. War IV, 655-8.
844. War IV, 592-620.
845. 1QpHab 7:1-2.

> The explanation of this [Hab. 2:3a] is that the last period will be long in coming, but will excel all that the Prophets said; for the Mysteries of God are marvelous.[846]

> The explanation of this [Hab. 2:3b] concerns the men of truth who observe the Torah, whose hands do not slacken in the service of Truth when the last period delays for them; for all the seasons of God come to pass at their appointed time according to His decree concerning them in the Mysteries of His providence.[847]

As a result of Nero's unexpected death and the postponement of the Roman plans for the siege, the time of the destruction of the city and Temple was no longer known with any certainty. It had been expected to occur in early AD 70, but this date became more and more unlikely as the months went by. The date in CD (i.e., ca. AD 75) was still a possibility, but how could one be sure? Because of this uncertainty, the "completion of the period," i.e., the end of the last generation, was unknown. As a result, the last period of history had been postponed as well, since it was to come after the expected destruction of Jerusalem and the Temple.[848] Unlike the scheme of CD, the writer of 1QpHab reverted to the older view that God's Day of Judgment would follow immediately after the forty-year war.

Taking into consideration the passages in 1QpHab alluding to the death of the Wicked Priest (i.e., Ananus) at the end of AD 67 or the beginning of AD 68, the three passages above allow us to date the composition of 1QpHab to probably the end of AD 68. For the writer of 1QpHab and his comrades, who were still in Jerusalem, "the last period will be long in coming" and "delays for them," as a result of the Emperor's unforeseen fate. In fact, it was just this postponement in the Roman attack that allowed them to escape from Jerusalem and attempt to rejoin the sect in the land of Damascus. Unfortunately, they probably failed in this endeavor.

We are now in a position to discuss the ordinance portion of CD in some detail. It is made up of two parts. One part is called the "rule of the settlement of

---

846. 1QpHab 7:7-8.
847. 1QpHab 7:11-4.
848. There was an intermediate opinion between the composition of CD and 1QpHab regarding when the last period of history would begin. The scribe of 4QpNah, who was writing in early AD 67, understood the withdrawal of Herod Agrippa II and his supporters from Jerusalem in AD 64-6 as the beginning of the last period. This withdrawal ended their rule over Israel (i.e., those baptized by John the Baptist or one of his successors). See 4QpNah, frags. 3-4, 4:1-6. 4QpNah, frags. 3-4, 3:3 further adds that the "evil deeds [of the Seekers-After-Smooth-Things] will be exposed to all Israel at the end of the period" (i.e., the end of the end of days).

Chapter 13. The Coming Visitation

the camps"[849] and the other part is called the "rule of the settlement of the cities of Israel."[850] The "camps" rule was for the sect while they were living in the land of Damascus "during the period of wickedness (i.e., the "period of wrath")[851] until there arises the Messiah of Aaron and Israel."[852] The "cities" rule was for the sect in Judea while they were conducting the forty-year war, but after they had gained possession of the land.

Based on the Cave 4 fragments, the ordinance portion of CD was originally in this order: cols. 15, 16, 9, 10, 11, 12, 13, and 14.[853] If 12:8-11 was taken out (see below), Col. 12 would then be compatible with the "cities" rule. The "cities" rule ends with 12:19-22, which starts with "[the regulations above are] the rule of the settlement of the cities of Israel." Then, immediately following 12:19-22, the column ends with "this is the rule of the settlement of the camps ... " (12:22-3 and 13:1) and the ordinance portion continues on with the "camps" rule. All of the columns before 12:1 are another part of the "camps" rule. Thus, col. 12 (i.e., the "cities rule) is sandwiched between two parts of the "camps" rule.

CD 12:8-11 is not compatible with the "cities" rule, as it is being understood here. I quote the passage below:

> Let no man sell clean beasts or birds to the Gentiles, that they may not sacrifice them. And the contents of his granary or his vat; let a man refuse with all his strength to sell them anything from them. And concerning his slave and his maidservant; let no man sell them to them because they have entered with him into the Covenant of Abraham.

This rule forbidding the sale of certain things to Gentiles would be applicable while the sect resided in the land of Damascus and was under the "camps" rule. Since the sectarians were living among Gentiles, rules had to be made for dealing — or should we say not dealing — with them. However, under the "cities" rule (when they had gained possession of the land and were conducting war against the nations of the world), it would not have been applicable. In a purified land, free of all uncleanness (which would certainly exclude Gentiles from dwelling in it), a rule for dealing with them would not

---

849. CD 12:22-3.
850. CD 12:19.
851. CD 1:5.
852. CD 12:23-13:1, 14:19, 19:10-1, 20:1.
853. Wise, Abegg, Jr. & Cook, *The Dead Sea Scrolls: A New Translation*, 65-72. There are some interesting rules found only in the Cave 4 fragments (pp. 61-5, 72-4 of the same source) that could be placed in the "camps" or "cities" rules according to the criteria described here as well.

have been needed. If it is a "camps" rule instead of a "cities" rule, Robert Eisler describes its purpose very well:

> "Non-cooperation" or "boycott" is strictly enjoined: "no cattle nor food may be sold to the gentile, no produce of one's threshing floor or one's wine-press, *not even for the price of all his fortune and possessions.*" Not for the whole wealth of a Roman or Greek is any meat or bread or wine to be sold to him, "because he would sacrifice it," i.e. dedicate it to his gods before eating or drinking it![854]

It is important to mention that, when the Cave 4 fragments are examined, no evidence is discovered that CD 12:8-11 was originally a part of col. 12.[855] Of course, because of the condition of the fragments, the rule could still have been part of the column originally.

CD 12:6-8 (i.e., the passage immediately preceding 12:8-11) is perfectly compatible with the "cities" rule. The sectarians would have regained possession of the land and would be conducting a war against the nations of the world. Having a rule for dealing with the killing of Gentiles and the confiscation of their property would be a necessity. I quote it below:

> Let no man stretch out his hand to shed the blood of any Gentile for the sake of riches and gain. And let him also take none of their possessions, that they may not blaspheme, unless it is according to the decision of the company of Israel.

As a "cities" rule, Robert Eisler is again right on the mark in explaining its purpose:

> If these regulations forbid the covenanters to shed the blood of the gentiles for the sake of gain and plunder, it goes without saying that they allowed them to kill the gentiles in a legitimate war ... for their faith and the land of their inheritance against an alien invader....
>
> More than that, the riches of the gentiles may be taken, i.e. requisitioned by order of the authority ("according to the decision of the council [company] of Israel").[856]

---

854. Robert Eisler, "The Sadoqite Book of the New Covenant: Its Date and Origin," *Occident and Orient* (Gaster Anniversary Volume), ed. B. Schindler (London: Taylor's Foreign Press, 1936), 131.
855. The relevant Cave 4 fragments (i.e., 4Q266 9 II and 4Q271 5 I) do not contain CD 12:8-11. See Martinez & Tigchelaar, eds., *The Dead Sea Scrolls Study Edition*, Vol. I, 571, 592-5, 620-3.
856. Eisler, "The Sadoqite Book of the New Covenant: Its Date and Origin," 131. It should be noted that the type of war Robert Eisler is referring to in this passage is a *guerilla* war to win the country's freedom from a foreign oppressor. The type of war I am referring to is a war of conquest to regain possession of the land. Nevertheless, the passage is applicable to either case.

CHAPTER 14. KHIRBET QUMRAN AND THE SCROLLS

Khirbet Qumran is the settlement that was discovered by the archaeologists near the scroll caves on the northwest shore of the Dead Sea. Based on the numismatic and other archaeological evidence, the periods of greatest occupation were the reign of Alexander Jannaeus (103-76 BC) and the period from 4 BC to ca. AD 70. 143 coins were discovered from the former period and 294 coins were discovered from the latter period.[857]

It is likely that Qumran was originally a military fortress that was put into operation under Alexander Jannaeus. Doubtless, the men selected to live there were loyal to him (i.e., Sadducees). Those opposed to Jannaeus were the Pharisees. When he died, his wife Alexandra became the Queen and his son Hyrcanus II became the high priest (76-67 BC). Under Alexandra's reign, the Pharisees became the real rulers of the country:

> Alexandra ... permitted the Pharisees to do as they liked in all matters, and also commanded the people to obey them; and whatever regulations, introduced by the Pharisees ... [but] abolished by her father-in-law Hyranus [John Hyrcanus I (135/4-104 BC)], these she again restored. And so, while she had the title of sovereign, the Pharisees had the power. For example, they recalled exiles, and freed prisoners, and, in a word, in no way differed from absolute rulers ... And throughout the entire country there was quiet except for

---

857. R. de Vaux, *Archaeology and the Dead Sea Scrolls* (London: Oxford University Press, 1973), 19, 22, 34, 37, 44-5. Another building was discovered one and a half miles to the south near the spring of 'Ain Feshkha. It was probably connected in some way with Khirbet Qumran. Based on the coin evidence there, the periods of greatest occupation were the same as the latter. There were 4 coins from the reign of Alexander Jannaeus (103-76 BC) and 83 coins from the period 4 BC to ca. AD 70 (R. de Vaux, *Archaeology and the Dead Sea Scrolls*, 60-87).

the Pharisees; for they worked upon the feelings of the queen and tried to persuade her to kill those who had urged Alexander to put the eight hundred to death [Jannaeus' crucifixion of his enemies in ca. 88 BC]. Later they themselves cut down one of them, named Diogenes, and his death was followed by that of one after the other....[858]

Only one coin was found at Qumran from the period of Queen Alexandra's reign.[859] Why has the coin evidence dropped off to almost nothing? It would appear that the new ruling establishment (i.e., the Pharisees) forced the pro-Jannaeus Sadducees of Qumran to abandon the site. Where did they go? They were probably the "remnant" mentioned in CD that escaped to the land of Damascus before Pompey's capture of Jerusalem in 63 BC.[860]

The site may have been re-settled in a small degree during the reign of the last Hasmonean king Antigonus (40-37 BC), since four coins minted by this king were discovered there.[861] The settlers probably abandoned the site in order to aid their king in Jerusalem shortly before Herod and the Romans laid a siege on the city in 37 BC.[862] It was probably Herod who ordered Qumran to be burned in order to stop any future re-settlements. Archaeologists did discover signs of a fire and an earthquake at this time.[863] The damage caused by the earthquake of 31 BC would have occurred when the site was already abandoned.[864]

Under the leadership of John the Baptist from 4 BC to AD 35, I find nothing to contradict the view that Khirbet Qumran became the main place of residence for the sect. However, after John's death (AD 35), when James the Righteous became the leader of the sect, the New Covenant made its residence in Jerusalem. The schismatics under Dositheus returned to Qumran and resided there until ca. AD 37, when they moved to the land of Damascus. After that, the New Covenant in Jerusalem probably used the Qumran settlement as a ritual purification center. It was a place where members of the New Covenant could go to perform their special purifications while in a state of ritual impurity. This state prohibited them temporarily from entering Jerusalem.[865]

---

858. Ant. XIII, 408-11, cf. War I, 110-4.
859. R. de Vaux, *Archaeology and the Dead Sea Scrolls*, 19.
860. CD 1:4. See the chapter titled *The First Ones*.
861. R. de Vaux, *Archaeology and the Dead Sea Scrolls*, 19. A coin minted by Antigonus (40-37 BC) was discovered at the building near 'Ain Feshkha as well (R. de Vaux, *Archaeology and the Dead Sea Scrolls*, 66).
862. Ant. XIV, 468-86; War I, 345-57.
863. R. de Vaux, *Archaeology and the Dead Sea Scrolls*, 20-4.
864. Ant. XV, 121-6; War I, 370-2.
865. The theory that Qumran was a ritual purification center was advanced by Edward E. Cook, "A Ritual Purification Center," *BAR* (November/December, 1996), 39, 48-51, 73-5.

It is usually thought that the Roman general Vespasian destroyed Qumran in the summer of AD 68, when he took Jericho and visited the Dead Sea.[866] This is based on the fact that the last Jewish coins at the settlement were from the third year of the revolt (AD 68-9) and that the earliest Roman coins at the settlement (from Caesarea and Dora) were from AD 67-8.[867] However, it is unlikely that coins that had just been minted in Jerusalem would have been found so soon in an outlying area such as Qumran.[868] Also, if the Romans destroyed Qumran in the summer of AD 68, it would be inexplicable why they did not continue on their route in order to take the fortress of Herodium to the southwest. This would have made it possible for them to surround Jerusalem on four sides instead of three sides only. Herodium was not taken until after the destruction of Jerusalem in AD 70. This evidence leads to the conclusion that Qumran was probably not destroyed by the Romans until Lucilius Bassus, the Roman legate, took Herodium in AD 71.[869] The coins mentioned above only provide evidence that Qumran was not destroyed *before* AD 68.[870]

In the 50s and 60s AD, some of those in the New Covenant may have joined the more radical Sicarii and have sort refuge with them on the fortress of Masada or escaped to Egypt with others of them. Most of the New Covenant escaped to the land of Damascus in AD 65-6, but some may have stayed behind and perished in the Jewish revolt against Rome. The caves were normally used as storehouses for many of the sect's scrolls, because the skins of animals slaughtered outside of Jerusalem could not be brought into the city.[871] Most of the scrolls were already in the caves by AD 65-6. However, prior to the siege of Jerusalem by the Romans in AD 70, some additional scrolls were placed in the caves. 4QpNah, 4QTest, and probably other scrolls were not placed in Cave 4 until sometime in AD 68 and the seven original Dead Sea Scrolls[872] were not placed in cave 1 until sometime in AD 69. After the Romans built the siege wall in June of AD 70,[873] it would have been next to impossible for anyone to get out of Jerusalem.

It is fortunate for us that no one ever retrieved the scrolls. Because of this, archaeologists were able to discover them in this century. However, why is it

---

866. War IV, 449-50, 475-7.
867. R. de Vaux, *Archaeology and the Dead Sea Scrolls*, 36-41.
868. Norman Golb, *Who Wrote the Dead Sea Scrolls?* (New York: Scribner, 1995), 12-3.
869. War VII, 163-4; Norman Golb, *Who Wrote the Dead Sea Scrolls?* 12-3; "The Problem of Origin and Identification of the Dead Sea Scrolls," *Proceedings of the American Philosophical Society* 124 (February 1980): 18, note 41, 23, note 73.
870. Norman Golb, *Who Wrote the Dead Sea Scrolls?* 12-3.
871. 11QT 47:7-18. Cook, "A Ritual Purification Center," 73.
872. They are the Habakkuk Commentary (1QpHab), the Rule of the Community (1QS), the War Scroll (1QM), the Hymns Scroll (1QH), the Genesis Apocryphon, and two Isaiah scrolls.
873. War V, 499-510.

that the scrolls were not retrieved after the crisis had passed? Perhaps the members of the New Covenant in the land of Damascus were victims of the Gentiles who massacred Jews throughout the cities of Syria in AD 66.[874] Also, after seeking refuge in Egypt during the war, the Sicarii were captured and handed over to the Romans by the Alexandrian Jews and were then tortured and killed.[875] Any of them who were one-time members of the New Covenant would have lost their lives as well. Finally, those sectarians who made the scroll deposits in AD 68 and 69 must have tried to join up with their comrades in the land of Damascus. Unfortunately, the Romans had subdued the Jordan Valley and all of Perea as far as Machaerus by the summer of AD 68.[876] Realizing the futility of making the journey and surviving it, the decision was made to make a last stand at Qumran. When the Romans attacked and destroyed the site in AD 71, these last sectarians must have been its defenders. Therefore, the likely answer why the scrolls were not retrieved is that no one was alive to do so.

The settlement of the conventional Essenes mentioned by Pliny the Elder (died AD 79) in *Natural History* (Book V) may have been discovered near Ein Gedi. Pliny states that "below the Essenes" lies Ein Gedi, which in his time was "another ash-heap" like Jerusalem.[877] The site, which is located about 2,500 feet above the original site of Ein Gedi (i.e., Tel Goren), is comprised of 28 cells and two pools scattered over the area. Most of the cells are small and each of them appears to have been the living quarters for a single person. However, there are a few larger ones and one of these may have been a community kitchen. Another important detail is that one of the two pools, which has a spring for a water source and a stone ramp for entering it, may have been a Jewish ritual bath (i.e., a mikveh). Other features of the site indicate that the approximately thirty residents lived simply without luxuries and were vegetarians. Unfortunately, one drawback is that no main building has been discovered where the community members could assemble to share their special Meal, recite prayers, and discuss different subjects. The answer given by Yizhar Hirschfeld, the director of the Ein Gedi excavation, is that the members gathered "in an open space at the center of the site, under shelter provided by perishable materials that have not survived."[878]

---

874. War II, 461-5, 477-80, 560-2.
875. War VII, 409-19.
876. War IV, 410-39, 443-58, 486-90.
877. This is an allusion to the devastation caused by the Jewish War (AD 66-70).
878. Hershel Shanks, "Searching for Essenes At Ein Gedi, Not Qumran," *Biblical Archaeology Review* 28 (2002): 18-27, 60. See also the essay titled "Ein Gedi 1998" by Yizhar Hirschfeld, which can be found on the following web site: The Orion Center for the Study of the Dead Sea Scrolls and Associated Literature, Hebrew University, Jerusalem. Web address: http://orion.mscc.huji.ac.il.

Finally, we need to discuss the Copper Scroll, which was discovered by archaeologists in Cave 3 in 1952. It is called the Copper Scroll, because it was the only scroll among the Dead Sea Scrolls that was written on a long copper sheet. Unfortunately, when it was discovered by the archaeologists, it was split into two rolls that then had to be sawed into strips in order to read its contents. The scroll is a list of hiding places for treasure that was mostly gold and silver. The total amount of these precious metals has been estimated to be between 58 and 174 tons! It is stated in the scroll that another copy of it was stored at the 65th and final hiding place. Neither the treasure nor the other copy has ever been found.

The theory offered by Manfred R. Lehmann is the most likely explanation of the Copper Scroll's contents. Based on the use of special words connected with Jewish law in the scroll, he put forward the theory that the treasure was the accumulation of certain offerings that continued to be sent to Judaea even though the Temple had been destroyed by the Romans in AD 70. This was done in the hope that a new Temple would be built in the near future. Lehmann summarizes his theory as follows:

> The Copper Scroll refers not to the Temple treasure collected while the Temple still stood nor to any hoards that were accumulated while the Temple was functioning, but to accumulations from the period following the year 70. The hope of a speedy rebuilding of the Temple was no doubt kept alive throughout the years following the Roman destruction, and appropriate offerings continued to flow in not only as a political and religious matter, but also as a legal matter in conformity with *halakhah* [Jewish law]. Accumulated redemption funds were systematically hidden and stored away for the day when they again could — legally and politically — be delivered to Jerusalem and/or the Temple, as intended by the respective donors. For this purpose, a detailed inventory, such as contained in the Copper Scroll, would obviously be required.[879]

---

879. Manfred R. Lehmann, "Where the Temple Tax Was Buried," *Biblical Archaeology Review* 19 (1993): 42. Unfortunately, the other part of his theory is less certain. A coin struck by Emperor Nerva (AD 96-8) has on one side of it the inscription that "the insult of the Jewish taxes has been annulled." According to Lehmann, the coin was issued to commemorate the discovery and confiscation of the secret offerings (i.e., taxes) for the Temple. They were considered to be an insult to Rome. However, the usual interpretation of this inscription is that it referred to the annual tax of one-half shekel that was levied on the Jewish population by Emperor Vespasian after the destruction of the Temple in AD 70. Previously, the Jews paid the tax to the Temple. It was the cruel manner of collecting the tax that was an insult to the Jewish population. This method of collection was abolished not the tax itself (see Lehmann, "Where the Temple Tax Was Buried," 43 note 16). For comments and criticisms of Lehmann's theory, especially regarding the Nerva coin, see "Queries & Comments," *Biblical Archaeology Review* 20 (1994): 20, 73-81.

If this view of the Copper Scroll is correct, there would have been no connection between it and the Dead Sea Scroll sect.

Important Scrolls and Their Dates of Composition

Scroll	Date Written	Leader	Brief Comment
11QT	22-21BC	Zadok (Saddok)	It is anti-Herodian.
1QM 2-9	4 BC	John the Baptist	It was written during the revolt after Herod the Great's death.
1QS 1:1-4:26, 5:20b-7:25, 1QSa, 1QSb	Probably AD 3	John the Baptist	The "New Covenant" was formed.
1QS 5:1-20a	AD 15/16	John the Baptist*	It was written as a result of the schism led by Judas/Jesus.
1QS 8:1-15a, 9:12-26	AD 35	Dositheus	James the Righteous took John's place after his death (AD 35). Dositheus was the leader of schismatics.
1QS 8:16b-9:11	Ca. AD 40	James the Righteous	The schism led by Dositheus was healed and he became the "Prophet" of the sect.
11QMelch	AD 35-42	James the Righteous	The "Herald" and the "One Anointed with the spirit," who was "cut off," is John.
4QMMT	Probably AD 41	James the Righteous	It was sent to Herod Agrippa I.
1QH	Before AD 60	James the Righteous	John "spoke" through James.
4QpPs^a	AD 61-2	James the Righteous	Written prior to James' trial before the Sanhedrin.
CD, 4Q174 with 4Q177	AD 65-6	Symeon, the son of Clopas	Symeon led a mass exodus of the sect to the land of Damascus.
1QM 1, 15-19	AD 65-6	Symeon, the son of Clopas	The "Chief Priest" is Symeon.
4QTest	Late AD 66	Symeon, the son of Clopas*	The "man accursed" is Herod the Great, and his two "sons" are Agrippa I and Agrippa II.
4QpNah	Early AD 67	Symeon, the son of Clopas*	It was written after the people appointed new leaders and generals to conduct the war against Rome.
1QpHab	Probably the end of AD 68	Symeon, the son of Clopas*	It alludes to the death of emperor Nero in June, AD 68.

The leader was in exile in the land of Damascus at the particular time.

Part II. Christianity

Chapter 15. The Family of Jesus

Jesus[880] was the first-born son[881] of Mary and Joseph, born in 12 BC.[882] It has been suggested that Jesus was actually the third of five sons born in the family,[883] but this does not explain how the enemies of Christianity arrived at the idea that Jesus was illegitimate or how the Christians themselves arrived at the idea of the virgin birth. In order for these two diverse beliefs to have arisen, Jesus must have been Mary's first-born son and she must have been found pregnant with him at some point after her betrothal to Joseph. Because Joseph accepted Jesus as his own son,[884] he was probably Jesus' father. Therefore, Mary and Joseph must have been together sexually before the betrothal. Because of the unexpected pregnancy, the marriage was quickly consummated. According to the gospel of Matthew, when "Mary had been betrothed to Joseph, before they came together she was found to be with child."[885] Based on the above understanding of the situation, the phrase "before they came together" would mean, "before they were married."

It is likely that the anti-establishment Essenes brought a unique marriage practice into the New Covenant with them. Josephus describes it as follows:

---

880. Jesus (Hebrew: Yeshua) is a later form of the name Joshua (Hebrew: Yehoshua). It means "Yahweh is salvation." The older form was replaced after the Babylonian exile.
881. Lk. 2:7, Mt. 1:25 in some versions.
882. Jerry Vardaman, "Jesus' Life: A New Chronology," *Cronos Kairos Christos* (Winona Lake: Eisenbrauns, 1989), 55-82.
883. Rendel Harris, *The Twelve Apostles* (Cambridge: W. Heffer & Sons, 1927), 64, 70.
884. Mt. 1:24-5, cf. Lk. 2:2-5.
885. Mt. 1:18, cf. Lk. 1:27, 2:5.

There is yet another order of Essenes, which, while at one with the rest in its mode of life, customs, and regulations, differs from them in its views on marriage. They think that those who decline to marry cut off the chief function of life, the propagation of the race.... They give their wives ... a three years' probation, and only marry them after they have by three periods of purification given proof of fecundity. They have no intercourse with them during pregnancy, thus showing that their motive in marrying is not self-indulgence but the procreation of children.[886]

Besides a three-year period of probation, which was like an extra long betrothal,[887] the woman also had to go through "three periods of purification"[888] in order to prove her fertility. This practice would be appropriate for a sect that was obsessed with ritual purity. In the case of Mary and Joseph, because of the unexpected pregnancy, this entire practice would not have been completed. According to Matthew, Joseph "took his wife, but knew her not until she had borne a son, and he called his name Jesus."[889] The phrase "but knew her not until she had borne a son" can be explained by the fact that according to the marriage practice described by Josephus above "they have no intercourse ... during pregnancy."

The five male children in the family were Jesus, Judas, James, Joseph, and Simon.[890] There were at least two sisters as well.[891] Later Christians could not accept the fact that Jesus had real brothers, because of the belief in the perpetual virginity of Mary.[892] In order to solve this problem, they created a brother of Joseph named Clopas, Cleophas, or Alpheus, whose wife was *another* Mary, and made them the actual parents of Jesus' brothers.[893] Even more astonishing, this second Mary was sometimes identified as the *sister* of Mary![894] Obviously,

---

886. War II, 160-1.
887. Marriage usually took place one year after the betrothal. Joachim Jeremias, *Jerusalem in the Time of Jesus* (Philadelphia: Fortress Press, 1969), 367-8.
888. Lev. 15:19: "When a woman has a discharge of blood which is her regular discharge from her body, she shall be in her impurity for seven days, and whoever touches her shall be unclean until evening."
889. Mt. 1:24-5.
890. The birth order of the last three brothers is not certain, but as will be seen, Judas must come after Jesus.
891. In Mk. 6:3, Jesus is called the "brother of James and Joses (Joseph: Mt. 13:55) and Judas and Simon (Simon and Judas: Mt. 13:55)," and "his sisters" are also mentioned.
892. As early as ca. AD 150, *The Infancy Gospel of James* states that Mary was still a virgin even after she gave birth to Jesus (19:18). See Robert J. Miller, ed., *The Complete Gospels* (San Francisco: Harper, 1994), 380-2, 393.
893. Another way used to solve the problem was to make this other Mary the *first* wife of Joseph and the mother of Joseph's other children (Harris, *The Twelve Apostles*, 64-6, 77).
894. Harris, *The Twelve Apostles*, 64-5.

Joseph probably did have brothers, but their real names are unknown to us. Mary may very well have had sisters, but certainly not one named Mary. Clopas, Cleophas, and Alpheus are probably aliases for Joseph. It is interesting that these names mean "successor" or "substitute."[895]

John 19:25 states the following:

> But standing by the cross of Jesus were his mother, and his mother's sister, *Mary the wife of Clopas*, and Mary Magdalene.

Based on the above information, the phrase in italics should be moved to the following place:

> But standing by the cross of Jesus were his mother, *Mary the wife of Clopas*, and his mother's sister, and Mary Magdalene.

Mary, the wife of Clopas (i.e., Joseph), was actually Jesus' mother *not* his mother's sister. John now agrees with the parallel passages in the synoptic gospels.[896] They state that the same three women were present at the crucifixion. They were Mary, the mother of James and Joseph (Jesus' mother); Salome, the mother of the sons of Zebedee (Jesus' mother's sister);[897] and Mary Magdalene.

A little known fact is that Jesus' brother Judas was his *twin* brother. In the gospels, he is simply called "Thomas," which comes from the word "twin" in Aramaic. Unfortunately, we are not told whom he was the twin of in the gospels. However, in the apocryphal *Acts of Thomas*, Thomas is definitely identified as the twin brother of Jesus and his name is Judas. The following passage can be found in the *Acts of Thomas*:

> And the king requested the groomsmen to go out of the bridal-chamber; and having gone forth, and the doors having been shut, the bridegroom raised the curtain of the bridal-chamber, that he might bring the bride to himself. And he saw the Lord Jesus talking with the bride, *and having the appearance of Judas Thomas*, who shortly before had blessed them, and gone out from them; and he says to him: Didst thou not go out before them all? And how art thou found here? And the Lord said to him: *I am not Judas, who is also Thomas; I am his brother.*

---

895. Harris, *The Twelve Apostles*, 72-7.
896. Mk. 15:40, Mt. 27:55.
897. Only when we compare the gospel of John with the synoptics can we tell that Jesus' mother's sister = the mother of the sons of Zebedee = Salome.

And the Lord sat down on the bed, and ordered them also to sit down on the seats; and He began to [speak to them....[898]

Furthermore, in this same source Judas Thomas is actually called the "twin-brother of Christ."[899]

Jesus' brother James was James the Righteous (usually referred to with the sobriquet "the Just"), who was the leader and high priest of the New Covenant from AD 35-62. He was killed by the establishment high priest Ananus in AD 62.

Nothing is known about Joseph. Perhaps he died at a young age.

Jesus' brother Simon was Symeon, the son of Clopas (i.e., Joseph), who led the New Covenant to the land of Damascus in AD 65-6. According to Hegesippus, "he suffered martyrdom when he was 120 years old, in the reign of Trajan Caesar [AD 98-117], when Atticus was consular legate [AD 99-103]."[900]

It is usually accepted that Joseph was descended from the tribe of Judah and from the family of David.[901] This would mean that his children would be so descended as well, but this is incompatible with the other belief that Jesus did not have a human father at all.[902] Furthermore, the genealogies of Jesus in Matthew[903] and Luke[904] are hopelessly irreconcilable. All one has to do is compare them to see that this is true.

Mary, on the other hand, was descended in some way from the tribe of Levi and the family of Aaron, because her "kinswoman" Elizabeth, the mother of John the Baptist, was descended from that tribe and family.[905]

The Judah/David descent of Joseph is impossible *on his father's side* based on important evidence about Jesus' brother James. According to Epiphanius, James "was permitted once a year to enter into the Holy of Holies, as the law commanded the high priests" and "he was empowered to wear the high priestly diadem upon his head."[906] Furthermore, in Epiphanius, the Syriac and Latin versions of Eusebius, Jerome, and Andrew of Crete, it is stated that James could

---

898. Rev. Alexander Roberts and James Donaldson, "Acts of the Holy Apostle Thomas," *The Ante-Nicene Fathers* (Grand Rapids: Eerdmans, 1981), Vol. VIII, 537 (italics mine).

899. Roberts and Donaldson, "Acts of the Holy Apostle Thomas," *The Ante-Nicene Fathers*, Vol. VIII, 542.

900. Eusebius, *Ecclesiastical History*, 2 Vols., trans. by Kirsopp Lake (Cambridge: Harvard University Press, 1975), Vol. I, 272-5 (III, 32.1-5); Emil Schurer, *The History of the Jewish People in the Age of Jesus Christ*, Vols. I, II, III.1, III.2, rev. and ed. by Geza Vermes, et al. (Edinburgh: T. & T. Clark, 1973/87), Vol. I, 516.

901. Mt. 1:1-17, 1:20; Lk. 2:4, 3:23-38.

902. Mt. 1:18-25, Lk. 1:26-35.

903. Mt. 1:1-17.

904. Lk. 3:23-38.

905. Lk. 1:5, 1:36.

enter the Holy of Holies, which only the high priest could do on the Day of Atonement.

According to Jewish law, the father determines the descent of the offspring in a legitimate marriage.[907] If the information about James given above is authentic and there is no reason to doubt it, then Joseph and his offspring must have been descended from the tribe of Levi and the family of Aaron, i.e., the tribe and family of the priesthood!

The priestly order *must* derive from the descent of the father, but the royal descent need not be so derived. Take the Hasmonaean priest-kings as an example. Mattathias, the founder of the line, was a priest of the course of Joarib through the male line.[908] Later, Simon, one of Mattathias' sons, was made *"leader and high priest for ever, until a trustworthy prophet should arise."*[909] According to Josephus, John Hyrcanus I, one of Simon's sons, "was accounted by God worthy of three of the greatest privileges, *the rule of the nation*, the office of high priest, and the gift of prophecy...."[910] Thus, royal descent could be granted by a special decree.

The mother's descent could have importance as well. Josephus states the following information about himself:

> Not only ... were my ancestors priests [on my father's side], but they belonged to the first of the twenty-four courses [Joarib] — a peculiar distinction — and to the most eminent of its constituent clans. Moreover, *on my mother's side* I am of *royal* blood; for the posterity of Asamonaeus [Hasmonaeans], from whom she sprang, for a very considerable period were *kings*, as well as high priests, of our nation.[911]

This shows that although priestly descent must be based on the father's lineage, royal descent could be based on the lineage of the mother.

The Dead Sea Scrolls support the idea that the royal Messiah must be descended from the tribe of Judah and family of David,[912] but this does not

---

906. Robert Eisler, *The Messiah Jesus and John the Baptist*, ed. by A. H. Krappe (London: Methuen & Co., 1931), 540-1.

907. Kiddushin 3:12: "If the betrothal was valid and no transgression befell [by reason of the marriage] the standing of the offspring follows that of the male [parent].... " See Herbert Danby, *The Mishnah* (Oxford, Oxford University Press, 1933), 327.

908. 1 Macc. 2:1; Ant. XII, 205.

909. 1 Macc. 14:41 (italics mine).

910. Ant. XIII, 299-300 (italics mine).

911. Vita, 1-2 (italics mine). In War I, 3, Josephus says he was a priest.

912. 4Q285, frag. 5; 4Q174 (Florilegium), 3:11-3; 4Q252 (Pesher on Genesis), 5:1-7; 4QpIs^a, frags. 7-10, 3:22-9.

necessitate that this descent be from the father. It could be derived from the mother just as well. The designation "Messiah of Aaron and Israel"[913] proves this to be the case. It means that he was to be a priest of Aaron on his father's side and a king of Israel on his mother's side.

It was Mary who was descended from the tribe of Judah and family of David, *not* Joseph.[914] This descent could have been on her mother or father's side. Mary could still have been related to Elizabeth (John the Baptist's mother) and descended from Levi/Aaron as well, if her other parent were Elizabeth's aunt or uncle.[915]

The belief that Joseph was descended from Judah/David may have originated sometime after the destruction of Jerusalem and the Temple (AD 70), when priestly descent would have had little meaning without a Temple. This would be especially true to Gentile believers. However, the royal descent from Judah/David would still have been important, because it was prophesied in Scripture.[916] The "grandsons" of Jesus' brother Judas, who were said to have been of the family of David and who were brought before Emperor Domitian (AD 81-96),[917] were probably so descended on *Mary's* side. This would also be the case with regard to Symeon, the son of Clopas (i.e., Joseph). Hegesippus states that he was "accused ... of being descended from David and a Christian...."[918]

The fact that Joseph, Jesus, and perhaps his brothers were carpenters[919] does not conflict with being priests also, because the latter usually practiced some other trade or work as well.[920] This would be especially true of priests who were members of the New Covenant. They were not allowed to officiate in the polluted Temple of Jerusalem[921] and would not have received the tithes and other gratuities that the priests were normally entitled to.

---

913. CD 12:23-13:1, 14:19, 19:10-1, 20:1.
914. The descent of Jesus from Judah/David on Mary's side would make more sense from the point of view of Christian tradition, since according to it Joseph was not Jesus' real father anyway!
915. In Hebrews 7:1-28, Jesus is said to be "descended from Judah" (Heb. 7:14) and by his sacrificial death "a priest forever, after the order of Melchizedek" (Heb. 7:17). O'Neill has theorized that in its original form Hebrews 7:1-28 did not try to prove that the priesthood had become obsolete by the death of the Messiah, but that he had expanded the priesthood. He was not only descended from Levi/Aaron on his father's side as the priests always were, but also from Judah/David on his mother's side. See J. C. O'Neill, "Jesus in Hebrews," *Journal of Higher Criticism*, Vol. 6/1, 1999, 64-82.
916. See, for example, Gen. 49:10, Jer. 23:5-6, 33:17-22, Ezek. 34:23-4.
917. Eusebius, *Ecclesiastical History*, Vol. I, 236-9 (III, 19.1-20.1-7).
918. Eusebius, *Ecclesiastical History*, Vol. I, 272-5 (III, 32.1-6).
919. Mk. 6:3, Mt. 13:55.
920. Jeremias, *Jerusalem in the Time of Jesus*, 206-7.
921. 1QS 9:3-5, CD 6:11-4.

Chapter 15. The Family of Jesus

Having described Jesus' likely genealogy above, is it possible to take it a step further? Were the Christians able to attach the kingly title to him with such fervor solely because he was descended from King David? Throughout the entire period from 200 BC to AD 70, we never hear of anyone from the family of David trying to regain his rightful place as the king of Israel. Nothing is mentioned during the period of the Hasmonaean priest-kings, during the reign of Herod the Great, or even during the period of the Roman governors. Certainly, descent from David had importance *doctrinally* as the Dead Sea Scrolls show, but David's actual descendants appear to have had little effect on the history of this period. The family *did* exist at this time. The *Mishnah* mentions the fact that they brought their wood offerings to the Temple on a special day (the 20th of Tammuz, i.e., June-July).[922] Robert Eisler gives us the following information:

> Since thus, like a few other clans, their impost fell due on a special day, and not, like that of the rest of the people, on the 15th of Ab [July-August], the reason for this arrangement evidently was that they owned so much real estate that the delivery of their wood required a great deal of time.[923]

If Joseph, Jesus, and his brothers were descended from the Hasmonaean priest-kings, we can understand better why royalty would have been so attached to Jesus during his lifetime. This would also explain much better why the descendants of Jesus were brought before Domitian (AD 81-96) and why Symeon, the son of Clopas (i.e., Joseph), suffered martyrdom under Trajan (AD 98-117). It was not really because of their descent from David, which history shows us had little relevance in terms of actual politics. It was because they were also descended from a much more dangerous royal line — the Hasmonaean priest-kings.[924] Herod the Great tried to wipe out this dynasty completely when he came to power and there is no reason to doubt that the people continued to revere it after his death.[925] Although it cannot be conclusively proved, I think the descent of Joseph, Jesus, and his brothers from the Hasmonaean line is a definite possibility.

---

922. Taanith 4.5 in Danby, *The Mishnah*, 200.
923. Eisler, *The Messiah Jesus and John the Baptist*, 322, note 1.
924. For the same reason, the descendants of David who, according to Eusebius, were arrested after the war by the order of Vespasian were probably really arrested because they were *Hasmonaean* heirs. If they were also descended from David, as was the case with Jesus' family, this fact was of little importance politically. See Eusebius, *Ecclesiastical History*, Vol. I, 233 (III, 12.1).
925. Alexander and Aristobulous, the two sons of Herod's wife, Mariamme, the Hasmonaean princess, were revered by the people (Ant. XVI, 6-11). Herod had them both executed by strangulation in 7 BC (Ant. XVI, 361-94, War I, 538-51).

Could there have been other important individuals who were involved in the politics of the time and who were descended from the Hasmonaeans? When mentioning the revolt after Herod the Great's death (4 BC), Bruce provides us with the following interesting statement:

> Whether all the risings that were precipitated by Herod's death can accurately be described as Zealot risings is uncertain; *that some of them were led by surviving scions of the Hasmonaean family is conceivable*, but the evidence for this view is insufficient.[926]

Let us remember two significant facts. First, the leaders of the revolt were Judas, the son of Ezekias; Simon of Perea, a former slave of Herod; and Athronges, a former shepherd. Second, Judas, the son of Ezekias, was probably the same person as Judas the Galilean, the founder of the Sicarii.

It is not difficult to understand why Josephus would not have mentioned the Hasmonaean descent of any of these individuals, if there were any truth in the claims. As we have seen, Josephus himself was descended from this dynasty of priest-kings and he would certainly not want to make it known that "surviving scions of the Hasmonaean family" were causing Rome trouble. Neither would he want to connect his lineage with the Sicarii (i.e., Judas the Galilean and his descendants), who are described by him as "the first" of the revolutionary groups to use violence against the Romans and their Jewish collaborators[927] and whom he blames for the destruction of his nation.[928] It would also not be to his purpose to admit the Hasmonaean descent of Jesus, whom he calls the "crucified wonder-worker" and who (so his followers believed) was destined to be the world ruler in opposition to Emperor Vespasian. His silence would make perfect sense, as he would not want to tarnish the noble reputation of his great family in the eyes of the Romans.

---

926. F. F. Bruce, *New Testament History* (New York: Anchor Books, 1972), 97 (italics mine).
927. War VII, 262, 325.
928. Ant. XVIII, 6, 9, 10, 25.

Chapter 16. Microletters

Dr. E. Jerry Vardaman, the founding director of the Cobb Institute of Archaeology at Mississippi State University (1974) and Professor of Religion until his retirement (1994), was the discoverer of microletters on first century AD coins (1984). Microletters are very small inscriptions placed on coins and other objects. They are so small that a magnifying glass is required to see them and, in case you may be wondering, magnifying glasses were indeed used in antiquity. Jerry Vardaman claims that the coins "are literally covered with microletters" and that "microletters existed on ancient coins, from the earliest times up through the Hellenistic and Roman periods, and beyond."[929]

Why were they placed on coins? There would appear to be at least four reasons:[930]

1. They were "placed on ancient dies to serve as guide letters."
2. They were "placed on coins ... to attest to the authenticity of the object."
3. They "eliminated the need for crowding all vital information on coins in the main legends."
4. They indicated "some kind of control in certain instances — such as a payment for something, or so much money allocated to a city."

In most cases, the microletters were placed on the original coin dies, but occasionally they were scratched on the coins before distribution from the mint.

---

929. Jerry Vardaman, "Jesus' Life: A New Chronology," *Cronos Kairos Christos*, eds. Jerry Vardaman, Edwin M. Yamauchi (Winona Lake: Eisenbrauns, 1989), 66.
930. Vardaman, "Jesus'Life: A New Chronology," 67.

What do they tell us? First, the accepted dates of the terms of office for the first five Roman governors will have to be changed. The accepted dates and the new dates are listed in the following table:[931]

Governor	Accepted Date	New Date
Coponius	AD 6-9	AD 6-9
Marcus Ambibulus	AD 9-12	AD 6-9
Annius Rufus	AD 12-15	AD 9-14
Valerius Gratus	AD 15-26	AD 14/15
Marcus Pontius Pilate	AD 26-36	AD 15/16-25/26

Second, Jesus is mentioned often in the microletters and he is referred to as "King Jesus," "King of the Jews," "Messiah," and even "Savior." Based on other information contained in the microletters, it can be determined that Jesus' "reign" (i.e., his public ministry) lasted for six years from AD 15/16 to AD 20/21. Pilate crucified him at Passover in April, AD 21 in his sixth year in office.[932]

AD 21 as the year of the crucifixion agrees with the publication by Emperor Maximinus Daia in AD 311 of what was in all likelihood Pilate's actual report of Jesus' trial. Eusebius called it a forgery.[933] However, if it was a forgery, why was a traditional date not given for the crucifixion like AD 29, 30, 32, or 33?[934] Except for the microletters, AD 21 is unique to *all* our sources. It is very unfortunate that the report no longer exists, since it could have provided us with other important information now lost.

One very interesting microletter was discovered on the rim of a Jewish shekel that was dated "year one" of the Jewish revolt (i.e., AD 66). It reads as follows:

> Year 6 of the procurator Mar(cus) Pontius Pilate, which is Year 1 of the death (or the cross, the crucifixion) of Jesus, the righteous one."[935]

"Year 6" of Pilate's governorship would be AD 20/21 (AD 15/16, 16/17, 17/18, 18/19, 19/20, 20/21), which was the year ("Year 1") of Jesus' death.

---

931. Jack Finegan, *The Archeology of the New Testament*, rev. ed. (Princeton: Princeton University Press, 1992), xxiv.

932. Finegan, *The Archeology of the New Testament*, xxv-xxvi.

933. Eusebius, *Ecclesiastical History*, 2 vols., trans. by Kirsopp Lake (Cambridge: Harvard University Press, 1975), Vol. I, 74-5 (I. 9.3-4), Vol. 2, 338-9 (IX.5.1), Vol. 2 340-3 (IX.7.1).

934. Robert Eisler, *The Messiah Jesus and John the Baptist*, ed. by A. H. Krappe (London: Methuen & Co., 1931), 16-7.

935. Finegan, *The Archeology of the New Testament*, xxv.

Why are these microletters so important? Jerry Vardaman answers this question as follows:

> These and other coins (which now can be more accurately dated) and their microletters provide the earliest nonbiblical, nonliterary testimonies of Jesus. ... What must be emphasized ... is ... that coins with microletters appear before any literary evidences presently known that mention Jesus.[936]

I will take this a step further and state unequivocally that they prove, *beyond doubt*, the very existence of Jesus! Before the discovery of microletters, a good case could be made that Jesus was a myth based on the nature of the sources available to us.[937] This is not the case anymore.

Jerry Vardaman further adds the following point:

> All these conclusions ... point to one exciting prospect, that more scholars will pursue the subject of microletters on coins and will, eventually, add to or change the pages of history from which we are still learning today.[938]

Unfortunately, this hope for further study does not appear to have materialized. Microletters are rarely if ever mentioned in the literature. Why is this so? I believe the reasons are as follows: For Christians, microletters would disprove the traditional dates that have been utilized for centuries and would call into question the trustworthiness of the gospels. For those who believe in the myth theory, microletters would prove Jesus' existence. Thus, neither side for reasons of their own wants to deal with them. Unfortunately, since there is a conspiracy of silence regarding microletters, many individuals who would be interested in them are unaware of their existence. Perhaps this chapter will at least remedy this problem.

---

936. Vardaman, "Jesus' Life: A New Chronology," 76.
937. See, for example, G. A. Wells, *Did Jesus Exist?* 2nd ed. (London: Pemberton, 1986).
938. Vardaman, "Jesus' Life: A New Chronology," 77.

CHAPTER 17. THE TRIAL AND CRUCIFIXION OF JESUS

The one fact from which all criticism of the trial and crucifixion of Jesus begins is that he was crucified for sedition against the Roman government of Judea. It is mentioned in all four gospels,[939] by Josephus,[940] and on microletters. Although the crucifixion is not mentioned specifically, the Roman historian Tacitus (ca. AD 55-120) does state in AD 116 that "Christus ... had undergone the death penalty in the reign of Tiberius, by sentence of the procurator [governor] Pontius Pilate."[941] Mark 15:26 states the following: "And the inscription of the charge against him read, 'The King of the Jews.'" In other words, Jesus was charged with making himself a king in opposition to Caesar.

Crucifixion was a barbaric form of execution. The victim usually did not give way to heart failure for two or three days, although death could be hastened by breaking the legs. The bones of a crucified man named Yehohanan (John, in Aramaic), who lived in the time of Jesus, were found during excavations northeast of Jerusalem in 1968.[942] The remains prove the brutality of crucifixion all too clearly.

From the death of Herod the Great (4 BC) to the Jewish revolt (AD 66-70), there were numerous insurrections against the Roman rule in Judaea. The penalty meted out to captured rebels was crucifixion. For example, Varus, the governor of Syria, had two thousand insurgents crucified not long after the death

---

939. Mk. 15:22-32, Mt. 27:33-44, Lk. 23:33-43, Jn. 19:17-24.
940. Ant. XVIII, 63-4; Slavonic Josephus (Josephus, Bk. III, Appendix, pp. 648-50).
941.Tacitus, *Histories, Annals*, trans. by C. H. Moore and J. Jackson (Loeb Classical Library) 4 vols. (Cambridge: Harvard University Press, 1979) V, 283 (Annals XV.44).
942.Vassilios Tzaferis, "Crucifixion — The Archaeological Evidence," *Biblical Archaeology Review* 11 (1985): 44-53.

of Herod the Great[943] and Tiberius Alexander, who was governor from AD 44-8,[944] had James and Simon, the two sons of the rebel Judas the Galilean, crucified.[945]

What makes the gospel story unusual is that Jesus, who is actually innocent of any seditious activity, is crucified in place of Barabbas, who was involved in a recent insurrection in Jerusalem.[946] Also, Pontius Pilate is portrayed as weak and indecisive in the gospels. This is hardly the character that one would expect of a Roman governor.

Since there are significant differences between the gospels, the four versions of Jesus before the Sanhedrin and his trial before Pilate have been reproduced in separate columns on the next page. The sections in italics are unique to that gospel and are not found in the other ones:

There are three elements common to all four versions that make them highly unlikely, if not impossible, historically:

1. Pontius Pilate was not the weak, indecisive governor portrayed in the gospels, but a tough, competent one, who was hated by the Jews.
2. There is no evidence for, nor is there likely to have been, a custom of freeing a prisoner by the Roman governor at the Passover.
3. Even though the Jewish authorities in all likelihood could not execute a Jew who had broken their ecclesiastical law, there is still no valid reason why they had to get the Romans to do it for them. To involve the Roman authorities, especially in the way the gospels depict it, would have been very difficult and politically foolish. What they did do, if required, was to use covert means to carry out an execution themselves.

Let us take each element one at a time.

Fortunately, we also have other information about Pilate from Josephus and Philo of Alexandria, the famous Jewish philosopher.

---

943. Ant. XVII, 295; War II, 75.
944. Based on the Slavonic Josephus about the followers of the "Wonder-worker" (i.e., Jesus), it can be determined that Tiberius Alexander governed jointly with the previous governor Cuspius Fadus in AD 44-ca. 46 and alone in AD ca. 46-48. Robert Eisler, *The Messiah Jesus and John the Baptist*, ed. by A. H. Krappe (London: Methuen & Co., 1931), 531-3.
945. Ant. XX, 102
946. Mk. 15:6-7, 11, 15; Mt. 27:15-7, 21, 26; Lk. 23:18-9, 24-5; Jn. 18:38-40.

Chapter 17. The Trial and Crucifixion of Jesus

Mt. 26:57 - 27:26	Mk. 14:43 -15:15	Lk. 22:54 -23:25	Jn. 18:12-19:16
Then those who had seized Jesus led him to Caiaphus the high priest, where the scribes and the elders had gathered.	And they led Jesus to the high priest; and all the chief priests and the elders and the scribes were assembled.	Then they seized him and led him away, bringing him into the high priest's house.	*So the band of soldiers and their captain and the officers of the Jews seized Jesus and bound him. First they led him to Annas; for he was the father-in-law of Caiaphus, who was high priest that year. It was Caiaphus who had given counsel to the Jews that it was expedient that one man should die for the people.*
PETER ENTERS THE COURTYARD OF THE HIGH PRIEST (Mt. 26:58)	PETER ENTERS THE COURTYARD OF THE HIGH PRIEST (Mk. 14: 54).	PETER ENTERS THE COURTYARD OF THE HIGH PRIEST (Lk. 22:54-5). PETER'S DENIAL (Lk. 22:56-62). JESUS IS MOCKED AND BEATEN (Lk. 22:63-5).	PETER AND *ANOTHER DISCIPLE* ENTER THE COURTYARD OF *ANNAS* (Jn. 18:15-8).
Now the chief priests and the whole council sought false testimony against Jesus that they might put him to death, but they found none, though many false witnesses came forward. At last two came forward and said, "This fellow said, 'I am able to destroy the temple of God, and to build it in three days.'" And the high priest stood up and said, "Have you no answer to make? What is it that these men testify against you?" But Jesus was silent. And the high priest said to him, "I adjure you by the living God, tell us if you are the Christ, the Son of God." Jesus said to him, *"You have said so. But I tell you, hereafter you will see the Son of man seated at the right hand of Power, and coming on the clouds of heaven."* Then the high priest tore his robes, and said, "He has uttered blasphemy. Why do we still need witnesses? You have now heard his blasphemy. What is your judgment?" They answered, "He deserves death."	Now the chief priests and the whole council sought testimony against Jesus to put him to death; but they found none. For many bore false witness against him, and their witness did not agree. And some stood up and bore false witness against him, saying, "We heard him say, 'I will destroy this temple that is made with hands, and in three days I will build another, not made with hands.'" Yet not even so did their testimony agree. And the high priest stood up in the midst, and asked Jesus, "Have you no answer to make? What is it that these men testify against you?" But he was silent and made no answer. Again the high priest asked him, "Are you the Christ, the Son of the Blessed?" And Jesus said, *"I am; and you will see the Son of man sitting at the right hand of Power, and coming with the clouds of heaven."* And the high priest tore his mantle, and said, "Why do we still need witnesses? You have heard his blasphemy. What is your decision?" And they condemned him as deserving death.	When day came, the assembly of the elders of the people gathered together, both chief priests and scribes; and they led him away to their council, and they said, "If you are the Christ, tell us." But he said to them, *"If I tell you, you will not believe; and if I ask you. You will not answer.* But from now on the Son of man shall be seated at the right hand of the Power of God." And they all said, "Are you the Son of God, then?" And he said to them, *"You say that I am."* And they said, "What further testimony do we need? We have heard it ourselves from his own lips."	The high priest then questioned Jesus about his disciples and his teaching. Jesus answered him, *"I have spoken openly to the world; I have always taught in synagogues and in the temple, where all Jews come together; I have said nothing secretly. Why do you ask me? Ask those who have heard me, what I said to them; they know what I said."* When he had said this, one of the officers standing by struck Jesus with his hand, saying, "Is that how you answer the high priest?" Jesus answered him, *"If I have spoken wrongly, bear witness to the wrong; but if I have spoken rightly, why do you strike me?"* Annas then sent him bound to Caiaphus the high priest.

JESUS IS MOCKED AND BEATEN (Mt. 26:67—8). PETER'S DENIAL (Mt. 26:69-75).	JESUS IS MOCKED AND BEATEN (Mk. 14:65). PETER'S DENIAL (Mk. 14:66-72).		PETER'S DENIAL (Jn. 18:25-7).
When morning came, all the chief priests and the elders of the people took counsel against Jesus to put him to death; and they bound him and led him away and delivered him to Pilate, the governor. *THE DEATH OF JUDAS* (Mt. 27:3-10).	And as soon as it was morning the chief priests, with the elders and scribes, and the whole council held a consultation; and they bound Jesus and led him away and delivered him to Pilate.	When day came, the assembly of the elders of the people gathered together, both chief priests and scribes; and they led him away to their council. Then the whole company of them arose, and brought him to Pilate.	*Then they led Jesus from the house of Caiaphas to the praetorium. It was early. They themselves did not enter the praetorium, so that they might not be defiled, but might eat the Passover.*
Now Jesus stood before the governor; and the governor asked him, "Are you the King of the Jews?" Jesus said to him, "You have said so." But when he was accused by the chief priests and elders, he made no answer. Then Pilate said to him, "Do you not hear how many things they testify against you?" But he gave them no answer, not even to a single charge; so that the governor wondered greatly.	And Pilate asked him, "Are you the King of the Jews?" And he answered him, "You have said so." And the chief priests accused him of many things. And Pilate again asked him, "Have you no answer to make? See how many charges they bring against you." But Jesus made no further answer, so that Pilate wondered.	*And they began to accuse him, saying, "We found this man perverting our nation, and forbidding us to give tribute to Caesar, and saying that he himself is Christ a king."* And Pilate asked him, "Are you the King of the Jews?" And he answered him, "You have said so." And Pilate said to the chief priests and the multitudes, "I find no crime in this man." *But they were urgent, saying, "He stirs up the people, teaching throughout all Judea, from Galilee even to this place."* JESUS BEFORE HEROD (Lk. 23:6-16).	*So Pilate went out to them and said, "What accusation do you bring against this man?" They answered him, "If this man were not an evildoer, we would not have handed him over." Pilate said to them, "Take him yourselves and judge him by your own law." The Jews said to him, "It is not lawful for us to put any man to death." This was to fulfill the word which Jesus had spoken to show by what death he was to die. Pilate entered the praetorium again and called Jesus, and said to him, "Are you the King of the Jews?" Jesus answered, "Do you say this of your own accord, or did others say it to you about me?" Jesus answered, "My kingship is not of this world; if my kingship were of this world, my servants would fight, that I might not be handed over to the Jews; but my kingship is not from the world." Pilate said to him, "So you are a king?" Jesus answered, "You say that I am a king. For this I was born, and for this I have come into the world, to bear witness to the truth. Every one who is of the truth hears my voice." Pilate said to him, "What is truth?"*

Chapter 17. The Trial and Crucifixion of Jesus

Now at the feast the governor was accustomed to release for the crowd any one prisoner whom they wanted. And they had then a notorious prisoner called Barabbas. So when they had gathered, Pilate said to them, "Whom do you want me to release for you, Barabbas or Jesus who is called Christ?" For he knew that it was out of envy that they had delivered him up. *Besides, while he was sitting on the judgment seat, his wife sent word to him, "Have nothing to do with that righteous man, for I have suffered much over him today in a dream."* Now the chief priests and the elders persuaded the people to ask for Barabbas and destroy Jesus. The governor again said to them, "Which of the two do you want me to release for you?" And they said, "Barabbas." Pilate said to them, "Then what shall I do with Jesus who is called Christ?" They all said, "Let him be crucified." And he said, "Why, what evil has he done?" But they shouted all the more, "Let him be crucified." *So when Pilate saw that he was gaining nothing, but rather that a riot was beginning, he took water and washed his hands before the crowd, saying, "I am innocent of this man's blood, see to it yourselves." And all the people answered, "His blood be on us and on our children!"* Then he released for them Barabbas, and having scourged Jesus, delivered him to be crucified.

Now at the feast he used to release for them any one prisoner whom they asked. And among the rebels in prison, who had committed murder in the insurrection, there was a man called Barabbas. And the crowd came up and began to ask Pilate to do as he was wont to do for them. And he answered them," Do you want me to release for you the King of the Jews?" For he perceived that it was out of envy that the chief priests had delivered him up. But the chief priests stirred up the crowd to have him release for them Barabbas instead. And Pilate again said to them, "Then what shall I do with the man whom you call the King of the Jews?" And they cried out again, "Crucify him." And Pilate said to them, "Why, what evil has he done?" But they shouted all the more, "Crucify him." So Pilate, wishing to satisfy the crowd, released for them Barabbas; and having scourged Jesus, he delivered him to be crucified.

But they all cried out together, "Away with this man, and release to us Barabbas" — a man who had been thrown into prison for an insurrection started in the city, and for murder. Pilate addressed them once more, desiring to release Jesus: but they shouted out, "Crucify, crucify him!" A third time he said to them, "Why, what evil has he done? I have found in him no crime deserving death; I will therefore chastise him and release him." But they were urgent, demanding with loud cries that he should be crucified. And their voices prevailed. So Pilate gave sentence that their demand should be granted. He released the man who had been thrown into prison for insurrection and murder, whom they asked for; but Jesus he delivered up to their will.

After he had said this, he went out to the Jews again, and told them, "I find no crime in him. But you have a custom that I should release one man for you at the Passover; will you have me release for you the King of the Jews?" They cried out again, "Not this man, but Barabbas!" Now Barabbas was a robber.

PILATE HAS JESUS SCOURGED (Jn. 19:1-3).

Pilate went out again, and said to them, "See, I am bringing him out to you, that you may know that I find no crime in him." So Jesus came out, wearing the crown of thorns and the purple robe. Pilate said to them, "Behold the man!" When the chief priests and the officers saw him, they cried out, "Crucify him, crucify him!" *Pilate said to them, "Take him yourselves and crucify him, for I find no crime in him." The Jews answered him, "We have a law, and by that law he ought to die, because he has made himself the Son of God." When Pilate heard these words, he was the more afraid; he entered the praetorium again and said to Jesus, "Where are you from?" But Jesus gave no answer. Pilate therefore said to him, "You will not speak to me? Do you not know that I have power to release you, and the power to crucify you?" Jesus answered him, "You would have no power over me unless it had been given you from above; therefore he who delivered me to you has the greater sin."* Upon this Pilate sought to release him, *but the Jews cried out, "If you release this man, you are not Caesar's friend; every one who makes himself a king sets himself against Caesar."*

			When Pilate heard these words, he brought Jesus out and sat down on the judgment seat at the place called The Pavement, and in Hebrew, Gabbatha. Now it was the day of Preparation of the Passover; it was about the sixth hour. He said to the Jews, "Behold your king!" They cried out, "Away with him, away with him, crucify him!" Pilate said to them, "Shall I crucify your king?" The chief priests answered, "We have no king but Caesar." Then he handed him over to be crucified.

The first incident comes at the beginning of Josephus' account of the governorship of Pontius Pilate. When Pilate arrived in Judea to begin his term of office as governor, he brought into Jerusalem by night the Roman standards that bore the image of the emperor. Out of respect for Jewish religious feelings, previous governors only brought standards into the city that did not have the emperor's image attached to them.[947] When the people saw these standards in the morning, they went to Caesarea and implored Pilate to take them out of Jerusalem. Only when Pilate realized that a massacre of the people would result (for they were willing to accept death rather than the violation of their religious law) did he finally relent and order the standards to be removed from Jerusalem.[948]

The second incident that Josephus tells us about occurred over the building of an aqueduct to bring water to Jerusalem. In order to pay for the work, Pilate took sacred money from the Temple. The Jews became outraged at this action and violently protested when he came to Jerusalem. Pilate had his soldiers disguise themselves as civilians and conceal clubs under their clothing. After distributing them throughout the crowd, the crowd was ordered to disperse. When they did not do so, the soldiers were given the signal and attacked the

---

947. See Ex. 20:4-5: "You shall not make for yourself a graven image, or any likeness of anything that is in heaven above, or that is in the earth beneath, or that is in the water under the earth; you shall not bow done to them or serve them; for I the LORD your God am a jealous God...." Cf. Dt. 4:16-8. According to Josephus, the Romans did sacrifice to their standards in the Temple court in August/September of AD 70 (War VI, 316).

948. Ant. XVIII, 55-9; War II, 169-71.

crowd. Many people were killed or wounded and the disturbance was quelled.[949]

The last incident that Josephus tells us about ended Pilate's term as governor. Believing in some false prophet[950] who told them that he knew were the sacred vessels of the Tabernacle were hidden by Moses on Mt. Gerizim, a large number of Samaritans gathered in the village of Tirathana to prepare to ascend the mountain. Before they could do so, Pilate sent troops, many were put to flight or killed, and those that were captured were executed. Although they were armed, the Samaritans protested to Vitellius, the legate (i.e., governor) of Syria, that "it was not as rebels against Rome but as refugees from the persecution of Pilate that they met in Tirathana." Vitellius ordered Pilate to Rome to explain his actions to Emperor Tiberius. When he reached Rome, the emperor was dead[951] and Pilate is no longer heard of again.[952]

Philo of Alexandria describes an incident regarding Roman shields during Pilate's governorship. It can be found in *The Embassy to Gaius*.[953] This incident, although similar to the standard affair mentioned by Josephus above, probably took place some time after it.[954]

Pilate set up in Herod's palace some shields coated with gold that had inscribed on them the emperor's name and the name of the person who dedicated them. There were no images on these shields. A Jewish delegation that was headed by four Herodian princes petitioned the governor to remove the shields, because they violated their customs.[955] Pilate refused to remove them.

---

949. Ant. XVIII, 60-2; War II, 175-7.

950. We will learn the likely identity of this false prophet in the chapter titled *Simon Magus*.

951. Jerry Vardaman takes the Greek word in Ant. XVIII, 89 that is usually translated as "died" or "passed away" ("But before [Pilate] reached Rome Tiberius had already *passed away*"), as "moved." The meaning would then be that Tiberius had *moved* from Rome to the island of Capri, not that he had died. Tiberius died on 16 March, AD 37. Josephus would then not be in contradiction to the microletters saying that Pilate was dismissed in AD 25/26 and not in AD 36. However, whether Vitellius' governorship of Syria can be placed as early as AD 25/26 is still an unresolved problem. See Jerry Vardaman, "Jesus' Life: A New Chronology," *Chronos Kairos Christos*, Jerry Vardaman and Edwin Yamauchi, eds. (Winona Lake: Eisenbrauns, 1989), 77-82.

952. Ant. XVIII, 85-9.

953. Philo, *The Embassy to Gaius*, Vol. X, F. H. Colson and J. W. Earp, trans., The Loeb Classical Library (Cambridge: Harvard University Press, 1971), 299-305 (pp. 151-5). The purpose of the embassy was to plead with Emperor Gaius (Caligula) not to force the Jews to give divine honors to him. It was initiated as a consequence of the violent disputes that were taking place between the Jews and Gentiles in Alexandria in AD 38-41 (Philo, *The Embassy to Gaius*, 114-36, pp. 57-69; Ant. XVIII, 257-60).

954. S. G. F. Brandon, *Jesus and the Zealots* (New York: Charles Scribner's Sons, 1967), 71-5.

955. Since the shields did not have images on them, it is difficult to understand why the Jews protested their being in the city.

They demanded that he produce the authority for his action and threatened him with an appeal to the emperor. This disturbed Pilate, because an appeal would make his maladministration known to Emperor Tiberius. Nevertheless, the Jews had to write to the emperor about the matter. Tiberius, who was extremely angry, ordered Pilate to remove the shields from Jerusalem to Caesarea.[956]

In describing the shield incident, Philo tells us that Pilate was "naturally inflexible [and] a blend of self-will and relentlessness."[957] He also mentions his "vindictiveness and furious temper."[958] In specifying accusations against his administration, he mentions "'the briberies, the insults, the robberies, the outrages and wanton injuries, the executions without trial constantly repeated [and] the ceaseless and supremely grievous cruelty."[959]

All of this information from secular sources gives us a portrait of Pilate totally at variance with the weak, indecisive Pilate portrayed in the gospels. He was firm in his desire to rule in his own way. The opinion of his subjects did not bother him in the least and a settlement of differences by mutual concessions was never attempted. It was only when the choice came down to ordering the removal of the standards or ordering a mass execution that Pilate removed the standards. When he later brought the shields into Jerusalem, it was the emperor himself who ended up ordering him to remove them even though his maladministration was supposedly made known to the emperor. In stopping revolts or even the beginnings of revolts, he was merciless, as can be seen by the aqueduct affair and the Samaritan affair.

Did Pilate needlessly harass the Jews in some cases? Josephus states that Pilate brought the standards into Jerusalem "in subversion of the Jewish practices."[960] Philo states that Pilate brought the shields into Jerusalem "not so much to honour Tiberius as to annoy the multitude."[961] In answer to this question, Morrison makes the following statement:

> It is hardly to be supposed that the procurator [Pilate], in the prosecution of his religious policy, was merely gratifying a feeling of personal animosity at the cost of adding immensely to his difficulties as a ruler. Such is not the course which a man of Pilate's experience was likely to adopt.[962]

---

956. Philo. *The Embassy to Gaius*. 299-305 (pp. 151-5).
957. Philo, *The Embassy to Gaius*, 301 (p. 151).
958. Philo, *The Embassy to Gaius*, 303 (p. 153).
959. Philo, *The Embassy to Gaius*, 302-3 (p. 153).
960. Ant. XVIII, 55.
961. Philo, *The Embassy to Gaius*, 299 (p. 151).
962. W. D. Morrison, *The Jews Under Roman Rule* (London, 1890), 145-6.

What seems more likely is that the Emperor changed his policy in regards to the standards and Pilate initiated the change on his arrival as the new governor. When the Jews would not accept this change, a less radical change was attempted later (i.e., the shields), but this attempt failed as well. Tiberius did not think it was worth the effort to cause bloodshed over either attempt — first the standards then the shields. If this was not the true situation, then why did Tiberius not recall Pilate for trying to harass the Jews?[963]

How do we explain the accusations of Pilate's maladministration? It is highly unlikely that Pilate could have ruled Judaea for as long as he did under Tiberius (10 years),[964] if he did what Philo says he did. We know that Tiberius went out of his way to appoint capable governors to the provinces.[965] Arnold makes the following statement:

> Whatever we may think of the life and character of Tiberius as a whole, there can be no question of the excellence of his government of the provinces. He had shown himself a friend of the provinces even before he was emperor; and his reign did not belie the hopes then raised.[966]

Regarding Philo's charges of maladministration, Morrision has this to say:

> Philo gives a long list of these misdeeds, which include oppression and cruelty of the worst kind. It is not likely that Pilate was a scrupulous official, but it is certain that he would not have dared to act in the manner described by Philo under the keen eyes of such a master as Tiberius.[967]

Finally, in regard to the shield affair, Brandon makes this important point:

> Although he [Philo] had emphasized Pilate's exceeding fear that a Jewish embassy would discover his misdeeds to the emperor, he describes him as continuing in his refusal to accede to the Jewish request for the removal of the shields. Surely, if he knew that he had exceeded his authority in the matter and that his other iniquities would thereby come to light, he would have prevented the sending of the embassy by a discreet concession? *His stubbornness, where he is*

---

963. S. G. F. Brandon, *Jesus and the Zealots* (New York: Charles Scribner's Sons, 1967), 69, 74-5.
964. Ant. XVIII, 89. Josephus mentions the practice of Emperor Tiberius to appoint governors for long terms of office (Ant. XVIII, 170-8).
965. T. Arnold, *The Roman System of Provincial Administration* (New York: Libraries Press, 1971), 140-2.
966. Arnold, *The Roman System of Provincial Administration*, 140.
967. Morrison, *The Jews Under Roman Rule*, 146, note 1.

represented as being in a weaker position vis-à-vis the Jewish leaders, contrasts strikingly with his abject submission when Caesar's name is invoked by the chief priests, to secure the condemnation of Jesus; cf. John xix. 12-13, 15.[968]

Clearly then, the weak, indecisive Pilate of the gospels is not historical. Why was this portrait created? It is not difficult to discover the reason. The Jews were utterly defeated by the Romans in the war of AD 66-70. Christians after this event wanted desperately to live in peace with Rome. How could they explain to the Romans that one of their governors had crucified the founder of their faith as a rebel against Rome? How could they make the Romans believe that they themselves had no desire to rebel against Rome? The gospel writers transformed Pilate into a weak, indecisive governor, who believed Jesus was innocent, but was forced to have him crucified against his better judgment, *because of Jewish malice*, despite the military force available to him to back up his decisions. The Jews were the perfect scapegoats after their defeat in the war.

> Now at the feast he used to release for them any one prisoner whom they asked. And among the rebels in prison, who had committed murder in the insurrection, there was a man called Barabbas.[969]

So according to Mark begins what is probably the most problematical and mysterious episode narrated in the gospels. Matthew adds that Barabbas was "a notorious prisoner," Luke adds that he was thrown in prison "for murder," and John adds that he was a "robber."[970]

As a last resort to try to release Jesus, Pilate made use of a Passover custom by which "he used to release for them any one prisoner whom they asked." In giving the crowd a choice between Jesus and Barabbas, Pilate hoped they would choose Jesus, but they chose Barabbas instead. He was forced to order the crucifixion of Jesus.

This Passover custom is not mentioned anywhere else but in the gospels. Suspicion is cast upon its actual existence by this lack of corroborating evidence. Here is what Wilson has to say about the custom:

---

968. Brandon, *Jesus and the Zealots*, 73, note 1 (italics mine except "vis-à-vis").
969. Mk. 15:6-7, cf. Mt. 27:15-6, Lk. 23:18-9.
970. Jn. 18:40. The designation "robber" means a "political revolutionary." See *The New Oxford Annotated Bible*, eds. Herbert G. May and Bruce M. Metzger (New York: Oxford University Press, 1973), 1314, note 40 for 18:1-19:42; Martin Hengel, *The Zealots*, trans. by David Smith (Edinburgh: T. & T. Clark, 1989), 24-46, 341.

Such an annual amnesty is unknown in all our other sources. The search for some substantiating evidence has been pursued to the remotest corners of Greek, Roman, and Jewish history, but on close examination none of the suggested references stand up as parallels to the Gospel accounts.[971]

Also, why would the Romans continue to respect such a custom? Certainly, in a province as tumultuous as Judaea such a custom would go against the whole idea of maintaining order. It is nonsense to believe that the Roman governor would free a Jewish rebel, because of some supposed ancient custom, and so allow him to continue undermining his authority. Furthermore, pardoning a convicted criminal was the sole prerogative of the Emperor.[972] On the other hand, if Barabbas had not yet been tried, Pilate would have had to make absolutely certain that the charges were without foundation before Barabbas could legitimately be freed. In any case, Pilate's freeing of Barabbas would have had no bearing on Jesus' case or visa versa.

The Passover custom was probably created in the gospels in order to make the Jewish guilt for Jesus' crucifixion, which the gospels want to support, appear undeniable. After all, in the gospel story the Jews prefer to free a rebel against Rome rather than the Son of God himself! What could be more proof of their guilt than this?

Like Judea, Egypt was also an imperial province ruled by a prefect (i.e., governor).[973] A study of the Egyptian papyri, which tell us something about the Roman government in Egypt, will help us to better understand how the Roman government in Judaea must have functioned.[974]

According to these papyri, Egypt was divided into three judicial districts and the governor visited the major city of each district to hold court. In each district was placed an official who was in charge of that district and who was appointed by the Emperor. These three large districts were divided into sub-districts. In charge of each sub-district was placed another official appointed by the governor.

The governor would go into one of the three districts along with the official of that district, the officials of the sub-districts, and other administrative aides.

---

971. William R. Wilson, *The Execution of Jesus* (New York: Charles Scribner's Sons, 1970), 140.
972. Richard W. Husband, *The Prosecution of Jesus* (Princeton: Princeton University Press, 1916), 270.
973. Normally, an official of high rank called a legate governed an imperial province. However, if its importance was considered to be small, an official of lower rank called a prefect or procurator governed it. This lesser official held the same authority over the province as a legate (Wilson, *The Execution of Jesus*, 5-6, 175-6; Husband, *The Prosecution of Jesus*, 174-5, 178-9).
974. All of the following information about the Roman government in Egypt comes from Husband, *The Prosecution of Jesus*, 137-81.

Each district would receive a visit from the governor. While there, the governor would examine the documents of each case that were prepared in advance and he would possibly delegate some of the most trivial cases to others. He would judge the important ones himself.

That the system worked efficiently is shown by the fact that the cases were handled quickly. When someone wanted to initiate a legal action against another, he addressed a complaint to the official of the sub-district where he resided. The official would prepare the legal documents in advance so that the case could be handled quickly when the governor arrived to hold court.

This evidence seems to show that the Sanhedrin and the lesser courts in Judea functioned in the same way as the officials of the districts of Egypt functioned. Husband states the situation as follows:

> The Romans found an ancient system of local tribunals in Judaea, and allowed them to maintain a partial activity, but reduced their power in criminal cases to that of preparing the documents and sifting the evidence, so that suits might be handled more expeditiously by the governor when he appeared in Jerusalem. Why the Romans permitted the ancient system of courts to remain must be only a matter of conjecture. But it may be that the Jewish courts still, as is commonly believed, treated ecclesiastical cases of smaller consequence, for the reason that the Romans decided that it would be least irritating and disturbing to racial feelings to allow the native courts to continue with a part of their former functions. The Jews would thus be more patient under foreign sway.[975]

Only the Roman governor had the authority to try a criminal case. In cases such as these, the Sanhedrin simply functioned as a grand jury and only prepared the evidence for the governor. As was explained in an earlier chapter, the Sanhedrin in all likelihood still had the power to judge infringements of the Mosaic Law under the Roman occupation, but it is highly unlikely that it could utilize capital punishment on anyone who was found guilty of a severe infringement of it. The only exception to this appears to have been that the Sanhedrin could use capital punishment on any foreigner who went beyond the stone balustrade into the inner court of the Temple. This court was reserved only to Jews.[976] Nevertheless, anytime the Sanhedrin had a reason to convene it first

---

975. Husband, *The Prosecution of Jesus*, 150-1.
976. Ant. XV, 417; War V, 193-4; VI, 125-6. An inscription in more than one language, which was placed at regular intervals in the stone balustrade, stated the following: "No foreigner is to enter within the balustrade and embankment around the sanctuary. Whoever is caught will have himself to blame for his death which follows" (Josephus, Bk. VIII, pp. 202-3, note d).

had to obtain approval from the governor. Doubtless, the purpose of requiring this approval was to keep tight control on the activities of the body.

The Romans were adamant in refusing to get involved in Jewish religious quarrels. In Acts 18:14-5, a Jewish crowd brought Paul into court accusing him of "inducing people to worship God in ways that are against the Law." Gallio, the Proconsul of Achaia, said, "if it had been a question of crime or grave misdemeanor, I should of course, have given you Jews a patient hearing, but if it is some bickering about words and names and your Jewish law, you see to it yourselves: I have no mind to be judge of these matters."

The Jewish authorities had no alternative but to use other means to inflict capital punishment on those who committed severe infringements of the Mosaic Law. There is evidence that they could and did use secret means to carry out the death penalty. This could be done through covert assassinations or unfortunate "accidents." James the Righteous was killed in just this fashion in AD 62.[977] A passage from the Talmud is very interesting in this regard. It says that when the Sanhedrin lost its power to inflict various forms of capital punishment, the condemned would still receive their due from God in the form of unexpected "accidents." I quote the passage below:

> ...whoever is guilty of being stoned either falls from the roof or a wild beast tramples him to death. Whoever is guilty of being burned to death either falls into the fire or is bitten by a snake. Whoever is guilty of being beheaded is either delivered up to the (pagan) government or assailed by robbers. Whoever is guilty of being strangled is either drowned or chokes to death.[978]

---

977. Arthur Palumbo, "1QpHab 11:2-8 and the Death of James the Just," *The Qumran Chronicle* (Vol. 3, No. 1-3, Dec. 1993) and pp. 64-74.
978. Eisler, *The Messiah Jesus and John the Baptist*, 544, note 2.

CHAPTER 18. THE HYPOTHESIS

The gospel of Mark clearly states that there was an insurrection in Jerusalem around the time of Jesus' activity in the city:

> And among the rebels in prison, who committed murder in the *insurrection*, there was a man called Barabbas.[979]

Furthermore, Barabbas appears to be the leader of this insurrection. The gospels do not explicitly state this, but Matthew calls him a "notorious prisoner,"[980] Luke states that he was "thrown into prison for an insurrection started in the city and for murder,"[981] and John calls him a "robber," which means a "political revolutionary."[982] Why would his name have been remembered, if he were not the leader of the insurrection?

What about Jesus' own activities in the city at this time? In the gospels, Jesus was supposed to have entered Jerusalem on an ass in order to fulfill Scripture about the coming of a triumphant king.[983] The people with great jubilation shouted the following: "Hosanna! Blessed be he who comes in the name of the Lord! Blessed be the kingdom of our father David that is coming!

---

979. Mk. 15:7 (italics mine), cf. Lk. 23:19.
980. Mt. 27:16.
981. Lk. 23:19.
982. Jn. 18:40. See *The New Oxford Annotated Bible*, eds. Herbert G. May and Bruce M. Metzger (New York: Oxford University Press, 1973), 1314, note 40 for 18:1-19:42; Martin Hengel, *The Zealots*, trans. by David Smith (Edinburgh: T. & T. Clark, 1989), 24-46, 341.
983. Zech. 9:9: "Rejoice greatly, O daughter of Zion! Shout aloud, O daughter of Jerusalem! Lo, your king comes to you; triumphant and victorious is he, humble and riding on an ass, on a colt the foal of an ass."

Hosanna in the highest!"[984] The gospel of John has "Hosanna! Blessed is he who comes in the name of the Lord, *even the King of Israel!*"[985] Was he not declaring himself king in opposition to Caesar?[986] Furthermore, according to Luke Jesus did not even disapprove of what the people are shouting:

> And some of the Pharisees in the multitude said to him, "Teacher, rebuke your disciples." He answered, "I tell you, if these were silent, the very stones would cry out."[987]

Matthew adds "all the city was stirred, saying, 'Who is this?'"[988] Then,[989] he entered the Temple and committed what could only be called a *seditious* act:

> And he entered the temple and began to drive out those who sold and those who bought in the temple, and he overturned the tables of the money-changers and the seats of those who sold pigeons; *and he would not allow any one to carry anything through the temple.*[990] And he taught, and said to them, "Is it not written, My house shall be called a house of prayer *for all the nations*?[991] But you have made it a den of robbers."[992]

Nevertheless, the gospels portray Jesus as a peaceful teacher and healer, who has no desire to get involved in insurgent activity. Did not Jesus teach "blessed are the peacemakers, for they shall be called sons of God."[993] In John 6:1-15, after Jesus performed the miracle of feeding the five thousand, it is stated that he, "perceiving then that they were about to come and take him by force to make him king ... withdrew again to the mountain by himself."[994]

---

984. Mk. 11:9-10, cf. Mt. 21:9, 19:38, Jn. 12:13.

985. Jn. 12:13 (italics mine).

986. That Zech. 9:9 refers to a triumphant king, who comes in humbleness and in peace on an ass, is beside the point. He came as a *king* and that was all the people were concerned with, as can be seen by their excitement.

987. Lk. 19:39-40.

988. Mt. 21:10.

989. In Mark, the cleansing of the Temple took place on the "following day" (Mk. 11:12). After the triumphal entry, Jesus "went into the Temple; and when he looked round at everything, as it was late, he went out to Bethany with the twelve" (Mk. 11:11). In John, the cleansing of the Temple took place toward the beginning of Jesus' ministry (Jn. 2:13-7) and was not connected with the triumphal entry that occurred toward the end of it (Jn. 12:12-9).

990. The phrase in italics is only in Mark.

991. The phrase in italics is only in Mark.

992. Mk. 11:15-7, cf. Mt. 21:12-3, Lk. 19:45-8, Jn. 2:13-7.

993. Mt. 5:9.

994. See also Mk. 6:32-44, Mt. 14:13-21, Lk. 9:10-17. Cf., the feeding of the four thousand in Mt 15:32-9, Mk. 8:1-10.

Chapter 18. The Hypothesis

There is an inconsistency here. He allows the people to declare him king yet disapproves of any overt action to become king. Did Jesus have a Dr. Jekyl and Mr. Hyde personality? I think not.

In two non-Christian sources, Jesus is described as a rebel against Rome. For example, the Platonic philosopher Celsus describes Jesus among other things as a "leader of sedition."[995] Also, the church father Lactantius informs us that Sossianus Hierocles, the governor of Bithynia (AD 303) and Egypt (AD 307) and a persecutor of Christians, reports that "Christ, driven out by the Jews, gathered a band of nine hundred men and committed acts of brigandage."[996] Brigandage here means rebellion or high treason.[997] In the light of this evidence, it is worth mentioning that in three ancient texts of Matthew the first name of the rebel Barabbas is Jesus![998]

The gospels tell us that there were two individuals named Jesus, who were closely involved in the affairs of the time — Jesus Christ, who was the crucified, peaceful teacher and healer and Jesus Barabbas, who was the released rebel. As was discussed in the last chapter, the gospel story of how Barabbas was released must be unhistorical. However, is the part about a peaceful teacher and healer being crucified in place of a rebel also unhistorical? I think not! The historical kernel of the Barabbas episode may indeed be that Jesus, the peaceful teacher and healer, *was* crucified in place of Jesus, the rebel. The gospel explanation of how this occurred is what is unhistorical. What did happen then?

Some early sources from the Christian Gnostics and from Islamic teachings state that someone, who was miraculously changed to resemble Jesus, was crucified in his place! In the second century AD, the Egyptian Gnostic Basilides taught that Simon of Cyrene, who carried the cross for Jesus,[999] was crucified in his place.[1000] The following passage is quoted from the Nag Hammadi Gnostic *Second Treatise of the Great Seth*. Jesus is allegedly speaking to an audience of Gnostic believers:

---

995. Ernst Bammel, C. F. D. Moule, eds., *Jesus and the Politics of His Day* (Cambridge: Cambridge University Press, 1985), 183.

996. Bammel, Moule, eds., *Jesus and the Politics of His Day*, 188.

997. Robert Eisler, *The Messiah Jesus and John the Baptist*, ed. by A. H. Krappe (London: Methuen & Co., 1931), 10-1.

998. Jesus Barabbas is found in Mt. 27:16, 17 in the Koridethi gospels (7th to 9th cent.), the "Lake group" minuscules (minuscules 1, 118, 131, 209, etc.), and the Sinaitic Syriac version (discovered in 1892).

999. Mk. 15:21, Mt. 27:32, Lk. 23:26.

1000. Geoffrey Parrinder, *Jesus in the Qur'an* (New York: Oxford University Press, 1977), 110.

For my death which they think happened, (happened) to them in their error and blindness, since they nailed their man unto their death. For ... they were deaf and blind. But in doing these things, they condemn themselves. Yes, they saw me; they punished me. It was another, their father, who drank the gall and the vinegar; it was not I. They struck me with the reed; it was another, Simon, who bore the cross on his shoulder, It was another upon whom they placed the crown of thorns. But I was rejoicing in the height over all the wealth of the archons and the offspring of their error, of their empty glory. And I was laughing at their ignorance.[1001]

Another interesting passage from the Nag Hammadi Gnostic *Apocalypse of Peter* is quoted below:

When he [Jesus, the Savior] had said those things, I [Peter] saw him seemingly being seized by them. And I said, "What do I see, O Lord, that it is you yourself whom they take, and that you are grasping me? Or who is this one, glad and laughing on the tree? And is it another one whose feet and hands they are striking?"

The Savior said to me, "He whom you saw on the tree, glad and laughing, this is the living Jesus. But this one into whose hands and feet they drive the nails is his fleshly part, which is the substitute being put to shame, the one who came into being in his likeness. But look at him and me."[1002]

The Koran has the following to say:

Verily we [the Jews] have slain Christ Jesus the son of Mary, the apostle of God; yet they slew him not, neither crucified him, *but he was represented by one in his likeness;* and verily they who disagreed concerning him, were in doubt as to this matter, and had no sure knowledge thereof, but followed only an uncertain opinion. They did not really kill him; but God took him up into himself: and God is mighty and wise.[1003]

Regarding the Islamic teachings, Parrinder has the following to say:

The idea of a substitute for the crucifixion has been adopted by many Muslim writers. Not only Simon the Cyrene, but Judas, Pilate, a disciple, or even an enemy of Jesus have been suggested for this office.[1004]

1001. James M. Robinson, ed., *The Nag Hammadi Library* (San Francisco: Harper & Row, 1977), 332 (55:30-56:20).
1002. Robinson, ed., *The Nag Hammadi Library*, 344 (81:4-20).
1003. George Sale, trans. *The Koran* (London: Frederick Warne and Co. Ltd., 1939), 94 (italics mine).
1004. Parrinder, *Jesus in the Qur'an*, 111.

Chapter 18. The Hypothesis

As an example, the views of the Muslim writer Tabari should be mentioned:

> Tabari said that Herod gave the order to kill Jesus but he hid himself. Simon then denied him and another betrayed him; Jesus was seized and dragged away to a cross. The Jews had a chief called Joshua and God took Jesus out of their sight, and gave his form and appearance to Joshua who was crucified in his place despite protests. Joshua stayed on the cross for seven days, and each night Mary, the mother of Jesus, came and wept at the foot of the cross, but on the eighth day Jesus descended from heaven to Mary and his disciples.[1005]

Could Jesus Barabbas have actually been Jesus' twin brother, Judas, and could Jesus have been crucified in his brother's place? A good case can be made that this was indeed what happened.[1006] It offers a rational answer to the question how a teacher of peace was crucified in place of a rebel against Rome. Using this idea, I propose the hypothesis below:

Because of the prominence of his family and his unique genealogy, Jesus, the first-born son of Mary and Joseph, was destined to be the Messiah of Israel.[1007] Children were normally baptized in the New Covenant at age ten. However, since the sect did not actually come into existence until AD 3, Jesus was probably baptized at this time. He would have been 14 years old.[1008] Because of his priestly descent, after baptism he would normally have begun the special initiation process for priests. However, due to the nature of the office he was destined to fill, he began the initiation process for laymen instead.

It was expected that his oath of entry into the Covenant would be taken in AD 8, when he was nineteen years old. However, to everyone's surprise he decided to forego the rite and leave the New Covenant. He had come to the realization that he could not accept many of the sect's doctrines. Its separatist, xenophobic, and militant views especially disturbed him. It is at this point that the following gospel verse should probably be placed: "And when his family heard about all this, they went to seize him, for they said, 'He is out of his mind.'"[1009]

1005. Parrinder, *Jesus in the Qur'an*, 111.
1006. In the sources referred to above, a double replaces Jesus, whereas in the hypothesis below, Jesus replaces a double. It seems to me that the real value of these sources is not to learn who takes the place of whom, but to realize a substitution occurred.
1007. Of course, because of his genealogy, Jesus could have just as easily become the High Priest of the sect. However, John the Baptist already held this office. After John's death (AD 35) Jesus' brother, James the Righteous, did take over John's office.
1008. 12 BC – 1 (there is no "0" year) + AD 3 = 14 years old.

The New Covenant merely wanted to perpetuate the Temple religious system, which included its purity laws. Presently, the impure and corrupt priestly establishment controlled the Temple, but the New Covenant planned to take control of the Temple away from them and to then operate it in the proper manner. Unfortunately, the system of separating people based on purity would still remain in effect. Borg describes the purity system as follows:

> The politics of holiness was a continuation in intensified form of a cultural dynamic that had emerged in Judaism after the exile. It was expressed most succinctly in the "holiness code" whose central words affirmed, *"You shall be holy, as I the Lord your God am holy."* The cultural dynamic was thus articulated in one of the classical patterns of religious thought, an *imitatio dei* or "imitation of God." God was holy, and Israel was to be holy. That was to be her ethos, her way of life. Moreover, holiness was understood in a highly specific way, namely as *separation*. To be holy meant to be separate from everything that would defile holiness. The Jewish social world and its conventional wisdom became increasingly structured around the polarities of holiness as separation: clean and unclean, purity and defilement, sacred and profane, Jew and Gentile, righteous and sinner.[1010]

Regarding Jesus' teachings, Borg makes the following point:

> ...there is something boundary shattering about the *imitatio dei* that stood at the center of Jesus' message and activity: "Be compassionate as God is compassionate." Whereas purity divides and excludes, compassion unites and includes. For Jesus, compassion had a radical sociopolitical meaning. In his teaching and table fellowship, and in the shape of his movement,[1011] the purity system was subverted and an alternative social vision affirmed. The politics of purity was replaced by a politics of compassion.[1012]

Out of compassion for all those disfranchised as a result of the purity system, i.e., the crippled, the blind, the deaf, the lepers, the outcasts, the poor, the unskilled, the masses who did not observe the Torah, and others,[1013] Jesus went on a journey of discovery. This period of his life has been called the "lost

---

1009. This is Stephen Mitchell's translation of Mk. 3:21. The Greek phrase translated as "his family" is literally "those with him" and can also be translated as "his friends" or "his relatives." See Stephen Mitchell, *The Gospel According to Jesus* (New York: HarperCollins, 1991), 48, 90, 192.

1010. Marcus J. Borg, *Jesus A New Vision* (San Francisco: Harper, 1987), 86-7.

1011. Unfortunately, as we will see in a later chapter, the later Christians disregarded Jesus' teaching about the kinship of human beings and began to separate people into believers and unbelievers who would be rewarded or condemned respectively in the Kingdom of God.

1012. Marcus J. Borg, *Meeting Jesus Again for the First Time* (San Francisco: Harper, 1994), 58.

1013. For an excellent discussion of all these groups, see Albert Nolan, *Jesus Before Christianity* (Maryknoll: Orbis Books, 1993), 27-36.

years," because nothing is known about it. During this time, it is possible that he joined the conventional Essenes,[1014] traveled to Egypt to learn the teachings of the Therapeutae (an Essene-like sect),[1015] or even traveled to the Far East to learn the teachings of Buddha.[1016] When he made his appearance again in AD 15/16, he was twenty-seven or twenty-eight years old.[1017]

At some point, the Jewish authorities became very concerned about Jesus, because he was attracting large crowds of people. The reason for this was his amazing ability to heal people of various maladies and his teachings about the Kingdom of God. Spies were sent out to investigate the situation. They further discovered that he prophesied about a coming destruction of Jerusalem and the Temple,[1018] he disobeyed the Torah on many points,[1019] and he did not keep the Sabbath in a proper manner.[1020] The Mount of Olives, just outside of Jerusalem, was the place where he most often healed and taught the people.

The Sanhedrin summoned Jesus to appear for trial for possible infringements of the ecclesiastical law. I think the strategy it used was that it decided not to seek approval from Pilate for a trial, as it was required to do, but for a private academic session only. It is likely that, if it did obtain the approval of Pilate for a trial, Roman guards would have been stationed there to make sure the body did not go beyond its legal jurisdiction. It used this strategy in order to avoid this situation. Of course, as a result of this maneuver, if Jesus chose not to

---

1014. Provided that we do not make the mistake of identifying the Dead Sea sect with the Essenes, then several traits of the conventional Essenes, as described by Philo, Josephus and Pliny, would indeed correspond to teachings of the historical Jesus. Some of these traits would include pacifism, piety, and communal life.

1015. For a description of the Therapeutae, see Emil Schurer, *The History of the Jewish People in the Age of Jesus Christ*, vols. I, II, III.1, III.2, rev. and ed. by Geza Vermes, et al. (Edinburgh: T. & T. Clark, 1973/87), Vol. II, 591-4.

1016. A theory has been put forward that "the original Jesus taught Buddhist ideas, lived the life of a Buddhist wandering monk, and instructed his disciples in following the Buddhist path." See Elmar R. Gruber & Holger Kersten, *The Original Jesus* (Great Britain: Element Books, 1995), 142-3. Indeed, many teachings of the historical Jesus correspond to Buddhist teachings.

1017. 12 BC + AD 15/16 = 27 or 28 years old.

1018. Lk. 19:41-4, Mk. 13:1-2=Mt 24:1-2=Lk. 21:5-6, 23:28-31, Mt. 26:52.

1019. See for example, Mk. 7:15, 21-3=Mt. 15:10-1, 19-20 where the food laws are declared invalid. Although in my opinion Mt. 11:18-9 (=Lk. 5:33-4) is not an actual saying of Jesus, it nevertheless records a genuine observation of the time. Also the Slavonic Josephus states the following: "Howbeit in many things he [Jesus] disobeyed the law [Torah] and kept not the Sabbath according to (our) fathers' custom" (Eisler, *The Messiah Jesus and John the Baptist*, 467).

1020. See, for example, Mk. 2:23-4=Mt. 12:1-2=Lk. 6:1-2, Mk. 2:27. According to DeLamotte, "external forms and works are usually of secondary concern to the mystic, and he may even regard them as positive hindrances." See Roy C. DeLamotte, *The Alien Christ* (Lanham: University Press of America, 1980), 28.

appear, there is nothing the Sanhedrin could have done about it. He must have appeared voluntarily.

After giving due process to the accused, the Sanhedrin found Jesus guilty of false prophecy. Dt. 18:20-2 gives the method for determining a false prophet and the means for dealing with him:

> But the prophet who presumes to speak a word in my name which I have not commanded him to speak, or who speaks in the name of other gods, that same prophet shall die. And if you say in your heart, "How may we know the word which the Lord has not spoken?" — when a prophet speaks in the name of the Lord, if the word does not come to pass or come true, that is a word which the Lord has not spoken; the prophet has spoken it presumptuously, you need not be afraid of him.

Since Jerusalem and the Temple were still standing. Jesus had spoken "presumptuously" and was condemned as a false prophet.[1021] Klausner provides more detail about the Jewish penalty handed out to one found guilty of this offense:

> The Law enacted that the blasphemer, the false prophet, the beguiler and seducer, were to be stoned. It was also held that "everyone that is stoned is also hanged," and all alike held that the blasphemer who had been stoned was (after death by stoning) also hanged. The *Mishna* goes into detail: "How do they hang him? They fix a beam in the ground and a piece of wood branches from it (R. Obadiah of Bertenora explains: "Like a peg coming out of the beam near the top") and the two hands are fastened together, and so they hang him."
> This is very like the form of the Roman cross which was not of the present conventional shape, but resembled the Latin or Greek capital T. The hanged victim suffered no pain since the hanging or crucifixion only took place after death had resulted from stoning; and the hanging only served to impress the onlookers during the body's short time of exposure: "They took it down at once, for if they suffered it to stay till night-time a negative commandment would thereby be broken, for it is written: His corpse shall not remain ... on the tree, but thou shalt surely bury it, for a curse of God is that which is hanged."[1022]

However, as was discussed in earlier chapters, the Sanhedrin lost its power to use capital punishment under the Roman occupation. They had no choice but to

---

1021. According to Dt. 13:1-5, even if someone's prophecy actually came true, he would still be considered a false prophet if he also incited the people to worship other gods. The power of prediction would have been given to him by God in order to test the faith of the people.
1022. Joseph Klausner, *Jesus of Nazareth* (New York: Bloch Publishing Co., 1989), 344-5.

Chapter 18. The Hypothesis

let Jesus go. Nevertheless, since the beginning of the occupation, it had used secret means to execute those condemned by it. The Jewish authorities kept an eye on Jesus and waited for the right time to execute the sentence on him in secret.

The episode in the gospels about Jesus being brought before the Sanhedrin is a distorted and incomplete account of the trial described above.[1023]

It may be wondered why Jesus, the son of Joseph, was condemned as a false prophet by the Sanhedrin. Another Jesus, the son of Ananias, who also predicted the destruction of Jerusalem and the Temple, was only "brought ... before the Roman governor [and] flayed to the bone with scourges." Let me quote what Josephus says about this individual:

> Four years before the war [AD 62], when the city was enjoying profound peace and prosperity, there came to the feast at which it is the custom of all Jews to erect tabernacles to God [Sukkoth or the Feast of Tabernacles, Tishri (Sept.-Oct.)], one Jesus, son of Ananias, a rude peasant, who, standing in the temple, suddenly began to cry out, "A voice from the east, a voice from the west, a voice from the four winds; a voice against Jerusalem and the sanctuary, a voice against the bridegroom and the bride, a voice against all the people." Day and night he went about all the alleys with this cry on his lips. Some of the leading citizens, incensed at these ill-omened words, arrested the fellow and severely chastised him. But he, without a word on his own behalf or for the private ear of those who smote him, only continued his cries as before. Thereupon, the magistrates, supposing, as was indeed the case, that the man was under some supernatural impulse, brought him before the Roman governor; there, although flayed to the bone with scourges, he neither sued for mercy nor shed a tear, but, merely introducing the most mournful of variations into his ejaculation, responded to each stroke with "Woe to Jerusalem!" When Albinus, the governor [AD 62-4], asked him who and whence he was and why he uttered these cries, he answered him never a word, but unceasingly reiterated his dirge over the city, until Albinus pronounced him a maniac and let him go. During the whole period up to the outbreak of war he neither approached nor was seen talking to any of the citizens, but daily, like a prayer that he had conned, repeated his lament, "Woe to Jerusalem!" He neither cursed any of those who beat him from day to day, nor blessed those who offered him food: to all men that melancholy presage was his one reply. His cries were loudest at the festivals. So for seven years and five months he continued his wail, his voice never flagging nor his strength exhausted, until in the siege [AD 70], having seen his presage verified, he found his rest. For, while going his round and shouting in piercing tones from the wall, "Woe once more to the city and to the people and to the temple," as he added a last word, "and woe to me also," a

---

1023. Mk. 14:53-65=Mt. 26:57-68=Lk. 22:54-5, 63-71=Jn. 18:19-24.

stone hurled from the *ballista* struck and killed him on the spot. So with those ominous words still upon his lips he passed away.[1024]

Jesus, the son of Joseph, drew large crowds. Jesus, the son of Ananias, was declared a "maniac" by the Roman governor and always kept to himself. It was only to be expected that the son of Joseph would be considered a dangerous false prophet, because of his effect on the masses. The son of Ananias would merely be considered a nuisance.

The "magistrates" (i.e., the members of the Sanhedrin) were more than happy to pass off the affair to the Roman governor, because they considered the son of Ananias to be guilty of disturbing the peace, not false prophecy. He was not considered culpable of the severe crime of false prophecy. Disturbing the peace, being a secular not a religious offense, probably fell under Roman jurisdiction. Nevertheless, the Sanhedrin would have had to initiate a grand jury process before it "brought him before the Roman governor."

Having dealt with the affair of Jesus, the son of Ananias, let us continue on with the hypothesis. Judas, Jesus' twin brother and the second oldest male in the family, took Jesus' place in the New Covenant and was expected to become the Messiah of Israel. He was baptized, as was Jesus in AD 3. However, unlike Jesus, he did take his oath of entry into the Covenant in AD 8, was enrolled in the Council of the Community in AD 9, and eventually, as a professed member, entered the ranks of government.

The main element of the New Covenant investiture of the Messiah of Israel was certainly his anointing with oil by the high priest.[1025] On his "arising"[1026] from the anointment, it was believed that God had "begotten" him (1QSa 2:12), i.e., he had become the Son of God[1027] and had been "turned into another man."[1028] Giving him a new name known as a "throne name" represented this transformation. Several examples of this practice can be found in the Old Testament.[1029]

1024. War VI, 300-9.
1025. "King, Kingship," *The Interpreter's Dictionary of the Bible*, 4 vols. (New York: Abingdon, 1962); 1 Kgs.1:39.
1026. The Hebrew root for "arise" or "stand" is used to refer to the Messiah's appearance, e.g., CD 20:1, 12:1, 4Q174 (Florilegium), 1:11-2, and 4QpIs^a, frags. 7-10, 3:22. The Hebrew root for "come" or "arrive" is also used, e.g., CD 19:11, 1QS 9:11, and 4Q252 (Pesher on Genesis), 5:1-7. I take this root to mean that he comes *to his office.*
1027. Ps. 2:7, 89:26-7, 2 Sam. 7:14.
1028. 1 Sam. 10:6, 9, 11.

Chapter 18. The Hypothesis

It is highly likely that one of these names given to the Messiah of Israel was Jesus, since he was to be the Savior of Israel[1030] and a military leader much like Joshua (i.e., Jesus), the Israelite leader and successor of Moses in the Old Testament. There is evidence that in the first century AD Joshua of Old Testament times was expected by some to return as the Messiah. Josephus mentions two individuals who appear to have given themselves out to be Joshua *redivivus*: Theudas[1031] and the "Egyptian."[1032]

In AD 15/16, an unexpected event caused Judas to leave the New Covenant and to prematurely declare himself the Messiah of Israel. Many laymen and perhaps some levites and priests joined him. He underwent a coronation rite and chose the throne name *Jesus*. His original name Judas fell out of use.[1033]

The incident that led him to make this move has already been described in the last chapter. Briefly, Pilate brought into Jerusalem standards with the image of the emperor. Previous governors had garrisoned their troops in the city without the standards bearing Caesar's image, because they were offensive to the Jewish religion. The Jews protested for a number of days and Pilate only ordered that the standards be removed from the city, when a massacre of the people was about to commence.[1034]

On the basis of Philo's statement,[1035] that these standards were placed *in the Temple*, it has been suggested that at least one of them was placed in the Antonia fortress that was connected to the Temple.[1036] There is evidence that some Jews believed that this standard with their emperor's image attached to it was a fulfillment of the prophecy in Daniel about the "abomination that makes desolate" being set up in the Temple.[1037] Judas/Jesus believed that the prophecy

---

1029. "King, Kingship," *The Interpreter's Dictionary of the Bible*; 2 Kgs. 23:34 (Eliakim became Jehoiakim); 24:17 (Mattaniah became Zedekiah); 2 Sam. 12:25 (Jedidiah became Solomon); and the contradiction between 1 Sam. 17 and 2 Sam. 21.19 could be resolved if Elhanan became David. 1 Chr. 20:5 attempts to correct this problem by stating that Elhanan actually slew "Lahmi the *brother* of Goliath."

1030. Jesus means, "Yahweh is salvation" or more simply put "Savior." Mt. 1:21 states that "you shall call his name Jesus [i.e., Savior], for *he will save* his people from their sins" (italics mine).

1031. Ant. XX, 97-9. For the possible identity of this individual, see the chapter titled *The Fate of the Son of Joseph*.

1032. Ant. XX, 169-72; War II, 261-3; Acts 21:8. For the probable identity of this individual, see the chapter titled *Simon Magus*.

1033. Thus, the view taken here is that Barabbas' original named was not Jesus but Judas.

1034. Ant. XVIII, 55-9; War II, 169-74.

1035. Euseb. *Dem. Evang.* viii. 2. 123, noted in Josephus, (Loeb Classical Library), Vol. IX, p. 45, note a.

1036. Eisler, *The Messiah Jesus and John the Baptist*, 312-20.

1037. Dan. 8:13, 9:27, 11:31, 12:11, cf. 9:17.

had been fulfilled. This desecration led him to leave the New Covenant and declare himself the Messiah.

The patronymic Barabbas can mean "son of the father," but Jerome tells us that in the Gospel according to the Hebrews,[1038] the name Barabbas is interpreted as "son of their teacher."[1039] How do we explain this name? Originally, the designation, which meant "son of the Father" (i.e., God),[1040] referred to Jesus, the peaceful teacher and healer, and the designation "Christ," which meant "Messiah" in Greek,[1041] referred to the Judas/Jesus, the rebel. When "Christ" became the acceptable designation for the Christian Jesus of the New Testament, the two designations were switched. "Barabbas" was then interpreted to mean "son of their teacher" (i.e., rabbi) and became the designation for the rebel Judas/Jesus, who was now supposed to have been the son of a notable rabbi. "Their" was added make certain that no one would think Jesus was this "teacher."[1042]

In a letter written to John Adams on January 24, 1814, Thomas Jefferson stated the method for identifying the authentic teachings of Jesus:

> The whole history of these books [the Gospels] is so defective and doubtful that it seems vain to attempt minute enquiry into it: and such tricks have been played with their text, and with the texts of other books relating to them, that we have a right, from that cause, to entertain much doubt what parts of them are genuine. In the New Testament there is internal evidence that parts of it proceeded from an extraordinary man; and that other parts are of the fabric of very inferior minds. It is as easy to separate those parts, as to pick out diamonds from dunghills.[1043]

1038. This gospel only survives in various quotations from the church fathers. See Robert J. Miller, ed., *The Complete Gospels* (San Francisco: Harper, 1994), 425-46.

1039. Jerome, *Commentary on Matthew* 27:16 from Miller, ed., *The Complete Gospels*, 446.

1040. Father (Aramaic: Abba) was a name for God used often by Jesus (Nolan, *Jesus Before Christianity*, 97). Furthermore, there is evidence that the designation son of God was used with reference to certain other holy men and miracle-workers and that God was even called Father (Abba) by them. See Geza Vermes, *Jesus the Jew* (Philadelphia: Fortress Press, 1981), 206-11.

1041. The word "Messiah" is the English transliteration of the Hebrew word and the word "Christ" is the English transliteration of the Greek word. Both words have the same meaning, i.e., the "Anointed One." Originally, the title referred to kings (1 Sam. 10:1, 1 Kgs. 1:39) and high priests (Ex. 29:7, Lev. 16:32, Ps. 133.2) who were anointed with oil at their investiture. Later, it came to refer to the expected deliverer promised by God in Judaism and to Jesus who was this deliverer in Christianity.

1042. This explanation for the use of "their" is given in Miller, ed., *The Complete Gospels*, 446, note 9.

1043. Quoted from Mitchell, *The Gospel According to Jesus*, 4.

As a result of these beliefs, Jefferson actually wrote a book titled *The Life and Morals of Jesus of Nazareth* in which he attempted to separate the authentic teachings of Jesus from the inauthentic ones in the four gospels. This book was not published until 1904. Before that, it remained in the private hands of Jefferson's descendants.

By utilizing the method that Jefferson described in his letter, it should be possible to extract the "diamonds" out of all the sources now available to us. Unfortunately, in studying these texts I have come to the somber conclusion that in many cases even though an authentic teaching seems to be just discernible its overall content does not allow a determination to be made. However, we are fortunate that many of the "diamonds" can still be found. Of course, it is not to be expected that there will be complete agreement between the views of different researchers as to what is authentic and what is not. However, the differences should not be great. The following teachings (though they are far from being complete) seem to pass the test of authenticity:

> Blessed are the poor in spirit,[1044] for theirs is the kingdom of heaven.
> Blessed are those who mourn, for they shall be comforted.
> Blessed are the meek, for they shall inherit the earth.
> Blessed are those who hunger and thirst for righteousness, for they shall be satisfied.
> Blessed are the merciful, for they shall obtain mercy.
> Blessed are the pure in heart, for they shall see God.
> Blessed are the peacemakers, for they shall be called sons of God.
> Blessed are those who are persecuted for righteousness' sake, for theirs is the kingdom of heaven.[1045]

> Come to me, all who labor and are heavy-laden, and I will give you rest. Take my yoke upon you, and learn from me; I am gentle and lowly in heart, and you will find rest for your souls. For my yoke is easy, and my burden is light.[1046]

> And he called the people to him again, and said to them, "Hear me, all of you, and understand: there is nothing outside a man which going into him can defile him; but the things which come out of a man are what defile him. For from within, out of the heart of man, come evil thoughts, fornication, theft, murder, adultery, coveting, wickedness, deceit, licentiousness, envy, slander,

---

1044. The phrase "the poor in spirit" is an Aramaic idiom meaning "those who surrender to God." See Rocco A. Errico, *The Message of Matthew* (Irvine: Noohra Foundation, 1991), 14, note 4.
1045. Mt. 5:3-10, cf. Lk. 6:20-1.
1046. Mt. 11:28-30.

pride, foolishness. All these evil things come from within, and they defile a man.[1047]

The Sabbath was made for man, not man for the Sabbath.[1048]

You have heard that it was said, 'An eye for an eye and a tooth for a tooth.'[1049] But I say to you, Do not resist one who is evil. But if any one strikes you on the right cheek, turn to him the other also; and if any one would sue you and take you're your coat, let him have your cloak as well; and if any one forces you to go one mile, go with him two miles. Give to him who begs from you, and do not refuse him who would borrow from you.[1050]

You have heard that it was said, 'you shall love your neighbor and hate your enemy.'[1051] But I say to you, Love your enemies, do good to those who hate you, bless those who curse you, pray for those who abuse you, so that you may be sons of your Father who is in heaven; for he makes his sun rise on the evil and on the good, and sends rain on the just and on the unjust. For if you love those who love you, what credit is that to you? For even sinners love those who love them. And if you do good to those who do good to you, what credit is that to you? For even sinners do the same. And if you lend to those from whom you hope to receive, what credit is that to you? Even sinners lend to sinners, to receive as much again. You, therefore must be perfect, as your heavenly Father is perfect [and] be merciful, even as even as your Father is merciful.[1052]

Pray then like this: Our Father who is in heaven. Let your name be holy. Let your kingdom come. Let Your will be, as in heaven also on earth. Provide us our needful bread from day to day. And forgive us our offenses as we have forgiven our offenders. And do not let us enter into temptation, but set us free from evil. Because yours are the kingdom and the power and the glory from all the ages,

---

1047. Mk. 7:14-5, 21-3=Mt. 15: 10-1, 19-20. Mk. 7:17-20 =Mt. 15:12-8 is omitted.
1048. Mk. 2:27. Mk. 2:28=Mt. 12:8=Lk. 6:5 is not included.
1049. Cf. Ex. 21:23-4: "If any harm follows [from the payment of a fine by a man who caused a woman with child to have a miscarriage], then you shall give life for life, eye for eye, tooth for tooth, hand for hand, foot for foot, burn for burn, wound for wound, stripe for stripe." Cf. Dt. 19:21: "Your eye shall not pity [a false witness], it shall be life for life, eye for eye, tooth for tooth, hand for hand, foot for foot." Cf. Lev. 24:19-20: "When a man causes a disfigurement in his neighbor, as he has done it shall be done to him, fracture for fracture, eye for eye, tooth for tooth; as he has disfigured a man, he shall be disfigured."
1050. Mt. 5:38-42=Lk. 6:29-30.
1051. No such commandment exists in the Old Testament, but one Dead Sea Scroll gives a sectarian rule very similar to it. It states that members of the sect are "to love all the sons of light, each according to his lot in the Council of God; and to hate all the sons of darkness, each according to his fault in the Vengeance of God" (1QS 1:9-11).
1052. This quotation is a composite of Mt. 5:43-4, Lk. 6:27-8, Mt. 5:45, Lk. 6:32-4, Mt. 5:48, and Lk. 6:36. Mt. 5:43-8=Lk. 6:27-8, 32-6. Borg translates Lk. 6:36 as "Be compassionate, even as your Father is compassionate." See Borg, *Jesus A New Vision*, 118 note 17.

throughout all the ages.[1053] For if you forgive men their trespasses, your heavenly Father also will forgive you; but if you do not forgive men their trespasses, neither will your Father forgive your trespasses.[1054]

Do not lay up for yourselves treasures on earth, where moth and rust consume and where thieves break in and steal, but lay up for yourselves treasures in heaven,[1055] where neither moth nor rust consumes and where thieves do not break in and steal. For where your treasure is, there will your heart be also.[1056]

No one can serve two masters; for either he will hate the one and love the other, or he will be devoted to the one and despise the other. You cannot serve God and mammon.[1057]

Enter by the narrow gate; for the gate is wide and the way is easy, that leads to destruction, and those who enter by it are many. For the gate is narrow and the way is hard, that leads to life, and those who find it are few.[1058]

For no good tree bears bad fruit, nor again does a bad tree bear good fruit; for each tree is known by its own fruit. For figs are not gathered from thorns, nor are grapes picked from a bramble bush. The good man out of the good treasure of his heart produces good, and the evil man out of his evil treasure produces evil; for out of the abundance of the heart his mouth speaks.[1059]

Judge not, and you will not be judged; condemn not, and you will not be condemned; forgive, and you will be forgiven; give, and it will be given to you; good measure, pressed down, shaken together, running over, will be put into your lap. For the measure you give will be the measure you get back. Why do you see the speck that is in your brother's eye, but do not notice the log that is in your own eye? Or how can you say to your brother, 'Brother, let me take out the speck that is in your eye,' when you yourself do not see the log that is in your own eye? You hypocrite, first take the log out of your own eye, and then you will see clearly to take out the speck that is in your brother's eye.[1060]

1053. Mt. 6:9-13=Lk. 11:2-4. This version of the Lord's Prayer is from the Peshitta-Aramaic text in Errico, *The Message of Matthew*, 21.
1054. Mt. 6:14-5=Lk. 11:25-6.
1055. The phrase "treasures in heaven" is an Aramaic idiom meaning "good deeds which never perish." See Errico, *The Message of Matthew*, 22 note 24.
1056. Mt. 6:19-21=Lk. 12:33-4.
1057. Mt. 6:24=Lk. 16:13. "Mammon" is derived from the Aramaic word, which means "money" or "riches." See *The New Oxford Annotated Bible*, 1178, note x.
1058. Mt. 7:13-4=Lk. 13:23-4.
1059. Lk. 6:43-5=Mt. 12:33-5 and 7:16-8.
1060. Lk. 6:37-8, 41-2=Mt. 7:1-5. Lk. 6:39-40=Mt. 15:14, 10:24-5 is omitted.

Ask, and it will be given you; seek, and you will find; knock, and it will be opened to you. For every one who asks receives, and he who seeks finds, and to him who knocks it will be opened. Or what man of you, if his son asks him for a loaf, will give him a stone? Or if he asks for a fish, will give him a serpent? If you then, who are evil, know how to give good gifts to your children, how much more will your Father who is in heaven give good things to those who ask him?[1061]

And as you wish that men would do to you, do so to them.[1062]

And he [Jesus] said, "There was a man who had two sons; and the younger of them said to his father, 'Father, give me the share of property that falls to me.' And he divided his living between them. Not many days later, the younger son gathered all he had and took his journey into a far country, and there he squandered his property in loose living. And when he had spent everything, a great famine arose in that country, and he began to be in want. So he went and joined himself to one of the citizens of that country, who sent him into his fields to feed swine. And he would gladly have fed on the pods that the swine ate; and no one gave him anything. But when he came to himself he said, 'How many of my father's hired servants have bread enough and to spare, but I perish with hunger! I will arise and go to my father.... And he arose and came to his father. But while he was yet at a distance, his father saw him and had compassion, and ran and embraced him and kissed him. And the son said to him, "Father, I have sinned against heaven and before you; I am no longer worthy to be called your son.' But the father said to his servants, 'Bring quickly the best robe, and put it on him; and put a ring on his hand, and shoes on his feet; and bring the fatted calf and kill it, and let us eat and make merry; for this my son was dead, and is alive again; he was lost, and is found.' And they began to make merry. Now his elder son was in the field; and as he came and drew near to the house, he heard music and dancing. And he called one of the servants and asked what this meant. And he said to him, 'Your brother has come, and your father has killed the fatted calf, because he has received him safe and sound.' But he was angry and refused to go in. His father came out and entreated him, but he answered his father, 'Lo, these many years I have served you, and I never disobeyed your command; yet you never gave me a kid, that I might make merry with my friends. But when this son of yours came, who has devoured your living with harlots, you killed for him the fatted calf!' And he said to him, 'Son, you are always with me, and all that is mine is yours. It was fitting to make merry and be glad, for this your brother was dead, and is alive, he was lost, and is found.'"[1063]

1061. Mt. 7:7-11=Lk. 11:9-13.
1062. Lk. 6:31=Mt. 7:12. Cf. Tobit 4:15 ("And what you hate, do not do to any one.") and Ecclesiasticus (Sirach) 31:15 ("Judge your neighbor's feelings by your own, and in every matter be thoughtful."). Fragments of these apocryphal books have indeed been discovered in the caves at Qumran. See Miller Burrows, *More Light on the Dead Sea Scrolls* (London: Secker & Warburg, 1958), 177.

Chapter 18. The Hypothesis

[A scribe asked Jesus], "Which commandment is the first of all?" Jesus answered, "The first is, 'Hear, O Israel: The Lord our God, the Lord is one; and you shall love the Lord your God with all your heart, and with all your soul, and with all your mind, and with all your strength.'[1064] And the second is this, 'You shall love your neighbor as yourself.'[1065] There is no other commandment greater than these."[1066]

Early in the morning he [Jesus] came again to the temple; all the people came to him, and he sat down and taught them. The scribes and Pharisees brought a woman who had been caught in adultery, and placing her in the midst they said to him, "Teacher, this woman has been caught in the act of adultery. Now in the law Moses commanded us to stone such.[1067] What do you say about her?" This they said to test him, that they might have some charge to bring against him. Jesus bent down and wrote with his finger on the ground. And as they continued to ask him, he stood up and said to them, "Let him who is without sin among you be the first to throw a stone at her." And once more he bent down and wrote with his finger on the ground. But when they heard it, they went away, one by one, beginning with the eldest, and Jesus was left alone with the woman standing before him. Jesus looked up and said to her, "Woman, where are they? Has no one condemned you?" She said, "No one, sir." And Jesus said, "Neither do I condemn you; go, and do not sin again."[1068]

But he, desiring to justify himself, said to Jesus, "And who is my neighbor?" Jesus replied, "A man was going from Jerusalem to Jericho, and he fell among robbers, who stripped him and beat him, and departed, leaving him half-dead. Now by chance a priest was going down that road; and when he saw him he passed by on the other side. So likewise a Levite, when he came to the place and saw him, passed by on the other side. But a Samaritan, as he journeyed, came to where he was; and when he saw him, he had compassion, and went to him and bound up his wounds, pouring on oil and wine; then he set him on his own beast and brought him to an inn, and took care of him. And the next day he

---

1063. Lk. 15:11-32.
1064. Cf. Deut. 6:4-5: "Hear, O Israel: The Lord our God is one Lord; and you shall love the Lord your God with all your heart, and with all your soul, and with all your might."
1065. Cf. Lev. 19:18: "You shall not take vengeance or bear any grudge against the sons of your own people, but you shall love your neighbor as yourself: I am the Lord." Cf. Lev. 19:34: "The stranger who sojourns with you shall be to you as the native among you, and you shall love him as yourself, for you were strangers in the land of Egypt: I am the Lord your God."
1066. Mk. 12:28-31=Mt. 22:34-40=Lk. 10:25-8.
1067. One must wonder, what happened to the man? Cf. Lev. 20:10: "If a man commits adultery with the wife of his neighbor, both the adulterer and the adulteress shall be put to death." Cf. Dt. 22:23-4: If there is a betrothed virgin, and a man meets her in the city and lies with her, then you shall bring them both out to the gate of the city, and you shall stone them to death with stones, the young woman because she did not cry for help though she was in the city, and the man because he violated his neighbor's wife; so you shall purge the evil from the midst of you."
1068. Jn. 8:2-11. Jn. 7:53-8:11 is omitted in some manuscripts or inserted somewhere else.

took out two denarii[1069] and gave them to the innkeeper, saying, 'Take care of him; and whatever more you spend, I will repay you when I come back.' Which of these three, do you think, proved neighbor to the man who fell among the robbers?" He said, "The one who showed mercy on him." And Jesus said to him, "Go and do likewise."[1070]

Therefore I tell you, do not be anxious about your life, what you shall eat or what you shall drink, nor about your body, what you shall out on. Is not life more than food, and the body more than clothing? Look at the birds of the air: they neither sow nor reap nor gather into barns, and yet your heavenly Father feeds them. Are you not of more value than they? And which of you by being anxious can add one cubit to his span of life? And why are you anxious about clothing? Consider the lilies of the field, how they grow; they neither toil nor spin; yet I tell you, even Solomon in all his glory was not arrayed like one of these. But if God so clothes the grass of the field, which today is alive and tomorrow is thrown into the oven, will he not much more clothe you, O men of little faith? Therefore do not be anxious, saying, "What shall we eat?" or "What shall we drink?" or "What shall we wear?" For all the nations of the world seek these things; and your Father knows that you need them. Instead, seek his kingdom, and these things shall be yours as well.[1071]

And behold, one came up to him, saying, "Teacher, what good deed must I do, to have eternal life?" And he said to him, "Why do you ask me about what is good? One there is who is good. If you would enter life, keep the commandments." He said to him, "Which?" And Jesus said, You shall not kill, You shall not commit adultery, You shall not steal, You shall not bear false witness, Honor your father and mother,[1072] and, You shall love your neighbor as yourself."[1073] The young man said to him, "All these I have observed; what do I still lack?" Jesus said to him, "You lack one thing; go, sell what you possess and give to the poor, and you will have treasure in heaven;[1074] and come, follow me." When the young man heard this he went away sorrowful; for he had great possessions. And Jesus said to his disciples, "Truly I say to you, it will be hard for a rich man to enter the kingdom of heaven. " Again I tell you, it is easier for a rope[1075] to go through the eye of a needle than for a rich man to enter the

---

1069. The denarius (pl. denarii) was a Roman coin made of silver.

1070. Lk. 10:29-37. The fact that it was a Samaritan who did right in this story, as opposed to a priest and a Levite, would be all the more biting to a Jew. Jews despised Samaritans in the first century AD. See Schurer, *The History of the Jewish People in the Age of Jesus Christ*, Vol. II, 19-20.

1071. This quotation is a composite of Mt. 6:25-31 and Lk. 12:30-1. Mt. 6:25-33=Lk. 12:22-31.

1072. Ex. 20:12-6, Dt. 5:16-20.

1073. Lev. 19:18, 34.

1074. The phrase "treasure in heaven" is an Aramaic idiom meaning "good deeds which never perish." See Errico, *The Message of Matthew*, 22 note 24.

1075. The Greek word here actually means "camel," but this is nonsense. However, in the Peshitta-Aramaic text the Aramaic word can mean not only "camel" but also "rope." The word "rope" makes sense here. See Errico, *The Message of Matthew*, 77 note 18.

kingdom of God." When the disciples heard this they were greatly astonished, saying, "Who then can be saved?" But Jesus looked at them and said to them, "With men this is impossible, but with God all things are possible."[1076]

> Truly, I say to you, whoever does not receive the kingdom of God like a child shall not enter it.[1077]

> Then Peter came up and said to him, "Lord, how often shall my brother sin against me, and I forgive him? As many as seven times?" Jesus said to him, "I do not say to you seven times, but seventy times seven."[1078]

Jesus' primary message was that when all people came to the full realization that they were brothers and sisters of each other and sons and daughters of the One Father, the Kingdom of God on Earth would finally come. Inner spiritual transformation in individuals was needed first. The Kingdom of God is "within you" in that it begins to grow from there, but it will in time be revealed in the world also (i.e., "in the midst of you").[1079] It is like a mustard seed, which when planted in the ground, is the smallest of all seeds. However, when it grows birds come to make nests in its branches.[1080] The inside and the outside would become one and the same. As more and more people changed inside, the world outside would change accordingly. This idea is very clearly stated in a saying from the Gospel of Thomas:

> Jesus said, "If your leaders say to you, 'Look, the Kingdom is in the sky,' then the birds of the sky will precede you. If they say to you, 'It is in the sea,' then the fish will precede you. Rather, the Kingdom is inside you and outside you. When you know yourselves, then you will be known, and you will understand that you are children of the living Father. But if you do not know yourselves, then you live in poverty, and you are the poverty.[1081]

Here is another saying from the Gospel of Mary that contains the same idea, although the term Son of Man is used instead of Kingdom:[1082]

1076. Mt. 19:16-26=Mk. 10:17-27=Lk. 18:18-27.
1077. Mk. 10:15=Mt. 18:3=Lk. 18:17.
1078. Mt. 18:21-2, cf. Lk. 17:4.
1079. Thus, both translations of Lk. 17:20-1 (i.e., "within you" and "in the midst of you") are correct.
1080. Mk. 4:30-2, Mt. 13:31-32, Lk. 13:18-9.
1081. *Thomas* 3:1-5 in Miller, ed., *The Complete Gospels*, 305.

Beware that no one lead you astray, saying 'Lo here!' or 'Lo there!' For the Son of Man is within you. Follow after him! Those who seek him will find him. Go then and preach the gospel of the kingdom.[1083]

When all God's offspring have finally accepted the truth about themselves, God Himself will take the final step. The entire world will be transformed into a paradise and evil will no longer exist. Death will be a thing of the past and everyone will live in perpetual peace, health, and happiness. Isaiah describes this new world very clearly:

For behold, I create new heavens and a new earth; and the former things shall not be remembered or come into mind. But be glad and rejoice forever in that which I create; for behold, I create Jerusalem a rejoicing, and her people a joy. I will rejoice in Jerusalem, and be glad in my people; no more shall be heard in it the sound of weeping and the cry of distress.[1084]

The wolf shall dwell with the lamb, and the leopard shall lie down with the kid, and the calf and the lion and the fatling together, and a little child shall lead them. The cow and the bear shall feed; their young shall lie down together; and the lion shall eat straw like the ox. The suckling child shall play over the hole of the asp, and the weaned child shall put his hand on the adder's den. They shall not hurt or destroy in all my holy mountain; for the earth shall be full of the knowledge of the LORD as the waters cover the sea.[1085]

Jesus' view seems to have been that when the Kingdom of God finally came in its fullness, i.e., when God transformed the old world into a new one, *none* of His sons and daughters would be left out of it. However, as will be discussed in an upcoming chapter, the later Christians distorted the teaching and believed that the righteous would inherit the Kingdom, but the wicked would suffer eternal punishment. Jesus endeavored to explain the idea in the following saying where "sheep" and "little ones" symbolize God's offspring:

What do you think? If a man has a hundred sheep, and one of them has gone astray, does he not leave the ninety-nine on the hills and go in search of the one

---

1082. According to DeLamotte, "among the most pivotal of the characteristics of unitive mysticism is the concept of the noumenal Self, 'the pure I' through which we meet God in states beyond normal consciousness" (see DeLamotte, *The Alien Christ*, 199). He brings forward evidence to show that the Son of Man, as well as the Kingdom of God, were not external, future realities, but terms used by Jesus to refer to this "noumenal self" as opposed to the "empirical self" of everyday experience (DeLamotte, *The Alien Christ*, 25-30, 199-218).
1083. Robinson, ed., *The Nag Hammadi Library*, 472 (8:15-20).
1084. Is. 65:17-9.
1085. Is. 11:6-9.

that went astray? And if he finds it, truly, I say to you, he rejoices over it more than over the ninety-nine that never went astray. *So it is not the will of your*[1086] *Father who is in heaven that one of these little ones should perish.*[1087] [Fear not, little flock, for it is your Father's good pleasure to give you the kingdom.][1088]

In their fanatical quest for holiness in the form of ritual purity, the people of Israel[1089] had forgotten the inner goodness that could still be found in people's hearts regardless of their supposed outer uncleanness. They had become hardened to this truth by separating people as clean or unclean based on this idea of outer purity. Furthermore, Israel was supposed to be a light to the nations,[1090] but instead, the people were waiting for a warrior Messiah, who would lead them in a victorious military campaign against the Romans. Jesus taught that if the people refused to change a terrible catastrophe would soon befall them in that Jerusalem and the Temple would be destroyed in a military attack:[1091]

> And when he drew near and saw the city he wept over it, saying, "Would that even today you knew the things that make for peace! But now they are hid from your eyes. For the days shall come upon you, when your enemies will cast up a bank about you and surround you, and hem you in on every side, and dash you to the ground, you and your children within you, and they will not leave one stone upon another in you; because you did not know the time of your visitation."[1092]

> And as some spoke of the temple, how it was adorned with noble stones and offerings, Jesus said, "As for these things which you see, the days will come when there shall not be left here one stone upon another that will not be thrown down."[1093]

1086. Other manuscripts have "my" here. See *The New Oxford Annotated Bible*, 1195, Mt. 18:14 text and note d.
1087. Mt. 18:12-4=Lk. 15:3-7 (italics mine).
1088. Lk. 12:32. I could not resist placing this saying here, because it fits in so well with the previous saying.
1089. It should be noted that "Israel" here is not to be understood in the way the New Covenant understood it, but in the usual sense.
1090. Is. 42:6-7: "I am the LORD, I have called you in righteousness, I have taken you by the hand and kept you; I have given you as a covenant to the people, a light to the nations, to open the eyes that are blind, to bring out the prisoners from the dungeon, from the prison those who sit in darkness."
1091. Borg, *Jesus A New Vision*, 156-65.
1092. Lk. 19:41-4.
1093. Lk. 21:5-6=Mk. 13:1-2=Mt. 24:1-2.

This catastrophe would not come as a consequence of the Father punishing them for their sins, but as a consequence of their own intentional thoughts and actions. In the East, this concept is called karma:

> *Karma* may be regarded as an absolutely just but impersonal cosmic operation according to which the fruits, or effects ripening of a volitional act or deed of body, speech or thought are suited to that act.[1094]

At the beginning of his mission, Jesus appointed messengers to bring this news to all the people of the world:

1. Twelve apostles were sent out to only the people of Israel.[1095]
2. Seventy (-Two) apostles were sent to the seventy (-two) countries of the world.[1096]

If the people of the world would only hear the message and act accordingly, the Great Transformation would occur. God's Kingdom on a new earth would become a reality. However, this was not to happen at this time. The Twelve soon returned to Jesus with little success in communicating the message even to their own countrymen.[1097] No mere message of universal brotherhood was going to change their feelings about the Romans or the Jewish establishment that corroborated with them. Love the Roman oppressors! What kind of nonsense was this! God send us your Messiah to destroy our enemies once and for all! The Seventy (-two), on seeing the poor results obtained by the Twelve, soon lost their faith and abandoned their worldwide mission.[1098] Neither the Twelve nor the Seventy (-two) had the mountain moving faith that Jesus had.[1099]

1094. R. C. Zaehner, ed., *Encyclopedia of the World's Religions* (New York: Barnes and Noble, 1988), 275.

1095. Mk. 6:7=Mt. 10:1=Lk. 9:1-2, Mt. 10:5-6. Mt. 10:5-6 only prohibited the twelve apostles from going to the Gentiles and the Samaritans. It did not place this restriction on Jesus' entire mission (see Eisler, *The Messiah Jesus and John the Baptist*, 350-1). However, Matthew was apparently not aware that Jesus also sent out the seventy (-two) apostles to the Gentiles. He utilized Mt. 10:5-6 and added verse 24 ("I was sent only to the lost sheep of the house of Israel") to the story of the Syrophoenician woman (Mt. 15:21-8, cf. Mk. 7:24-30 where the verse is missing) in order to limit Jesus' mission only to Israel. This exclusive view, erroneously put in Jesus' mouth by Matthew, probably originated with his twin brother. Other examples of this mistake will be given later in this chapter.

1096. Lk. 10:1. The Jews believed that there were seventy (-two) countries with seventy (-two) different languages surrounding Israel. See Eisler, *The Messiah Jesus and John the Baptist*, 348.

1097. Mk. 6:30=Lk. 9:10. The apostles told Jesus "all that they had done and taught" (Mk. 6:30) and "what they had done" (Lk. 9:10). The abruptness of these statements without further elaboration (e.g., stories of their successes in preaching and healing) reveals the truth all too clearly. They were unsuccessful and returned to Jesus prematurely.

Chapter 18. The Hypothesis

Several days before the Passover in AD 21, Jesus was on the Mount of Olives healing and teaching the people. When they witnessed his amazing ability to heal[1100] and perform other miraculous acts,[1101] they became politically excited thinking that he could use his power to free them from the Romans. The festival of Passover was always a time of increased political agitation, because the people could not help but remember how their ancestors had miraculously obtained their freedom from the Egyptian Pharaoh. Did not Moses heal[1102] and perform other miracles[1103] during the exodus from Egypt? Perhaps Jesus, as Moses *redivivus*,[1104] could free them in a similar manner now. It could be that the rebels, who had been dispersed throughout the crowd, purposely suggested this idea to them. In any case, getting the people politically agitated was precisely what they wanted. On realizing that things were seriously deteriorating, Jesus could do little but to withdraw from the excited crowd.[1105]

Judas/Jesus, the leader of the rebels, quickly took Jesus' place and led the people on a far different course than his brother had ever planned to take them. The result was a full-fledged revolt against the Romans and the Jewish establishment. Armed with weapons that had been hidden on the Mount of

---

1098. Lk. 10:17-20, which states that the Seventy (-two) returned to Jesus with joy regarding the success of their mission, is only wishful thinking on the part of Luke.

1099. Mt. 17:20, Lk. 17:5-6, Mk. 11:22-3, Mt. 21:21.

1100. According to Larson, "there are serious scholars who maintain that physical cures, beyond the understanding of medical science, have taken place as a result of an overwhelming faith or emotional experience. Psychoanalysis has proved that people become lame, blind, bedridden, or will suffer heart trouble, dizziness, and many other ailments as a result of neuroses, and that the symptoms will vanish when the emotional pressure causing them is relieved. Is it then very difficult to believe that the man cured of palsy was simply a neurotic, long paralyzed by his inner conflicts?" He further adds in the next paragraph "and the same reasoning applies even more to the casting out of devils, that is, giving peace of mind to the mentally distraught. There can be no doubt that the calm and powerful gaze of Jesus, reflecting a mind certain of its power, could act as a restorative to broken personalities. Especially would this be true, once His reputation as a healer began to spread among the poor." See Martin A. Larson, *The Story of Christian Origins* (Washington, D.C: a Joseph J. Binns/ New Republic Book, 1977), 323.

1101. It is possible to explain Jesus' miracles naturally without recourse to supernaturalism or deception. W. Barnes Tatum gives some natural explanations in his discussion of Jesus' miracles: "The resuscitation of the dead by Jesus may actually have involved persons who were not dead but in a coma. ... In feeding the multitudes, Jesus did not really multiply the fish and the loaves of bread.... He set an example of sharing his food which was followed by others in the crowd until all were satisfied. Neither did Jesus really walk on the water of the Sea of Galilee.... He walked along the shore or on a sand bar. Nor did Jesus really still the storm by his word of command.... The subsiding of the storm was pure coincidence. " See W. Barnes Tatum, *In Quest of Jesus: A Guidebook* (Atlanta: John Knox Press, 1982), 160. I will let the reader decide whether the natural or the supernatural explanation makes the most sense.

1102. E.g., Ex. 4:6-7, Num. 21:6-9.

1103. E.g., Ex. 7:20, 8:5-7,8:16-9, 9:23-6, 10:13-5,22-3, 14:21-2, Ex. 15:22-5, Ex. 16:9-36, Ex. 17:1-7.

Olives and that they now hid under their garments, they moved towards the city. Their purpose was to enter Jerusalem and take it over. Two strategic sites were taken within the city: the Temple with its Antonia fortress in the north and the tower of Siloam in the south.[1106]

The Roman troops stationed at Herod's place in the western part of the city were unable to put down the revolt.[1107] The Sanhedrin sent word to Pilate at Caesarea on the coast to come immediately to suppress it. With the additional troops and siege machinery Pilate was able to crush the revolt by the afternoon of Passover eve, which was the 15th of April in AD 21.[1108] Many Galileans were massacred in the Temple and eighteen Jerusalemites were killed, when the tower of Siloam was overthrown.[1109] However, Judas/*Jesus*, the leader of the revolt, could not be found.[1110] He probably escaped through tunnels below the city.[1111]

Pilate wanted the leader captured, the city was under martial law, and as the Jewish authorities knew, Pilate dealt harshly in matters of rebellion. In endeavoring to pacify the populace, many innocent people might be killed along with the guilty. What was to be done?

About this time, some men, who had been a part of the tragic events in Jerusalem but who were able to escape, went to tell Jesus, who was somewhere outside of the city, what had happened. Luke has preserved this incident for us:

> There were some present at that very time who told him [Jesus] of the Galileans whose blood Pilate had mingled with their sacrifices. And he

---

1104. According to the Slavonic Josephus (see the next chapter), some people described Jesus in the following manner: "Our first lawgiver [Moses] is risen again and displays many healings and (magic) arts...."

1105. See the story in Jn. 6:1-15 where, after miraculously feeding about five thousand people (Mk. 6:30-44, Mt. 14:13-21, Lk. 9:10-17), Jesus withdrew from a politically excited crowd. Cf., the feeding of the four thousand in Mt 15:32-9=Mk. 8:1-10.

1106. Eisler, *The Messiah Jesus and John the Baptist*, 500-10, 570-1.

1107. Robert Eisler gives reasons why in AD 21 the Roman garrison was stationed at Herod's palace at the west of the city and not at the fortress of Antonia that was attached to the Temple. The Antonia fortress was only in the hands of the Jewish Temple guard at the time —many of whom may have actually joined the revolt! See Eisler, *The Messiah Jesus and John the Baptist*, 481-2, 486-9.

1108. Eisler, *The Messiah Jesus and John the Baptist*, 502, 505, 513 (note 3), 571.

1109. Eisler, *The Messiah Jesus and John the Baptist*, 500-10, 570-1.

1110. It should be noted here that in this hypothesis the arrest and imprisonment of Barabbas is considered unhistorical.

1111. Josephus mentions Judas, the son of Ari. When "in command of a company at the siege of Jerusalem [AD 70]," "*he secretly escaped through some of the underground passages*" (War VII, 215, italics mine). He also explains the Roman decision to build a siege wall around Jerusalem in June of AD 70. Although the Romans could guard the main exits to and from the city, "the Jews from necessity and their knowledge of the locality *would contrive secret routes*; and, should supplies be furtively smuggled in, the siege would be still further protracted" (War V, 497-8, italics mine).

answered them, "Do you think that these Galileans were worse sinners than all the other Galileans, because they suffered thus? I tell you, No; but unless you repent you will all likewise perish." [And they told him about] those eighteen upon whom the tower in Siloam[1112] fell and killed them? [And he answered them,] "Do you think that they were worse offenders than all the others who dwelt in Jerusalem? I tell you, No; but unless you repent you will all likewise perish."[1113]

Through the coming forward of an intermediary, Caiaphas, the high priest, learned an amazing fact. Judas/Jesus, the leader of the revolt, was the twin brother of Jesus, who had been condemned earlier by the Sanhedrin for false prophecy! The massage from Jesus to Caiaphas was that he would be willing to deliver himself up and take his brother's place in order to end the crisis and save the people from any further Roman reprisals:

> Greater love has no man than this, that a man lay down his life for his friends.[1114]

The Sanhedrin had already condemned Jesus to death earlier. The problem had always been how to carry out the sentence. Caiaphas made the following statement to the council:

> You know nothing at all, you do not understand that it is expedient for you that one man should die for the people, and that the whole nation should not perish.[1115]

The Jewish authorities would have Jesus arrested at night on the Mount of Olives,[1116] they would have a brief consultation to prepare a false indictment,[1117] and finally they would deliver Jesus to Pilate for the Roman trial in place of Judas/Jesus. The secret plan was put into operation.

From the unknown intermediary who brought the offer to Caiaphas developed the myth that someone (i.e., Judas Iscariot) betrayed Jesus. Actually,

---

1112. Presumably, the southeastern corner of Jerusalem was called Siloam, thus giving rise to the phrase "tower *in* Siloam" (italics mine). The name was probably derived from the fact that the pool of Siloam was located there as well (War II, 340, V, 140, 145, 252, 410, 505, VI, 363, 401). See also John J. Rousseau and Rami Arav, *Jesus and His World* (Minneapolis: Fortress Press, 1995), 149, 157-61.

1113. Lk. 13:1-5. I have followed Robert Eisler's interpretation of this passage (Eisler, *The Messiah Jesus and John the Baptist*, 500-510). In *The New Oxford Annotated Bible*, eds. May and Metzger, the mention of the eighteen Jerusalemites who were killed by the collapse of the tower of Siloam is part of Jesus' *response* to the people who brought him the news about the Galileans who had been massacred by Pilate. It seems to me that Eisler's interpretation makes more sense.

1114. Jn. 15:13.

1115. Jn. 11:49-50.

the Greek verb used in the gospels means "delivered up" and only in Luke 6:16 is Judas Iscariot called a traitor.[1118] The designation "Iscariot" could mean a number of things. One possible meaning is that it is derived from the Latin word "sicarius" that means "dagger-man."[1119] Another meaning is that it is derived from the Aramaic word that means "deceit" or "falsehood."[1120] Judas could be called the "dagger-man" or the "false one." Judas Iscariot is simply another name used in the gospels for Judas/Jesus, the twin brother of Jesus. He would have been an excellent choice for the role of the betrayer as the myth developed.

Jesus took the place of his brother and was arrested on the Mount of Olives with little resistance. All four gospels agree that one of those with him drew a sword and cut off the ear of the high priest's slave.[1121] In John, this individual is even said to have been Simon Peter.[1122] Against Jesus' own wishes, some of his followers may have carried swords for protection against robbers.[1123] It is not unlikely that one of them tried to protect him when he was being arrested, but it is unlikely that it was one of his closest supporters. Jesus probably informed them beforehand at the Last Supper[1124] about what was going to occur. Since, in the negotiations with Caiaphus Jesus' supporters were probably granted immunity from arrest, it can be understood why this individual who used his sword was not arrested along with Jesus. Unfortunately, this use of the sword actually helped the Jewish authorities identify Jesus to the Romans as the leader of the revolt.[1125]

1116. Mk. 14:43-53, Mt. 26:47-57, Lk. 22:47-54, Jn. 18:1-12. Mk. 14:43 and Mt. 26:47 state that Judas with a "crowd with swords and clubs from the chief priests (and the scribes, Mk. only) and the elders" arrested Jesus. Lk 22:47 and 52 state that the "chief priests and officers of the temple and elders" were with the "crowd" that arrested him. Finally, Jn. 18:3 and 12 state that "a band of soldiers (and their captain) and some officers from the chief priests and the Pharisees (or "and the officers of the Jews") arrested Jesus. It was probably officers of the Jewish Temple guard that arrested Jesus.
1117. This short deliberation is alluded to in Mk. 15:1=Mt. 27:1-2.
1118. G. A. Wells, *Did Jesus Exist?* 2nd ed. (London: Pemberton, 1986), 132.
1119. S. G. F. Brandon, *Jesus and the Zealots* (New York: Charles Scribner's Sons, 1967), 39, 204 note 1.
1120. G. A. Wells, *Did Jesus Exist?* Rev. ed.(London: Pemberton, 1986), 133.
1121. Mk. 14:47, Mt. 28:51, Lk. 22:50, Jn. 18:10.
1122. Jn. 18:10.
1123. Josephus states that even the conventional, peaceful Essenes "carry nothing whatever with them on their journeys, *except arms as a protection against brigands*" (War II, 125-6, italics mine). However, it is possible that he is here confusing the conventional Essenes with the anti-establishment Essenes.
1124. Mk. 14:17-25, Mt. 26:20-29, Lk. 22:14-38, Jn. 13:1-38.
1125. Lk. 22:35-8 about Jesus ordering his disciples to actually purchase swords was simply created as an example of fulfilled Scripture, as the passage itself attests (v. 37). The Scriptural verse is Is. 53:12 ("And he was reckoned with transgressors").

Chapter 18. The Hypothesis

At the Roman trial, Jesus remained silent on hearing the charges.[1126] It took little time for his supposed guilt to be proved, since the evidence for it was overwhelming. He was crucified for being the "King of the Jews,"[1127] i.e., a rebel against Rome. Pilate ordered him and two others to be crucified.[1128] The two others who were crucified with Jesus had each commanded a section of the city that had been taken by the rebels (i.e., the Temple with its Antonia fortress in the north and the tower of Siloam in the south).[1129] Jesus' life ended before dawn on the 16th of April, Passover of AD 21.[1130] He would have been 32 years old.[1131] Pilate was satisfied in believing that the supposed leader of the revolt was caught and executed. Caiaphus was satisfied that his nation was saved from Roman retribution and that a false prophet received his just punishment.

The view taken here is that Jesus did not perform the "entry into Jerusalem" and the "cleansing of the Temple" episodes. It is nonsense to believe that a teacher of peace would have initiated actions that would have caused the people to become politically agitated and would have given the authorities an excuse to take violent action against them. The "entry into Jerusalem" episode[1132] was probably created as a fulfillment of biblical prophecy[1133] and the "cleansing of the Temple" episode[1134] was most likely a distorted account of an action performed by Judas/Jesus in the Temple but later transferred to Jesus in the gospels.[1135]

As we have seen, Judas/Jesus had taken control of the Temple with an armed force for a time. It is likely that his next step was to put an end to the past abuses perpetrated by the corrupt priestly establishment and institute new practices in

---

1126. Mk. 15:2-5, Mt. 27:11-4, Jn. 19:9-10.
1127. Mk. 15:26, Mt. 27:37, Lk. 23:38, Jn. 19:19.
1128. Mk. 15:27, Mt. 27:38, Lk. 23:32 33, 39-43, Jn. 19:18.
1129. Eisler, *The Messiah Jesus and John the Baptist*, 510, 571.
1130. According to Robert Eisler, the discrepancy between the Synoptics that Jesus was crucified on the Passover (Mk. 14:12-6=Mt. 26:17-9=Lk. 22:7-13, Mk. 15:1=Mt. 27:1-2=Lk. 23:1) and John that it was the day before the Passover (Jn. 19:14) can be explained if we remember an important fact. In Jewish tradition the day begins at sunset and in Greek and Roman tradition it begins at sunrise. The period common to both would then be Passover night and in this case it was the night that fell between the 15th and 16th of April. Therefore, if the crucifixion, as well as all the activities preceding it, occurred during that time, the discrepancy between the sources would be explained. The Synoptics would simply have followed the Jewish tradition and John the Greek/Roman tradition (Eisler, *The Messiah Jesus and John the Baptist*, 299-302, 513, 571-2).
1131. 12 BC – 1 (there is no "0" year) + AD21 = 32 years old.
1132. Mk. 11:1-10, Mt. 21:1-9, Lk. 19:28-38, Jn. 12:12-9.
1133. Zech. 9:9.
1134. Mk. 11:15-9, Mt. 21:12-3, Lk. 19:45-8, Jn. 2:13-7.
1135. Another distorted account of an action most likely performed by Judas/Jesus but transferred to Jesus is the account in Gospel Oxyrhynchus 840, 2:1-9 (Miller, ed., *The Complete Gospels*, 420-1) about Jesus taking his disciples into the "inner sanctuary" of the Temple.

their place. Depending on whose point of view is being referred to, the action could have been interpreted as one of purification or destruction. To the followers of Judas/Jesus, the purpose of it was to *purify* the Temple.[1136] In the gospels, this view of the event was transformed into the "cleansing of the Temple" episode that was supposedly performed by Jesus. The same tendency can also be seen in the Acts where the followers of Jesus were erroneously portrayed like the Jews as being devoted to the Temple and regularly worshipping in it.[1137] On the other hand, to the establishment priests, the purpose of the action was to *destroy* the Temple. In the gospels, this view of the event was transformed into testimony provided to the Sanhedrin that was described as false.[1138] These witnesses supposedly heard Jesus say, 'I will destroy this temple that is made with hands, and in three days I will build another, not made with hands.'"[1139] The same tendency can also be seen in the *Gospel of Peter* where it is stated that the apostles after the crucifixion were supposedly being searched for "as ones wishing to burn down the temple."[1140]

Even some sayings put in Jesus' mouth may have actually originated with his twin brother. Let us take three examples:

1. Mt. 10:34:[1141] "Do not think that I come to bring peace on earth; I have not come to bring peace, but a sword." Some people had probably heard Jesus speaking of peace at an earlier date and they assumed they were now seeing the same person in front of them. They asked him to speak on the subject of peace again. Judas/*Jesus* corrected their error by uttering this saying.
2. Mk. 8:34:[1142] "If any man would come after me, let him deny himself and take up his cross and follow me." This saying would make perfect sense

---

1136. From the rabbinical sources, Robert Eisler accepted as authentic at least one passage as referring to Jesus from several that have been cited by scholars, i.e., Baraitha — B. Abodah Zarah 16b, 17a. In this passage, Jacob of Kephar Sekhanjah, who is identified as a disciple of Jesus, quotes a saying to R. Eli'ezer b. Hyrkanos in order to solve a problem regarding the interpretation of Dt. 23:18 (i.e., "You shall not bring the hire of a harlot ... into the house of the LORD your God in payment for any vow...."). Jacob further added that his teacher Jesus taught it to him. The saying is as follows: "She gathered it as the hire of an harlot, and they shall return it to the hire of an harlot (Mic. 1:7): it has come from dirt, and to the place of dirt it shall go." According to Eisler, at an earlier date Jacob probably heard his teacher utter the saying when witnessing the offering of a prostitute being rejected on the basis of Dt. 23:18. The idea being expressed is that an impure priesthood residing in a polluted Temple has no legitimate grounds for rejecting the offering of an impure woman. Filth is merely being added to more filth. Thus, the saying is a denunciation of the priesthood and Temple (Eisler, *The Messiah Jesus and John the Baptist*, 8-9, 593-4). My only departure from Eisler's analysis is that I understand the saying as having actually originated with Judas/*Jesus* not Jesus. The original compilers of this Baraitha erroneously identified the originator of the saying with the Jesus of Christianity. Anyway, the tone of the saying certainly supports my identification.

coming from Judas/Jesus. The "grim challenge," as Brandon put it,[1143] to take up one's cross was one that all rebels against Rome had to deal with, because it was on a cross that they would undoubtedly die if captured.

3. Mt. 19:29-30:[1144] "And every one who has left houses or brothers or sisters or father or mother or children or lands, for my name's sake, will receive a hundredfold, [and inherit eternal life].[1145] But many that are first will be last, and the last first." Jesus probably did expect his apostles to renounce everything they owned to follow him.[1146] Also, when the young rich man asked him what he lacked to gain eternal life, Jesus told him to sell all he owned, give it to the poor, and follow him.[1147] According to Mitchell, "Jesus intuited that the man's only attachment was to his wealth, and that if he could give it up he would step right into the kingdom of God."[1148] Furthermore, it was "a teaching for this particular man at this particular moment."[1149] However, the saying quoted above takes renunciation to another level that is difficult to explain if it came from Jesus, but it would not be so if it came from his twin brother. It was applicable to "everyone" not just prospective apostles and the giving of possessions to the poor was not asked for. The proper milieu of this saying becomes clear if we examine Mattathias' announcement to the Jerusalemites made at the onset of the revolt against the Syrians in 167 BC:

1137. Acts 2:46, 3:1, 5:12, 20-1, 25, 21:23-4, 26. The Romans seem to have also accepted this portrayal of the followers of Jesus as being devoted to the Temple. According to the fourth century Christian writer, Sulpicius Severus, the Roman general, Titus, convened a council to discuss the fate of the Temple during the siege of AD 70. According to Severus, Titus and some others "opposed [the view that the temple should be preserved], holding the destruction of the temple to be a prime necessity in order to wipe out more completely the religion of the Jews *and the Christians*; for they urged that these religions, although hostile to each other, nevertheless sprang from the same sources; the Christians had grown out of the Jews: if the root were destroyed, the stock would easily perish" (italics mine). Quoted from Tacitus, *Histories, Annals*, trans. by C. H. Moore and J. Jackson (Loeb Classical Library) 4 vols. (Cambridge: Harvard University Press, 1979) III, 220-1 (Fragments of the Histories). Josephus, probably in order to avert the accusation of cruelty to Titus, states that the latter wanted to preserve the Temple and was appalled when it was incinerated (War VI, 236-43, 250-66). See also S. G. F. Brandon, *The Fall of Jerusalem and the Christian Church*, 2nd ed. (London: S.P.C.K., 1968), 120-1,123; Eisler, *The Messiah Jesus and John the Baptist*, 552-4.

1138. Mk. 14:57, cf. Mk. 14:56, Mt. 26:60. In the view of the Christians, it was proper for the Savior to predict the destruction of the Temple (Lk. 21:5-6=Mk. 13:1-4=Mt. 24:1-3), but it was in no way proper for him to be the *destroyer* of it. Thus, the gospels describe this testimony as being untrue.

1139. Mk. 14:57-8, cf. Mt. 26:60-1. Cf. Acts 6.14, where some men accuse Stephen of saying that "Jesus of Nazareth will destroy this place [the Temple]...." See also Mk. 15:29-30=Mt. 27:39-40.

1140. *Gospel of Peter* 7:2 in Miller, ed., *The Complete gospels*, 404.

1141. Cf. Lk. 12:51.

1142. Cf. Mt. 10:38, 16:24, Lk. 9:23, 14:27.

1143. Brandon, *Jesus and the Zealots*, 145.

1144. Cf. Mk. 10:29-31, Lk. 18:29b-30, 13:30, Cf. also Lk. 14:33.

1145. If I am correct in suggesting that this saying in its pristine form actually came from Jesus' twin brother, then the phrase in brackets ("and inherit eternal life") must be a later addition to the saying.

Then Mattathias cried out in the city with a loud voice, saying: "Let every one who is zealous for the law and supports the covenant *come out* with me!" And he and his sons *fled to the hills and left all that they had in the city*. Then many who were seeking righteousness and justice *went down to the wilderness to dwell there*, they, their sons, their wives, and their cattle, because evils pressed heavily upon them. And it was reported to the king's [Antiochus IV Epiphanes'] officers, and to the troops in Jerusalem the city of David, that men who had rejected the king's *command had gone down to the hiding places in the wilderness*.[1150]

Mt. 19:29-30 is what survives of an original announcement made by Judas/Jesus to the people: Leave all possessions behind and come out into the wilderness to prepare for a war of liberation against the Romans. This renunciation included family members opposed to the enterprise. If the revolt was successful, they would get their possessions back and be awarded with considerably more than they had before. All the lands, houses, and other possessions once owned by the Jewish establishment, who had collaborated with the Romans, would be distributed to the people. Indeed, "many that are first will be last, and the last first."[1151]

At regular intervals in the stone balustrade surrounding the inner court of the Temple were placed warning inscriptions in Greek, Latin, and Jewish (actually Aramaic) forbidding foreigners to enter within.[1152] According to the Slavonic Josephus,[1153] above one set of the warning inscriptions was affixed a fourth one in the same languages. It stated the following:

1146. Mk. 10:28=Mt. 19:27=Lk. 18:28.
1147. Mk. 10:17-27=Mt. 19:16-26=Lk. 18:18-27.
1148. Mitchell, *The Gospel According to Jesus*, 234.
1149. Mitchell, *The Gospel According to Jesus*, 234.
1150. 1 Macc. 2:27-31 (italics mine).
1151. For a hypothetical reconstruction using Mt. 19:29-30, 1 Macc. 2:27-9, and other passages of an announcement Judas/Jesus made to the people at a later time of grave crisis, see the chapter titled *The Fate of the Son of Joseph*.
1152. Ant. XV, 417; War V, 193-4; VI, 125-6. The inscription stated the following: "No foreigner is to enter within the balustrade and embankment around the sanctuary. Whoever is caught will have himself to blame for his death which follows" (Josephus, Bk. VIII, pp. 202-3, note d).
1153. Eisler, *The Messiah Jesus and John the Baptist*, 516. See also Josephus, Bk. III, p. 657.

Chapter 18. The Hypothesis

> Jesus a king who did not reign[1154] was crucified [by (the) Jews][1155] because he foretold (the) destruction of (the) city and the desolation of (the) temple.[1156]

This inscription endeavored to explain the crucifixion of Jesus as proper according to the Mosaic Law. Jesus, by predicting the destruction of Jerusalem and the Temple, which everyone could see did not occur, was guilty of being a false prophet according to Dt. 18:20-2.[1157] As mentioned above, the penalty for such a crime was stoning followed by hanging the corpse on a stake. The hanging on the stake portion of the penalty was understood as crucifixion in the inscription. Thus, the Jewish authorities inscribed on stone —short and to the point — in the very edifice Jesus predicted would be destroyed the true crime that *they* (not the Romans) found him guilty of. In order to be viewed by everyone, the inscription was probably attached sometime after AD 25/26 (i.e., Pilate's last year in office) at one of the entrances (actually stairways of fourteen steps) that went through the stone balustrade and up to the inner court.[1158]

An interesting letter exists that was written by a Hellenized Syrian named Mara bar Serapion to his son Serapion at some point after AD 73. Mara bar Serapion was in prison when he wrote the letter. He wrote it to urge his son to strive for wisdom in life and to prove to him that all those who persecute men of wisdom are punished in some way. As proof of the latter, he used the fates of Socrates, Pythagoras, and Jesus as examples. I quote the applicable portion of the letter below:

> What advantage did the Athenians gain from putting Socrates to death? Famine and plague came upon them as a judgment for their crime. What advantage did the men of Samos gain from burning Pythagoras? In a moment their land was covered with sand. *What advantage did the Jews gain from executing their wise King? It was just after that that their kingdom was abolished.* God justly avenged these three wise men: the Athenians died of hunger; the Samians were overwhelmed by the sea; *the Jews, ruined and driven from their land, live in complete dispersion.* But Socrates did not die for good; he lived on in the teaching of Plato.

1154. This statement shows that the establishment priests were well aware of Jesus' genealogy.
1155. The phrase in brackets ["by (the) Jews"] was probably a Christian interpolation inserted to implicate the Jews for the crucifixion of Jesus (Eisler, *The Messiah Jesus and John the Baptist*, 521).
1156. Robert Eisler believed that the Slavonic Josephus reproduced only a shortened version of what the actual inscription contained (Eisler, *The Messiah Jesus and John the Baptist*, 520).
1157. Eisler, *The Messiah Jesus and John the Baptist*, 521-3.
1158. Robert Eisler thought the inscription was placed at the very entrance that Jesus supposedly used to reach the Holy Place within the inner court (Eisler, *The Messiah Jesus and John the Baptist*, 517-8).

Pythagoras did not die for good; he lived on in the statue of Hera. *Nor did the wise King die for good; he lived on in the teaching which he had given.*[1159]

It is doubtful that Mara bar Serapion obtained is information about the "wise King" (i.e., Jesus) from Christians. Otherwise, he would certainly have mentioned the resurrection and not just the "teaching which he had given." He also would have known that the Romans crucified Jesus not the Jews. The correct source of Mara bar Serapion's information was put forward by Robert Eisler:

> At this early date we can hardly think of any other source save that inscription on Jesus, 'the king who did not reign,' written in three languages [Greek, Latin and Aramaic] and constantly pointed out to a succession of Jewish and gentile visitors to the temple of Jerusalem ... a monument which may still be hidden today beneath the ruins of the Herodian temple or built into some wall and awaiting its rediscovery.[1160]

1159. F. F. Bruce, *Jesus and Christian Origins Outside the New Testament* (Grand Rapids: Eerdmans, 1977), 30-1 (italics mine).
1160. Eisler, *The Messiah Jesus and John the Baptist*, 525.

CHAPTER 19. THE SLAVONIC JOSEPHUS

Robert Eisler's theory about the Slavonic (Old Russian) version of Josephus is that it was translated from manuscripts of the first Greek edition of the *Jewish War*, which was called the *Halosis* or *The Capture (of Jerusalem)* and was published in AD 72. However, it could have been as early as AD 71, because Josephus strove to have it ready for the Triumph of Vespasian and Titus in Rome. The *Halosis* was a Greek rewriting of Josephus' original Aramaic rough draft that was made almost entirely by assistants hired for the purpose, since Josephus did not have adequate knowledge of the language. After its initial publication, it was continually revised and then republished in a new form during the reign of Emperor Domitian (AD 81-96). This later Greek edition of the *Jewish War* became our present standard version. An Aramaic rendering of the *Halosis* (*not* the Aramaic rough draft), which was meant for the Aramaic speaking people of the East in order to persuade them not to revolt against Rome, was also published in AD 72.[1161]

The Slavonic Josephus contains some unique passages about John the Baptist, Jesus, and the early Christians, which are not found in the *Jewish War*. In fact, the latter is completely silent about these subjects. Eisler concluded that Christian scribes tampered with them in the *Halosis* by omitting some unfavorable items and interpolating others that were more in line with the faith.[1162] A Lithuanian scribe of a Judaizing heresy in the church translated the *Halosis* with these excisions and additions from the Greek into the Old Russian

---

1161. All of the above can be found in Robert Eisler, *The Messiah Jesus and John the Baptist* ed. by A. H. Krappe (London: Methuen & Co., 1931), 26-31, 113-47.
1162. Eisler, *The Messiah Jesus and John the Baptist*, 223-31, 381-92, 457-71, 514-21, 527-31, 547-50.

between 1250 and 1260. While doing this work, he interpolated one passage about Jesus' resurrection and added certain glosses in other parts of the Slavonic text.[1163]

Eisler endeavored to restore the Slavonic passages about John the Baptist, Jesus, and the early Christians to their original form through a detailed analysis of the text. He then made them the basis of a novel and controversial theory of Christian origins.[1164] In other chapters, various passages from the Slavonic Josephus have been discussed along with Eisler's restorations of them where applicable. With regard to the Slavonic Jesus passage to be discussed below, he thought that Josephus derived the original form of it from the actual records of Jesus' trial in the Roman archives.[1165]

It must be admitted that most scholars have not accepted Eisler's theory and believe that the Slavonic Josephus is either a medieval Christian or Jewish forgery — the purpose of which was to make Josephus testify either for or against the Christian faith. The most complete attempt to refute his theory is a 284-page book by J. W. Jack that was written in 1933.[1166] John P. Meier summarized the present scholarly consensus regarding the Slavonic Josephus and Eisler's utilization of it in the following way:

> Despite the spirited and ingenious attempt of Robert Eisler in the 1920s and 1930s to defend the authenticity of much of the Jesus material in the Slavonic *Jewish War*, almost all critics today discount his theory.[1167]

After carefully examining the various opinions, I must accept Eisler's theory for the following reasons:

1. When the actual Slavonic passage about Jesus is examined,[1168] the "non-committal attitude" towards him, as Brandon called it, can easily be noticed.[1169] Surely, if it were a Jewish forgery, a scribe would have

---

1163. Eisler, *The Messiah Jesus and John the Baptist*, 147-69, 216-9.
1164. For a summarization of his theory, see Eisler, *The Messiah Jesus and John the Baptist*, 562-90.
1165. Eisler, *The Messiah Jesus and John the Baptist*, 381-92, 466-71.
1166. J. W. Jack, *The Historic Christ* (London: James Clarke & Co., 1933. See also J. M. Creed, "The Slavonic Version of Josephus' History of the Jewish War," *Harvard Theological Review* 25 (1932): 277-319. For a recent discussion of Eisler's theory, see E. Bammel, "The revolution theory from Reimarus to Brandon," in Ernst Bammel and C. F. D. Moule, eds. *Jesus and the Politics of His Day* (New York: Cambridge University Press, 1984), 32-7.
1167. John P. Meier, "Jesus in Josephus: A Modest Proposal," *Catholic Biblical Quarterly* 52 (1990): 77-8.
1168. For the passage in its present form (i.e., the unrestored version), see Eisler, *The Messiah Jesus and John the Baptist*, 383-5 and Josephus, Bk. III, Appendix, p. 648-50.

written something more derogatory. One only has to examine the medieval Jewish life of Jesus known as the *Toledoth Jeshu* to realize the truth of this statement.[1170] On the other hand, a Christian scribe would have followed the gospel evidence more closely. Why would a Christian state that Jesus had 150 "helpers,"[1171] who are completely unheard of in all the Christian sources,[1172] or that Jesus' supporters planned a revolt in Jerusalem that Pilate suppressed at the outset by slaying many of them? Whoever may have written the passage in the form we presently have it, the "non-committal attitude" proves it was not a Jewish or a Christian forger. Nevertheless, it does contain Christian interpolations. For example, the statement that Jesus' "works were divine"[1173] could only have come from a believer. Also, at the trial Pilate freed Jesus after pronouncing him "[a benefactor, but not] a malefactor [nor] a rebel [nor] covetous of king(ship)."[1174] Needless to say, a Jewish forger would not have called Jesus a "benefactor." The impartiality and the additions taken together can best be explained if we accept the view that the passage in its original form was derogatory from a Christian point of view, but was neutralized by editing later on. In this way, it is possible that a Jewish forger wrote it *in its original form*, but not necessarily Josephus. The evidence that Josephus was indeed the writer is provided by the answer to another question. Why would a Jewish forger have taken the time and effort to revise Josephus' entire *Jewish War* in order to insert a few derogatory passages about John the Baptist, Jesus, and the early Christians into it? Surely, he could have obtained the same result if he simply inserted them into a standard copy of the *War*. Brandon stated that such a hypothetical work on the part of a Jewish scribe would be "one of the most

---

1169. S. G. F. Brandon, *Jesus and the Zealots* (New York: Charles Scribner's Sons, 1967), 367-8.

1170. For example, according to one version of the *Toledoth Jeshu*, Yeshu (Jesus) was able to obtain the unutterable Name of God on the Foundation Stone in the Temple. Its use gave the person in possession of it the power to do anything he wanted. In order to defeat Yeshu, the Sages gave Judah Iskarioto the Name also. By using the power of the Name, Yeshu and Iskarioto were able to fly. While doing so, they both tried making the other fall to the ground. However, neither one could do so, because their power came from the same source. As a last resort, Iskarioto "defiled" Yeshu and they both fell to earth and forgot the Name. Here is another example from the same source: In order to execute Yeshu (Jesus), the Sages first tried using a tree, but it broke, as a result of Yeshu declaring while he had the Name that no tree would support him. Next, they tried a carob-stalk and because it was really a plant and not a tree, they hung him on it until he died. See Morris Goldstein, *Jesus in the Jewish Tradition* (New York: The Macmillan Co., 1950), 147-66.

1171. "Many helpers of the wonder-worker" (i.e., Jesus) are also mentioned during the reign of Emperor Claudius in AD 41-54 (Eisler, *The Messiah Jesus and John the Baptist*, 528-9). See also Josephus, Bk. III, Appendix, pp. 651-2.

1172. Eisler, *The Messiah Jesus and John the Baptist*, 470-1.

1173. This phrase is a Christian interpolation according to Eisler (Eisler, *The Messiah Jesus and John the Baptist*, 389-91).

1174. The portions in brackets are the Christian interpolations according to Eisler (Eisler, *The Messiah Jesus and John the Baptist*, 385).

laboriously senseless compositions known in the whole field of literary creation."[1175] There is no adequate answer why a Jewish forger or any forger for that matter would undertake such a project.[1176] The best explanation is that Josephus was the author of the Slavonic Josephus in its original form.

2. There are passages found in the Slavonic Josephus that are not in the *War* and do not have any relationship at all to the religions of Judaism and Christianity. For example, when Antipater, the father of Herod the Great, was before Caesar in ca. 47 BC, the Slavonic Josephus adds the statement that Caesar "remitted the tax to his [Antipater's] country."[1177] Even though this is probably incorrect, why would a Jewish or a Christian scribe have interpolated it into the Slavonic Josephus? Another example is Herod's dream that revealed his brother Joseph's death to him in advance. Whereas in the *War* only the bare fact that Herod had a dream is mentioned, in the Slavonic text the dream is described in some detail.[1178] What would have been the reason for a Jewish or a Christian scribe to expand upon the story in this way? As a final example, the stratagem of the "three-pronged irons" that was used by Vitellius against Otho in the battle of Bedriacum (AD 69) should be mentioned.[1179] Its use allowed the former to totally defeat the latter.[1180] Again, there is simply no explanation why a Jewish or a Christian scribe would have interpolated this passage into the Slavonic Josephus. However, a scribe would have *copied* all these passages, if he believed he was preserving authentic statements of Josephus.[1181]

3. The Slavonic Josephus provides a candid confession how Josephus was able to surrender to the Romans. The event occurred after the Romans captured Jotapata in Galilee in AD 67.[1182] Josephus was hiding in a cave with some other Jews and desired to surrender to the enemy. However,

---

1175. S. G. F. Brandon, *The Fall of Jerusalem and the Christian Chruch*, 2nd ed. (London: S.P.C.K., 1968), 116-7. Brandon based his argument on the two *actual* Slavonic passages about Jesus and the early Christians. However, why a Jewish scribe would undertake the task of revising the *War* in order to insert these "vague" passages (as Brandon describes them) is even more inexplicable.

1176. In Josephus, Bk. III, Appendix, pp. 635-58, twenty-two passages are reproduced from the Slavonic Josephus that are not found in the standard copy of the *War* and on pp.659-60 a large number of passages are listed that are found in the latter but not in the former.

1177. This Slavonic addition is located at War I, 200. Eisler, *The Messiah Jesus and John the Baptist*, 170-1.

1178. This Slavonic addition is located at War I, 328. Eisler, *The Messiah Jesus and John the Baptist*, 172-3. See also Josephus, Bk. III, Appendix, pp. 635-6.

1179. This Slavonic addition is located at War IV, 547. Eisler, *The Messiah Jesus and John the Baptist*, 180-1. See also Josephus, Bk. III, Appendix, pp. 656-7.

1180. It is worth noting that the use of this device is not mentioned in any of our other sources (Josephus, Bk. III, Appendix, p. 656, note e).

1181. For other examples of similar passages, see Eisler, *The Messiah Jesus and John the Baptist*, 170-82.

1182. War III, 316-39.

his companions threatened to kill him if he attempted to do so. They preferred to commit suicide rather than give themselves up to the Romans. In order to save himself, Josephus suggested that they cast lots to determine the order in which they would dispatch each other.[1183] The suggestion was accepted. What followed is different in the *War* and in the Slavonic Josephus. In the former, it is stated that Josephus *"(should one say by fortune or by the providence of God?), was left alone with one other;* [continued below]."[1184] The latter has the statement that Josephus *"counted the numbers with cunning, and thereby misled them all."*[1185] Both versions continue on in roughly the same way: "and, anxious neither to be condemned by the lot nor, should he be left to the last, to stain his hand with the blood of a fellow-countryman, he persuaded this man also, under a pledge, to remain alive."[1186] It is inexplicable why a later Jewish or Christian scribe would desire to diminish Josephus' character by adding this detail in the Slavonic Josephus. The best explanation is that the confession came from Josephus and "the crudeness of the original account of Josephus' contemptible conduct after the fall of Jotapata may ... have been felt to need toning down."[1187]

There are admittedly some puzzling passages (e.g., the two invectives against the Romans)[1188] and some passages with historical errors in the Slavonic Josephus (e.g., the statements that Herodias' first husband was Philip the Tetrarch[1189] and that Herod Agrippa I had no son).[1190] On initial examination, their existence would cause one to question whether the Slavonic Josephus could have actually originated with Josephus.[1191] However, on further examination there are no insurmountable problems in believing that this was indeed the case.

1183. War III, 340-90.
1184. War III, 391 (italics mine).
1185. Josephus, Bk. III, Appendix, p. 654 (italics mine). A very brief summary of Josephus' life after this event is as follows: When the Romans took him prisoner, he was brought before Vespasian where he predicted that the Roman general would become emperor (War III, 392-408, see p. 180). After the war, he received lodging, a pension, and Roman citizenship from the new emperor (The Life, 422-3). This gave him the leisure necessary to produce his famous literary works.
1186. War III, 391, cf. Josephus, Bk III, Appendix, p. 654.
1187. G. A. Williamson, *Josephus The Jewish War* (Harmondsworth: Penguin Books, 1959), 403 (Appendix, The Slavonic Additions).
1188. Josephus, Bk. III, Appendix, pp. 639-41.
1189. Josephus, Bk. III, Appendix, pp. 646-8. The first husband of Herodias was actually a half-brother of Herod Antipas called Herod (Ant. XVIII, 136). Mk. 6:17 and Mt. 14:3 make the same error that he was Philip the Tetrarch. While her first husband was still alive, she married Herod Antipas.
1190. Josephus, Bk. III, Appendix, pp. 651-2. Herod Agrippa II was actually his son (Ant. XIX, 354, War II, 220). He also had three daughters.
1191. Jack, *The Historic Christ*, 50-2, 125-6, 149 note 2.

The two invectives against the Romans in his Aramaic rough draft were certainly never intended for inclusion in the *Halosis*. Greek assistants wrote the latter almost entirely, because Josephus had such a poor knowledge of the language.[1192] It is conceivable that the invectives could have gotten into the *Halosis* by a mistake or prank on the part of his assistants and Josephus was unable to catch the error in time.[1193]

Those who deny that the historical errors mentioned above originated with Josephus simply refuse to take into consideration the errors, exaggerations, differences, and contradictions found in his writings when they are compared.[1194] Let me quote this very revealing statement by G. A. Williamson:

> It must be confessed that our book [the *Jewish War*] contains much that has not the stamp of truth, though fortunately the discerning reader is in little danger of being imposed on. From one who boasted so proudly of his own achievements in the art of deception we should hardly expect a high standard of objectivity. Many statements in the *War* are contradicted in our author's other works, and we cannot always say 'He had new sources of information and corrected his mistakes,' for he gives irreconcilable accounts of events in which he himself was the chief actor, and we cannot escape the conclusion that in one account or both he is perverting the truth, and perverting it for a purpose. Where we do not find contradictions the account may still fail to convince us. He obviously draws freely on a vivid imagination for events that he did not witness.... Figures of every sort he habitually exaggerates. ... I ventured to draw attention to several instances, and it should be observed that so far from correcting these figures in his later works, he often increases them-like a story-teller who in each retelling of the tale feels compelled to make it more impressive still.[1195]

Certainly Josephus' Aramaic rough draft, which was not even intended for publication, would have had its share of errors. Some of them could have accidentally gotten into the *Halosis*, but were corrected or deleted in the later *War*.

It is likely that Eisler's restoration of the Slavonic passage about Jesus does correspond as close as can be expected to what Josephus actually wrote and to what was recorded in the actual official Jewish and Roman documents. One reason is that Josephus' original statements about Christianity must have been derogatory. Origen (died ca. AD 254) in two places stated that Josephus did *not* believe that Jesus was the Christ.[1196] However, by ca. AD 324 Eusebius quoted

---

1192. Against Apion, I, 50, War I, 3, 454, Ant. XX, 263.
1193. Eisler, *The Messiah Jesus and John the Baptist*, 128-40.
1194. Eisler, *The Messiah Jesus and John the Baptist*, 181-2, 183-200, 205-8, 217-8, 229.
1195. Williamson, *Josephus The Jewish War*, 13-4.

Josephus as stating that Jesus *was* the Christ.[1197] Furthermore, Josephus was an establishment Pharisee hostile to all the rebels, deceivers, and impostors whom he believed brought his country to ruin. He surely would have conceived of Jesus (rightly or wrongly) as being one of them.[1198]

However, does it tell us the whole truth? The following passage opened my eyes to the possibility that it might not:

> It comes then to this — that there seems a real possibility that we have in these Slavonic passages some first-century evidence from Josephus himself of the historicity of Jesus and the start of the Christian Church. If this is so, it is a matter of considerable importance in view of the meagerness of the non-Christian witness to these facts. *But as regards the actual information conveyed in the relevant passages great hesitancy must be exercised.* I would not say that they can have nothing accurate to contribute — the whole question needs to be looked at again very carefully. But in the main the account we have here seems to be just the garbled second-hand half-correct version which we might have expected under the circumstances, based upon rumours and hearsay and unreliable gossip.[1199]

The writer certainly goes too far in saying that the Slavonic Josephus is a "garbled second-hand half-correct version ... based upon rumours and hearsay and unreliable gossip." However, there is some truth to his statement that "as regards the actual information conveyed ... great hesitancy must be exercised." In another place, the same writer states that one should not "be too easily confident that [Josephus'] views afford us an accurate representation of the historical facts."[1200] This is undoubtedly true, if the hypothesis described in the previous chapter has historical credibility.

The priestly establishment had to portray Jesus as the true ringleader of the revolt in Jerusalem instead of his twin brother. This was done by creating a *composite portrait* of both brothers in the writ of indictment that was presented to Pilate. After all, Pilate had spies who could have quickly figured out the secret plan, if the Jewish authorities were not very careful in how they presented the evidence. The "man of magical power" (i.e., Jesus) and the "robber thirsting for

---

1196. Emil Schurer, *The History of the Jewish People in the Age of Jesus Christ*, vols. I, II, III.1, III.2, rev. and ed. by Geza Vermes, et al. (Edinburgh: T. & T. Clark, 1973/87), Vol. I, 430-2; Brandon, *The Fall of Jerusalem and the Christian Church*, 110-4.

1197. Eusebius, *The Ecclesiastical History*, 2 vols., trans. by Kirsopp Lake (Cambridge: Harvard University Press, 1975), Vol. I, 83 (11.7-8).

1198. Eisler, *The Messiah Jesus and John the Baptist*, 23-4, 27-8.

1199. Rev. R. Dunkerley, "The Riddles of Josephus," *Hibbert Journal* 53 (1954-5), 134 (italics mine).

1200. Dunkerley, "The Riddles of Josephus," 133.

the crown" (i.e., Judas/Jesus) were merged into one person. As a result of this composite portrait, the identification of Jesus as a rebel against Rome can be traced back to the official writ of indictment handed to Pilate by the Sanhedrin![1201] Josephus simply transferred the composite portrait in the official documents into his own works.

I quote Robert Eisler's *restored* version of the Slavonic Josephus below. It was written in AD 72:[1202]

> At that time, too [during the governorship of Pontius Pilate], there appeared a certain man *of magical power*, if it is permissible to call him a man, *whom (certain) Greeks call a son of God*,[1203] *but his disciples the true prophet*[1204], *(said to) raise the dead and heal all diseases*. His nature and his form were human; *a man of simple appearance, mature age*,[1205] small stature, three cubits high, hunchbacked, with a long face, long nose, and meeting eyebrows, so that they who see him might be affrighted, with scanty hair (but) with a parting in the middle of his head, after the manner of the Nazirites, and with an undeveloped beard.[1206] Only in semblance was he superhuman, (for) he gave some astonishing and spectacular exhibitions. But again, if I look at his commonplace physique I (for one) cannot call him an angel. And everything whatsoever he wrought through some invisible power, he wrought through some word and a command. Some said of him, "Our first lawgiver [Moses] is risen again and displays many healings and (magic) arts," others that "he is sent from God." Howbeit in many things he disobeyed the law [Torah] and kept not the Sabbath according to (our) fathers' custom. Yet he himself did nothing shameful or high-handed,[1207] but by (his) word he prepared everything.
>
> And many of the multitude followed after him and accepted his teaching, and many souls were excited, thinking that thereby the Jewish tribes might be

---

1201. An authentic section of the Jesus passage in Ant. XVIII, 63-4 should be noted here. It states that "on the *indictment* of the principle men among us, Pilate had sentenced him [Jesus] to the cross" (italics mine).

1202. Eisler, *The Messiah Jesus and John the Baptist*, 27, 466-8. The parts in italics are Robert Eisler's additions to the Slavonic text. For the unrestored version, see Eisler, *The Messiah Jesus and John the Baptist*, 383-5 and Josephus, Bk. III, Appendix, pp. 648-50.

1203. Josephus was not correct here in ascribing this title to only the Greek followers of Jesus. As we have seen in the last chapter, the designation "Barabbas," which means "son of the Father" (i.e., God), originally referred to Jesus before it was transferred to Judas/Jesus (i.e., the actual Barabbas of the gospels).

1204. The title "true prophet" was probably really used by the Christians to refer to Jesus. However, I think there was a very good reason why Josephus specifically selected this title here instead of another one like "Messiah" for example, which is actually found in the *Antiquities* passage (Ant. XVIII, 63-4, see below). The reason is that in the Slavonic passages he wanted to show the sharp contrast between Jesus' disciples who proclaimed him a *true* prophet and the Jewish authorities who condemned him as a *false* one. In this connection, the reader is reminded of another Slavonic passage quoted in the last chapter (Josephus, Bk. III, p.657). In it, the crucifixion of Jesus is explained as the hanging of a false prophet for predicting the destruction of the city and the Temple.

1205. Since Jesus was 33 years old in AD 21, this probably means that he looked older than his age.

freed from Roman hands. But it was his custom most (of the time) to abide over against the city on the Mount of Olives, and there too he bestowed his healings upon the people. And there assembled unto him of helpers one hundred and fifty[1208] and a multitude of the mob.

Now when they saw his power, how that he accomplished whatsoever he would by a (magic) word, and when they had made known to him their will, that he should enter into the city, cut down the Roman troops and Pilate and rule over us, he disdained us not.[1209] *And having all flocked into Jerusalem, they raised an uproar (against Pilate), uttering blasphemies alike against God and against Caesar....*[1210]

And when thereafter knowledge of it came to the Jewish leaders, they assembled together with the high priest and spake: We are powerless and (too) weak to withstand the Romans. But seeing that "the bow is bent,"[1211] we will go and impart to Pilate what we have heard, and we shall be safe, lest he hear (of it) from others and we be robbed of our substance and ourselves slaughtered and the children (of Israel) dispersed.

And they went and imparted (the matter) to Pilate, and he sent and had many of the multitude slain. And he had that wonder-worker brought up, and after instituting an enquiry concerning him, he passed (this) sentence upon him: "He is a malefactor [a sorcerer],[1212] a rebel, a robber thirsting for the crown." And they took him and crucified him according to the custom of (their) fathers.

1206. Josephus' physical portrait of Jesus that Robert Eisler restored by utilizing certain Byzantine chroniclers and other early sources is not a flattering one. What gives it credibility is that the statements of some early Christians themselves confirm it (e.g., Tertullian, died ca. AD 225 and Origen, died AD 254). Surely, they would have portrayed Jesus in a more flattering way, if they were free to do so. For his detailed restoration of Josephus' portrait of Jesus, see Eisler, *The Messiah Jesus and John the Baptist*, 393-456. If the portrait is an authentic description of Jesus' physical appearance, then the image of the 5 ft., 11 in. man on the Shroud of Turin cannot be Jesus, who would have been only "three cubits high" or less than 5 ft. tall! Radiocarbon dating of the Shroud has placed it only in the 13th or 14th century AD (*The Boston Globe*, October 14, 1988). This portrait of Jesus, if authentic, would then be additional evidence (if we can trust the accuracy of the radiocarbon dating) that the Shroud was a medieval forgery. Although the twin brothers did not have to resemble each other *in every detail*, the resemblance had to be close enough for one of them to be taken for the other.

1207. This statement that "he himself did nothing shameful or high-handed" must mean that Jesus' twin brother did not murder any Roman soldiers, as some sources want us to believe (Lk. 23:19 and Acts 3:14). Although the idea that Barabbas was in prison is unhistorical, the idea that he was only "*among* the rebels ... who had committed murder in the insurrection" (i.e., he did not kill Roman soldiers himself) is probably correct (see Mk. 15:7). As the myth of Barabbas developed, he was turned into a murderer.

1208. I think the 150 "helpers" of Judas/Jesus (there is no known connection with Jesus) were the officers in his army. If we assume he had a 1200 man army, there would have been 157 officers in it, i.e., 1 head of thousands, 12 heads of hundreds, 24 heads of fifties, and 120 heads of tens. Sossianus Hierocles (quoted by the church father Lactantius) stated that Jesus (actually Judas/Jesus) had 900 armed men and the medieval *Toldoth Jeshu* states that he had 2000 (see Eisler, *The Messiah Jesus and John the Baptist*, 10, 107, 363 note 2, 370 note 1). The actual number appears to have been between both of these extremes. I quoted the Lactantius passage in the last chapter.

For the sake of completeness, I would now like to quote Robert Eisler's *restored* text about Jesus from the *Antiquities*. It was written in AD 93-4:[1213]

> Now about this time arose (an occasion for new disturbances) a certain Jesus, a wizard of a man, if indeed he may be called a man (who was the most monstrous of all men, whom his disciples call a son of God, as having done wonders such as no man hath ever yet done). ... He was in fact a teacher of astonishing tricks to such men as accept the abnormal with delight. ... And he seduced many Jews and many also of the Greek nation, and (was regarded by them as) the Messiah. ... And when, on the indictment of the principal men among us, Pilate had sentenced him to the cross, still those who before had admired him did not cease (to rave). For after three days, he had appeared to them alive, as the divinely-inspired prophets had foretold — these and ten thousand other wonderful things — concerning him. And even now the race of those who are called 'Messianists' after him is not extinct.

I summarize the above hypothesis as follows:
1. Jesus, a peaceful healer and teacher, was crucified in place of his twin brother Judas/Jesus, a rebel against Rome.
2. Robert Eisler's *restored* Slavonic passage about Jesus is a *composite portrait* of both brothers that is derived from the actual legal documents of Jesus' trial before Pilate.
3. The composite portrait was created by the Sanhedrin in the writ of indictment that was handed to Pilate in order to portray both brothers as one and the same person.

1209. This is where the inaccuracy of the official documents comes out the clearest. If the true events had been recorded in the passage, it would have said something like this: "but he [Jesus] did not heed it and withdrew from the multitude, but his twin [Judas/Jesus] led them on in violence. And having all flocked into Jerusalem, they raised an uproar...." The phrase "but he did not heed it" actually replaces "he disdained us not" in one of the manuscripts of the Slavonic Josephus (Eisler, *The Messiah Jesus and John the Baptist*, 384).

1210. Robert Eisler found a statement by the Byzantine compiler, Suidas, that according to Josephus "Jesus officiated in the sanctuary with the priests" and he believed that something about this was originally found in the lacuna here (Eisler, *The Messiah Jesus and John the Baptist*, 467, 482-3, 620-1). Based on his priestly genealogy, I found no reason to doubt that Judas/Jesus, when he gained control of the Temple, may have indeed performed priestly activities in it. Other actions performed by him may also have been recorded here.

1211. Cf. Ps. 11:1-3: "In the LORD I take refuge; how can you say to me, 'Flee like a bird to the mountains; for lo, the wicked *bend the bow*, they have fitted their arrow to the string, to shoot in the dark at the upright in heart; if the foundations are destroyed, what can the righteous do'?" (italics mine). This allusion to the Psalms passage is an additional piece of evidence for authenticity of the Slavonic Josephus in its original form (Eisler, *The Messiah Jesus and John the Baptist*, 467-8).

1212. Eisler, *The Messiah Jesus and John the Baptist*, 468. This charge of sorcery relates solely to Jesus, but it proves that Pilate accepted the composite portrait.

1213. Eisler, *The Messiah Jesus and John the Baptist*, 28, 62 (including note 1 of that page). The phrases in parentheses are not in the traditional text (Ant. XVIII, 63-4).

4. The purpose of this strategy was to assure the crucifixion of Jesus as the supposed leader of the revolt.

Unfortunately, this composite portrait, which was derived from the actual records of Jesus' trial, could only induce Josephus and the Romans to view the Christians as insurgents against Rome, regardless of the truth of the matter. Later, the activities of Judas/Jesus after AD 21 and to some extent the preaching of the Christians themselves after Jesus' crucifixion and resurrection (topics to be discussed in upcoming chapters) could only make matters worse.

We have examined one method the Christians used to attempt to counter this allegation in an earlier chapter. They created the highly unlikely, if not impossible, story of a Roman governor who believed Jesus was innocent and used extraordinary means to try to free him (i.e., the Passover custom). In spite of the military force available to him to back up his decisions, he was still forced to have Jesus crucified because of Jewish malice.

Chapter 20. The Fate of the Son of Joseph

The Gentile inhabitants of Jamnia, a coastal town in Judea, set up a crude altar to Emperor Gaius (Caligula, AD 37-41). Some of the Jews, who were the principal residents of the town, destroyed it, since it appeared to them to signify the emperor's divinity. In revenge for this desecration, Gaius ordered Petronius, the legate (governor) of Syria, to set up a huge statue with his effigy in the Temple of Jerusalem.[1214]

In the winter of AD 39-40, Petronius marched with two or three legions to Ptolemais on the Mediterranean coast in Galilee to carry out the order. A multitude of Jews arrived to protest this insane plan. Petronius, being a reasonable man and realizing that the Jews would in no way allow this sacrilege to occur, procrastinated for as long as he could. However, the Jews continued to protest most strenuously. Petronius, in seeing their resoluteness and in realizing the bloodshed that would result if the imperial order was carried out, decided to send a letter to Gaius asking him to revoke it.

Meanwhile, Herod Agrippa I, who was in Rome at the time, attempted to get Gaius to revoke the order. A letter addressed to the latter from the former is preserved in Philo's *The Embassy to Gaius*.[1215] Among other things, the statue affair is compared to the shield incident that occurred under Emperor Tiberius when Pilate was the governor of Judea:

1214. There are three historical sources about this affair. They are Philo, *The Embassy to Gaius*, Vol. X, F. H. Colson and J. W. Earp, trans., The Loeb Classical Library (Cambridge: Harvard University Press, 1971), 184-338, (pp. 95-169); Ant. XVIII, 261-309; and War II, 184-203. Unfortunately, they do not completely agree with each other.

1215. Philo, *The Embassy to Gaius*, 276-329 (pp. 139-65).

> So both objects were safeguarded [when Tiberius ordered Pilate to remove the shields from Jerusalem], the honour paid to the emperor and the policy observed from of old in dealing with the city.
> Now at that time [under Tiberius] it was shields on which no likeness had been painted; now it is a colossal statue [under Gaius]. Then too [under Tiberius] the installation was in the house of the governors;[1216] now [under Gaius] they say it is to be in the inmost part of the temple in the special sanctuary itself [the Holy of Holies], into which the Grand Priest enters once a year only on the Fast as it is called [the Day of Atonement], to offer incense and to pray according to ancestral practice for a full supply of blessings and prosperity and peace for all mankind.[1217]

The argument being offered is as follows: Emperor Tiberius ordered the shields, which were much less of an infringement on the Jews' religious customs, to be removed from Jerusalem. Surely then, Emperor Gaius was obliged to act accordingly with respect to the statue, which went beyond all measure of impiety.

Agrippa I was able to change Gaius' mind. The latter sent a letter to Petronius telling him that the order was canceled. However, when Gaius received the letter from Petronius asking him to revoke the very order that he had already canceled in his own letter to him, he became enraged. He sent another letter to Petronius ordering him to commit suicide for his disobedience to him. Fortunately for Petronius, as well as the Jews, Gaius was assassinated in January of AD 41. Because of bad weather, the messengers who carried the Gaius' letter were delayed. Petronius received the news of his death before he received the order to commit suicide. As fate would have it, Petronius was now no longer obliged to set up the statue in the Temple or to end his life.

Josephus does not say that the Jews were prepared to take up arms over this affair, but he does state that they were willing to sacrifice their lives for their beliefs:

> Petronius, having checked their clamour, said, "Will you then go to war with Caesar?" The Jews replied that they offered sacrifice twice daily for Caesar

---

1216. The "house of the governors" is also called "Herod's palace in the holy city." See Philo. *The Embassy to Gaius*, 306, 299 (pp. 155, 151). It was located in the western part of the city and it was where the Roman governor stayed while in Jerusalem. Robert Eisler gives reasons why in AD 21 the Roman garrison was stationed there also and not at the fortress of Antonia that was attached to the Temple. See Robert Eisler, *The Messiah Jesus and John the Baptist*, ed. A. H. Krappe (London: Methuen, 1931), 481-2, 486-9.

1217. Philo. *The Embassy to Gaius*. 305-6 (pp. 153-5).

and the Roman people, but that if he wished to set up these statues, he must first sacrifice the entire Jewish nation; and that they presented themselves, their wives and the children, ready for slaughter.[1218]

However, Tacitus does not agree with Josephus:

> Then, when Caligula ordered the Jews to set up his statue in their temple, *they chose rather to resort to arms*, but the emperor's death put an end to their rising.[1219]

In the first printed edition of the mediaeval Hebrew translation of Josephus known as the *Josippon*, there is an interesting passage about the followers of the "son of Joseph" during the reign of Emperor Gaius (AD 37-41). I quote it below:

> In those days there were wars and quarrels in Judaea between the Pharisees and the "robbers of our people" who followed the son of Joseph, etc. ... [chief among them was] 'Ele'azar, who committed great crimes in Israel until the Pharisees overpowered him.[1220]

Brandon made the following comment about the *Josippon*:

> The *Josippon* has ... a certain relevancy ... in that it is certain that Christian censors removed from it passages which they regarded as offensive to Christian doctrine....[1221]

In the passage from the *Josippon* quoted above something has probably been removed after the abbreviation "etc."

Robert Eisler understood the significance of the passage in the following way:

> The essential and hitherto entirely unknown fact is that the Jewish *Josippon* refers to the followers of Jesus as 'bandits of our nation' ... a transparent allusion (in the usual rabbinical way) to the prophecy of *Daniel* xi.14: 'and in those days many shall stand up against the king of the South, also the children of the bandits among thy people ... shall rebel in order to realize the vision, but they shall stumble.' Such an allusion was easy to understand by any reader learned in the Scriptures, who would then be quick to take the hint and to identify the

---

1218. War II, 196-7.
1219. Tacitus, *Histories, Annals*, trans. by C. H. Moore and J. Jackson (Loeb Classical Library) 4 vols. (Cambridge: Harvard University Press, 1979) III, 191 (Histories V.9, italics mine).
1220. Eisler, *The Messiah Jesus and John the Baptist*, 96.
1221. S. G. F. Brandon, *The Fall of Jerusalem and the Christian Church* (London: S.P.C.K., 1968), 122.

'king of the South' with the 'Edomite' ruler [Herod Agrippa I],[1222] and to rejoice at the prophesied failure of those 'bandits,' 'eager to realize the vision.'[1223]

What caused the "robbers (bandits) of our people (nation)" to take up arms was Emperor Gaius' attempt to have his statue erected in the Temple. It appears that they believed the statue was the "abomination that makes desolate" prophesied by Daniel.[1224]

That "wars and quarrels" broke out between the authorities (referred to as the "Pharisees" in the passage) and the "robbers (bandits)" is not difficult to understand. The situation was very serious. Josephus states that the people refused to farm the land and as a result, a famine was expected to occur.[1225]

It is likely that the son of Joseph issued an announcement to the populace something like the following hypothetical reconstruction:

> Let every man who is zealous for the Torah and supports the Covenant come out to the hills with me! Let us prepare for battle in the wilderness! We must not allow the desolating sacrilege spoken by the prophet Daniel[1226] to be set up in the holy place, where it ought not to be! We will obtain our sustenance from what grows wild. God will aid us in our righteousness endeavor. Truly, I say to you, there is no one who has left houses or brothers or sisters or mother or father or children or lands, for the sake of this undertaking, who will not receive a hundredfold after we have destroyed the ungodly out of the land. For many that are first will be last, and the last first.[1227]

If a large number of the male population heeded the son of Joseph and went out to live in the wilderness, this would make matters even worse. It is to be expected that the Jewish establishment would do whatever was required to put an end to this affair.

I take the view that the son of Joseph of the *Josippon* passage is not Jesus, but his twin brother Judas/Jesus. He escaped from Jerusalem in AD 21 and continued to cause the authorities problems even after that. J. W. Jack criticized Robert Eisler's interpretation of the word "followed" in the passage as "leaned" or inclined after" in the following way:

1222. Herod Agrippa I was descended from Herod the Great, whose family came from Idumaea, an area *south* of Jerusalem. Therefore, he could be called an "Edomite," i.e., an Idumaean.
1223. Eisler, *The Messiah Jesus and John the Baptist*, 100.
1224. Eisler, *The Messiah Jesus and John the Baptist*, 101; Dan. 8:13, 9:27, 11:31, 12:11, cf. 9:17.
1225. War II, 200-1, Ant. XVIII, 271-2.
1226. Dan. 8:13, 9:27, 11:31, 12:11, cf. 9:17.
1227. This announcement is a composite of the following passages: 1 Macc. 2:27-9, 3:8; 2 Macc. 5:27; Mt. 24:15=Mk. 13:14; Mk. 10:29-31=Mt. 19:29-30=Lk. 18:29b-30, 13:30.

Chapter 20. The Fate of the Son of Joseph

> The text ... referring as it does to a band of robbers, clearly points to the meaning "had as their leader, " but seeing that this would represent Jesus as still living and at the head of brigands in the time of Caligula, ten or more years after the crucifixion (or nearly twenty, according to Eisler's own scheme of chronology), and would thus exhibit the legendary character of the text, he is forced to adopt the questionable interpretation referred to.[1228]

If Jesus' twin brother was the son of Joseph, then Jack's objection is not valid.

Those who heeded the announcement of Judas/*Jesus* made haste with him into the wilderness and prepared for war against the Romans in order to stop them from erecting the statue (i.e., the desolating sacrilege) in the Temple. Fortunately, Gaius' sudden death ended the prospect of war.

The 'Ele'azar who joined Judas/*Jesus* was Eleazar, the son of Deinaeus. Josephus states that he was a "brigand chief, who for twenty years had ravaged the country."[1229] He also mentions an incident regarding Eleazar and the Samaritans. In revenge for killing Galileans who were going through Samaritan country on the way to a festival in Jerusalem, some Jews led by Eleazar attacked some Samaritan villages and killed the inhabitants.[1230] Eventually, he was captured by the governor, Felix (AD 52-60), and sent to Rome for trial.[1231]

With regard to the fate of Judas/*Jesus*, the son of Joseph, at least three possibilities present themselves. The first one has to do with an interesting incident that occurred in AD 46 that is described by Josephus:

> During the period when Fadus was procurator [governor] of Judaea [AD 44-6], a certain impostor named Theudas persuaded the majority of the masses to take up their possessions and to follow him to the Jordan River. He stated that he was a prophet and that at his command the river would be parted and would provide them an easy passage. With this talk he deceived many. Fadus, however, did not permit them to reap the fruit of their folly, but sent against them a squadron of cavalry. These fell upon them unexpectedly, slew many of them and took many prisoners. Theudas himself was captured, whereupon they cut of his head and brought it to Jerusalem.[1232]

1228. J. W. Jack, *The Historic Christ*, (London: James Clarke & Co., Ltd., 1933), 179.
1229. Eisler, *The Messiah Jesus and John the Baptist*, 102-3; War II, 253.
1230. War II, 235-6; Ant. XX, 121.
1231. War II, 253; Ant. XX, 161.
1232. Ant. XX, 97-8; Acts 5:36. Acts states that Theudas had about four hundred men.

It would appear that Theudas, believing that he was Joshua (i.e., Jesus) *redivivus*, attempted to reenact a miracle of the Old Testament Joshua by leading his followers dryshod across the Jordan River.[1233]

In the gospels, Judas the brother (or son) of James has two other names: Lebbaeus and most importantly, Thaddaeus. All one has to do to see this is to compare Luke's list of the Twelve with the lists of Mark and Matthew.[1234] In fact, Judas the *brother* of James is in all likelihood a duplication of Judas Thomas, the twin brother of Jesus. This would explain why he is called the brother of James, since one of Jesus' brothers was James the Righteous. If we then look a little further, we discover the following important information:

> The name Thaddaeus may be a diminutive of *Theudas* or *Theodore* [e.g., Johnny is a diminutive of John], derived from the Aramaic noun *tad* which means "breast" and which would mean "dear" or "beloved," that is one close to the heart of the one who named him.
> The other name, Lebbaeus, may be a derivation of the Hebrew noun *leb*, which means heart, and in that case it would bear the same meaning as Thaddaeus.[1235]

The evidence shows that Theudas may be an alias for Judas/Jesus and, if so, we know how he died. The Roman governor Fadus beheaded him in AD 46. He would have been 57 years old at the time.[1236]

As possible support for this view, there are early sources that state Jesus was actually crucified in the reign of Emperor Claudius (AD 41-54) *not* Tiberius (AD 14-37) and two of them even date the crucifixion in AD 46![1237] Could these sources have confused the real Jesus with Judas/Jesus who *was* executed at this time?

It is worth mentioning that Josephus describes other "deceivers and imposters" during the governorship of Felix (AD 52-60) who duped the masses like Theudas (i.e., Judas/Jesus?) did. According to Josephus, they "led [the multitude] out into the desert under the belief that God would there give them tokens of deliverance." Felix "put a large number to the sword."[1238] Furthermore,

---

1233. Jos. 3:1-17.
1234. Lk. 6:14-6, Mk. 3:16-9, Mt. 10:2-4. In certain Latin manuscripts of Matthew, Thaddaeus-Lebbaeus is called Judas the Zealot. See Rendel Harris, *The Twelve Apostles* (Cambridge: W. Heffer & Sons, 1927), 34.
1235. William Stevart McBirne, *The Search for the Twelve Apostles* (Wheaton: Living Books, 1973), 196.
1236. 12 BC – 1 (there is no "0"year) + AD 46 = 57 years old.
1237. E. Bammel, "Jesus as a political agent in a version of the Josippon" in E. Bammel and C. F. D. Moule, eds., *Jesus and the Politics of His Day* (Cambridge: Cambridge University Press, 1985), 207.
1238. War II, 258-60.

the "Egyptian" put himself off as another Joshua (i.e., Jesus) *redivivus* by attempting to miraculously make the wall of Jerusalem fall like Joshua did to the wall of Jericho.[1239] Josephus also mentions another "impostor" who appeared during the governorship of Festus (AD 60-2):

> Festus also sent a force of cavalry and infantry against the dupes of a certain impostor who had promised them salvation and rest from troubles, if they chose to follow him into the wilderness. The force which Festus dispatched destroyed both the deceiver himself and those who had followed him.[1240]

The second possibility regarding the fate of Judas/*Jesus* is that at some point after the affair regarding Emperor Gaius and the statue (AD 39-41), his remorse for allowing his brother to suffer and die in his place caught up with him and he took his own life. The two different versions of Judas Iscariot's death may be distorted accounts of this suicide.[1241]

The third possibility regarding his fate is that at some point after the statue affair, he may have actually converted to Christianity after a long period of doubt about Jesus' resurrection (cf. Jn. 20:24-9). This would explain why the name Thomas, which comes from the Aramaic word for "twin," made it in the apostle lists in the Gospels and the Acts.[1242] Furthermore, Judas Thomas was believed to be a notable Christian personage, since the Gnostic *Gospel of Thomas* prologue states the following: "These are the secret sayings that the living Jesus spoke and Didymos[1243] Judas Thomas recorded."[1244] Also, Christian tradition has it that he was a great missionary who journeyed most notably to eastern Syria and India. His tomb is reputed to be located in Mylapore, India.[1245]

1239. Ant. XX, 169-72, War II, 261-3.
1240. Ant. XX, 188. Also see War VII, 437-50 about Jonathan, a weaver of Cyrene, who led many of the "indigent class" into the desert. Many of his followers were killed or taken prisoner by the Romans and he was finally tortured and burned at the stake.
1241. Mt. 27:3-10, Acts 1:16-20.
1242. Mk. 3:16-9, Mt. 10:2-4, Lk. 6:14-6, Acts 1:13.
1243. "Didymos" comes from the Greek word for "twin," as "Thomas" comes from the Aramaic word that means the same thing.
1244. *Thomas* Prologue in Robert J. Miller, ed., *The Complete Gospels* (San Francisco: Harper, 1994), 305.
1245. McBirne, *The Search for the Twelve Apostles*, 142-73.

Chapter 21. Simon Magus

Simon Magus (i.e., the Magician)[1246] was said to be "the first and most esteemed" of the "thirty[1247] chief men" of John the Baptist.[1248] According to the *Recognitions of Clement*, he said this about himself:

> For I am able to render myself invisible to those who wish to lay hold of me, and again to be visible when I am willing to be seen. If I wish to flee, I can dig through the mountains, and pass through rocks as if they were clay. If I should throw myself headlong from a lofty mountain, I should be borne unhurt to the earth, as if I were held up; when bound, I can loose myself, and bind those who had bound me; being shut up in prison, I can make barriers open of their own accord; I can render statues animated, so that those who see suppose that they are men. I can make new trees suddenly spring up, and produce sprouts at once. I can throw myself into the fire, and not be burnt; I can change my countenance, so that I cannot be recognized; but I can show people that I have two faces ... And what need of more words? Whatever I wish, that I shall be able to do.[1249]

1246. Acts 8:9-11.

1247. All references to the *Recognitions of Clement* and the *Clementine Homilies* are from Alexander Roberts and James Donaldson, *The Ante-Nicene Fathers*, vol. VIII (Grand Rapids: Eerdmans Publishing Co., 1951), 98-100, 232-3. Although the *Recognitions* and the *Homilies* give different explanations of why there were thirty chief men or disciples (Hom. 2:23, Rec. 2:8), another more likely explanation presents itself. Perhaps the number thirty is derived from the fact that the solar calendar that was utilized by the New Covenant was made up of thirty-day months. S. J. Isser, *The Dositheans: A Samaritan Sect in Late Antiquity* (Leiden: Brill, 1976), 24, note 33. Every three months, which made up a season, an intercalary day was added, making a total of 364 days (91 + 91 + 91 + 91 = 364). Emil Shurer, *The History of the Jewish People in the Age of Jesus Christ*, vols. I, II, III.1, III.2, rev. and ed. by Geza Vermes, et al. (Edinburgh: T. & T. Clark, 1973/87), Vol. I, 600-1.

1248. Hom. 2:23. In the *Recognitions*, it was not John, but Dositheus who established the sect when John was killed (Rec. 2:8).

We also know that Simon was a Samaritan.[1250] At some point, the apostle Philip baptized him in Samaria.[1251]

Josephus describes the following incident that occurred in AD 25/26 (i.e., Pilate's last year in office):[1252]

> The Samaritan nation too was not exempt from disturbance. For a man who made light of mendacity and in all his designs catered to the mob, rallied them, bidding them go in a body with him to Mount Gerizim, which in their belief is the most sacred of mountains. He assured them that on their arrival he would show them the sacred vessels which were buried there, where Moses had deposited them. His hearers, viewing this tale as plausible, appeared in arms. They posted themselves in a certain village named Tirathana, and, as they planned to climb the mountain in a great multitude, they welcomed to their ranks the new arrivals who kept coming. But before they could ascend, Pilate blocked their projected route up the mountain with a detachment of cavalry and heavy-armed infantry, who in an encounter with the firstcomers in the village slew some in a pitched battle and put the others to flight. Many prisoners were taken, of whom Pilate put to death the principle leaders and those who were most influential among the fugitives.[1253]

This Samaritan false prophet, who Josephus does not state was captured or killed, may very well have escaped and was probably Simon Magus.[1254] He probably fled to Egypt at this time.[1255] As a result of this affair, Pilate was ordered to return to Rome to face charges made on him by the Samaritans.[1256]

Both the *Recognitions* and the *Clementine Homilies* describe a violent confrontation between Dositheus and Simon, when the latter returned from Egypt. The *Recognitions* describes it as follows:

> But Dositheus, when he perceived that Simon was depreciating him, fearing lest his reputation among men might be obscured (for he himself was supposed to be the *Standing One*),[1257] moved with rage, when they met as usual at the school, seized a rod, and began to beat Simon; but suddenly the rod seemed to

---

1249. Rec. 2:9.
1250. Hom. 2:22, cf. Rec. 2:7.
1251. Acts 8:12-3.
1252. Jerry Vardaman, "Jesus' Life: A New Chronology," *Cronos Kairos Christos*, Jerry Vardaman and Edwin M. Yamauchi, eds. (Winona Lake: Eisenbrauns, 1989), 77-82.
1253. Ant. XVIII, 85-9.
1254. Robert Eisler, *The Messiah Jesus and John the Baptist*, ed. by A. H. Krappe (London: Methuen & Co., 1931), 577, 592-3.
1255. Hom. 2:24. cf. Hom. 2:22: Simon "disciplined himself greatly in Alexandria [in Egypt]."
1256. Ant. XVIII, 85-9.

pass through his body, as if it had been smoke. On which Dositheus, being astonished says to him, "Tell me if thou art the *Standing One*, that I may adore thee." And when Simon answered that he was, then Dositheus, perceiving that he himself was not the Standing One, fell down and worshipped him, and gave up his place as chief to Simon, ordering all the rank of thirty men to obey him; himself taking the inferior place which Simon formerly occupied. Not long after this he died.[1258]

It will be remembered from an earlier chapter that when John the Baptist died (AD 35), James the Righteous became the leader of the New Covenant and Dositheus became the leader of schismatics for a time. The confrontation between Dositheus and Simon caused a split in Dositheus' faction of the New Covenant. Some members remained with Dositheus and others went over to Simon. Eventually, the schism was healed and the former became the Prophet of the New Covenant. The latter and his faction remained a separate sect. Dositheus must have died soon after becoming the Prophet, because the *Recognitions* states that he died "not long after" the confrontation with Simon.[1259]

One reason for the hostility between the both of them was probably Simon's excessive libertine beliefs that were simply incompatible with the Dositheus' strict legalism. Allegro characterizes the libertine views of Simon as follows:

> Thenceforth they could afford to reject the world and its values, since, in God as seen in Simon, they had been offered salvation by grace, not earned by their own efforts, but freely given to those who had Knowledge of God. This was the true *gnosis*, and for those who had attained its blessed state, there was no further need of the Law, and they could spurn social conventions.[1260]

1257. According to the *Recognitions*, Simon "uses this name [i.e., the Standing One] as implying that he can never be dissolved, asserting that his flesh is so compacted by the power of divinity, that it can endure to eternity. Hence, therefore, he is called the *Standing One*, as though he cannot fall by any corruption" (Rec. 2:7, cf. Hom. 2:22) Jesus in the gospel of John teaches the same doctrine. "Truly, truly, I say to you, he who hears my word and believes him who sent me, has eternal life; he does not come into judgment, but has passed from death to life" (Jn. 5:24, cf. 8:52, 11:25-6). This is important additional evidence for determining the true identity of the "Jesus" of John's gospel (see below). It is not known how Dositheus understood the designation "Standing One."

1258. Rec. 2:11. cf. Hom. 2:24.

1259. The *Homilies* states that Dositheus died "not many days after" the confrontation with Simon (Hom. 2:24). The *Recognitions* is probably more accurate here (Rec.2:11).

1260. John Allegro, *The Dead Sea Scrolls and the Christian Myth* (Buffalo: Prometheus Books, 1984), 142-3.

It is significant that a former prostitute from Tyre named Helen accompanied Simon on his travels.[1261]

The "Paraclete" (i.e., the Counselor) mentioned several times in the gospel of John[1262] is usually identified with the Holy Spirit who, after the death and resurrection of Jesus, would appear to the apostles in their time of need to help and comfort them.[1263] However, Robert Eisler had this to say about the designation:

> It seems impossible to express more strongly the fact that the paraclete, the foretold *alter ego* of Jesus, is not a ghost, but a man. No visions of a disembodied *pneuma* [spirit], but a living man, a re-incarnation of Jesus, will testify that the first paraclete, Jesus, was and is the true Messiah, just as the disciples, the eyewitnesses of his life, will witness for him. It is this *man* who will, according to the evangelist, supplement the teaching of Jesus by further revelations; it is this man who will confound the world, convict it of its sin and convince it concerning righteousness.[1264]

In his view, the Paraclete is to be identified with Simon Magus.[1265]

Jerome (ca. AD 342-420) records that Simon said this about himself:

> I am the Logos [Word] of God; I am the Beautiful One; *I am the Paraclete*; I am the Almighty; I am the All of God.

He furthers records that Simon came "in the name of Jesus" and stated that he was the Christ.[1266]

Cyril, the bishop of Jerusalem (ca. AD 315-86), has this to say about Simon Magus:

> Of all heresy the archheretic is Simon Magus. ... For he dared to say that it was he who appeared in the guise of the Father on Mount Sinai, later on among the Jews —not in the flesh, but in semblance[1267] —as the Messiah Jesus, and after that as the Holy Spirit [actually the *pneuma* or spirit of Jesus],[1268] which

---

1261. Edwin M. Yamauchi, *Pre-Christian Gnosticism*, 2nd ed. (Grand Rapids: Baker Book House,1983), 59. Hom. 2:23. In the *Recognitions* (Rec. 2:8, 9, 12), she is called Luna.
1262. Jn. 14:16, 26, 15:26, 16:7.
1263. F. F. Bruce, *New Testament History* (Garden City: Anchor Books, 1969), 208.
1264. Robert Eisler, "The Paraclete Problem," *The Quest* 21 (January 1930): 124.
1265. Robert Eisler, "The Paraclete Claimant-Simon Magus," *The Quest* 21 (April 1930): 225-243.
1266. Eisler, "The Paraclete Claimant-Simon Magus," 227 (italics mine).
1267. This view that Jesus while on earth only "seemed" to have a body of flesh and blood is known as Docetism.
1268. Eisler, "The Paraclete Problem," 118-20.

the Christ promised to send [*as the Paraclete*].[1269] And he misled the city of Rome, etc.[1270]

This statement of Cyril is in agreement with those of Irenaeus (ca. AD 130-ca. 200), Hippolytus (ca. AD 170-ca. 236), Theodoret (ca. AD 393-ca. 466), and Augustine (AD 354-430).[1271]

0Simon believed that after the death and resurrection of Jesus, the latter's spirit became embodied in him and that, as the Paraclete (i.e., Jesus *redivivus*), he would give a more complete revelation of Jesus' teachings. If one of the sources that was utilized by the writer of the John's gospel originated with the followers of Simon, this would solve a number of problems regarding this gospel. Some of these will be discussed below:

1. The mystery why Jesus' sayings in John's gospel are so completely different from his sayings in the synoptic gospels can be answered, if the idea is accepted that they were actually uttered by Simon. Robert Eisler explained this idea as follows:

    ... there is no longer any difficulty in explaining why the Jesus Christ of the Fourth Gospel is so different from the lovable, humble and modest hero of the Synoptics, -that is, from the historical Jesus; why the Johannine Christ is constantly asserting his own claims and demonstrating his own superiority, why — if such a modern expression may be permitted —he is constantly advertising his own self, through the ever-recurrent use of the most solemn form of divine self-revelation, —the 'I am's:[1272] I am the Bread from Heaven; I am the Bread of Life; I am the Good Shepherd; I am the true Vine; I am the Life and the Resurrection; I am the Door; I am the Way; I am the Truth; I am the Light of the World. This arrogant, self-asserting, self-glorifying, perpetually shouting preacher, who lashes himself into a frenzy before working his miracles, is not the true Jesus. It is a dimmed and distorted likeness, a super-imposition on the original of the picture of the 'other paraclete': — that is to say, a combination portrait of Jesus and the 'reincarnated Jesus,' — the gnostic Simon Magus.[1273]

1269. Robert Eisler placed the phrase "*as the Paraclete*" in italics in his quotation from Cyril, but stated on the next page that the "term 'paraclete' ... is not used by Cyril of Jerusalem" (Eisler, "The Paraclete Problem," 229).
1270. Eisler, "The Paraclete Claimant-Simon Magus," 228.
1271. Eisler, "The Paraclete Claimant-Simon Magus," 227-9.
1272. Jn. 6:35, 8:12, 10:9, 10:11, 11:25, 14:6, 15:5.
1273. Eisler, "The Paraclete Claimant-Simon Magus," 231.

2. The doctrine taught by Jesus in John's gospel that he (i.e., the Son of God) and God the Father were basically one and same person agrees remarkably well with Simon Magus' teaching about his own identity. However, it is completely unknown to the Jesus of the synoptic gospels. In John, Jesus stated that "I and the Father are one."[1274] Likewise, according to Jerome Simon said this about himself: "I am the Almighty; I am the All of God" and Cyril stated that he "appeared in the guise of the Father on Mount Sinai."[1275]

3. In John's gospel, Jesus is actually called a Samaritan by the Jews[1276] and his "own country" is understood to be Samaria not Galilee! John 4:43-5 can only be understood if the writer believed that Samaria was Jesus' home:

> After the two days he departed [from Samaria, as evidenced by the previous verses] to Galilee. For Jesus himself testified that a prophet has no honor in his own country. So when he came to Galilee, the Galileans welcomed him.... [1277]

4. It is not a coincidence that in John's gospel John the Baptist (i.e., Simon Magus' former master) baptized not only at "Bethany [actually Bethabara][1278] beyond the Jordan,"[1279] which is in agreement with the synoptic gospels,[1280] but also at "Aenon near Salim, because there was much water there."[1281] According to Eusebius, Aenon and Salim were located in northern Samaria not far from Scythopolis.[1282]

5. Finally, contempt for the Jews can be noticed in the gospel.[1283] This is certainly strange, because Jesus was himself a Jew. However, Simon, who was a Samaritan, would certainly have partaken in the familiar Samaritan hatred for the Jews.[1284]

In AD 49 under Emperor Claudius (AD 41-54), Simon Magus went to Rome claiming to be not only the Christ (i.e., the Messiah) but Jesus *redivivus* as

---

1274. Jn. 10:30, cf. 8:16-9, 29, 58, 10:33, 38, 12:44-5, 14:7-11.
1275. Eisler, "The Paraclete Claimant-Simon Magus," 234-5.
1276. Jn. 8:48.
1277. Eisler, "The Paraclete Claimant-Simon Magus," 232-3.
1278. Jack Finegan, *The Archeology of the New Testament*, rev. ed. (Princeton: Princeton University Press, 1992), 12-3.
1279. Jn. 1:28, cf. 10:40.
1280. Mk. 1:5, Mt. 3:5-6, Lk. 3:3.
1281. Jn. 3:23.
1282. Finegan, *The Archeology of the New Testament*, 15-6; Eisler, "The Paraclete Claimant-Simon Magus," 233.
1283. Jn. 5:41-7, 8:39-47.

well. He seems to have caused a serious disturbance within the Jewish population there that forced the emperor to expel the Jews from Rome.[1285] Suetonius (ca. AD 120) stated that "because the Jews of Rome were indulging in constant riots at the instigation of Chrestus ... he [Claudius] expelled them from the city."[1286] If, as was probably the case, the designation "Christus" (i.e., Christ) was actually intended instead of "Chrestus,[1287] then the identity of this personage was almost certainly Simon. On the other hand, it remains a mystery who Chrestus could have been.

Sometime during the period when Felix was the governor (AD 52-60) Josephus recorded that the following event occurred:

> At this time came to Jerusalem from Egypt a man who declared that he was a prophet and advised the masses of the common people to go out with him to the mountain called the Mount of Olives, which lies opposite the city at a distance of five furlongs. For he asserted that he wished to demonstrate from there that at his command Jerusalem's walls would fall down, through which he promised to provide them an entrance into the city.[1288] When Felix heard of this he ordered his soldiers to take up their arms. Setting out from Jerusalem with a large force of cavalry and infantry, he fell upon the Egyptian and his followers, slaying four hundred of them and taking two hundred prisoners. The Egyptian himself escaped from the battle and disappeared.[1289]

According to Robert Eisler, the "Egyptian" was actually Simon[1290] and his end can be determined from other important sources:[1291]

> The leader, who again managed to escape ... may once more have been the omnipresent Simon ... who was constantly defying fate in this manner, and who

---

1284. Shurer, *The History of the Jewish People in the Age of Jesus Christ*, Vol. II, 19-20; Eisler, "The Paraclete Claimant-Simon Magus," 232. For a complete discussion of Robert Eisler's theory of the "Paraclete" see the above referenced articles in *The Quest*, as well as Robert Eisler, "The Evangel of Kerinthos: The Book of Lazarus-The Beloved Disciple," *The Quest* 21 (July 1930): 340-57. Some of the research in this last article was replaced by later research in Robert Eisler, *The Enigma of the Fourth Gospel* (London: Methuen & Co. Ltd., 1938).

1285. Eisler, *The Messiah Jesus and John the Baptist*, 581; F. F. Bruce, *New Testament History* (Garden City: Anchor Books, 1969), 297-9. The expulsion of the Jews from Rome is briefly mentioned in Acts 18:2.

1286. Suetonius, *Claudius*, 25:4 quoted from Bruce, *New Testament History*, 297.

1287. According to Bruce, "*Christus* [was] not unnaturally confused with the common slave-name *Chrestus*, which was pronounced in practically the same way" (Bruce, *New Testament History*, 297).

1288. The Egyptian planned to make the wall of Jerusalem miraculously collapse just like Joshua did to the wall of Jericho (Jos. 6:20). He was a Joshua (i.e., Jesus) *redivivus*.

1289. Ant. XX, 169-72, cf. War II, 261-3. In Acts 21:38, the Roman tribune who arrested the apostle Paul confused him with the Egyptian.

at a much later date fell into the hands of the Jews and appears to have been stoned and hanged at Lydda as a false prophet seeking to seduce the people to the worship of foreign Gods.[1292]

We are now in a position to say more about the *Recognitions* passage that was quoted in its entirety in the very first chapter (Rec.1:54). It is indeed a somewhat confusing chapter and it contains some errors,[1293] but nevertheless it gives us some valuable information:

1. It tells us about the anti-establishment Sadducees, Pharisees, and Samaritans, who joined the New Covenant.
2. It connects these anti-establishment groups with John the Baptist.
3. It connects Dositheus and Simon with John the Baptist.
4. It mentions sectarians who endeavored to surpass others in their desire to be righteous[1294] and who separated themselves from contact with the people (i.e., all outsiders) in order to accomplish this desire.[1295] These are certainly characteristics of the New Covenant.
5. It mentions sectarians who did not reveal their interpretations of the Mosaic Law to the people.[1296] Again, this was a characteristic of the New Covenant.

1290. Josephus may have referred to Simon again during the governorship of Felix as "a Cyprian Jew named Atomus [Simon in a few manuscripts], who pretended to be a magician" (Ant. XX, 142-3). According to Josephus, this individual successfully persuaded Drusilla, Herod Agrippa II's sister, to divorce her husband, King Azizus of Emesa, and marry Felix, the governor. In Acts 24:24, Drusilla is identified as the Jewish wife of Felix. H. Waitz suggested that this Atomus or Simon may have been Simon Magus as far back as 1904 [see Josephus, (Loeb Classical Library), Vol. X, pp. 76-7, note e].

1291. Eisler, *The Messiah Jesus and John the Baptist*, 592-3 (Appendix II).

1292. Eisler, *The Messiah Jesus and John the Baptist*, 583.

1293. For example, it mentions that the anti-establishment Sadducees and Samaritans "deny the resurrection of the dead." This was indeed the case for the *conventional* Sadducees, but not for the anti-establishment variety. It was probably the case for the *conventional* Samaritans as well, since they only accepted the Torah (i.e., the Pentateuch) as binding on them. See Schurer, *The History of the Jewish People in the Age of Jesus Christ*, Vol. II, 17, 19, 407-12.

1294. E.g., 1QSa 1:3: "They are the men of His Counsel who keep His covenant in the midst of wickedness in order to aton[e for the ear]th."

1295. E.g., 1QS 5:18: "For all who are not counted in His Covenant *shall be set apart*, together with all that is theirs ... " (under John the Baptist); 1QS 8:13: "They *shall be separated* from the midst of the habitation of perverse men to go into the desert ..." (under Dositheus); 1QS 9:8-9: " ... let their possessions not be mingled with those of the men of deceit who have not purified their way *to be separated* from perversity and walk in perfection of way" (under James the Righteous); CD 6:14-5: "Truly, they shall be careful... *to separate* themselves from the sons of the Pit ... ," (under Symeon, the son of Clopas) (all italics mine). Although the sect resided in Jerusalem under the leaderships of James and Symeon, the members probably still avoided contact with outsiders by settling in their own private sector of the city and dealing only with fellow sectarians in that sector.

1296. E.g., 1QS 9:17: "And let him [the sectarian] not rebuke the men of the Pit nor dispute with them; let him conceal the maxims of the Torah from the midst of the men of perversity."

6. It mentions the "one true prophet" predicted by Moses. It will be remembered that John the Baptist was called the "Unique Teacher" or the "Unique One." The word "unique" probably corresponds to "one" in the "one true prophet." The same Hebrew word may be in mind.[1297] Furthermore, it will be remembered that Dositheus was called the "Prophet" when the schism was healed.
7. It mentions some "disciples of John, who seemed to be great ones." The designation "Great Ones" could be an alternative translation for "Many" that is used numerous times in 1QS and much less often in CD.[1298]
8. It mentions that some disciples of John "proclaimed their own master as the Christ [Messiah]." According to the beliefs of the New Covenant, they believed John was a Messiah of Aaron and one of the earthly embodiments of the heavenly being Melchizedek.

1297. Robert Eisler, 'The Sadoqite Book of the New Covenant: Its Date and Origin," *Occident and Orient* (Gaster Anniversary Volume), ed. B. Schindler (London: Taylor's Foreign Press, 1936), 125, 127.
1298. A. Dupont-Sommer, *The Essene Writings from Qumran*, trans. by G. Vermes (Gloucester: Peter Smith, 1973), 85, note 1.

CHAPTER 22. SAUL, PAUL, THE PILLARS, AND THE TWELVE

As stated in an earlier chapter, if the identification of James the Righteous as the Teacher of Righteousness of the Dead Sea Scrolls is correct, then James and the New Covenant could not have been connected with the followers of the historical Jesus (i.e., the Christians) in any way. I gave reasons above, and I will not repeat them here. If this is the case, then there is a problem. The documents that allegedly give us the history of Christianity after Jesus' crucifixion and resurrection (i.e., the Acts of the Apostles and the Epistles of Paul, especially Galatians) clearly portray James as a leader of the Jewish Christian church in Jerusalem. How can this problem be explained?

It is significant that in the synoptic gospels Peter (Cephas) and James and John, the sons of Zebedee, are Jesus' most intimate apostles.[1299] However, in the Acts and Galatians James, the brother of Jesus, takes the place of James, the son of Zebedee.[1300] In fact, except for being listed with the other apostles in Acts 1:13, James, the son of Zebedee, is not mentioned again until Acts 12:1-2, when he is beheaded by Herod Agrippa I. Also, after Acts 8:14, John, the brother of James, is not mentioned again either.[1301] Even more curious, James, the brother of Jesus, somehow supplants Peter (Cephas) and becomes the leader of the church![1302]

The belief that James the Righteous held this leadership position probably arose as an accepted Christian view sometime after the destruction of Jerusalem

---

1299. Mk. 5:37, 9:2, 13:3 (Andrew included), 14:33, Mt. 17:1, 26:37, Lk.8:51, 9:28.
1300. Acts 12:17, 15:13, 21:18, Gal. 1:19, 2:9, 12.
1301. John is mentioned in Acts 1:13, 3:1, 11, 4:13, 19.
1302. Mt. 16:18-9, Acts 15:13, 21:18, Gal. 2:9, 12, cf. Thomas 12:1-2. In Acts, a group called the "elders" are mentioned as leading the church along with James (Acts 15:2, 22, 21:18). In Acts 11:30, the elders are mentioned without James.

in AD 70. However, the evidence shows that it was an erroneous belief. Perhaps it arose in the following way: Because James and the New Covenant awaited the coming of a Messiah of Israel, the later Christians simply could not accept the idea that this coming personage was not to be identified with Jesus. This was especially true, since James was Jesus' brother and a noteworthy religious leader of the time.

The truth appears to be that the "Pillars"[1303] of the Christians had always been Peter (Cephas) and James and John, the sons of Zebedee. They were a smaller group within the Twelve[1304] and apparently held more authority than the other members. The name Pillars was probably understood in the following way:

> As God once "established the world," the covenant community Israel, on the basis of the three Patriarchs [Abraham, Isaac, and Jacob], so in the messianic period, inaugurated by the resurrection of Jesus ... God was thought ... as having "established the world" anew ... on the basis of three new pillars.[1305]

Furthermore, the name may have been borrowed from the New Covenant, because the Teacher of Righteousness was actually given this title in 4QpPS^a 3:15-6: "the Priest, the Teacher of [Righteousness, whom] God [ch]ose as the Pillar."[1306]

The name Cephas is derived from the word Rock in Aramaic and the name Peter is derived from the same word in Greek. Cephas is found in Paul's epistles[1307] and in the gospel of John.[1308] Peter is found in the gospels along with the name Simon. In Matthew 16:17-9, Jesus gave the name Peter to someone called Simon Bar-Jona. Actually, Simon Bar-Jona and Peter (Cephas) are probably two different individuals who were made into one by the growing church in Rome. We now know that Cephas was a regular name used in the first century AD.[1309] The title Bar-Jona (actually barjona) means extremist.[1310] As mentioned above, Peter (Cephas) was one of the leaders of the followers of Jesus.

1303. Gal. 2:9.
1304. Mk. 3:16-9=Mt. 10:2-4=Lk. 6:14-6, Acts 1:13.
1305. Roger D. Aus, "Three Pillars and Three Patriarchs: A Proposal Concerning Gal 2^9," *Zeitchift für die neutestamentliche wissenschaft* 70 (1979): 256-7.
1306. Maurya P. Horgan, *Pesharim: Qumran Interpretations of Biblical Books* (Washington, DC: Catholic Biblical Assoc. of America, 1979), 197-8, 219.
1307. Gal. 1:18, 2:9, 11, 14, I Cor. 1:12, 9:5, 15:4.
1308. Jn. 1:42.
1309. *Biblical Archaeology Review*, September/October, 1992, pp. 38-44.
1310. Robert Eisler, *The Messiah Jesus and John the Baptist*, ed. by A. H. Krappe (London: Methuen & Co., 1931), 252-3.

Simon, who is mentioned by Josephus,[1311] is there described as a very religious Jew from Jerusalem, who denounced Herod Agrippa I as being ritually unclean. He was probably a member of the radical Sicarii or Zealots, which explains why he is called barjona, i.e., extremist. This same individual, who was not really a follower of Jesus, is also to be identified with Simon the Zealot[1312] and Simon the Cananaean[1313] in the gospel lists of apostles.

James and John, the sons of Zebedee, were known as the Bo-anerges, which the gospel of Mark translates as the Sons of Thunder.[1314] The name Bo-anerges could actually be a corruption of the Aramaic B'nai-rogez, which means the sons of anger.[1315]

Several questions remain unanswered about the membership of the Twelve. For example, is Levi, the tax collector,[1316] the same person as Matthew, the tax collector?[1317] Also, is Nathanael, who is referred to only in John,[1318] the same person as Bartholomew? The main reason Levi is usually identified with Matthew and Nathanael with Bartholomew is to keep the number of Jesus' apostles no higher than twelve and to reconcile John to the synoptic gospels. However, there is no real evidence for the identification of Levi with Matthew other than that they were both tax collectors. The identification of Nathanael with Bartholomew is based only on the fact that Philip and Bartholomew are always named together in the synoptic gospels,[1319] and in John[1320] it is Philip who brings Nathanael to Jesus.

Furthermore, the evidence shows that different names of the Twelve refer to the same person and some alleged members are not really members at all. For example, Judas the brother of James = Thomas = Thaddaeus = Lebbaeus = Judas Iscariot. As we have seen, this person is actually Judas, the twin brother of Jesus, who was not a follower of his brother unless he converted to Christianity at a later date. Also, James the son of Alphaeus, who is allegedly a member of the

---

1311. Ant. XIX, 332-4. Robert Eisenman identified this Simon of Josephus with Peter. See "James the Just in the Habakkuk *Pesher*" in Robert Eisenman, *The Dead Sea Scrolls and the First Christians* (Rockport: Element, 1996), 125-6, note 22.
1312. Lk. 6:15.
1313. Mk. 3:18, Mt. 10:4. Cananaean = Zealot. See S. G. F. Brandon, *Jesus and the Zealots* (New York: Charles Scribner's Sons, 1967), 42-4.
1314. Mk. 3:17.
1315. Stephen Mitchell, *The Gospel According to Jesus* (New York: HarperCollins, 1991), 157.
1316. Mk. 2:14, Lk. 5:27.
1317. Mt. 9:9.
1318. Jn. 1:43-51, 21:2.
1319. Mk. 3:18, Mt. 10:3, Lk. 6:14.
1320. Jn. 1:45.

Twelve, is actually James the Righteous, the brother of Jesus, and as we have seen, he was not a follower of Jesus either.

There were probably resurrection appearances to the Twelve and other believers, but what exactly they were is difficult to determine. Most likely, they were *not* bodily appearances,[1321] but appearances of Jesus' immaterial form or spirit, or even inner mystical experiences similar to Paul's revelation of his Christ Jesus (see below). In the Gnostic *Letter of Peter to Philip*, Jesus appears to his disciples as a "great light" and in the Gnostic *Wisdom of Jesus Christ*, he appears as a "great angel of light."[1322]

The seventy (-two) other apostles[1323] were probably disbanded after Jesus' death and resurrection, because there is no evidence that they continued on in any form after these events.

As a result of the crucifixion and the resurrection appearances, the Christians had to determine in some way what meaning these remarkable events they experienced had for themselves, the Jewish people, and even the world. A radical revision of Jesus' original message was thus unavoidable.[1324]

In due course, they came to the conclusion that what they witnessed had been prophesied in Scripture. Jesus first appeared on earth in gentleness as the "Suffering Servant" of Isaiah[1325] and had been crucified. A portion of the Isaiah passage reads as follows:

> He was despised and rejected by men; a man of sorrows, and acquainted with grief; and as one from whom men hide their faces he was despised, and we esteemed him not. Surely he has borne our griefs and carried our sorrows; yet we esteemed him stricken, smitten by God, and afflicted. But he was wounded for our transgressions, he was bruised for our iniquities; upon him was the chastisement that made us whole, and with his stripes we are healed. All we like sheep have gone astray; we have turned away every one to his own way; and the Lord has laid on him the iniquity of us all.[1326]

1321. If there were bodily appearances, they were probably seeing Jesus' twin brother and imagined they were seeing Jesus. See Eisler, *The Messiah Jesus and John the Baptist*, 448-53, 571-2.

1322. Elaine Pagels, *The Gnostic Gospels* (New York: Vintage Books, 1981), 19.

1323. Lk. 10:1.

1324. In the 18th century, H. S. Reimarus, the first scholar to critically investigate the gospels, made a thorough distinction between what Jesus taught and what the apostles later preached. However, he also believed that the resurrection was a complete fraud perpetrated by the apostles to preserve their new careers established by Jesus. See Charles H. Talbert, ed. *Reimarus: Fragments*, trans. by Ralph S. Fraser (Philadelphia: Fortress Press, 1970), 64-5, 248-58. I cannot accept his view of the resurrection. Whatever it was, it was authentic to the apostles.

1325. Is. 52:13-53:12, Lk. 24:25-7, 44-7, Acts 3:18, 8:26-39.

1326. Is. 53:3-6.

He was now in heaven with God, but would return in the near future as the triumphant "Son of Man" in order to complete his mission:

> I saw in the night visions, and behold, with the clouds of heaven there came one like a son of man, and he came to the Ancient of Days and was presented before him. And to him was given dominion and glory and kingdom, and all peoples, nations, and languages should serve him; his dominion is an everlasting dominion, which shall not pass away, and his kingdom one that shall not be destroyed.[1327]

In this role, he would carry out the Last Judgment. All the wicked (i.e., all non-believers) would suffer eternal punishment in the underworld and the righteous (i.e., all believers) would live in eternal peace and prosperity in God's Kingdom on earth:

> When the Son of man comes in his glory, and all the angels with him, then he will sit on his glorious throne. Before him will be gathered all the nations, and he will separate them one from another as a shepherd separates the sheep from the goats, and he will place the sheep at his right hand, and the goats at the left. Then the King will say to those at his right hand, 'Come, O blessed of my Father, inherit the kingdom prepared for you from the foundation of the world....' Then he will say to those at his left hand, 'Depart from me, you cursed, into the eternal fire prepared for the devil and his angels....' And they will go away into eternal punishment, but the righteous into eternal life.[1328]

I Enoch 69:27-9 is very similar to the above passage:

> (Then) there came to them a great joy. And they blessed, glorified, and extolled (the Lord) on account of the fact that the name of that (Son of) Man was revealed to them. He shall never pass away or perish from before the face of the earth. But those who have led the world astray shall be bound in chains; and their ruinous congregation shall be imprisoned; all their deeds shall vanish from before the face of the earth. Thenceforth nothing that is corruptible shall be found; for that Son of Man has appeared and has seated himself upon the throne of his glory; and all evil shall disappear from before his face; he shall go and tell to that Son of Man, and he shall be strong before the Lord of the Spirits.[1329]

1327. Dan. 7:13-4, cf. Mk. 13:24-7=Mt. 24:29-31=Lk. 21:25-8.
1328. Mt. 25:31-46.
1329. James H. Charlesworth, ed., *The Old Testament Pseudepigrapha*, 2 vols. (Garden City: Doubleday & Co., 1985), Vol. 1, 49.

Jesus had originally taught that the Kingdom or the Son of Man was a spiritual reality to be found within individuals. When they found it, inner transformation would come and in time would transform the entire world. Unfortunately, this teaching was now totally distorted. Jesus was now the Son of Man himself, who would return in the future to carry out the Last Judgment and bequeath the Kingdom to the righteous. However, this was not the only revision that was made.

A careful analysis of the synoptic gospels[1330] reveals that there are two portraits of Jesus intertwined that are mutually irreconcilable. They are as follows:

Jesus #1	Jesus #2
Teaches forgiveness and non-judgment. Examples: (1) Then Peter came up and said to him, "Lord, how often shall my brother sin against me, and I forgive him? As many as seven times?" Jesus said to him, "I do not say to you seven times, but seventy times seven" (Mt. 18:21-2=Lk. 17:4). (2) Judge not, that you be not judged. For with the judgment you pronounce you will be judged, and the measure you give will be the measure you get (Mt. 7:1-2=Lk. 6:37-8).	Condemns and judges. Examples: (1) And if any one will not receive you or listen to your words, shake off the dust from your feet as you leave that house or town. Truly, I say to you, it shall be more tolerable on the day of judgment for the land of Sodom and Gomorrah than for that town [that does not receive the apostles] (Mt. 10:14-5=Lk. 10:10-2). (2) Again, the kingdom of heaven is like a net which was thrown into the sea and gathered fish of every kind; when it was full, men drew it ashore and sat down and sorted the good into vessels but threw away the bad. So it will be at the close of the age. The angels will come out and separate the evil from the righteous, and throw them into the furnace of fire; there men will weep and gnash their teeth (Mt. 13:47-50).
Teaches that God is the Father of all. Examples: (1) Our Father who is in heaven, Let your name be holy (Mt. 6:9=Lk. 11:2).[a] (2) But I say to you, Love your enemies ... so that you may be sons of your Father who is in heaven; for he makes his sun rise on the evil and on the good, and sends rain on the just and on the unjust. (Mt. 5:43-5=Lk. 6:27).	Teaches that he is exclusively God's son. Examples: (1) All things have been delivered to me by my Father; and no one knows the Son except the Father, and no one knows the Father except the Son and any one to whom the Son chooses to reveal him (Mt. 11:27=Lk. 10:22). (2) So every one who acknowledges me before men, I also will acknowledge before my Father who is in heaven; but whoever denies me before men, I also will deny before my Father who is in heaven (Mt. 10:32-3=Lk. 12:8-9).

1330. The Chester Beatty Papyrus (P^{45}) from the third century AD contains the "oldest consecutive text of the four gospels," but it "evidences a different text for each [of them]." Earlier than the third century AD there are only a few fragments of the gospels. Evidence for the existence of the gospels first shows up in other sources only after AD 150. W. G. Kümmel, *Introduction to the New Testament*, 17th ed., trans. by H. C. Kee (New York: Abingdon, 1975), 187, 485-92, 517-8.

Chapter 22. Saul, Paul, the Pillars, and the Twelve

Teaches peace and non-resistance.	Condones and uses violence.
Examples: (1) Blessed are the peacemakers, for they shall be called sons of God (Mt. 5:9). (2) You have heard that it was said, "An eye for an eye and a tooth for a tooth." But I say to you, Do not resist one who is evil. But if one strikes you on the right cheek, turn to him the other also; and if any one would sue you and take your coat, let him have your cloak as well; and if any one forces you to go one mile, go with him two miles (Mt. 5:38-41=Lk. 6:29). (3) You have heard that it was said, "you shall love your neighbor and hate your enemy." But I say to you, Love your enemies, do good to those who hate you, bless those who curse you, pray for those who abuse you, so that you may be sons of your Father who is in heaven ... (Mt. 5:43-4, Lk. 6:27-8, Mt. 5:45).	Examples: (1) And he said to them, "When I sent you out with no purse or bag or sandals, did you lack anything?" They said, "Nothing." He said to them, "But now, let him who has a purse take it, and likewise a bag. And let him who has no sword sell his mantle and buy one. ... And they said, "Look, Lord, here are two swords." And he said to them, "It is enough" (Lk. 22:35-8). (2) Do not think that I have come to bring peace on earth; I have not come to bring peace, but a sword (Mt. 10:34, cf. Lk. 12:51). (3) And he entered the temple and began to drive out those who sold and those who bought in the temple, and he overturned the tables of the money-changers and the seats of those who sold pigeons; and he would not allow any one to carry anything through the temple (Mk. 11:15-6=Mt. 21:12=Lk. 19:45=Jn. 2:13-7).
Teaches the commandment to honor father and mother. Examples: (1) And behold, one came up to him, saying, "Teacher, what good deed must I do, to have eternal life?" And he said to him, "Why do you ask me about what is good? One there is who is good. If you would enter life, keep the commandments." He said to him, "Which?" And Jesus said, "You shall not kill, You shall not commit adultery, You shall not steal, You shall not bear false witness, *Honor your father and mother*,[b] and, You shall love your neighbor as yourself." (Mt. 19:16-20=Mk. 10:17-9=Lk. 18:18-20, italics mine). (2) Then the Pharisees and scribes came to Jesus from Jerusalem and said, "Why do your disciples transgress the tradition of the elders? For they do not wash their hands when they eat." He answered them, "And why do you transgress the commandment of God for the sake of your tradition? For God commanded, '*Honor your father and your mother*,'[c] and, '*He who speaks evil of father or mother, let him surely die.*'[d] But you say, 'If any one tells his father or his mother, What you would have gained from me is given to God, he need not honor his father.' So, for the sake of your tradition, you have made void the word of God. You hypocrites! ..." (Mt. 15:1-9=Mk. 7:1-12, italics mine).	Teaches hatred of father and mother and the breaking of ties with them (and even with the rest of the family) in order to be a disciple.[e] Examples: (1) If any one comes to me and does not hate his own father and mother and wife and children and brothers and sisters, yes, and even his own life, he cannot be my disciple (Lk. 14:26, cf. Mt. 10:37, "He who loves father or mother more than me is not worthy of me"). (2) Do you think that I have come to bring peace on earth? No, I tell you, but rather division; for henceforth in one house there will be five divided, three against two and two against three; they will be divided, father against son and son against father, mother against daughter and daughter against her mother, mother-in-law against her daughter-in-law and daughter-in-law against her mother-in-law Lk. 12:51-3=Mt. 10:34-5). (3) And his mother and brothers came; and standing outside they sent to him and called him. And the crowd was sitting about him; and they said to him, "Your mother and your brothers are outside, asking for you." And he replied, "Who are my mother and my brothers?" And looking around on those who sat about him, he said, "Here are my mother and my brothers! Whoever does the will of God is my brother, and sister, and mother" (Mk. 3:31-5=Mt. 12:46-50=Lk. 8:19-21).

    a. This portion of the Lord's Prayer is from the Peshitta-Aramaic text. See Rocco A Errico, *The Message of Matthew* (Irvine: Noohra Foundation, 1991, 21.
    b. Ex. 20:12, Dt. 5:16.
    c. Ex. 20:12, Dt. 5:16.
    d. Ex. 21:17, Lev. 20:9.
    e. These sayings inculcating hatred and divisions between family members probably originated when Jewish and/or Gentile believers, who desired to formally become Christians, received great disapproval and even severe chastisement from their non-believing kin (especially their fathers and mothers) for wanting to join the new sect. The only recourse for them was to sever all connections with their blood relations and to view the Christian community as their new family.

It is obvious that both of these portraits could not be of the same individual. So how do we explain their existence in the gospel record? The answer seems to be that when the followers of Jesus tried to tell their neighbors what their leader had taught them while on earth, they made very little progress.

The reason was that Jesus' teachings of peace, non-resistance, and forgiveness were not what their listeners wanted to hear. They were waiting for a Messiah, who would lead them in a victorious military campaign against the Romans and their Jewish collaborators. The message of the historical Jesus (i.e., Jesus #1) was not getting much response and the temptation to transform him into Jesus #2 was overwhelming. The result was that the two portraits became commingled when the gospels were written, even though they contradicted each other. The Jesus #1 portrait was probably preserved for no other reason than its authenticity.

So it was that until Jesus returned to carry out the Last Judgment, the commission of the Twelve was to bring the message to as many people as they were able to — first to the Jews[1331] and then to all the nations.[1332] Since baptism was the means of entry into the new faith,[1333] their goal was to baptize as many converts as possible. As we have seen, other titles were used to refer to Jesus besides the Son of Man, such as the True Prophet, the Son of the Father (God), and the Messiah (Christ).

The Christians were actually very successful in selling their recreated Jesus to the masses. Soon after the Jewish revolt (AD 66-70), Josephus could state, "what more than all else incited [the Jews] to the war was an ambiguous oracle, likewise found in their sacred scriptures,[1334] to the effect that at that time one from their country would become ruler of the world."[1335] The Slavonic Josephus adds that the world ruler was believed to be either "that crucified Wonder-worker Jesus" or the Roman emperor "Vespasian"![1336] In the opinion of Josephus, "the oracle ... in reality signified the sovereignty of Vespasian, who was proclaimed Emperor on Jewish soil."[1337] Unfortunately, by offering the choice between Jesus and Vespasian, as to who would be the ruler of the world,

---

1331. A belief came into existence that Jesus had told his disciples not to leave Jerusalem for twelve years. See Hugh J. Schonfield, *The Jesus Party* (New York: Macmillan, 1974), 168. Cf. Lk. 24:47, where it is stated that "repentence and forgiveness of sins should be preached in his [Jesus'] name to all nations, *beginning from Jerusalem*" (italics mine).

1332. Mt. 28:19-20, Lk. 24:47, Mk. 16:15.

1333. Mk. 16:16, Mt. 28:19, Acts 2:37-41, 8:12-3.

1334. This was probably Gen. 49:10: "The scepter shall not depart from Judah, nor the ruler's staff from between his feet, until he comes to whom it belongs; and to him shall be the obedience of the peoples" (Eisler, *The Messiah Jesus and John the Baptist*, 554-61).

1335. War VI, 311-2.

1336. Eisler, *The Messiah Jesus and John the Baptist*, 547-8. See also Josephus, Bk. III, p. 658. Herod the Great was included as the third candidate, but was probably omitted from later editions of the work by Josephus due to a protest by Herod Agrippa II and his supporters (Eisler, *The Messiah Jesus and John the Baptist*, 549-50).

1337. War VI, 313-4. Cf. War IV, 592-604.

Josephus actually laid the blame for the war on the Christians![1338] This implicit allegation was doubtless not true, but the fact Josephus could propose it must mean that the Christians had made considerable progress in preaching their crucified Jesus to the people. This Slavonic addition provides us with another example of Josephus' disparaging view of Christianity.

In the years following AD 70, it was realized that Jesus was not going to return as the Son of Man as soon as had been expected. As a result of this delay, the idea developed that prior to this great event there would be a period of terrible suffering and unknown length, which would include among other things wars, famines, earthquakes, and persecutions.[1339] Furthermore, there was a real need to comfort other Christians who were losing hope that the Last Judgment was going to occur very soon if at all. In order to soothe their fear, Jesus was made to say, "there are some standing here who will not taste death before they see the Kingdom of God."[1340] Although they would have been children or infants at the time, "some" believers would indeed have been alive during Jesus' lifetime. Of course, their number would have continued to diminish as the years moved past AD 70. In another place and for the same reason, Jesus was also made to say, "this generation will not pass away before all these things take place."[1341] According to Wells, "every reader would feel that he belonged to 'this generation'.... "[1342] It would be further consoling to know that God in his mercy had even 'shortened" the period of suffering that would precede the Last Judgment "for the sake of the elect," i.e., believers.[1343]

It has always been difficult to explain why, if Paul's Jesus was based on an actual historical person, he tells us nothing about that person, his teachings, or his miracles even when it would have helped his theological argument. Furthermore, his Jesus was not even tied to any particular time or setting. All we are told is that the "rulers of this age"[1344] (i.e., the demonic powers) crucified him.[1345]

1338. Robert Eisler, *The Messiah Jesus and John the Baptist*, 550-4.
1339. All of this is detailed in what is called the Synoptic Apocalypse (Mk. 13:5-37=Mt. 24:4-36=Lk. 21:8-36).
1340. Lk. 9:27. Mark and Matthew are both slightly different. Mark has "there are some standing here who will not taste death before they see the kingdom of God *come with power*" (Mk. 9:1, italics mine). Matthew has "there are some standing here who will not taste death before they see *the Son of Man coming in his kingdom*" (Mt. 16:28, italics mine).
1341. Mk. 13:30-2=Mt. 24:34-6=Lk. 21:32-3.
1342. G. A. Wells, *Did Jesus Exist?* rev. ed. (London: Pemberton, 1986), 84.
1343. Mk. 13:20=Mt. 24:22.
1344. I Cor. 2:6, 8.
1345. Wells, *Did Jesus Exist?* 18-20, 64; Brandon, *Jesus and the Zealots*, 11 note 4, 151.

Based on these facts and the generally accepted belief that Paul's epistles are the earliest documents of Christianity written in AD 50-60, one recent writer has theorized that Jesus was a myth with no historical reality whatsoever. Historical attributes were added only later, when the gospels were written after AD 70 but before AD 125.[1346] With the discovery of microletters on first century AD coins, this theory has been completely disproved. However, it was a valid theory before their discovery, because it is a fact that Paul's epistles do not corroborate the gospel evidence about Jesus' life and teachings. How do we explain Paul's silence about these subjects?

The Jesus of Paul appears to have been a divine being[1347] (i.e., God's Son), whom the Father sent "in the likeness of sinful flesh."[1348] His purpose was to save mankind from bondage to the "rulers of this age" (i.e., the demonic powers) and to bring them knowledge of Himself. According to Paul, "but we impart a secret and hidden wisdom of God, which God decreed before the ages for our glorification. None of the rulers of this age understood this; for if they had, they would not have crucified the Lord of glory."[1349] He also states that "though [Christ Jesus] was in the form of God, [he] did not count equality with God a thing to be grasped, but emptied himself, taking the form of a servant, being born in the likeness of men. And being found in human form he humbled himself and became obedient unto death, even death on the cross. Therefore God has highly exalted him...."[1350] Not recognizing the lofty identity of this being when he rose from the dead, the demonic powers were defeated and mankind was freed from enslavement to them.

Regarding the source of his beliefs, Paul says, "the gospel which was preached by me is not man's gospel. For I did not receive it from man, nor was I taught it, but it came though a revelation of Jesus Christ."[1351] In other words, it was *not* followers of an historical Jesus who taught him anything about this being, but it was the entity himself who imparted the knowledge to him! Certainly, it is not very likely that Paul would have described an actual Jewish contemporary of his who had brothers, ate, and slept, etc., as "Christ the power

---

1346. Wells, *Did Jesus Exist?* 65, 92.

1347. Davies, quoting Bultmann, describes Paul's conception of the divine being revealed to him as follows: "The Kyrios (Lord) Jesus Christos is conceived as a mystery deity, in whose death and resurrection the faithful participate through the sacraments." See R. Bultmann, *Primitive Christianity in its Contemporary Setting*, trans. by R. H. Fuller (New York, 1956), 177; quoted in A. Powell Davies, *The First Christian: A Study of St. Paul and Christian Origins* (New York: New American Library, 1959), 156.

1348. Rom. 8:3, cf. Phil. 2:7.
1349. I Cor. 2:7-8.
1350. Phil. 2:6-9.
1351. Gal. 1:11-2.

of God and the wisdom of God"[1352] and "the image of the invisible God, the first born of all creation."[1353] The divine being that Paul was preaching about was *not* the historical Jesus.[1354]

One scholar has theorized that Paul believed his Jesus was not crucified and resurrected on the earth at all, but at the bottom plane of the ethereal part of the universe that was situated just above the earth. This plane, as well as the earth, was where the demonic powers were in control. This theory is probably correct. Doherty describes this ancient view of the universe as follows:

> ...the spiritual part of the universe was popularly seen as divided into several levels — usually seven. As a deity descended from the higher reaches of pure spirit, he passed through ever degenerating spheres of the heavens, and could take on an increasing likeness to lower, material forms as well as an ability to suffer fleshly fates, such as pain and death. The lowest level of the spirit realm was the air, or "firmament," between the earth and the moon. This was the domain of the demon spirits — in Jewish parlance, of Satan and his evil angels — and it was regarded as closely connected to the earthly sphere. The demonic spiritual powers belonged to the realm of flesh and were thought of as in some way corporeal, though they possessed 'heavenly' versions of earthly bodies.[1355]

Paul's statement that "even though we once regarded Christ from a human point of view, we regard him thus no longer"[1356] does not mean that he disregarded (as a result of the resurrection) any knowledge of an historical Jesus,[1357] which is usually the way this verse is interpreted. What it does mean is that his Jesus was not to be judged by the usual worldly standards. This is proved by the first part of the verse, which states "from now on ... we regard *no one* from a human point of view."[1358] In other words, judgments based on earthly

---

1352. I Cor. 1:24.
1353. Col. 1:15. It should be noted here that scholars consider Paul's authorship of Colossians "debatable" (Kümmel, *Introduction to the New Testament*, 250-1).
1354. The fact that Jesus was the name of both Paul's deity and the historical Jesus is not evidence that they were identical, as many would like to think. The name was a very common one. Josephus mentions 21 individuals with it [see Josephus, *General Index* (Loeb Classical Library), Vol. X, pp. 279-80]. Furthermore, according to Davies, "it is abundantly evident that as well as being a proper name it is a "mystery" word with cryptic connotations clustered about the central meaning of *Deliverer* or *Savior*" (Davies, *The First Christian: A Study of St. Paul and Christian Origins*, 183; see p. 140, note 53). Also, as we have seen, "Christ" is not a name at all, but a title meaning the "Anointed One." It came to refer to the expected deliverer promised by God.
1355. Earl Doherty, *The Jesus Puzzle* (Ottawa: Canadian Humanist Publications, 1999), 103.
1356. II Cor. 5:16.
1357. Brandon, *Jesus and the Zealots*, 182-3.
1358. II Cor. 5:16 (italics mine). See Wells, *Did Jesus Exist?* 97-9.

criteria were of no use to believers anymore. According to Paul, the reason for this new viewpoint was that "if any one is in Christ, he is a new creation; the old has passed away, behold, the new has come."[1359]

According to Acts, it was supposedly on Paul's way to Damascus to arrest Christians who had escaped there that he had a vision. Although there are three slightly different versions of this incident recorded in the Acts,[1360] they all agree that Paul saw a bright flash of light and heard Jesus speak to him. Depending on the version consulted, those who were with him saw or heard something too. As a result of this experience, the one who had supposedly been a fierce persecutor of Christians became an ardent believer and in due time would become the acknowledged apostle to the Gentiles.

However, the epistles lead us to the more accurate view that Paul's revelation of his Jesus was an *inner* experience[1361] not an experience outside of him, as it is described in the Acts. Perhaps in this mystical state, he experienced his Jesus as a very lofty entity in God's presence. He states that "God has highly exalted him and bestowed on him the name which is above every name, that at the name of Jesus every knee should bow, in heaven and on earth and under the earth, and every tongue confess that Jesus Christ is Lord, to the glory of the Father."[1362]

In the Acts, Paul is also called Saul. It is usually understood that Saul was Paul's original Jewish name and Paul was his Roman one,[1363] since Paul was a Roman citizen by birth.[1364] Acts first mentions a "young man named Saul" at Acts 7:58 and begins to call Saul Paul at Acts 13:9, which is probably the beginning of a new source utilized by the writer of Acts. The portrait of Saul/Paul in Acts is probably a *composite* one created by the growing church in Rome. It does not represent the *historical* Saul *or* Paul.

The historical Paul, a Jewish tentmaker from the city of Tarsus in Cilicia,[1365] was the teacher of a special *gnosis* (i.e., knowledge) of the divine being called Jesus Christ or Christ Jesus that we have described above.

The historical Saul, who is mentioned by Josephus,[1366] was the brother of someone called Costobar and a member of the Herodian royal family. He was

---

1359. II Cor. 5:17.
1360. Acts 9:1-22, 22:4-16, 26:9-18. In all three versions of the incident, Paul is actually called Saul (see below).
1361. See II Cor. 12:2-5 and Gal. 1:16.
1362. Phil. 2:9-11.
1363. F. F. Bruce, *New Testament History* (Garden City: Anchor Books, 1969), 234-6.
1364. Acts 22:28.
1365. Acts 18:3, 21:39, 22:3, Rom.11:1, II Cor. 11:22.

part of a delegation sent to Herod Agrippa II to ask him to send troops to crush the Jewish revolt in AD 66. After Cestius Gallus' defeat in the same year, Saul deserted to the Romans along with some others. At their request, Cestius sent them to Emperor Nero to report on the events that had transpired.

Saul's very real persecution of the New Covenant in Judaea and the land of Damascus was the source for Paul's supposed pre-conversion persecution of the Christians in Judea and Damascus.[1367] He probably undertook these brutal activities while under the employ of the establishment high priests, especially the "Wicked Priest" Ananus. Saul is mentioned in the *Recognitions of Clement* as the "enemy," who throws James down from the top of the Temple steps! In this source, James was not killed, but afterwards he was "still lame on one foot."[1368] This story seems to be a fictitious version of the actual event that was discussed in an earlier chapter.[1369] The historical Saul was the hired thug[1370] of the high priest Ananus, who pushed James the Righteous down from the pinnacle of the Temple!

It was to be expected that there would soon be conflict between Paul, the Twelve, and their respective followers, although there was actually no relationship between them. The Twelve would criticize Paul by saying that they had actually seen and heard the Messiah and therefore had the authentic teachings, whereas Paul only had a mythical experience as support for his teachings. Paul would comment back that his teaching was a special revelation from God through His Son, which was planned by God before time began and which negated all other human teachings.

1366. War II, 418, 556, 558; Ant. XX, 214. Robert Eisenman identified this Saul of Josephus at least tentatively with Paul. See "Paul as Herodian" in Eisenman, *The Dead Sea Scrolls and the First Christians*, 241-3.

1367. Acts 8:1-3, 9:1-22, 22:4-16, 26:9-18, Gal. 1:13, 17, I Cor. 15:9, II Cor. 11:32-3, Phil. 3:6.

1368. Rev. Alexander Roberts and James Donaldson, *The Ante-Nicene Fathers* (Grand Rapids: Eerdmans, 1981), Vol. VIII, 95-6 (chap. 70-3). A marginal note in chap. 70 in one of the manuscripts states that this enemy was Saul and chap. 71 confirms this by stating that the "enemy" received a commission from the chief priest to go to Damascus in order to arrest the followers of Jesus. In reality, this commission of Saul's was to arrest followers of the New Covenant in the land of Damascus *not* the followers of Jesus, but the incident still allows us to identify the "enemy" with Saul.

1369. Another fictitious version of the same event is Acts 6:1-8:3 where Stephen is a substitute for James. See Hans-Joachim Schoeps, *Jewish Christianity*, trans. by Douglas R. A. Hare (Philadelphia: Fortress Press, 1969), 42-6.

1370. In a feud that developed between the two high priests Jesus, the son of Damnaeus (ca. AD 62-3), and his successor Jesus, the son of Gamaliel (ca. AD 63-4), Josephus states that "Costobar and Saul also on their own part collected gangs of villians. They themselves were of royal lineage ... but were lawless and quick to plunder the property of those weaker than themselves" (Ant. XX, 213-4).

It would appear that the Twelve actually attempted to convert Paul's followers to their views. This conflict shows up in the epistles. Those who teach a "different gospel" and "another Jesus" are mentioned.[1371] "False apostles,"[1372] "workers of evil,"[1373] and "enemies of the cross of Christ"[1374] are mentioned, as well as "those who were reputed to be something"[1375] and "superlative apostles" (both ironically intended).[1376]

These derogatory epithets were probably used for other rival teachers also. For example, someone named Apollos appears to have caused considerable strife within some of Paul's churches by teaching his own unique brand of the faith.[1377]

James, the leader of the New Covenant in Jerusalem, was probably well aware that it would be beneficial to recruit Jews from the Diaspora into the New Covenant. Even Gentiles that were willing to become Jews, i.e., to be baptized, circumcised[1378] and to learn the Torah, would be worth locating. It cannot be excluded that some of these derogatory epithets were directed against missionaries from James as well. Perhaps Paul stressed a *crucified* Christ (i.e., Messiah),[1379] because some of his opponents (i.e., missionaries from James in this instance) were teaching that the true Messiah could not be crucified.[1380]

Sometime during his reign (AD 41-4), Herod Agrippa I had James and John, the sons of Zebedee, beheaded.[1381] Although Acts states only that James was executed, there is evidence that both brothers were actually put to death.[1382] After they were executed, the king arrested Peter (Cephas), but somehow he was able to escape and "departed and went to another place."[1383] Since Acts also adds that the king "laid violent hands upon *some* who belonged to the

---

1371. Gal. 1:6-8, II Cor. 11:3-4.
1372. II Cor. 11:13.
1373. Phil. 3:2, II Cor. 11:13.
1374. Phil. 3:18.
1375. Gal. 2:6.
1376. II Cor. 11:5, 12:11.
1377. I Cor. 1:12, 3:1-9, 21-3, 4:6; Acts 18:24-8.
1378. As we have seen, circumcision was not an absolute requirement to join the sect, since there were a small number of baptized but uncircumcised Gentile proselytes in it. However, although they could associate with Israel, they were not themselves Israelites, because they were not circumcised.
1379. I Cor. 1:23 ("we preached Christ *crucified*") and I Cor. 2:2 ("for I decided to know nothing among you except Jesus Christ and him *crucified*").
1380. A crucified Messiah would be "accursed by God" (Dt. 21:23, cf. 11QT 64:12). Paul actually admits that such a Messiah is "a stumbling block to Jews" (I Cor. 1:23), but in his view "Christ redeemed us from the curse of the law, having become a curse for us ..." (Gal. 3:13).
1381. Acts 12:2.
1382. Robert Eisler, *The Enigma of the Fourth Gospel* (London: Methuen & Co., 1938), 59-77, 95-8.
1383. Acts 12:3-19.

church,"[1384] other members of the church may have been persecuted as well. It was most likely their messianic propaganda about Jesus, as well as their indifferent attitude towards the Jewish religious rituals and practices,[1385] that actually initiated the king's violent attack against the church.

With the arrival of Cuspius Fadus and Tiberius Alexander, who were sent by Emperor Claudius (AD 41-54) and who ruled as joint governors from AD 44-ca. 46 (Tiberius Alexander was the sole governor from AD ca. 46-48),[1386] a new policy appears to have gone into effect. According to the Slavonic Josephus, they "kept the people in peace, by not allowing any departure in anything from the pure laws." It further goes on to say, "but if notwithstanding anyone did deviate from the word of the Law [i.e., the Torah] and information was laid before the teachers of the Law, they punished or banished him, or sent (him) to Caesar."[1387] Henceforth, the Roman government and the Jewish hierarchy, working in concert, would enforce the Jewish religious law in addition to the Roman provincial law for the benefit of both parties.[1388] Roman jurisdiction would now extend to cases that involved an infringement of the Torah as interpreted by the Jewish authorities. Obviously, the Romans must have come to the realization that the enemies of the Jewish establishment were the enemies of Rome as well.

This new policy was especially dangerous for the followers of Jesus because of their laxity in practicing the Torah. However, the deviation from religious observance that was intended by the policy probably included any interpretation that reduced the collection of tithes and other gratuities due to the Jewish hierarchy or that otherwise threatened their authority in some way. Thus, James and the New Covenant were probably in jeopardy at this time as well.

In this same period, the restored Slavonic Josephus provides us with the following information about the followers of Jesus:

> And since in the time of him [Emperor Claudius] many helpers of the wonder-worker aforementioned had appeared and spoken to the people of their Master, (saying) that he was alive, although he had been dead, and "he will free you from bondage," many of the multitude hearkened to the(ir)

1384. Acts 12:1 (italics mine).
1385. They were unconcerned with these things, as Jesus had been. The Slavonic Josephus states the following about Jesus: 'Howbeit in many things he disobeyed the law [Torah] and kept not the Sabbath according to (our) fathers' custom" (Eisler, *The Messiah Jesus and John the Baptist*, 467).
1386. Eisler, *The Messiah Jesus and John the Baptist*, 531-3.
1387. Eisler, *The Messiah Jesus and John the Baptist*, 528-9. See also Josephus, Bk. III, Appendix, p. 651.
1388. Eisler, *The Messiah Jesus and John the Baptist*, 531-8.

preaching and took heed of their directions, for they were of the humble(r sort), some mere tailors, others sandal-makers, (or) others artisans.[1389]

How should we understand the statement that Jesus would release them "from bondage"? When he returned to carry out the Last Judgment, all the wicked (i.e., all non-believers) would suffer eternal punishment in the underworld and the righteous (i.e., all believers) would live in eternal peace and prosperity in God's Kingdom on earth. So it was that deliverance from the "bondage" of evil was to be the destiny of all believers.[1390]

Paul probably visited Jerusalem near the end of his life.[1391] If he did bring a collection with him on this visit, it was probably intended to be a gift to the Jewish people by way of the Temple of Jerusalem. It was not intended for the "saints" in Jerusalem.[1392] In Paul's defense to the Roman governor, he stated the following: "Now after some years I came to bring *to my nation* alms and offerings."[1393] Note here that there is no mention of the "saints," as is the case in the Epistles. This idea was probably a later addition to Paul's epistles.

When Paul was discovered in the Temple, a riot ensued. According to Acts, "the Jews from Asia, who had seen him in the temple, stirred up all the crowd, and laid hands on him, crying out, 'men of Israel, help! This man who is teaching men everywhere against the people and law and this place; moreover he also brought Greeks into the temple, and he has defiled this holy place.'"[1394] He was then arrested and eventually sent to Rome on the basis of his appeal to the emperor. A Roman citizen like Paul had this right of appeal.[1395] Tradition has it that he was beheaded in Rome by order of Emperor Nero. Tradition also has it that Peter (Cephas) was crucified by order of Nero about the same time.[1396]

1389. Eisler, *The Messiah Jesus and John the Baptist*, 529. For the unrestored version, see Josephus, Bk. III, Appendix, p. 651-2.

1390. Robert Eisler understood the statement that "he [Jesus] will free you from bondage" as referring to "liberation from the yoke of ... well-known worldly oppressors" (Eisler, *The Messiah Jesus and John the Baptist*, 540). This view is correct with regard to all believers who would be totally free of any political or economic injustice with Jesus sitting on the throne as their benevolent king in the Kingdom of God.

1391. Acts 21:15 ff.

1392. Rom. 15:25-33, I Cor. 16:1-4, II Cor. 8-9.

1393. Acts 24:17. Acts 11:27-30 may have some value, if the "brethren" receiving the aid were really *all* Jews.

1394. Acts 21:27-8.

1395. Bruce, *New Testament History*, 358-9.

1396. Eusebius, *The Ecclesiastical History*, 2 vols., trans. by Kirsopp Lake (Cambridge: Harvard University Press, 1975), Vol. I, 181-3 (II, 25.5-8).

Chapter 22. Saul, Paul, the Pillars, and the Twelve

The belief first recorded by Eusebius[1397] and then by Epiphanius[1398] that the first Jewish Christians migrated en masse to the Hellenistic city of Pella in the Decapolis in order to escape the Roman siege of Jerusalem (AD 70) has been deemed historical by some scholars[1399] and unhistorical by others.[1400] Since Epiphanius tells us that Jewish Christians probably from the second to the fourth centuries did reside over a large land area east of the Jordan,[1401] an emigration from Jerusalem at an earlier time would certainly be a possible explanation for their existence there. However, as a result of the new Dead Sea Scroll evidence, it seems clear that the actual mass exodus of the New Covenant to the land of Damascus (AD 65-66) was the source for the alleged emigration of the pre-war Jerusalem church to Pella.

What motivated them to make this erroneous connection? According to Ludemann, "with the death of the first Christian generation and the apostles, a problem arose in early Christianity, especially in view of conflicting opinions. Who and what Christian community can lay claim to be the true successor of the apostles?"[1402] In AD 130, Emperor Hadrian built the city of Aelia Capitolina on the ruins of Jerusalem and prohibited all Jews from entering the city.[1403] According to Eusebius, the Christian church there was completely Gentile.[1404] It was important for the prestige of these Gentile Christians to claim an unbroken continuity between the church of Jerusalem before the Jewish War (AD 66-70) and the church of Aelia Capitolina after it. They accomplished this by claiming that the first Jewish Christians were saved from the ravages of the war by escaping to Pella. Epiphanius mentions their return to Jerusalem soon after it.[1405] Eusebius does not state this, but gives the impression of continuity

---

1397. Eusebius, *The Ecclesiastical History*, Vol. I, 199-200 (III, 5.3).

1398. See the passages from Epiphanius quoted by Gerd Ludemann, "The Successors of Pre-70 Jerusalem Christianity: A Critical Evaluation of the Pella-Tradition," *Jewish and Christian Self-Definition*, ed. by E. P. Sanders, Vol. I (Philadelphia: Fortress Press, 1980), 161-73, 245-54.

1399. E.g., Sidney Sowers, "The Circumstances and Recollection of the Pella Flight," *Theologische Zeitschrift* 26 (1970): 305-20; Hugh J. Schonfield, *The Jesus Party* (New York: Macmillan, 1974), 230-8.

1400. E.g., S. G. F. Brandon, *The Fall of Jerusalem and the Christian Church*, 2nd ed. (London: S.P.C.K., 1968), 168-73, 263-4; *Jesus and the Zealots*, 208-17.

1401. It extended southwards from Syria in the north to Arabia in the south. It is interesting that Epiphanius mentions the city of Cochaba in Basanitis (Batanaea), which is located right in the land of Damascus. See Hans-Joachim Schoeps, *Jewish Christianity*, trans. by Douglas R. A. Hare (Philadelphia: Fortress Press, 1969), 24-30.

1402. Ludemann, "The Successors of Pre-70 Jerusalem Christianity ... ,"172.

1403. Emil Shurer, *The History of the Jewish People in the Age of Jesus Christ*, vols. I, II, III.1, III.2, rev. and ed. by Geza Vermes, et al. (Edinburgh: T. & T. Clark, 1973/87), Vol. I, 534-57.

1404. Eusebius, *The Ecclesiastical History*, Vol. I, 313 (IV, 6.4), 465-6 (V, 12.1).

1405. Sowers, "The Circumstances and Recollection of the Pella Flight," 310.

by listing fifteen Jewish Christian bishops of Jerusalem up to the expulsion of the Jews from Aelia Capitolina[1406] and fifteen Gentile Christian bishops after that.[1407]

From where did the Christians get the idea that Pella was the place of residence at the time of the supposed emigration? The New Covenant would surely not have settled at any time in Pella, which was a resolute pro-Roman Hellenistic city.[1408] It is possible that Christians living there from the second to the fourth centuries created the story in order to claim they were the true heirs of the Jerusalem Christians.[1409] However, another possible explanation has to do with the geographical location of Pella. The main route to the city of Damascus in Syria went through it: " ... the great highway from Scythopolis to Damascus went through Pella, which was situated where the road crossed into Transjordan...."[1410] In the gospels, when the "desolating sacrilege spoken of by the prophet Daniel[1411] [was found] standing in the holy place,"[1412] Jesus is supposed to have commanded the Christians to "flee to the mountains."[1413] According to Sowers, except for the mountains of Jerusalem, "one would have to look to the Transjordanian mountains to find the nearest such range. Pella qualifies as a city of refuge ... since it is in the foothills of these mountains."[1414]

1406. Eusebius, *The Ecclesiastical History*, Vol. I, 311 (IV, 5.3-4). The Jewish Christian bishops of Jerusalem in the order they held office were James, Simeon, Justus, Zacchaeus, Tobias, Benjamin, John, Matthias, Philip, Seneca, Justus, Levi, Ephres, Joseph, and Judas.

1407. Eusebius, *The Ecclesiastical History*, Vol. I, 465-7, 467 note 1 (V, 12.1-2). The Gentile Christian bishops of Aelia Capitolina in the order they held office were Marcus, Cassian, Publius, Maximus, Julian, Gaius, Symmachus, Gaius, Julian, Capito, Maximus, Antoninus, Valens, Dolichianus, and Narcissus. According to Ludemann, "the fact that according to Eusebius ... there are fifteen Gentile Christian bishops (after the fifteen Jewish Christian bishops) until Narcissus, who became bishop at the end of the second century, makes one think that the parallelism (and this list) is not due to history but to the construction of the fifteenth Gentile bishop Narcissus ..." (Ludemann, "The Successors of Pre-70 Jerusalem Christianity ... ," 251 note 48).

1408. Sowers, "The Circumstances and Recollection of the Pella Flight," 309.

1409. Brandon, who gave cogent reasons why the Jewish Christians of Jerusalem could not have escaped to Pella en masse from AD 66 to 70, weakened his argument somewhat by suggesting that Jewish Christians from communities in Galilee and Samaria may have settled there during the same time period. He further theorized that these emigrants would have been absorbed into the Gentile Christian church of Pella. When the latter to a large extent moved to Aelia Capitolina after the war, it was able to lay claim to being the legitimate heir of the "Mother Church of Jerusalem." This assertion was based primarily on its earlier assimilation of the Jewish Christian refugees (Brandon, *The Fall of Jerusalem and the Christian Church*, 170-3; *Jesus and the Zealots*, 212-6).

1410. Schoeps, *Jewish Christianity*, 27.

1411. Dan. 8:13, 9:27, 11:31, 12:11, cf. 9:17.

1412. Mt. 24:15 = Mk. 13:14. Mk. replaces "standing in the holy place" with "set up where it ought not to be."

1413. Mt. 24:16 = Mk. 13:14=Lk. 21:21.

1414. Sowers, "The Circumstances and Recollection of the Pella Flight," 319.

Therefore, because of Pella's distinctive geographical location, the selection of the city as the place of asylum in the emigration story is understandable.[1415]

1415. Rev. 12:1-17 has been interpreted as depicting the flight of the church to Pella (Sowers, "The Circumstances and Recollection of the Pella Flight," 315, 320), but it could be a source for the story rather than a description of an actual event. In the passage, "the serpent [Satan] poured water like a river out of his mouth" to destroy a "woman" fleeing for safety into the wilderness. Fortunately, the "earth opened its mouth and swallowed the river" and saved her from destruction. The imagery has been interpreted in the following way: The woman is the Christian Church; the river, which is depicted first as dangerously high but then as fordable, is the Jordan River; and the place of refuge in the wilderness is Pella.

CHAPTER 23. THE CREATION OF CHRISTIANITY

Why are the documents that allegedly give us the history of Christianity after Jesus' crucifixion and resurrection (i.e., the Acts of the Apostles and the Epistles of Paul, especially Galatians) so at variance with what has been described in the last chapter?

There appears to be no evidence for the existence of the Acts of the Apostles before AD 175[1416] and the earliest manuscript that is known is from the third century AD (i.e., the Chester Beatty Papyrus, P^{45}).[1417] A good case can be made that Acts' narrative of the progress of Christianity after the crucifixion and resurrection of Jesus is largely legendary and based on what the growing church in Rome (i.e., Catholic Christianity) believed it to be ca. AD 150.[1418]

Curiously, the writer of Acts does not appear to have known of the epistles of Paul.[1419] This fact may mean that either Paul's epistles did not exist when Acts was written or, what is more likely, that they were not yet considered relevant documents from the point of view of Catholic Christianity.

Thirteen epistles or letters are assigned to Paul in the New Testament. They are Romans, I and II Corinthians, Galatians, Philippians, I and II Thessalonians, Philemon, Colossians, Ephesians, I and II Timothy, and Titus. The scholarly consensus is that the Pastoral Epistles (i.e., I and II Timothy and

---

1416. Doherty, *The Jesus Puzzle* (Ottawa: Canadian Humanist Publications, 1999), 270.

1417. W. G. Kümmel, *Introduction to the New Testament*, 17th ed., trans. by H. C. Kee (New York: Abingdon, 1975), 187, 517-8. Kümmel states that "for Acts [this papyrus] is the oldest witness of the 'Short,' 'Egyptian' text."

1418. Doherty, *The Jesus Puzzle*, 269-74.

1419. Kümmel, *Introduction to the New Testament*, 189.

Titus) are not genuine writings of Paul and the genuineness of Colossians, Ephesians, II Thessalonians is "debatable."[1420] Therefore, seven epistles (i.e., Romans, I and II Corinthians, Galatians, Philippians, I Thessalonians, and Philemon) are unquestionably considered to be authentic writings of Paul.

The evidence is meager for the existence of Paul's epistles before ca. AD 140, when the Gnostic heretic Marcion (died ca. AD 160) is known to have collected ten epistles of Paul except for the Pastoral Epistles.[1421] Before Marcion's collection appeared, the only epistles that we have evidence for are Romans, I Corinthians, and Ephesians, and this evidence comes mainly from the writings of the Apostolic Fathers specifically the First Letter of Clement and the seven Letters of Ignatius.[1422] However, the authenticity of the writings of the Apostolic Fathers has been questioned by some.[1423] II Peter mentions "all [Paul's] letters,"[1424] but this New Testament letter has been dated by at least one scholar to AD 150 at the earliest.[1425] Also, we cannot be sure what epistles of Paul are actually intended by the word "all." The earliest manuscript that we have of the Pauline Epistles dates from ca. AD 200 (i.e., the Chester Beatty Papyrus, P[46]).[1426] Nevertheless, it is usually accepted that there was a collection in existence (i.e., the *Corpus Paulinum*) by ca. AD 100.[1427]

One writer has stated the main issue regarding the Pauline Epistles as follows:

> The problem concerning the Pauline literature consists in determining the exact manner in which it was altered, rewritten, and expanded before it was accepted by the Catholic Church. For, oddly enough, although it preceded all other portions of the New Testament, it was the last to achieve authority; and not only are several of the epistles wholly spurious, but those which are genuine were drastically revised.[1428]

Another writer described the controversy regarding the Pauline literature in the second century AD and later as follows:

1420. Kümmel, *Introduction to the New Testament*, 250-1.
1421. Kümmel, *Introduction to the New Testament*, 480-1.
1422. Kümmel, *Introduction to the New Testament*, 480-1.
1423. Hermann Detering, "The Dutch Radical Approach to the Pauline Epistles," *Journal of Higher Criticism* 3/2 (Fall 1996): 8.
1424. II Peter 3:15-6.
1425. Wells, *Did Jesus Exist?* rev. ed. (London: Pemberton, 1986), 68 note 22.
1426. Kümmel, *Introduction to the New Testament*, 517-8.
1427. G. Kuntz, *The Text of the Epistles* (London: Oxford University Press, 1953), 14-5.
1428. Martin A. Larson, *The Story of Christian Origins* (Washington, D.C: a Joseph J. Binns/New Republic Book, 1977), 437.

> At one extreme were groups of Jewish Christians who rejected Paul because of his views regarding justification and the law. At the opposite extreme, Marcion was convinced that Paul was the only true apostle. In something of a mediating position were the precursors of Catholic Christianity, who accepted the apostleship and the letters of Paul but only after, in various ways, 'domesticating' or 'taming' the more radical features of the apostle's thought. It is clear that at least two significantly different versions of the Pauline corpus circulated in the second century: that accepted by Marcion (no longer extant) and that recognized by his opponents (the only surviving version). Marcion's enemies accused him of excising offensive (to him) materials from the letters; he no doubt accused them of adding these materials. We cannot simply assume that Marcion's opponents were completely correct in their charges, particularly in light of the fact that our knowledge about Marcion comes precisely from these opponents; indeed, there may have been some degree of truth in both charges. We only know that the surviving text of the Pauline letters is the text promoted by the historical winners in the theological and ecclesiastical struggles of the second and third centuries. Marcion's text disappeared — another example, no doubt, of the well-documented practice of suppressing and even destroying what some Christians regarded as deficient, defective, deviant, or dangerous texts. ... In short, it appears likely that the emerging Catholic leadership in the churches 'standardized' the text of the Pauline corpus in the light of 'orthodox' views and practices, suppressing and even destroying all deviant texts and manuscripts. Thus it is that we have no manuscripts dating from earlier than the third century; thus it is that all of the extant manuscripts are remarkably similar in most of their significant features; and thus it is that the manuscript evidence can tell us nothing about the state of the Pauline literature prior to the third century.[1429]

I endeavored to show in the previous chapter that the historical Paul was a teacher of a special *gnosis* (i.e., knowledge) of the divine being Jesus Christ or Christ Jesus. This view of Paul makes understandable the fact that the first ones to appropriate Paul's epistles were the Gnostics (most notably Marcion) *not* the Catholic church![1430] The second century AD Gnostics found one of their own in Paul.

Because it was probably believed that Paul's Jesus had been crucified and resurrected in another plane of existence, there was at least one difference between the teachings of Paul and Marcion, as well as the other second century

---

1429. William O. Walker, Jr. "The Burden of Proof in Identifying Interpolations in the Pauline Letters," *New Testament Studies* vol. 33 (1987): 613-4.
1430. Detering, "The Dutch Radical Approach to the Pauline Epistles," 8, 20 note 40.

AD Gnostics. The latter believed that Jesus *did* enter the earthly plane, but only as an apparition. This view is known as Docetism, which is derived from the Greek word for "seemed." In other words, the Gnostics believed that Jesus only "seemed" to have a body of flesh and blood while on earth.[1431]

How much in the epistles attributed to Paul actually originated with him? As far back as 1929, one scholar, after a very detailed analysis of them, determined that only a portion of Romans[1432] and I Corinthians[1433] came from Paul.[1434] Perhaps this analysis was too critical and more authentic Pauline material could have been accepted. However, what seems clear is that Paul's epistles in their present form would probably be quite different from his original autograph copies. They appear to have been Gnostic documents through and through before they were tampered with by the growing church in Rome.

There is no evidence that the Epistle to the Galatians existed until Marcion put together his collection of Paul's Epistles ca. AD 140.[1435] Could it be that Galatians did not originate with Paul at all, but with the followers of Marcion? If so, its main purpose would have been to defend their image of Paul against the portrayal of him found in the Catholic Acts of the Apostles. In the Acts, Paul is subordinated to the apostles in Jerusalem (symbolizing Rome in the second century AD!). However, in Galatians he is under no one's authority but God's.[1436] Detering states the case as follows:

> My opinion is that the Epistle to the Galatians (in its original form) must be understood ... as a *Marcionite polemic pamphlet*. The (Marcionite) author of Galatians defends himself against the annexation of the apostle [Paul] and the falsification of his image by the Catholics. Contra the allegation of his dependence on the apostles (as Acts would have it), he straight away starts his letter by pointing out that his apostle is an "apostle not of men neither by men" (Gal. 1:1). What is more, he has Paul give information about the historical circumstances of his relationship to the Jerusalem apostles before him, viz. the exact information now needed by the Marcionites in order to legitimate themselves as a *sovereign* church. In the Marcionite version of Galatians ... Paul, after his revelation that came straight from God (1:16), did "not take up contact" with the Jerusalem Christians. That appears from the fact that ... he

---

1431. Doherty, *The Jesus Puzzle*, 107, 268, 305-7.
1432. Rom. 1:16-2:29 (possible omission of 2:1-16), 6:1-7:6, 8:3-28, 38-9, 12:1-2.
1433. I Cor. 2:1-16, 12:1-31, 14:1-4, 7-9, 23-5.
1434. L. Gordon Rylands, *A Critical Analysis of the Four Chief Pauline Epistles* (London: Watts & Co., 1929), 102-8, 199-202, 416.
1435. Kümmel, *Introduction to the New Testament*, 480-1.
1436. Detering, "The Dutch Radical Approach to the Pauline Epistles," 9-11.

Chapter 23. The Creation of Christianity

did not go immediately to Jerusalem. Only after fourteen years (2:1) did he go ... because of the problem of circumcision.[1437]

The only change I would make is that the Marcionites could have found an authentic Gnostic epistle of Paul's that they enlarged to suit their purposes. In fact, church sources actually state that Marcion had "found" or "discovered" the Epistle to the Galatians.[1438] If in their reworked epistle the Marcionites did in fact associate Paul with the Christians of Jerusalem, then according to the theory being advocated here, they would have been just as wrong in this regard as the Catholics!

As a result of all that has been discussed above, the following pieces of finformation should certainly be considered later additions to Paul's original epistles:

1. The list of the resurrection appearances.[1439]
2. All mention of the Lord's Supper and its institution.[1440]
3. All evidence of fellowship between Paul and the apostles of Jesus, most notably Paul's first and second visits to Jerusalem to meet with them.[1441]
4. The confrontation of Paul with Peter (Cephas) in Antioch.[1442]
5. Paul's persecution of the church before his conversion.[1443]
6. Paul's time in Damascus, and perhaps Arabia as well.[1444]
7. The statement of the Son of God's descent from king David.[1445]
8. The statement that the Jews in Judea killed Paul's Jesus.[1446]

Except for a few authentic epistles of the historical Paul (surviving as portions of the present epistles), which were written at some point before the destruction of Jerusalem in AD 70, all the other documents that make up the New Testament came into being sometime after that date. Through a complex

---

1437. Detering, "The Dutch Radical Approach to the Pauline Epistles," 10.
1438. Detering, "The Dutch Radical Approach to the Pauline Epistles," 8.
1439. I Cor. 15:3-11.
1440. I Cor. 11:17-34, 10:14-22.
1441. Gal. 1:17. 18-24, 2:1-10, I Cor. 9:1-7, I Th. 2:14-5. However, as was seen in the previous chapter, I take the designation "Pillars" (Gal. 2:9) and their names — James, Cephas (Peter), and John — to be authentic.
1442. Gal. 2:11-21.
1443. Gal. 1:13-14, I Cor. 15:9, Phil. 3:5-6.
1444. II Cor. 11:32-3, Gal. 1:17.
1445. Rom. 1:3.
1446. I Th. 2:14-5. This passage is even inaccurate for the historical Jesus, since based on earlier chapters only the Jewish *leaders* could be held responsible for his death, not all the Jews in Judea.

process of writing and revising these documents over a period of at least one hundred years, Christianity as evidenced by the New Testament came into being. In this process, a story of Christian beginnings emerged that was largely fictionalized, but acceptable to the growing church in Rome. Depictions were invented in this story for James the Righteous; Paul; Saul; Peter (Cephas); James and John, the sons of Zebedee; Simon Bar-Jona; Simon Magus; Barabbas; Judas Iscariot; and others.

To summarize, I would like to briefly describe the four sects discussed in the preceding chapters that believed in a Messiah figure before AD 70 and provided source material for the creation of the fictionalized story of Christian beginnings. As we have seen, historically there was no connection at all between the New Covenant, the Pauline Sect, and Historical Christianity. They only became merged when the official story of its beginnings had developed in the church in Rome:

1. The New Covenant, i.e., the Dead Sea Scroll Sect. James the Righteous certainly believed in a coming Messiah of Israel, who would free the righteous from the Romans and their Jewish collaborators. Judas the Galilean, the founder of the Sicarii, and Judas/Jesus, the twin brother of Jesus, were expected to be this personage in their time. However, they caused schisms in the sect and went out on their own. It is possible that other unknown individuals filled this position as well. However, like Judas the Galilean and Judas/Jesus they would have been declared false Messiahs for not successfully completing their messianic roles. James the Righteous became the leader of the Christians in the official story of it origins. Judas/Jesus became Barabbas in the New Testament and some sayings and actions attributed to Jesus may actually have originated with him.
2. The Pauline Sect. Paul received a special revelation from God of His Son, "Christ Jesus," who was crucified by demonic powers at the bottom plane of the ethereal part of the universe that was their domain along with the earth just below it. They were not aware of the true identity of this personage whom they crucified. When he rose from the dead, the demonic powers were defeated and lost control over their domains. Mankind was now freed from enslavement to them and could worship God the Father without restriction. His epistles were drastically revised to support the official story of Christian beginnings.
3. Historical Christianity. The three Pillars (i.e., Peter-Cephas and James and John, the sons of Zebedee) and the rest of the Twelve, who were subordinated to them, were the leaders of historical Christianity after the death and resurrection of Jesus. An explanation was needed in order to understand the incredible events they had witnessed. The answer they

came up with was as follows: Although Jesus had been crucified as the Suffering Servant of Isaiah, his resurrection proved that he was indeed the Son of Man and the Messiah (Christ). In due course, he would return triumphantly to punish the wicked (i.e., all non-believers) and to reward the righteous (i.e., all believers) at the Last Judgment. The former would suffer unending damnation in the underworld, but the latter would inherit God's eternal Kingdom on earth with Jesus sitting on his throne. Unfortunately, in arriving at their belief system the original teachings of Jesus were seriously distorted and a more popular portrait of him was created that better met the needs of the Twelve in their missionary endeavors.

4. The Simonian Sect. Simon Magus taught that he appeared on Mt. Sinai as the Father, then as the Messiah Jesus (though not in the flesh, but in appearance only), and later as the Paraclete (i.e., the Counselor). His followers believed that the spirit of the historical Jesus became embodied in him and that as Jesus *redivivus* he would expand upon Jesus' original teachings. It is likely that many of his followers had been believers in the historical Jesus before they joined him. At least one of the sources of John's gospel was derived from the followers of Simon.

Summary

The evidence shows that John the Baptist established the Dead Sea Scroll sect, which called itself the New Covenant, at the turn of the first century AD. Anti-establishment factions from all the sects of the time — the Pharisees, the Sadducees, and the Essenes — joined it, as well as certain Galileans, Samaritans and others. Although it was actually a new sect, it claimed to have originated as far back as 187 BC — twenty years before the Maccabean revolt (167 BC).

John's main tenet was this: By not properly observing the Torah in all its aspects according to his strict interpretation, the people coming to him for baptism and taking pride in their supposed Jewish ancestry had actually lost their identity as descendants of Abraham. John required them all to undergo a baptism of proselytes in order to become Jews again. Their repentance and acceptance of baptism would allow them to be members of the new Israel in which they would be able to practice the Torah in every detail. By proving their devotion to the Holy Word, God would send them a Messiah of Israel (i.e., a rightful King). He would take back their country from the Romans and the Jewish establishment that made concessions with them and in due time would become the ruler of the world.

We now know that baptism was only the *first step* in a long initiation process that might be taken by men in the sect. Only the outer public activity of John is recorded in the gospels and by the Jewish historian Josephus. The inner secretive organization of the New Covenant was unknown until the Dead Sea Scrolls came to light.

After the death of John the Baptist in AD 35, James the Righteous (usually referred to with the sobriquet "the Just"), a brother of Jesus, became the leader and high priest of the New Covenant.

The view has long been held that Jesus was not of true priestly descent. If this is so, then how was it possible for a brother of Jesus to occupy the high priestly office of the sect? A careful review of the evidence shows that Jesus' father Joseph *was* an authentic priest, i.e., he was descended from the tribe of Levi and the family of Aaron. Consequently, his sons Jesus, Judas, James, Joseph, and Simon were priests as well. Furthermore, because Jesus' mother Mary was descended from the tribe of Judah and the family of David and *not* Joseph as it is usually thought, the brothers could legitimately hold the kingly office also.

After James' death in AD 62, Symeon, the son of Clopas, another brother of Jesus, became the leader and chief priest and led a mass exodus of the sect to the "land of Damascus" in AD 65-6. This large land area was probably situated primarily on the eastern side of the Sea of Galilee and the Jordan River starting from just above the city of Pella in the Decapolis and extending northeastwards to just below the city of Damascus in Syria.

Church sources tell us that Symeon was the *cousin* of Jesus not his brother, even though Jesus *did* in fact have a brother named Simon (Simon is just another form of the name Symeon). However, I am persuaded that this belief developed only when the church for doctrinal reasons endeavored to make Jesus' actual brothers into his cousins. It did this by interpreting the word "brother" to mean "kin" and by creating a fictional brother of Joseph called Clopas, who was then said to be the actual father of Jesus' brothers. In reality, the name Clopas is probably an alias for Joseph, the father of Jesus.

Furthermore, James and Symeon are portrayed as Christians, i.e., believers in Jesus. I take this idea to be unhistorical also. Later Christians could simply not accept the idea that relatives of Jesus — be they cousins or brothers — were *not* Christians. In actuality, James, Symeon, and even John the Baptist could not have regarded Jesus — who left the New Covenant and did not follow the Torah on many points — as anything but a false prophet.

This view goes a long way to explain the beliefs of the Mandaean community living in the Tigris-Euphrates valley. To this day they venerate John the Baptist as a great prophet, but regard Jesus as a liar or false Messiah.

It turns out that another unhistorical tenet is that the Christians migrated en masse to the Hellenistic city of Pella in the Decapolis before the Roman siege of Jerusalem (AD 70). As I understand it, the actual mass exodus of the New

Covenant to the land of Damascus (AD 65-6) was the source for the alleged flight of the first Christians across the Jordan River.

Not long after James the Righteous became the leader of the sect, Ananus, who was born into a prominent high priestly family in Jerusalem, caused a schism in the New Covenant. He took a large number of priests, levites, and laymen with him. They joined or rejoined the Jewish establishment in Jerusalem as a sort of private association. Ananus actually became the establishment High Priest for three months in AD 62.

It was through his machinations that James the Righteous was killed. The historical Saul (*not* the composite Saul/Paul of Acts), a hired ruffian of Ananus, pushed him off the pinnacle of the Temple and another of his men finished him off with a wooden club when he hit the pavement below. This was the penalty meted out to James for entering the Temple Holy of Holies on the Day of Atonement as the rightful High Priest was authorized to do. Although the Sanhedrin formally condemned him and his accomplices to be stoned for the action several months later, it could not carry out the death penalty. Under the Roman occupation, it lost the power to do so. The executions of those condemned by it had to be carried out by clandestine means. James' death was handled in just this way and it is clearly alluded to in a passage of the Habakkuk Commentary (11:2-8) from the Dead Sea Scrolls.

It turns out that James was the Teacher of Righteousness and Ananus was the Wicked Priest/Man of Lies in the Dead Sea Scrolls. It is this identification of James with the Teacher of Righteousness that makes spurious the Christian claim that he was a believer in Jesus.

Although left curiously unmentioned by scholars, the discovery of microletters on first century AD coins has finally proven *beyond doubt* the actual existence of Jesus. Most importantly, they reveal to us the actual time period of his public ministry and the date of his crucifixion (at Passover in April, AD 21). Furthermore, they give us valuable information that corrects the dates of the periods when some Roman governors held office.

I offer this hypothesis about Jesus: He was expected to be the Messiah of Israel. However, because he could not accept many of the sect's doctrines, he left the New Covenant and went on a journey of discovery. Since nothing is known about it, this period of his life has been called the "lost years." He appeared again in AD 15/16 to begin his mission.

Jesus' twin brother Judas, the second oldest male in the family, took his place in the New Covenant and was expected to become the Messiah of Israel. However, in AD 15/16, he caused a schism in the New Covenant, took many laymen and perhaps some levites and priests with him, and prematurely declared himself to be the Messiah of Israel. Taking the "throne name" *Jesus*, he became a rebel against the Romans and the Jewish establishment that made concessions with them. In the gospels, Barabbas actually represents Jesus' twin brother.

Jesus' message was this: When all people came to the full realization that they were brothers and sisters of each other and sons and daughters of the One Father, the Kingdom of God on earth would finally come. Inner spiritual transformation in individuals was needed first. As more and more people changed inside, the world outside would change accordingly. When the light had finally come to all people, God Himself would take the final step. The earth would be transformed into a paradise and evil would be eradicated forever. Death would be a thing of the past and everyone would live in perpetual peace, health, and happiness. When this transformation finally came, all God's offspring would partake in it.

In the first century AD, the Jews were practicing a fanatical form of ritual purity that allowed them to reject people based on their seeming uncleanness as determined by their purity code. The unfortunate results of this practice were the arbitrary separating of people into two groups (i.e., the clean and the unclean) and the disregard for the inner goodness of people.

Furthermore, the coming of a warrior Messiah was also hoped for, who would wipe out all the impure Gentiles and free the nation from the power of the Romans and their Jewish appeasers. However, Israel was really supposed to bring enlightenment to the Gentiles not war.

Jesus taught that if they refused to change their ways a terrible catastrophe would befall them, i.e., Jerusalem and the Temple would be destroyed in a military attack. This catastrophe would not come as a consequence of the Father punishing them for their sins, but as a consequence of their own intentional thoughts and actions. In the East, this concept is called karma.

He began his mission by sending out messengers — twelve to his countrymen and seventy (-two) to the nations of the world. Unfortunately, in not having the unshakable faith of their master, they soon returned with little success in conveying the message to the masses.

Meanwhile, Jesus was gaining a reputation as a great healer also. Larger and larger crowds would gather around him to watch him cure people of various maladies, as well as to listen to him teach about the Kingdom of God. He was also stirring up controversy by disobeying the Torah on many points and not keeping the Sabbath properly.

The Jewish authorities became concerned about Jesus' activities. He was summoned to appear before them for trial where he was condemned as a false prophet. However, since they were not able to impose the death penalty under the Roman occupation, they let him go and waited for the chance to bring about his death secretly.

Several days before Passover in AD 21, Jesus was healing and teaching the people on the Mount of Olives just outside of Jerusalem. When they saw his amazing ability to heal and perform other miraculous acts, the idea came over them that perhaps he could use his mysterious power to free them from the Romans. Their political excitement escalated to the point where Jesus was forced to withdraw from the crowd. Suddenly, Judas/*Jesus* made his move. He took his brother's place and his men, who were dispersed throughout the crowd, tried to excite the people even more. The result was a full-fledged revolt. They all took up weapons that had been hidden on the Mount of Olives and entered Jerusalem.

Two sites were taken in the city: the Temple with its Antonia fortress in the north of the city and the tower of Siloam in the south. The Roman troops stationed at Herod's palace in the west of the city were not strong enough to put down the revolt. The Sanhedrin sent a message to the governor Pilate, who was at Caesarea on the coast. With the aid of additional troops and siege machinery, he was able to crush the revolt by the afternoon of Passover eve (the 15th of April, AD 21). Unfortunately, the leader of the revolt could not be found, because he escaped through secret tunnels underneath the city. Pilate was infuriated that the situation had gotten so far out of hand and that the leader was still at large. In endeavoring to pacify the populace, many innocent people might be killed along with the guilty. What was to be done?

The answer came from Jesus himself and was sent to the high priest Caiaphus through an intermediary. He would be willing to deliver himself up and take the place of his brother Judas/*Jesus* in order to stop further bloodshed. The Jewish authorities accepted the offer and the secret plan was put into operation. At the Roman trial, Jesus was sentenced to be crucified as a rebel against Rome and his life came to an end before dawn on the 16th of April, Passover of AD 21. Pilate was satisfied that the supposed leader of the revolt was executed and Caiaphus was satisfied that a false prophet received his due and that his country was saved from Roman retribution.

After the resurrection appearances, the three Pillars (i.e., Peter-Cephas and James and John, the sons of Zebedee) and the rest of the Twelve, who were subordinated to them, became the leaders of the Christians. In order to make sense out of everything they experienced, they came to believe that, although Jesus had been crucified as the "Suffering Servant" of Isaiah, his resurrection proved that he was indeed the "Son of Man" and the Messiah (Christ). At the Last Judgment, he would return triumphantly to punish the wicked (i.e., the unbelievers) and reward the righteous (i.e., the believers). The former would suffer eternal punishment in the underworld and the latter would inherit God's Kingdom on earth forever. Unfortunately, in reaching this explanation of the events they witnessed the original teachings of Jesus were significantly altered and a more acceptable portrait of him was created to aid in their proselytizing efforts. At some point during his reign (AD 41-4), Herod Agrippa I beheaded James and John, the sons of Zebedee, and at a later date, tradition has it that Peter-Cephas was crucified by the order of Emperor Nero.

It is not known what ultimately happened to Judas/*Jesus*, but there are at least three possibilities:

1. He is to be identified with the troublemaker Theudas, who was beheaded by the Roman governor Fadus in AD 46.
2. He took his own life.
3. He eventually converted to Christianity and became a famous apostle of the faith.

The gospel of John has always been a problem, because it is so different from the three synoptic gospels. Two questions that need to be asked are the following: Why are Jesus' utterances in John so completely different from Jesus' utterances in the synoptic gospels? Also, who or what is the Paraclete (i.e., the Counselor) who was expected to appear sometime after the death and resurrection of Jesus? The ranting and raving egomaniac of John was *not* Jesus and the Paraclete was *not* a disembodied spirit (i.e., the Holy Spirit). Simon Magus (i.e., the Magician) is the one to be identified with both of these. His followers believed that the spirit of the historical Jesus became embodied in him and that, as Jesus *redivivus*, he would add further revelations to Jesus' original teachings. It turns out that at least one of the sources utilized by the writer of John's gospel originated with the followers of Simon Magus.

Paul was never actually a believer in the historical Jesus. He received a special revelation from God of His Son Jesus Christ or Christ Jesus, who was crucified by demonic powers at the bottom plane of the ethereal part of the universe that was their domain and was situated just above the earth. Since they were not aware of the personage whom they crucified, when he rose from the dead the demonic powers were defeated. Since they controlled the earth also, they could no longer enslave mankind. The barrier that had existed between God and man had been broken. It was only later, when his authentic epistles were drastically revised, that Paul was made into a believer in the historical Jesus. According to tradition, he was beheaded in Rome by order of Emperor Nero about the same time as Peter-Cephas was crucified.

Through a complex writing and revising process starting after the destruction of Jerusalem in AD 70 and continuing well into the second century AD, New Testament Christianity came into existence along with its official story of beginnings that was largely legendary.

Chronological Chart of Rulers

Ruler	Ruler's Title	Date
The Syrian King, Antiochus IV Epiphanes, attacks Jerusalem and loots the Temple.	--	169 BC
Mattathias	--	167-166 BC
Judas Maccabeus	--	166-161 BC
Jonathan	Ruler and High Priest	161-143/2 BC
Simon	Ruler and High Priest	143/2-135/4 BC
John Hyrcanus I	Ruler and High Priest	135/4-104 BC
Aristobulus I	King and High Priest	104-103 BC
Alexander Jannaeus	King and High Priest	103-76 BC
Salome Alexandra	Queen (Hyrcanus II, High Priest)	76-67 BC
Aristobulus II	King and High Priest	67-63 BC
The Roman General Pompey captures Jerusalem.		63 BC
Hyrcanus II	High Priest	63-40 BC
Antigonus	King and High Priest	40-37 BC
Herod the Great	King	37-4 BC
Herod Antipas	Ruler of Galilee and Peraea	4 BC-AD 39
Archelaus	Ruler of Judaea, Samaria, and Idumaea	4 BC-AD 6
First Series of Roman Governors	Governors of Judaea, Samaria, and Idumaea	AD 6-41
Herod Agrippa I	King	AD 41-4
Second Series of Roman Governors	Governors of all Palestine	AD 44-66
Herod Agrippa II	King of several areas and as the "curator of the temple," appointed High Priests in Jerusalem	AD 50-(?)92/3
The Jewish Revolt. The Roman General Titus destroys Jerusalem and the Temple.		AD 66-70

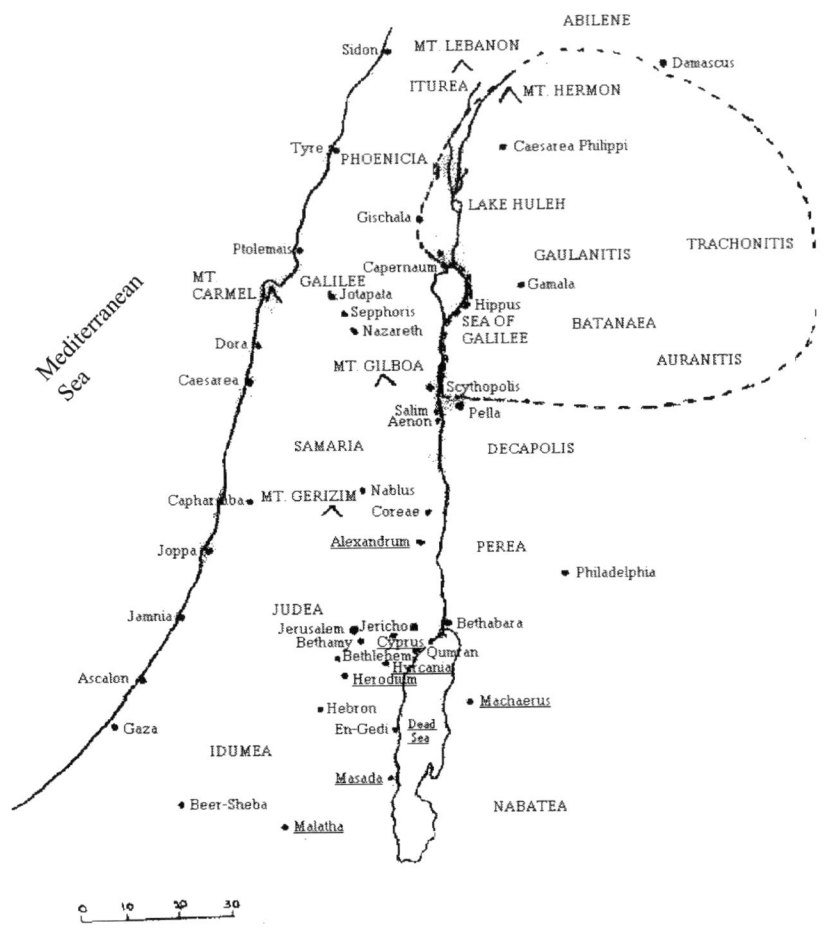

Major cities in Israel - first century A.D.

Notes

1. The area inside the broken line is the "Land of Damascus" (also called the "Desert of the Peoples").
2. Underlined names are fortresses.

Summary

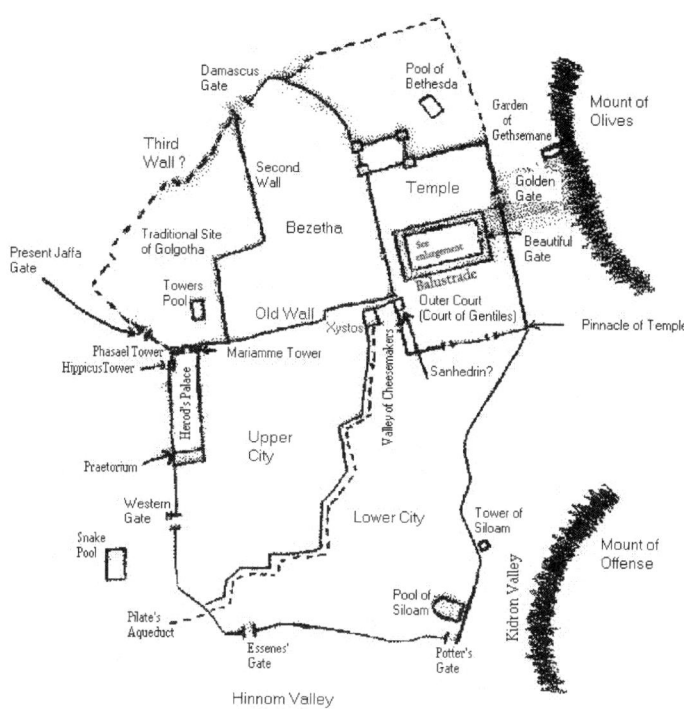

Map of Jerusalem - first century A.D.

Below: Temple layout

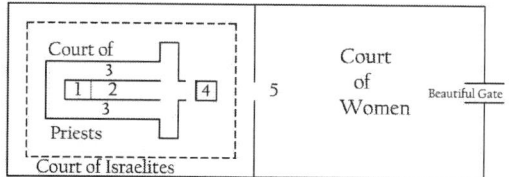

1. Holy of Holies
2. Holy Place
3. Priests' Chambers
4. Altar
5. Corinthian Gate

Bibliography

Books

Achtemeier, Paul J. *The Quest for Unity in the New Testament Church.* Philadelphia: Fortress Press, 1987.

Allegro, J. M. *The Dead Sea Scrolls: A Reappraisal.* 2nd. ed. New York: Penguin Books, 1964.

    The Treasure of the Copper Scroll. 2nd. ed. New York: Doubleday & Co., 1964.

    Discoveries in the Judaean Desert. Qumran Cave 4. Vol. V. Oxford: Clarendon Press, 1968.

    The Dead Sea Scrolls and the Christian Myth. Buffalo: Prometheus Books, 1984.

Arnold, T. *The Roman System of Provincial Administration.* New York: Libraries Press, 1971.

Bammel, E., and Moule, C. F. D., eds. *Jesus and the Politics of His Day.* Cambridge: Cambridge University Press, 1985.

Borg, Marcus J. *Jesus A New Vision.* San Francisco: Harper, 1987.

    Meeting Jesus Again for the First Time. San Francisco: Harper, 1994.

    Conflict, Holiness, and Politics in the Teachings of Jesus. Harrisburg: Trinity Press International, 1998.

Brandon, S. G. F. *Jesus and the Zealots.* New York: Charles Scribner's Sons, 1967.

    The Fall of Jerusalem and the Christian Church. 2nd ed. London: S.P.C.K., 1968.

Brown, Francis. *The New Brown-Driver-Briggs-Gesenius Hebrew and English Lexicon.* Peabody: Hendrickson Publishers, 1979.

Brownlee, William H. *The Midrash Pesher of Habakkuk.* Missoula: Scholars Press, 1979.

Bruce, F. F. *New Testament History.* Garden City: Anchor Books, 1969.

    Jesus and Christian Origins Outside the New Testament. Grand Rapids: Eerdmans, 1977.

Burrows, Millar. *The Dead Sea Scrolls.* New York: Viking Press, 1955.

    More Light on the Dead Sea Scrolls. London: Secker & Warburg, 1958.

Buttrick, G., ed. *Interpreter's Dictionary of the Bible.* 4 vols. New York: Abingdon, 1962; supp. vol. By K. Crim, ed., 1976.

Charlesworth, James H., ed. *The Old Testament Pseudepigrapha.* 2 vols. Garden City: Doubleday & Co., 1985.

Cook, Edward E. *Solving the Mysteries of the Dead Sea Scrolls*. Grand Rapids: Zondervan Publishing House, 1994.

Cook, S. A., Adcock, F. E., and Charlesworth, M. P., eds. *The Cambridge Ancient History*. Vols. VII-X. Cambridge: University Press, 1952.

Danby, Herbert. *The Mishnah*. Oxford: Oxford University Press, 1933.

Davies, A. Powell. *The First Christian: A Study of St. Paul and Christian Origins*. New York: New American Library, 1959.

Davies, Philip R. *1QM, the War Scroll from Qumran — Its Structure and History*. Rome: Biblical Institute Press, 1977.

Davis, W. S. *A Day in Old Rome*. New York: Biblio and Tannen, 1963.

DeLamotte, Roy C. *The Alien Christ*. Lanham: University Press of America, 1980.

De Vaux, R. *Archaeology and the Dead Sea Scrolls*. London: Oxford University Press, 1973.

Doherty, Earl. *The Jesus Puzzle*. Ottawa: Canadian Humanist Press, 1999.

Driver, G. R. *The Judaean Scrolls-The Problem and a Solution*. New York: Schocken Books, 1965.

Dupont-Sommer, A. *The Dead Sea Scrolls-A Preliminary Survey*. trans. by E. Margaret Rowley. Oxford: Basil Blackwell, 1952.

The Essene Writings from Qumran. trans. by G. Vermes. Gloucester: Peter Smith, 1973.

Eisenman, Robert. *The Dead Sea Scrolls and the First Christians*. Rockport: Element, 1996.

Eisler, Robert. *The Messiah Jesus and John the Baptist*. Eng. ed. by A. H. Krappe. London: Methuen & Co., 1931.

The Enigma of the Fourth Gospel. London: Methuen & Co., 1938.

Ehrman, Bart D. *Jesus Apocalyptic Prophet of the New Millennium*. Oxford: University Press, 1999.

Elliger, K., and Rudolph, W. eds. *Biblical Hebraica Struttgartensia*. Stuttgart: Deutsche Bibelgesellschaft, 1984.

Errico, Rocco A. *The Message of Matthew*. Irvine: Noohra Foundation, 1991.

Let There Be Light. Santa Fe: Noohra Foundation, 1994.

Eusebius. *The Ecclesiastical History*. 2 vols. trans. by Kirsopp Lake. Cambridge: Harvard University Press, 1975.

Finegan, Jack. *The Archeology of the New Testament*. rev. ed. Princeton: Princeton University Press, 1992.

Furneaux, Rupert. *The Roman Siege of Jerusalem*. New York: David McKay Co., 1972.

Gaster, Theodor H. *The Dead Sea Scriptures*. 3rd. ed. New York: Anchor Books, 1976.

Ginzberg, Louis. *An Unknown Jewish Sect*. New York: Jewish Theological Seminary, 1976 (revised and updated translation of the author's 1922 German edition).

Golb, Norman. *Who Wrote the Dead Sea Scrolls?* New York: Scribner, 1995.

Goldstein, Morris. *Jesus in the Jewish Tradition*. New York: The Macmillan Co., 1950.

Gospel Parallels A Synopsis of the First Three Gospels. New York: Thomas Nelson & Sons, 1949.

Gruber, Elmar R. & Kersten, Holger. *The Original Jesus*. Great Britain: Element Books, 1995.

Harris, Rendel. *The Twelve Apostles*. Cambridge: W. Heffer & Sons, 1927.

Harvey, Andrew. *Son of Man The Mystical Path to Christ*. New York: Jeremy P. Tarcher/Putnam, 1998.

Hengel, Martin. *The Zealots*. trans. by David Smith. Edinburgh: T. & T. Clark, 1989.

Hollady, W. L., ed. *A Concise Hebrew and Aramaic Lexicon of the Old Testament*. Grand Rapids: Eerdmans, 1971.

Horgan, Maurya P. *Pesharim: Qumran Interpretations of Biblical Books*. Washington: Catholic Biblical Assoc. of America, 1979.

Husband, R. W. *The Prosecution of Jesus*. Princeton, 1916.

Isser, S. J. The Dositheans: A Samaritan Sect in Late Antiquity. Leiden: Brill, 1976.

Jack, J. W. *The Historic Christ: An Examination of Dr. Robert Eisler's Theory*. London: James Clarke & Co., 1933.

Jeremias, Joachim. *Jerusalem in the Time of Jesus*. Philadelphia: Fortress Press, 1969.

Josephus, Flavius. *Jewish Antiquities. Jewish War. The Life. Against Apion*. trans. by H. St. J. Thackeray, R. Marcus, and L. H. Feldman. 10 vols. (Loeb Classical Library) Cambridge: Harvard University Press, 1925-65.

Kautzsch, E., ed. *Gesenius' Hebrew Grammar*. 2nd. ed. Oxford: Clarendon Press, 1910.

Kee, Howard, C. *The Origins of Christianity: Sources and Documents*. Englewood Cliffs: Prentice-Hall, 1973.

Klausner, J. *Jesus of Nazareth: His Life, Times, and Teachings*. trans. by H. Danby. New York: Bloch Publishing Co., 1989.

Kobelski, Paul J. *Melchizedek and Melchiresa*. Washington, DC: The Catholic Biblical Association of America, 1981.

Kümmel, W. G. *Introduction to the New Testament*. 17th ed. trans. by H. C. Kee. New York: Abingdon, 1975.

Kuntz, G. *The Text of the Epistles*. London: Oxford University Press, 1953.

Larson, Martin A. *The Story of Christian Origins*. Washington, D.C: a Joseph J. Binns/New Republic Book, 1977.

Mack, Burton L. *The Lost Gospel The Book of Q & Christian Origins*. San Francisco: Harper, 1993.

Maier, Johann. *The Temple Scroll: An Introduction, Translation & Commentary*. Sheffield: JSOT Press, 1985.

Martinez, Florentino Garcia and Tigchelaar, Eibert J. C., eds. and trans. *The Dead Sea Scrolls Study Edition*. 2 vols. Leiden: Brill, 1997.

Mattingly, H. *Roman Imperial Civilization*. London: Edward Arnold, 1959.

May, Herbert G., and Metzger, Bruce M., eds. *The New Oxford Annotated Bible*. New York: Oxford University Press, 1973.

McBirnie, William Stevart. *The Search for the Twelve Apostles*. Wheaton: Living Books, 1973.

Mead, G. R. S. *The Gnositc John the Baptizer*. London: John M. Watkins, 1924.

Metzger, Bruce M., ed. *The Oxford Annotated Apocrypha*. New York: Oxford University Press, 1977.

Miller, Robert J., ed. *The Complete Gospels*. San Francisco: Harper, 1994.

Mitchell, Stephen. *The Gospel According to Jesus*. New York: HarperCollins, 1991.

Morrison, W. D. *The Jews Under Roman Rule*. London, 1890.

Nolan, Albert. *Jesus Before Christianity*. Maryknoll: Orbis Books, 1993.

Pagels, Elaine. *The Gnostic Gospels*. New York: Vintage Books, 1981.

Parrinder, Geoffrey. *Jesus in the Qur'an*. New York: Oxford University Press, 1977.

Pike, Diane Kennedy, and Kennedy, R. Scott. *The Wilderness Revolt*. New York: Doubleday & Co., 1972.

Philo. *The Embassy to Gaius*. Vol. X. F. H. Colson and J. W. Earp, trans. (The Loeb Classical Library) Cambridge: Harvard University Press, 1971.

Powell, Mark Allen. *Jesus as a Figure in History*. Louisville: John Knox Press, 1998.

Rabin, C. *Qumran Studies*. New York: Schocken Books, 1957.

Rhoads, David M. *Israel in Revolution: 6-74 C. E.* Philadelphia: Fortress Press, 1976.

Roberts, Rev. Alexander, and Donaldson, James. *The Ante-Nicene Fathers*. Vol. VIII. Grand Rapids: Eerdmans, 1981.

Robinson, James M., ed. *The Nag Hammadi Library*. San Francisco: Harper & Row, 1977.

Roth, Cecil. *The Dead Sea Scrolls: A New Historical Approach.* New York: W. W. Norton & Co., 1965.

Rousseau, John J. and Arav, Rami. *Jesus and His World.* Minneapolis: Fortress Press, 1995.

Rowley, H. H. *The Teacher of Righteousness and the Dead Sea Scrolls.* Manchester: Manchester University Press, 1957.

The Zadokite Fragments and the Dead Sea Scrolls. Oxford: Blackwell, 1952.

Rylands, L. Gordon. *A Critical Analysis of the Four Chief Pauline Epistles.* London: Watts & Co., 1929.

Sale, George, trans. *The Koran.* London: Frederick Warne and Co. Ltd., 1939.

Schechter, S. *Documents of Jewish Sectaries.* Vol. I. Cambridge University University Press, 1910; reprint, KTAV Publishing House, 1970.

Schiffman, Lawrence H. *Who Was a Jew? Rabbinic and Halakhic Perspectives on the Jewish-Christian Schism.* Hoboken: KTAV Publishing House, 1985.

Schoeps, Hans-Joachim. *Jewish Christianity.* trans. by Douglas R. A. Hare. Philadelphia: Fortress Press, 1969.

Schonfield, Hugh J. *Secrets of the Dead Sea Scrolls.* London: Jewish Chronicle Publications, 1956.

The Jesus Party. New York: Macmillan, 1974.

Schurer, Emil. *The History of the Jewish People in the Age of Jesus Christ.* Vols. I, II, III.1, III.2, rev. and ed. by Geza Vermes, et al. Edinburgh: T. & T. Clark, 1973/87.

Schweitzer, Albert. *The Quest of the Historical Jesus.* First Complete Edition. John Bowden, ed. Minneapolis: Fortress Press, 2001.

Silberman, Neil Asher. *The Hidden Scrolls.* New York: G. P. Putman's Sons, 1994.

Talbert, Charles H. ed. *Reimarus: Fragments.* Ralph S. Fraser, trans. Philadelphia: Fortress Press, 1970.

Tacitus, *Histories, Annals.* trans. by C. H. Moore and J. Jackson (Loeb Classical Library) 4 vols. Cambridge: Harvard University Press, 1979.

Tatum, W. Barnes. *In Quest of Jesus: A Guidebook.* Atlanta: John Knox Press, 1982.

Thiering, B. E. *Redating the Teacher of Righteousness.* Sydney: Theological Explorations, 1979.

Vardaman, Jerry and Yamauchi, Edwin M., eds. *Chronos, Kairos, Christos.* Winona Lake: Eisenbrauns, 1989.

Vermes, Geza. *Jesus the Jew.* Philadelphia: Fortress Press, 1981.

The Dead Sea Scrolls in English. 3rd ed. New York: Penguin Books, 1987.

The Dead Sea Scrolls: Qumran in Perspective. Philadelphia: Fortress Press, 1981.

Wells, G. A. *Did Jesus Exist?* 2nd ed. London: Pemberton, 1986.

Williamson, G. A. *Josephus The Jewish War.* Harmondsworth: Penguin Books, 1959.

Wilson, R. M. *The Execution of Jesus.* New York: Charles Scribner's Sons, 1970.

Wise, Michael, Abegg, Jr., Martin, and Cook, Edward. *The Dead Sea Scrolls: A New Translation.* San Francisco: Harper, 1996.

Wright, N. T. *Who Was Jesus?* Grand Rapids: Eerdmans, 1993.

Yadin, Yigael. *The Temple Scroll: The Hidden Law of the Dead Sea Sect.* New York: Random House, 1985.

Yamauchi, Edwin M. *Pre-Christian Gnosticism.* 2nd ed. Grand Rapids: Baker Book House, 1983.

Zaehner, R. C., ed. *Encyclopedia of the World's Religions.* New York: Barnes and Noble, 1988.

Articles

Aus, Roger D. "Three Pillars and Three Patriarchs: A Proposal Concerning Gal. 2^9." *Zeitchift für die neutestamentliche wissenchaft.* 70 (1979): 252-61.

Beckwith, R. T. "The Significance of the Calendar for Interpreting Essene Chronology and Eschatology." *Revue de Qumran* 10 (1980): 167-202.

Cook, Edward E. "A Ritual Purification Center." *Biblical Archaeology Review* (Nov./Dec.1996): 39, 48-51, 73-5.

Creed, J. M. "The Slavonic Version of Josephus' History of the Jewish War." *Harvard Theological Review* 25 (1932): 277-319.

Detering, Hermann. "The Dutch Radical Approach to the Pauline Epistles." *Journal of Higher Criticism.* 3/2 (Fall 1996): 163-93 (1-23, downloaded from the following web address: http://www.depts.drew.edu/jhc).

Doughty, Darrell. "Pauline Paradigms and Pauline Authenticity." *Journal of Higher Criticism* 1 (Fall 1996): 95-128.

Drower, E. S. "Mandaean Polemic." *Journal of the School of Oriental and African Studies* 25 (1962): 438-48.

Dunkerley, R. "The Riddles of Josephus." *Hibbert Journal* 53 (1954-5): 127-34.

Eisler, Robert. "The Paraclete Problem." *The Quest* 21 (January 1930): 113-28.

"The Paraclete Claimant-Simon Magus." *The Quest* 21 (April 1930): 225-43.

"The Evangel of Kerinthos: The Book of Lazarus-the Beloved Disciple." *The Quest* 21 (July 1930): 340-57.

"The Sadokite Book of the New Covenant-Its Date and Origin." *Occident and Orient* (Gaster Anniversary Volume) B. Schindler, ed. London: Taylor's Foreign Press, 1936, 110-43.

Ford, J. Massingberd. "Can We Exclude Samaritan Influence from Qumran?" *Revue de Qumran* 6 (1967): 109-29.

Golb, Norman. "The Problem of Origin and Identification of the Dead Sea Scrolls." *Proceedings of the American Philosophical Society* 124 (February 1980): 1-24.

"Who Hid the Dead Sea Scrolls?" *Biblical Archaeologist* 48 (1985): 68-82.

Hengel, M. Charlesworth, J. H. and Mendels, D. "The Polemical Character of 'On Kingship' in the Temple Scroll: An Attempt at Dating 11Q Temple." *Journal of Jewish Studies* 37 (1986): 28-38.

Kingdon, H. P. "Had the Crucifixion a Political Significance?" *Hibbert Journal* 35 (1936/37): 556-67.

Lehmann, Manfred R. "Where the Temple Tax Was Buried." *Biblical Archaeology Review* 19 (1993): 38-43.

Ludemann, Gerd. "The Successors of Pre-70 Jerusalem Christianity: A Critical Evaluation of the Pella-Tradition." *Jewish and Christian Self-Definition.* Ed. by E. P. Sanders. Vol. I. Philadelphia: Fortress Press, 1980: 161-73, 245-54.

Mead, G. R. S. "The Gnostic John the Baptizer." *The Quest* (October 1925): 1-24.

"The First Gnostic Community of John the Baptizer." *The Quest* (January 1926): 179-97.

Meier, John P. "Jesus in Josephus: A Modest Proposal." *Catholic Biblical Quarterly* 52 (1990): 76-103.

Milgrom, J. "The Temple Scroll." *Biblical Archaeologist* 41 (1978): 105-20.

North, Robert. "The Qumran 'Sadducees.'" *Catholic Biblical Quarterly* 17 (1955): 164-88.

O'Neill, J. C. "Jesus in Hebrews." *Journal of Higher Criticism* 6/1 (Spring 1999): 64-82.

Palumbo, Arthur. "1QpHab 11:2-8 and the Death of James the Just." *The Qumran Chronicle* Vol. 3, No. 1-3 (December 1993): 139-52.

Qimron, E. and Strugnell, J. "An Unpublished Halakhic Letter from Qumran." *Biblical Archeology Today: Proceedings of the International Congress on Biblical Archeology Jerusalem, April 1984*. Jerusalem: Israel Exploration Society, 1985: 400-7.

Rabinowitz, I. "A Reconsideration of 'Damascus' and '390 Years' in the 'Damascus' ('Zadokite') Fragments." *Journal of Biblical Literature* 73 (1954): 11-35.

Schiffman, Lawrence. "The Significance of the Scrolls." *Bible Review* 6, no. 5 (October 1990): 18-27, 52.

Shanks, Hershel. "Searching for Essenes At Ein Gedi, Not Qumran." *Biblical Archaeology Review* 28 (2002):18-27, 60.

Silberman, L. H. "Unriddling the Riddle, A Study in the Structure and Language of the Habakkuk Pesher." *Revue de Qumran* III, no. 11 (1961): 323-64.

Sowers, Sidney. "The Circumstances and Recollection of the Pella Flight." *Theologische Zeitschrift* 26 (1970): 305-20.

Tzaferis, Vassilios. "Crucifixion — The Archaeological Evidence." *Biblical Archaeology Review* 11 (1985): 44-53.

Walker, Jr., William O. "The Burden of Proof in Identifying Interpolations in the Pauline Letters." *New Testament Studies* 33 (1987): 610-8.

Williamson, H. G. M. "The Translation of 1QpHab, 5, 10." *Revue de Qumran* 9 (1977): 263-5.

Wilson, A, M. and Wills, L. "Literary Sources of the Temple Scroll," *Harvard Theological Review* 75 (1982): 275-88.

INDEX

11QMelch, 148, 149, 150, 153, 164
4Q Testmonia (4QTest), 137
4QMMT, 14, 142, 164

Acts of the Apostles, 253, 273, 276
Aelia Capitolina, 270
Against Apion, 5, 295
Albinus, 88, 96, 105, 106, 126, 141, 199
Alexander Jannaeus, 12, 22, 57-60, 65, 66, 159, 287
Alpheus, 168
Annius Rufus, 176
Antigonus, 12, 66, 160, 287
Antiochus III, 65
Antiochus IV Epiphanes, 48, 52,-54, 58, 59, 220, 287
Antiochus VII Sidetes, 57-58
Antipater II, 67
Antony, 66, 71
Apocalypse of Peter, 194
Archelaus, 18, 19, 31, 41, 42, 73, 74, 76, 287
Aristobulus II, 12, 60, 61, 140, 287
Aristobulus III, 140
Athronges, 18, 19, 76, 174
Augustus, 18, 19, 70-72, 76, 80, 122

Bannus, 42, 45
Barabbas, 180-182, 187, 188, 191, 193, 195, 202, 278, 284
Basilides, 193
Berenice, 141, 143
Bo-anerges, 255
Boethus, 12, 13, 18, 20, 48, 63, 68
Boethusians, 12, 13
Borg, Marcus J., 196, 293
Branch of David, 113
Brandon, S. G. F., 102, 104, 186, 219, 224, 237, 293
Brownlee, William H., 5, 293
Builders of the Wall, 48

C. Sosius, 123
Caiaphus, 181, 215, 216, 217, 285
Celsus, 193
Cestius Gallus, 123, 135, 154, 266
Chief Priest, 75, 76, 77, 113, 164
Claudius, 240, 248, 268
Clementine Homilies, 244
Cleophas, 168
Clopas, 48, 75, 85, 86, 113, 139, 151, 152, 154, 164, 168, 169, 170, 172, 173, 282
Congregation of Traitors, 48
Coponius, 19, 105, 176
Copper Scroll, 163, 164, 293
Council of the Community, 26- 29, 33, 34, 37, 44, 78, 127, 200
Cuspius Fadus, 268
Cypros, 31, 67, 143

Damascus, 4, 48, 49, 50, 52-55, 56, 61, 72, 75, 79, 81, 84-87, 113, 115, 139, 152, 153, 156, 157, 160-162, 164, 170, 265, 266, 270, 271, 277, 282, 283, 298
Damascus Document (CD), 4, 49
Day of Atonement, 101, 106, 107, 108, 149, 153, 171, 236, 283
Day of Judgment, 146, 147, 149, 151, 154, 156
De Vaux, R., 294
Demetrius I Soter, 56, 59
Demetrius III Eucerus, 57, 58, 133
Domitian, 172, 173, 223
Doris, wife of Herod, 68
Dositheus, 14, 15, 48, 83, 84, 85, 87, 113, 160, 164, 244, 245, 250, 251
Dupont-Sommer, A., 4, 5, 22, 115, 116, 294

Egyptian (The), 249
Eisenman, Robert, 91, 294
Eisler, Robert, 3, 4, 19, 29, 41, 42, 73, 81, 96, 98, 101, 103, 105, 106, 109, 158, 173, 222-224, 228, 230, 232, 237, 238, 239, 246, 247, 249, 294, 295, 297
Elizabeth, mother of John the Baptist, 170, 172

End of Days, 48
Ephraim and/or Manasseh, 36, 111
Epistle to the Galatians, 276, 277
Essenes, 4, 9, 10, 11, 12, 15, 16, 17, 18, 20-22, 27, 66, 162, 167, 168, 197, 281, 294, 297, 298
Eusebius, 97, 98, 101, 170, 176, 228, 248, 269, 270, 294

First Letter of Clement, 274
First Ones, 48, 49
First Visitation, 48

Gessius Florus, 50, 131
Gospel of Mary, 209
Gospel of Peter, 218
Gospel of Thomas, 209, 241

Habakkuk Commentary (1QpHab), 5
Hasmonaeans, 12, 51, 113, 171, 174
Herald (The), 148, 149, 164
Herod Agrippa I, 19, 88, 107, 135, 138, 142, 143, 144, 227, 235, 238, 253, 255, 266, 267, 286, 287
Herod Agrippa II, 88, 107, 135, 138, 144, 266, 287
Herod Antipas, 18, 31, 81, 115, 149, 287
Herod the Great, 2, 11-13, 17-19, 31, 66, 67, 94, 123, 138, 140, 144, 164, 173, 174, 179, 226, 287
Hilkiah, 64, 149
House of Absalom, 94, 95
House of Judah, 50, 147
House of Peleg, 48
Hymn Scroll (1QH), 115

Idumaeans, 67, 111, 135
II Peter, 274
Interpreter (The), 48, 84, 113, 152, 293
Interpreter of the Torah, 48, 113, 152

James and John, sons of Zebedee, 140, 253, 254, 255, 267, 278, 285
James the Righteous, 3, 48, 83, 87, 91, 96, 113, 116, 145, 150, 160, 164, 170, 190, 240, 245, 253, 256, 266, 278, 282, 283
Jerusalem, 4, 9, 14, 17, 20-23, 31, 35, 46, 48, 54, 55, 56, 57, 58, 59, 60, 61, 65, 68, 74, 75, 76, 80, 83, 86, 87, 95-97, 101, 104, 122-128, 133-135, 138-142, 151, 154-156, 160-163, 172, 179, 180, 183, 185, 189, 191, 197-199, 201, 207, 210, 211, 214, 215, 217, 220-223, 225, 229, 231, 235, 236, 238, 239, 241, 246, 249, 253, 255, 260, 267, 269, 270, 271, 276, 277, 282-285, 287, 293, 294, 295, 297, 298
Jesus, 3, 14, 45, 80, 83, 86, 91, 97, 99, 101-103, 106, 111, 125, 126, 167-170, 172-174, 176-182, 187, 188, 191-203, 206-219, 221-224, 228-229, 232-233, 237-241, 246-248, 253-256, 258-269, 271, 273, 275, 277-279, 282-286, 293-297

Jesus, son of Ananias, 199
Jesus, son of Thebuthi, 125
Jewish Antiquities, 5, 295
Jewish War, 5, 223, 224, 225, 228, 270, 295, 296, 297
John Hyrcanus I, 56, 57, 65, 67, 159, 171, 287
John the Baptist, 14, 19, 20, 22, 25, 26, 29, 37, 41, 45, 48, 73, 76, 78-80, 83, 87, 91, 102, 108, 113, 115, 116, 133, 145, 149, 150-152, 160, 164, 223-225, 243, 245, 248, 250, 251, 281, 282, 294
John the Essene, 16
Jonathan, 20, 22, 57, 66, 287
Josephus, Flavius, 295
Joshua, 63, 137, 138, 153, 195, 201, 240, 241
Josippon, 237, 238
Judah, 33, 48, 52, 53, 54, 85, 92, 93, 96, 138, 139, 153, 170-172, 282
Judas Iscariot, 215, 241, 255, 278
Judas Maccabeus, 54, 55, 56, 59, 150, 287
Judas the Galilaean, 10, 19, 21
Judas/Jesus, 164, 201, 202, 213-220, 230, 232, 233, 238-241, 278, 285, 286

Karma, 212
Khirbet Qumran, 83, 159, 160
Kingdom of God, 197, 209, 210, 262, 284
Kings of the Peoples, 48
Kittim, 58, 75, 121-125, 128
Koran, 194, 296

Lactantius, 193
Last Generation, 48
Lebbaeus, 240, 255
Letters of Ignatius, 274
Life (The), 5, 203, 295
Lion of Wrath, 58, 131, 132, 134

M. Aemilius Scaurus, 22
Malthace, 31, 68
Man of Lies, 48, 91, 95, 151, 152, 283
Man of Mockery, 48, 91
Man who Preaches Lies, 48
Mandaeans, 84, 102
Mara bar Serapion, 221, 222
Marcion, 5, 274-277
Marcionites, 276-277
Marcus Ambibulus, 176
Marcus Pontius Pilate, 176
Mariamme, the Hasmonean princess, 143
Masada, 11, 21, 70, 161
Mattathias, 48, 51, 54, 55, 113, 150, 171, 219, 220, 287
Maximinus Daia, 176
Melchizedek, 116, 148, 149, 150, 251, 295
Menaham the Essene, 12
Messiah of Aaron, 48, 78, 87, 89, 113, 149, 152,

153, 157, 172, 251
Messiah of Aaron and Israel, 48, 113, 149, 152, 153, 157, 172
Messiah of Israel, 21, 31, 44, 77-79, 81, 87, 89, 145, 149, 195, 200, 201, 254, 278, 281, 283
Microletters, 175, 177

Nahum Commentary (4QpNah), 4
Nazirite vow, 44
Nebuchadnezzar, 48, 50, 51, 55, 76, 113, 151, 152, 153, 155
Nebuchadnezzar king of Babylon (symbolic designation for the Roman emperor), 51
Nero, 48, 50, 76, 93, 151, 155, 156, 164, 266, 269, 286, 287
New Covenant, 20-23, 27, 29, 34-36, 47, 49, 77, 83, 88, 91, 95, 102, 104, 108, 111, 113, 127, 133, 139, 143, 144, 149, 160-162, 164, 167, 170, 172, 195, 196, 200-202, 245, 250-254, 266-268, 270, 271, 278, 281-283, 297
Nobles, 48

Octavian, 71

Paleography, 1
Paraclete, 246, 247, 279, 286, 297
Pastoral Epistles, 273, 274
Paul, 190, 253, 254, 256, 262-269, 273-278, 283, 286, 293, 294, 295
Pauline Epistles, 274, 296, 297
Pella, 50, 269, 270, 271, 282, 297, 298
Perfectly Holy Men, 89
Period of Wrath, 48
Peter (Cephas), 140, 253-254, 267, 269, 277-278
Petronius, 71, 235, 236
Pharisees, 9, 11-14, 18, 20, 21, 57-61, 65, 99, 102, 133, 140, 159, 160, 192, 207, 237, 238, 250, 260, 281
Philip, 31, 81, 227, 244, 255, 256, 294
Pillars, 253, 254, 278, 285, 297
Pompey, 48, 59, 60, 61, 86, 122, 123, 160, 287
Porcius Festus, 104
Preacher of Lies, 112
Prince of All the Congregation, 113, 153
Princes, 48, 72, 77
Princes of Judah, 48
Prophet, 89, 113, 137, 139, 164, 245, 251, 261, 294
Psalms Commentary (4QpPsa), 4

Quirinius, 10

Radiocarbon dating, 1
Returnees of Israel, 48
Rod, 48, 113
Root of Planting, 48, 113
Rule of the Community (1QS), 4
Rule of the Congregation (1QSa), 4

Sadducees, 9, 11-14, 19, 20-22, 60, 61, 105, 159, 160, 250, 281, 297
Salome Alexandra, 22, 287
Samaritans, 14, 20, 36, 56, 184, 239, 244, 250, 281
Saul, 253, 265, 266, 278, 283
Sceptre, 48, 113
Schurer, Emil, 68, 88, 296
Second Treatise of the Great Seth, 193
Seekers-After-Smooth-Things, 36, 58, 59, 61, 132, 133, 135
Sicarii, 11, 15, 17, 21, 23, 35, 36, 79, 161, 162, 174, 255, 278
Simon Bar-Jona, 254, 278
Simon Magus, 243, 244, 246, 247, 248, 278, 279, 286, 297
Simon of Cyrene, 193
Simon of Perea, 18, 76, 174
Simon the Cananaean, 255
Simon the Zealot, 255
Slavonic Josephus, 3, 5, 43, 67, 81, 220, 223, 224, 226, 227, 229, 230, 261, 268
Son of Man, 101, 103, 209, 210, 257, 258, 261, 262, 279, 286, 294
Sons of Thunder, 255
Sons of Zadok, 48
Sossianus Hierocles, 193
Star, 48, 80, 87, 113
Suffering Servant, 256, 279, 286
Symeon (Simon), Son of Clopas, 37, 48, 75, 77, 85, 86, 89, 100, 113, 139, 151, 152, 154, 164, 170, 172, 173, 252, 284

Tabari, 195
Tacitus, 179, 237, 296
Teacher of Righteousness, 2, 3, 48, 73, 85, 91, 94, 95, 101, 106-113, 116, 253-254, 283, 296
Temple Scroll (11QT), 4, 63, 101
Thaddaeus, 240, 255
Therapeutae, 197
Theudas, 201, 239, 240, 286
Thiering, B. E., 66, 76, 296
Thomas, 169, 170, 202, 240, 241, 255, 294
Tiberius, 21, 59, 80, 179, 180, 184, 185, 186, 235, 236, 240, 268
Tiberius Iulius Alexander, 59
Trajan, 170, 173
Twelve (The), 84, 212, 240, 253, 254, 255, 256, 261, 266, 278, 285, 294, 295

Unique Teacher, 48, 73, 113, 151, 251

Valerius Gratus, 176
Vardaman, Jerry, 175, 177, 296
Varus, 18, 76, 123, 179
Vespasian, 100, 155, 161, 174, 223, 261
Visitation, 21, 34, 35, 48, 145, 146, 147, 151, 152

Voice of the Teacher, 48, 113

Well (The), 48
Wicked Priest, 2, 91, 92, 96, 106, 107, 109, 110, 111, 112, 126, 127, 147, 148, 156, 266, 283
Wise, Michael, 4

Yawan, Chief of the Kings of, 48

Zadok (Saddok), 113, 164
Zaw, 48, 91
Zealots, 11, 15, 111, 127, 128, 135, 255, 293, 294

Made in the USA
Lexington, KY
18 March 2011